The Sphinx

The Sphinx

The Life of Gladys Deacon
– Duchess of Marlborough

HUGO VICKERS

**HODDER &
STOUGHTON**

ZULEIKA

First published in Great Britain in 2020 by Hodder & Stoughton
An Hachette UK company
By joint imprimatur with Zuleika

1

A CIP catalogue record for this title is available from the British Library

Hardback ISBN 978 1 529 39070 4
Trade Paperback ISBN 978 1 529 39071 1
eBook ISBN 978 1 529 39075 9

Typeset in Bembo MT by Hewer Text UK Ltd, Edinburgh
Printed and bound in Great Britain by Clays Ltd, Elcograf S.p.A.

Hodder & Stoughton policy is to use papers that are natural, renewable
and recyclable products and made from wood grown in sustainable forests.
The logging and manufacturing processes are expected to conform
to the environmental regulations of the country of origin.

Hodder & Stoughton Ltd
Carmelite House
50 Victoria Embankment
London EC4Y 0DZ

Zuleika
Thomas House
84 Eccleston Square
London SW1V 1PX

www.hodder.co.uk
zuleika.london

To June Dillon
(1933–2018)
Sister-in-charge of O'Connell Ward
St Andrew's Hospital
who made it possible

Contents

PART THREE: THE PURSUIT OF
PROFIT AND POSSESSIONS

PART FOUR: RENUNCIATION

Preface

It has been a privilege and joy to rewrite this biography forty years on, one reason being the release of many new papers, the other that a number of people were breathing down my neck first time round, who could have frustrated my work, and they aren't breathing at all any more.

In the Archives at Blenheim I read all of Gladys's letters to the 9th Duke of Marlborough during the First World War, aware that the only other person to have read them was the 9th Duke 100 years before. I found Gladys's letters to Count Hermann von Keyserling in the University of Darmstadt, and read them online, without leaving my London apartment. I revisited I Tatti in the summer of 2018, with my daughter Alice, who helped me transcribe 15,000 words of letters from Mary Berenson to her mother. The National Archives of Paris at Pierrefytte-sur-Seine contained a cache of letters from Gladys in the Comtesse Greffulhe papers – another chest of gold. I visited Colorado Springs to inspect the papers of Charles and Virginia Baldwin. And more besides.

I discovered Gladys in 1968 and my interest in her has never waned. I began research in 1975, talked to her between 1975 and 1977, and the book was published in London in September 1979, in New York in 1980 and as a slightly revised paperback version in 1987. This edition has been completely rewritten.

Hugo Vickers
October 2019

Introduction

Gladys Deacon? . . . She never existed.

I was sixteen when I chanced upon an astonishing reference in *Chips: The Diaries of Sir Henry Channon*. Chips, that most social of MPs, spotted the former Gladys Deacon in a jeweller's in Bond Street in 1943. He got a shock:

> I saw an extraordinary marionette of a woman − or was it a man? It wore grey flannel trousers, a wide leather belt, masculine overcoat, and a man's brown felt hat, and had a really frightening appearance, but the hair was golden dyed and long: what is wrongly known as platinum; the mouth was a scarlet scar. Bundi [his dog] began to growl, and as I secretly examined this terrifying apparition, I recognized Gladys Marlborough, once the world's most beautiful woman . . . the toast of Paris. The love of Proust, the *belle amie* of Anatole France.[1]

Chips went over to reintroduce himself. 'She looked at me, stared vacantly with those famous turquoise eyes that once drove men insane with desire and muttered in French: "I have never heard that name", she flung down a ruby clip she was examining and bolted from the shop . . .'[2]

This story fascinated me − in a few lines it implied a life of sharp contrasts − but I mistrusted it. I wondered if the vacant stare was hiding something. I wanted to know more about this Miss Deacon who had changed from 'the world's most beautiful woman' into 'a terrifying apparition'. It is hard to explain why one character fires the imagination while another makes no impact. On that day, she went into my head and stayed there. She appealed to me in the same way as three figures of fiction I had encountered as a child. These were Charlotte Brontë's first Mrs Rochester in *Jane Eyre*, enclosed in an upper room at Thornfield Hall and emerging with evil intent; Daphne du Maurier's unseen Rebecca, her clothes still in her bedroom at Manderley; and Charles Dickens's Miss Havisham, in her decaying bridal gown at Satis House in *Great Expectations*. To these I add Yvonne de Galais, the elusive dream girl in Alain-Fournier's haunting novel, *Le Grand Meaulnes*. They had all had opportunities and all had come to grief. Yet their mysterious presences still influenced the lives of others. None could be successfully brushed under the carpet as Gladys Deacon seemed to have been. Again, the contrast between the young and beautiful Gladys and this witch-like creature was intriguing. I wanted to know how and why this metamorphosis had taken place. I also wanted to find her, if indeed she was still alive.

As the result of reading *Chips*, I found myself consumed with curiosity. I know now what I did not know then – that I was setting out on a life-changing adventure. Everything that has shaped my later life, not to mention my career, stemmed from reading that passage, though the seeds had been planted earlier by Brontë, du Maurier and Dickens.

Gladys Deacon had been an extraordinarily famous beauty in her day, but she had faded into complete obscurity. Her name still appeared in *Kelly's Handbook* but no address was shown and few people knew anything about her. But I found an address in Chacombe, near Banbury, and in March 1968 I wrote to her. In my diary I noted:

> After breakfast my letter to Gladys, Duchess of Marlborough was returned by the Official Returned Postal Packet service and the reason given was that she had 'gone away'. This puzzles me a lot though it is not surprising in the circumstances. Throughout the day I was fascinated by her . . .[3]

In the summer I prevailed upon an understanding aunt to drive me to Blenheim Palace to make enquiries there. A sympathetic though slightly surprised guide told us that the duchess was a very old lady, living in a small village in Oxfordshire under the name of Mrs Spencer. The Marlboroughs supported her financially, she said, but had nothing to do with her. She was surrounded by dogs, which she walked at night, carrying a small lamp. The guide also said that on bank holidays an old lady arrived at the palace swathed in furs and announced that, years ago, she had been duchess there. She wondered if this was Mrs Spencer. It wasn't.

Chacombe was not far away. I persuaded my aunt to drive us there. We located the house. There was some activity but we did not feel brave enough to ring any door bells. I promised myself that when I was old enough to drive a car, I would return there to discover the truth. Meanwhile I delved into books on Proust in the school library, found some nuggets of interest and made an abortive attempt to start this book. My material stretched to less than two pages.

Not until February 1975 did I make the journey to Chacombe. I again located the house and peered nervously over the wall. Then I visited the pub, which was unaccustomed to receiving visitors other than its regulars. I enquired if 'Mrs Spencer', as she liked to call herself, still lived at the Grange. The publican looked at me suspiciously, evidently confused by my interest. I found this hard to justify but muttered that she had once been a very beautiful and intelligent person and rather famous. He then replied: 'No, she's been gone a long time now.' I assumed that he meant dead and my heart sank accordingly, but he continued: 'She's gone to a hospital up Northampton way.' He had not heard of her death, but reckoned she would be a great age if still alive.

I tried to persuade myself that my curiosity was satisfied and returned to London. There I chanced to relate the story to a friend who, to my astonishment, told me that he had once heard a story of a Duchess of Marlborough being evicted from Blenheim Palace. I checked the dates. It had to have been Gladys Deacon.

This was too much. I decided then and there that I would write her life. Looking back, it was a brazen, arrogant decision. Though I started with slender knowledge, I was able to follow up the clues, and each time I started to dig, a hidden gem emerged from the undergrowth of time. Soon it became clear that no part of this woman's life had been normal. Nor would she have been so interesting, I suspect, had she married Marlborough at twenty-one and retired gracefully to the dower house after his death. My task was to lift the veil that had fallen over her.

The most terrifying question concerned her present whereabouts. If she was still alive, how old was she? Where was she? Was she *compos mentis*? Would I ever be allowed into her presence? I was pessimistic.

Several people told me that there was a well-known hospital in Northampton. Eventually this was identified as St Andrew's. I plucked up courage and telephoned the hospital, said I thought the Duchess of Marlborough was a patient there and asked if I could come and see her to tell her I wanted to write her biography. The secretary neither confirmed nor denied her presence, but suggested I put my request in writing. This I did and by the end of the month I was excited to learn that she was still alive and that my application was being considered. Furthermore, I received a letter from her nephew, Count John Pálffy, in which he said: 'The purpose of your letter has indeed retained my fullest attention and interest . . .' He suggested a meeting.

Wasting no further time, I flew to Lausanne, wondering how to convince this nephew that Gladys Deacon had had a life interesting enough for a book. I found him in his office at the bank where he was a director and later he drove me to his family's home on the lake. He needed no convincing. He was more than aware of the scope of his aunt's life and gave me a number of clues and introductions. He was surprised that someone so young (I was then twenty-three) should wish to write such a book and, as I later discovered, slightly concerned as to why. He warned me that I would do well to brush up on my Keyserling and Hofmannsthal before visiting his aunt. 'She's as cute as a cat,' he said. 'She'll look right through you.' I came away, encouraged, 'my only fear the enormity of the task'.[4]

I put myself on a crash course on the people she knew, all of them interesting. I studied everything that I thought relevant. Then my other aunt wisely told me that if the duchess was indeed ninety-four, there was not a moment to lose, prepared or unprepared. 'People of ninety-four have a habit of dying,' she said. It would be more than disappointing not to meet her.

So I asked if I could go and see her, and to that end visited the office of the family lawyer, who enjoyed the Dickensian name of Mr Sharp, to be armed with a letter. Mr Sharp had never met the duchess and looked at me as if to say: 'Can anyone want to go and visit her?' Others were saying: 'Be careful of her' and 'Don't underestimate her.' I experienced a vivid nightmare three nights before the visit in which I came face to face with the duchess in hospital, a fragile invalid yet restored to youth and beauty. I found myself being observed by eyes that sometimes showed anger and sometimes deceived: all of which left me yet more frightened.

The actual visit took place on Sunday, 6 July. I drove to Northampton in trepidation. My appointment was for two o'clock. Punctually, I drove through the gates and up to the front door of the impressive building. Presently, the chief nursing officer, Mrs Newton, took charge of me and we began the long walk to O'Connell Ward, along spacious carpeted corridors. We passed patients playing cards, reading or wandering about as though they were in a large country hotel. One beautiful lady (Diana Astor) rested on a window seat, reading *Tatler*. Some made polite greetings, others were silent. The occasional hostile face glared from a bedroom, angry to see us pass. I had never been in a psychiatric hospital before and was not at ease. Mrs Newton warned me: 'You'll find her very ugly, but she has beautiful eyes.' I asked if the duchess was expecting me. 'I thought it better not to tell her,' she replied. 'She's very temperamental, the duchess. She may tell you she's dead. You may have had a completely wasted journey.'

Having travelled along a seemingly endless succession of corridors, which involved the unlocking and relocking of several doors, we arrived in the stark, clinical atmosphere of O'Connell Ward, a psycho-geriatric ward on the first floor. A chirpy Japanese nurse informed us: 'The duchess is in the Green Room.' Only one or two patients were indoors; the rest were out in the sun.

The duchess was seated in her chair by the door with a white linen cloth over her face, asleep, with her feet resting on a stool. All I could see of her was her white hair, and I was surprised at how small she was. Mrs Newton roused her and I knelt down beside her.

She began to raise the cloth. I saw her jaw, which was distorted, partly due to wax injections she had taken in her youth and partly due to old age. As the cloth was lifted higher, I found myself being stared at by those eyes, which were so blue that any description of them would be inadequate. She gazed at me for a moment, then cried out: 'Later, later, later!' She dropped the cloth and returned to sleep.

At this point Sister Dillon, in charge of the ward, arrived and said they would put her to bed, because she was happier there, and we could try again in half an hour. Meanwhile I wandered in the garden, where I met a clergyman who thought I was a patient, or a patient who thought he was a clergyman, or a genuine clergyman who was also a patient, I still do not know. We had a brief conversation which did nothing to settle my nerves.

The second visit took place three-quarters of an hour later. We retraced the long journey through the hospital's corridors and this time went to the duchess's bedroom. Mrs Newton ushered me into the small rectangular room and left me there while she went to find the sister. From another room there emerged a maniacal scream reminiscent of all film versions of *Jane Eyre*, while I came face to face with Gladys Deacon.

She was in bed, dressed in a pink nightgown and wide awake. I went over to her and gave her some photographs I had taken of her sphinx at Blenheim. She took them, looked at them, and handed them back with the words: 'I don't like them.' Then Sister Dillon came in and sat down on the bed. She gave her the message that I was going to write about her, but this got no response. Then she showed her another photograph I had brought, one of her eye painted in the portico of Blenheim. Gladys looked at it and suddenly began to laugh. Then she asked for some doughnuts, which were to have jam and sugar in them. 'Tell me what I'm going to dream about tonight?' she asked, and then: 'How's the Mississippi?' After a while, she dismissed the sister, adding: 'Take him with you, will you.'[5]

My first conclusion was that she was quite senile, and I left feeling rather hollow inside. Only later did I wonder if she had not been taking in rather more than she liked to let on. I resolved to visit her again.

My next visit, the following October, signified something of a breakthrough. Gladys was sitting in a corner of the lounge with her hair in a bun. She was wearing a white dress with black spots, stockings, slippers and a blue shawl. There were flowers on the table and she was surrounded by nurses. They had clearly gone to a lot of trouble in advance of the visit. In their midst, Sister Dillon was telling her that a visitor was on his way, a Mr Vickers, who was going to write a book about her. I entered the room just as Gladys was saying: 'But I don't see why I should be disturbed by Mr Vickers.' I sat down beside her. Her head turned to look at me and she continued slowly in a different tone: 'And he doesn't think so either.'

'He's come to see you,' said the sister.

'Well, I don't like this story,' she said.

I produced photographs – of Hugo von Hofmannsthal, David Garnett, Sigmund Freud, Harold Nicolson, Marcel Proust and Consuelo Vanderbilt. She had great fun denying that she had ever seen any of them. She laughed at the picture of Proust, and enquired: 'Is that you?' She liked the dress in the picture of Consuelo, so we tried it again.

Gladys decided that Consuelo was a consul. She beckoned to one of the male nurses and asked him if he had ever seen the lady in the photograph. Prompted by me, he said: 'It's Consuelo.' With much laughter she continued: 'Did you ever see a consul dressed like that? No! That's a very fine consul. I'm not smart enough to hobnob with consuls!'

She pointed to the picture of Proust and addressed a young nurse. 'When you get married, you go to a fellow like that!' Soon afterwards she gave me back the picture and said: 'Thank you very much. You've given me a better laugh than I've had since I came here.' She offered me a cup of tea, asked me to stay with her and we began the slow process of making friends.

Because I brought photographs, she referred to me in those early days as 'the photographer'. Three visits later she recognised me and gave me a huge greeting. My visits began to extend to several hours at a time and she invited me to keep coming to see her. Because she was deaf, every question had to be written in capital letters in a black felt-tipped pen. She often missed oral questions, but her eyesight was phenomenal and she read without spectacles. She would read the questions slowly and then reply if she wanted to, usually in English or French, which was fine, but occasionally in German, which I could not understand. She spoke all languages so fluently that some of the nurses thought she was French and others that she was German. They were surprised when I told them she was American. They also used to ask about her 'car accident'. Gladys had four tiny scars on her chin, two on each side. It was where they had cut out the paraffin wax after her injections went wrong.

In January 1976 she started to address me as *tu* not *vous* when speaking French, and just before I went to America in March, she took my hands in hers, put them to her forehead and declared: 'Friends for ever!' All in all, I visited Gladys sixty-five times.

Never for a moment did I expect that she would lift her self-imposed ban on discussing the past. Yet in February 1976 I showed her a book on d'Annunzio* and told her that I was reading it. She suddenly told me she used to know him in Rome and asked me what I thought of him. I almost jumped into the air. I spluttered out the inadequate comment: 'A good poet, but perhaps a less good politician?' She brushed this aside and continued:

> He had spark, but not fire. In this respect he was like Winston Churchill. Winston . . . he was not a great man . . . He had weight, yes, but he was not a gentleman. I knew him well enough. He used to come to that place where we were [Blenheim]. He liked to lay down the law![6]

Hitler, however, she thought was a great man. 'He had a telling personality. When you think how hard it is to create a rising in a small village, well, he had the whole world up in arms. He was larger than Winston. Winston couldn't have done that!' She went on to describe insanity as 'a disease of the brain, like a lock'. Then she urged me to take over the hospital. 'Hoof them out,' she said. I pointed at some young nurses. 'Not them, they're small fry!'[7]

Once a little light had been shed on the past, I realised that she would respond to books, liked looking at pictures and discussing the different characters. Most of all she liked looking at art books and the works of artists. Gradually I worked my way through the artists, writers and society figures of her day, a process mutually enjoyed and with many tangents and diversions. At the end of a meeting, which sometimes lasted as long as four hours, it was invariably I who was tired and not Gladys.

Only one subject remained taboo unless she mentioned it, and that was her identity. She was never to be directly associated with her past. She might say: 'Rodin liked to precipitate himself on every woman he met. You know, hands all over you.' But if I said, 'Ah! You knew

---

* Gabriele d'Annunzio (1863-1938), Italian poet, writer, and politician who immortalised himself at his villa, Il Vittoriale, on Lake Garda, Italy.

him then?' she would either shut up like a clam or say, 'I never met him, but a close woman friend of mine told me.' And when I dared to ask her once: 'Where is Gladys Deacon?' she looked at me with a twinkle in her eye and said slowly: 'Gladys Deacon? . . . She never existed.'[8]

The Baldwins, Deacons and Parkers

BALDWIN

Sylvester Baldwin (d. 1638)
m. Sarah Bryan

Richard Baldwin (1622–65)
m. Elizabeth Alsop (1625–88)

Zachariah Baldwin (1660–1722)
m. (1) Mary Atkins (1652– ante 1691)

Zachariah Baldwin II (1681–1766)
m. Mary Marvin

Zachariah Baldwin III (1709–56)
m. Rebecca Crane (1707–91)

Ezekiel Baldwin (1736–1822)
m. Martha Hayward (1745–1820)

Daniel Baldwin (1753–1815)
Captain N.J. Continental Infantry
m. Phoebe Fraunces (1764–1816)

DEACON

Edwin Baldwin (1790–1848)
m. Caroline Carey (1795–1869)

Captain David Deacon
US Navy
(1871–1840)
m. Anna Hutchinson

Charles H. Baldwin (1822–88)
Rear-Admiral
m. (1) Pamelia Tolfree (1835–73)
m. (2) Mary Morgan Reade
'Marraine' (1845–1924)

Emma L. Baldwin (1821–90)
m. Elias.S. Higgins (1815–89)

Adolphus Deacon
(1815–39)

Eugene Higgins (1860–1948)

Charles A. Baldwin (1860–1934)
m. Virginia Hobart (1872–1958)
(later wife of Prince Zourab Tchkotoua)
(1897–1975)

Florence Baldwin ═══ m. ═══ Edward Parker Deacon
(1859–1918)   (1844–1901)

John (1893–1906)   Charles (1897–1943)

GLADYS MARIE DEACON
Duchess of Marlborough
(1881–1977)

(Ida) Audrey Deacon
(1883–1904)

Edward Parker Deacon
(1885–87)

PARKER

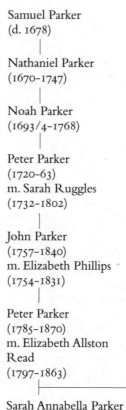

Samuel Parker
(d. 1678)

Nathaniel Parker
(1670-1747)

Noah Parker
(1693/4-1768)

Peter Parker
(1720-63)
m. Sarah Ruggles
(1732-1802)

John Parker
(1757-1840)
m. Elizabeth Phillips
(1754-1831)

Peter Parker
(1785-1870)
m. Elizabeth Allston
Read
(1797-1863)

Edward Preble Deacon —— m. —— Sarah Annabella Parker
(1813-51)   (1821-1900)

Ellen Parker
(1831-1903)
m. Albert van Zandt
(1828-1900)

Harleston Deacon   Ida Deacon
(1848-1926)   (1847-83)
m. Susanne Knox
(1861-1954)

Louise van Zandt
(1855-1905) (eloped
1886)
m. Neilson Winthrop
(1849-1936)

Gerald Winthrop
(1880-1938)

Edith Florence Deacon   Dorothy Evelyn Deacon
(1887-1965)   (1891-1960)
m Henry G. Gray   m. (1) Prince Antoni Albrecht Radzwill (div)
(1875-1954)   (1885-1935)
                            m. (2) Count Paul Pálffy
                            (1890-1968)

The Spencer-Churchills*

6th Duke of Marlborough
(1793–1857)
m. (1) Lady Jane Stewart
(1798–1844)
m. (2) Hon Charlotte Flower　　　　m. (3) Jane Stewart
(1818–50)　　　　　　　　　　　　(1818–97)

7th Duke of Marlborough, KG　　　Lord Edward Spencer-Churchill
(1822–83)　　　　　　　　　　　　(1853–1911)
m. Lady Frances Vane　　　　　　　m. Augusta Warburton
(1822–99)　　　　　　　　　　　　(1854–1941)

8th Duke of Marlborough　　　　　　　　　　　　　　Lady Cornelia Spencer-Churchill
(1844–92)　　　　　　　　　　　　　　　　　　　　(1847–1927)
m. (1) Lady Albertha Hamilton　m. (2) Lilian Hammersley　m. 1st Baron Wimborne
(div. 1883) (1847–1932)　　　　(1854–1909)　　　　　　1835=1914)

Ivor Guest, 1st　　　　　　Rt Hon Frederick Guest
Viscount Wimborne　　　　　(1875–1937)
(1873–1939)　　　　　　　　m. Amy Phipps
m. Hon Alice Grosvenor　　　(1872–1959)
(1880–1948)

9th Duke of Marlborough, KG　　Lady Frances Spencer-Churchill　　Lady Lilian Spencer-Churchill
(1871–1934)　　　　　　　　　　(1870–1954)　　　　　　　　　　(1873–1951)
m. (1) Consuelo Vanderbilt　　　m. Sir Robert Gresley, Bt　　　　m. Cecil Grenfell
(div. 1920)　　　　　　　　　　(1866–1936)　　　　　　　　　　(1864–1924)
(1877–1964)

m. (2) **GLADYS DEACON**
(1881–1977)

10th Duke of Marlborough　　　　　　　　Lord Ivor Spencer-Churchill
(1897–1972)　　　　　　　　　　　　　　(1898–1956)
m. (1) Lady Mary Cadogan　m. (2) Laura Canfield　m. Elizabeth Cunningham
(1900–61)　　　　　　　　(1915–90)　　　　　　(1914–2010)

11th Duke of Marlborough　　　　　　　Lady Sarah Roubanis　　Lady Caroline Waterhouse
(1926–2014)　　　　　　　　　　　　　(1921–2000)　　　　　　(1923–92)
m. (1) Susan Hornby (div)
(1929–2005)　　　　m. (2) Athina Livanos (div)
　　　　　　　　　(1929–74)
　　　　　　　　　m. (3) Countess Rosita Douglas (div)
　　　　　　　　　(b. 1943)
　　　　　　　　　m. (4) Lily Mahtani
　　　　　　　　　(b. 1957)

12th Duke of Marlborough　　　　Lady Henrietta Spencer-Churchill
(b. 1955)　　　　　　　　　　　　(b. 1958)
m. (1) Rebecca Few-Brown (div)
(b. 1957)
m. (2) Edla Griffiths
(b. 1968)

Lord Randolph Spencer-Churchill
(1849-95)
m. Jennie Jerome
(1854-1921)

Lady Rosamond Spencer-Churchill
(1851-1920)
m. 2nd Baron de Ramsey
(1848-1925)

Lady Sarah Spencer-Churchill
(1865-1929)
m. Lt-Col Gordon Wilson
(1865-1914)

Sir Winston Spencer-Churchill, KG
(1874-1965)
m. Clementine Hozier
(1885-1977)

John Spencer-Churchill
(1880-1947)
m. Lady Gwendoline Bertie
(1885-1941)

Hon Reginald Fellowes
(1884-1953)
m. Princess Marguerite de Broglie
(1890-1962)

Clarissa Churchill (b. 1920)
m. 1st Earl of Avon, KG (1897-1977)

Lady Norah Spencer-Churchill
(1875-1946)
m. Francis Bradley-Birt
(1874-1963)

Guy Bertrand Spencer †
(1881-1950)

Lady Rosemary Muir
(b. 1929)

Lord Charles Spencer-Churchill
(1940-2016)

* Select family tree showing the Spencer-Churchills mentioned in the text
† Dotted line indicates illegitimate child

PART ONE

Early Days

Deacon House, Boston

Gladys by Boldini, 1899

I

A REMARKABLE YOUNG PERSON

Edward Parker Deacon advanced into the room, his eyes darting
from side to side in a cursory examination that was interrupted
when his wife, her composure regained for the moment, blew out
the candle.

'Permit me,' said the hotel secretary in the background. 'I have
another candle.'

'Thank you,' said Edward Deacon, 'we'll see how good the
hunting is in the sitting room.'

He found his quarry cowering behind a couch. Three shots
signalled the end of a two-year chase and Edward Deacon reap-
peared in the doorway, a smoking pistol in his right hand.

'I suggest', he said to the hotel secretary, 'that you summon the
gendarmes. M. Émile Abeille seems to be dead.'

—'Heartbreaks of Society'[1]

Murder is a disruptive business in a family. For eleven years Gladys
had been living in Paris, travelling with her family to the high spots
of Europe and occasionally crossing to America. And then it all
ended. Any stability she had known dissolved overnight and she was
propelled into a new life, separated from her mother and sent with
her father to a foreign land.

In February 1892, then aged eleven, Gladys was staying in the
Hôtel Splendide in Cannes, with her mother, her three sisters and her
mother's step-mother. On the night of 17 February her father shot
her mother's lover dead in the hotel. He handed himself in, while her
mother wrote to her hostess of the following day to say she regretted
she would be unable to attend a luncheon party. Gladys and her sisters
were taken away from the hotel by their step-grandmother. Soon
afterwards Gladys found herself deposited in a convent in Paris.

Gladys Deacon was an exceptionally beautiful, intelligent and gifted child, an American who could have walked out of a novel by Henry James. She was born in Paris at the Hôtel Brighton in the rue de Rivoli, opposite the Tuileries Gardens, on Monday, 7 February 1881. Her mother, Florence Deacon, a good looking twenty-one-year old, was thrilled at the sight of the baby with its arms outstretched and its little hands opening and closing. Later she recalled to Gladys 'the rapture I felt these many years ago when first I held you in my arms. I can never think about it without emotion.'[2]

Gladys gave many contradictory dates for her birth, anything from 1888 on a visa application to 1890 on her marriage certificate. On her ninety-fifth birthday in 1976, she sat at the head of a long table and gazed at the cake with its handful of candles. Earlier she had pretended she had forgotten when her birthday was. 'How could I know? I couldn't say: "Here I am!"' She dismissed the matter with an alternative theory: 'I was not born, I happened.'[3]

Edward Parker Deacon and his wife Florence were rich Americans who chose to live in Europe as many discriminating Americans did at the height of the belle époque. It was an era of respectable idleness and security when the upper crust (*Le Gratin*), existed stylishly in the world of salons and smart restaurants, of magnificent balls, exclusive clubs, and strolls in the Bois de Boulogne. The Deacons would travel, according to the season, to Cannes, Nice or Trouville. They might visit Genoa or Homburg, Geneva or St Moritz. They crossed the Atlantic for the season at Newport or to visit Mrs Deacon's brother, Charles Baldwin, at Clara County, California.

Gladys was the most beautiful and the most brilliant of the four Deacon sisters, and each of them was destined to glitter – and shock – in European or American society. Next was Audrey, born in Pau, France, on 30 November 1883. In childhood she was close to Gladys and frequently covered up for her mischievous elder sister, though later they fell out. Audrey possessed a more regal beauty than Gladys's. She had brilliant dark eyes and a classic brow. Being tall, she was teased by her sisters: 'What's it like up there in the heavens?'

Edith was born in Cannes on 16 February 1887. Her devotion to her mother was total, while she disliked Gladys, who was a superb mimic, and did not fail to include her mother in her repertoire. The youngest child, Dorothy, was not born until March 1891; there was a brother, Edward Parker, who was born in Paris, but died young in May 1887.*

Gladys's first home was 14 rue Pierre-Charron, just off the Champs-Élysées. During her early years she called herself Marie-Gladys, the names by which she was baptised in the American Episcopal Church of the Holy Trinity on 20 March 1881.† Later she swapped the names round and settled for Gladys on its own, which she pronounced 'Glaydis' in the style of Americans such as Gladys Vanderbilt Szechenyi. The children were brought up in a mixture of French and English.

When Gladys was six months old, the Deacons took a house in Grosvenor Street, in London. A goat cart took Gladys and Mrs Deacon's dog for rides in Hyde Park. Years later, Gladys pieced together this phase in conversation with her nurse, Irma Deodat, who was with the family from 1887:

> I had a very pretty wet nurse & Papa insisting that Irma sd never let her & me out of her sight. Mamma gets a lovely pale blue brocade with silver flowers, Papa very jealous & poor Mamma obedient as a lamb.
>
> Papa dislikes the cooking & they take lodgings which prove satisfactory. They go to Windsor for a visit. Papa & Mamma prefer the Otto Fitzgeralds'‡ hospitality because they are warmer there.
>
> I get cantankerous & develop dyspepsia. Papa says Nounou [her nurse] has flirted with some footy in London during the week's absence.[4]

She was not always happy, though. Years later, during the First World War, she wrote: 'I feel as I used to when a little, little girl, & it rained. Lonely, depressed, lost in space.'[5]

---

* This boy eludes reference on ancestry sites, but his existence was acknowledged by the next generation of the family, in the Parker genealogy and in contemporary press cuttings.
† She was baptised by the Rev. John B. Morgan (a cousin of J. P. Morgan), rector from 1873 to 1912, who raised money to turn the church into the American Cathedral.
‡ Lord Otho FitzGerald (1827–81), son of 3rd Duke of Leinster, a Liberal politician, and his wife Ursula (d. 1883). Irma must have recalled visits that Gladys would have been too young to remember.

The Deacons came from New Jersey, and were dashing figures who moved up in the world. Gladys's grandfather, Edward Preble Deacon, married a Miss Parker from a famous family of Parkers in Boston, and they lived at the fabulous Deacon House. Through her mother, Florence Baldwin, Gladys was part of a grand New England family, originally from Aston Clinton, in Buckinghamshire. (See Appendix: Gladys's Ancestors, pages 323–9, for a fuller account of these families.)

The Baldwins and the Parkers provided Gladys with a family tree proven back many generations. Her background gave her the confidence that she was of high birth and permitted her to cast aspersions on the origins of less well-connected Americans. A favourite expression in later life was to describe someone pejoratively as 'middle class'. From her mother she inherited great beauty and from her father a sense of adventure and a bizarre intelligence.

Edward Parker Deacon, austere, dark and intelligent, had the straight eyebrows and powerful, bright blue eyes which his daughter inherited. His hair was brown and he had a pronounced nose. In his youth, then known as 'Ned', he attended school at the Berkeley Institute, in Newport, where Henry James was a fellow pupil. He went on to Brown University, then joined the 1st Massachusetts Cavalry as a second lieutenant. He served in the various battles of the Peninsula and Virginia campaigns in the Civil War. He participated in the capture of Fort Harrison in two days' fighting during which the commander and two thirds of his staff were killed, before resigning his commission in June 1865.[6]

Having profited from the sale of Deacon House and still owning property in Boston, he led a life of leisure, financed by annuities, was a member of Boston's famous Somerset Club and frequently travelled abroad. He was considered one of New England's most eligible bachelors, but he was reserved and distant, combining elements of his dashing father with his deeply unstable mother, Sarahann Parker.

His mother's eccentricities became a source of embarrassment in Boston society. She insisted on being addressed as 'Mrs de Konn', would scream at people in the street and had a curious predilection for sliding on the icy gutter in Sumner Street, obliging her footman to await her arrival feet first at the end of the slide, to catch her in his arms. In 1861 she took her family to Europe with her and eventually settled in England. After years of epilepsy and eighteen months of diabetes mellitus, she died on 18 May 1900 at Wyke House, Isleworth, Middlesex, a large, claustrophobic lunatic asylum, where nobody knew or cared who she was. She was the first of three generations of Deacons to end their days in a sanatorium, all for different reasons.

Edward Parker Deacon was fond of yachting and it was on such a trip that he met sixteen-year-old Florence Baldwin, daughter of Admiral Charles H. Baldwin, the richest man in the US Navy. Nobody was particularly pleased when he led her to a specially constructed altar at the Fifth Avenue home of her father and made her his wife on 29 April 1879. By then he was thirty-five and she a mere twenty.

Florence's mother, Pamelia Tolfree, had been a great belle – 'a beauty of the wax doll type with a profusion of golden hair worn in short fluffy curls all over her head'.[7] She died in 1873. In 1875 the admiral married Mrs Mary Morgan Reade (known as Marraine), and they divided their time between New York and Newport, Rhode Island. They also came to London, where, in 1883, Marraine was presented to the Princess of Wales at a Buckingham Palace drawing room, and at Cowes in August 1884 the future Edward VII honoured Admiral Baldwin with a dinner on his yacht.[8]

Marraine was a devoted stepmother to Florence and her brother, Charley (though as time went on she nurtured reservations about Florence due to her extravagance). Considerably rich in her own right, she was a close friend of Eliot Gregory, an effete society portrait painter, who wrote about international society as 'The Idler'. Marraine was witness to most of the drama in the Deacon family.

Florence's brother, Charles Adolphe Baldwin, known as Charley, was born in San Francisco in 1861, educated at Harrow and became a collector of etchings, paintings, bronzes and enamels. In 1896 he married Virginia Hobart, daughter of a millionaire California gold-mine operator. They lived in Santa Clara County, to which Florence paid several visits with her children in the 1880s and 1890s. Then, in 1901, because Virginia suffered from tuberculosis, the young Baldwins moved to Colorado Springs, arriving with two automobiles to the astonishment of the locals. Virginia's considerable fortune enabled Charley to commission the architect Thomas MacLaren to construct Claremont, his home at Broadmoor, modelled on the Grand Trianon at Versailles (but an eighth of its size), with *parquet de Versailles* wooden floors. The house was completed in 1907.*

Virginia being so rich, both Charley and she were important in the lives of his sister Florence and her daughters, Florence turning frequently to her brother when funds were low.

The newly married Deacons left for Paris on 29 June, where they ran into Henry James. He noted that Deacon was there 'with the prettiest young wife (a Miss Baldwin of Newport) in all creation'. He was amazed to find that Deacon was 'literary'.[9] The new Mrs Deacon was not an intelligent woman, but she was cultured. She adorned her beauty at great expense. She was a famed customer at all the smart Paris shops and, like Eleanora Duse and some of Proust's heroines, she loved the serpentine dresses of Fortuny. She once bought an entire dressing-table set in vermeil, despite possessing three of them already. Social columnists monitored her and expressed concern that the lascivious eye of the Prince of Wales had fallen upon her; they hoped she would not become one of his mistresses. By 1885 her father, the Admiral, was writing: 'Florence . . . goes much in French society. I think she is rather inclined to drop her own Country people.'[10]

It is easy to pour scorn on her, for her values, ambitions and aspirations are hard to admire. Later in life she spent with no regard for the future and ran up enormous debts, scrounging on her more solid relations. Yet she survived many grave crises and disasters that would have driven a lesser woman to take the veil. 'How cruel life was to her! How unjust!' wrote Gladys in the aftermath of her death.[11]

Florence Deacon sought the company of artists, musicians and writers, such as Auguste Rodin, Bernard Berenson and Maurice Lobre. She was a particular friend of Robert de Montesquiou, who remembered her as a likeable, worthy enough woman. It was through

---

* The Baldwins had two sons – Charles Hobart Baldwin (1897-1943), an architect in San Francisco, who had a gold mine in Nevada and was a director of the Hobart estates; & John Tolfree Baldwin (1898-1906), who died when his burro bolted in a stampede and he was dragged 200 yards along rocks. Widowed in 1934, Virginia remarried in 1949, to Prince Zourab Tchkotoua (1896-1975), a Russian-Georgian prince who was also an artist and a racing-car enthusiast twenty-one years her junior. They separated in 1952 and Virginia died in her large Victorian apartment in San Francisco in 1958. Claremont is now the Colorado Springs School.

her mother that Gladys met many of her artist friends, but in the early years she knew well the frustration of being presented in the drawing room, then spirited away to the nursery by Irma, while the grown-ups continued their conversations. Sometimes she and her sister Audrey crept downstairs before a dinner party, taking surreptitious bites from peaches on the dining-room table, amused at the thought of the guests later finding tooth-marks.[12]

Gladys's parents had widely differing tastes, Mr Deacon preferring the company of his own countrymen. Due to the immense amount of publicity that attended the Deacons in the 1890s there is no dearth of 'authoritative statements' about their way of life.

About a month after the wedding in 1879, Mr Deacon is reported to have knocked his wife down because he did not like her hairstyle. In the hotels in which they stayed, he forbade the servants to wait on her and would not even allow a basket of wood to be brought to her room without written instructions from him. In the winter of 1884, spent in Paris, Mrs Deacon was about to leave for a ball when she found that one of the children's nurses had gone off duty without permission. Mr Deacon insisted that she should go on her own, promising to join her later. When he had failed to appear by one o'clock she returned home to find him barricaded in their apartment. When at last she got in, Mr Deacon was found 'rushing about undressed, in a state of frenzy'.

In May 1887 their little boy died. Mr Deacon was not in the least bit sympathetic when he found his wife alone, weeping. He reproached her for her tears, then beat her so cruelly that she was marked for days. He was further accused by Mrs Deacon's friends of intemperance and cruelty to the children. Gladys used to relate to villagers at Chacombe that he was tough to all the sisters and frequently thrashed them.

In the midst of these troubles, on 17 November 1888, Mrs Deacon's father, Admiral Baldwin, died at 590 Fifth Avenue, New York, at the age of sixty-eight. His death meant that Mrs Deacon inherited $235,408.22, a third share of his immense fortune.[13] From that moment on, Mr Deacon refused to contribute one cent towards household expenses or the support of his family. Further allegations of violence were made against him.

However exaggerated, the picture is not a happy one. Mrs Deacon is said to have tried hard to subdue her husband's dangerous temper.

Throughout their subsequent troubles, the couple were united on one thing only: that their children should be well cared for. Mrs Deacon was also desperate to avoid any scandal that might jeopardise her place in society. Somehow there was no scandal, and even Mr Deacon conceded that until 1888 his wife's behaviour had been exemplary. Only later did he accuse her of improper conduct with a number of men unknown to him; but foremost in the list of lovers was a man with whom he was only too well acquainted.

Émile François Abeille was introduced to the Deacons at Villers-sur-Mer in 1888 by the Baronne Edmond de Rothschild. He was a young French attaché, born in Paris on 3 January 1845, and thus forty-seven in February 1892, a bachelor who had long indulged in the high life and a mere three months younger than Mr Deacon. According to Gladys, the Abeilles had Jewish blood. Émile's father had worked with Georges Haussmann, who had rebuilt so much of Paris, and then amassed a considerable fortune in the laying down of the Suez Canal. His mother was a Parisian, who shared with Mrs Deacon the dubious honour of being satirised by Robert de Montesquiou in *Les Quarante Bergères* [Forty Shepherdesses].

An intelligent man, Abeille had given up the diplomatic service in favour of a life of travel, sport, summer resorts and lovely ladies, one of whom, the Comtesse du Bari, was to assist in his undoing. He was not a handsome man, his pockmarked face and sallow complexion inspiring Mr Deacon to nickname him the 'Yellow Dwarf'.[14] Yet he had a way with women, and after evenings at the theatre, he would visit 'notorious persons of Parisian night life'.[15]

Émile Abeille wasted no time in becoming a close friend of both Mr and Mrs Deacon and a regular visitor to their home. As she stated later: 'My husband was quite aware of the frequency of his visits at Paris as well as at Cannes. He was always received at our house as an intimate friend.'[16] When Mr Deacon received an anonymous letter warning him about his wife and Abeille, she reproached him for not understanding the 'Parisian flirt'. He forbade Florence to see Abeille, and it seems that for two years she obeyed him.

All would no doubt have been well but for the fact that Mrs Deacon foolishly left a letter in her secretaire, which began: 'My Darling why have you broken with me?' Her husband identified this as having come from Abeille, but once more Florence Deacon appeased her husband, stating that it was impertinent of Abeille to have written to her, but what could she do?

In March 1891 the Deacons moved to an apartment at 142 rue de Grenelle in the heart of the Faubourg Saint-Germain. There, on 12 April 1891, Mrs Deacon's youngest child Dorothy* was born. Gladys was ill at the time, and Mr Deacon found the domesticity too much for him so he left to spend a fortnight in a hotel.

A month after Dorothy's birth, a piece of lingerie reminded Mr Deacon of Abeille's threatening presence. One evening, at about ten o'clock, he came home from a Rothschild party to find Abeille hiding behind the curtain. Mr Deacon later stated: 'I noticed the curtains moved. I rushed to the curtain, and found M. Abeille, whom I had not seen for two years. I walked straight up to my wife and said: "Look at this man! Now I doubt the paternity of your child!"'[17] He went in search of his stick, but on his return, not surprisingly, Abeille had gone.

Mrs Deacon claimed that Abeille had called on her because she was unwell and she had invited him to come up. He had only hidden because he remembered Mr Deacon's unjust suspicions. She enlisted the help of her brother, Charley, and her stepmother, to point out to her husband that he did not understand that he must not alienate his wife's affections by his persistent jealousy. Mr Deacon was duly humbled and allowed his wife to see Abeille, but only at the tea-hour.

Abeille then engaged chambers in the rue d'Anjou, near the boulevard Malesherbes, under a pseudonym. Here Mrs Deacon visited him, unwisely confessing to Mrs Kate Moore[†] that she used to swing naked on a seat for Abeille's greater enjoyment.

Mrs Deacon's doctor recommended a change of air and despatched her to St Moritz with her baby. Mr Deacon's doctor diagnosed that

---

* Dorothy Evelyn Deacon (1891–1960) married, first, 1910, Prince Antoni Albrecht ('Aba') Radziwill (1885–1935); and after an annulment, married, as his second wife, Count 'Pali' Pálffy ab Erdoed (1890–1968).

† Kate Moore, a jolly millionairess from Pittsburgh and a noted social climber with a loose tongue. John Singer Sargent, who painted her more than once, described her as 'like a great frigate under full sail'. [Letter to Henry James.]

he had inflammation of the stomach, so he left for Homburg with Gladys, Audrey and Edith.

At this point, the Comtesse du Bari, a former mistress of Abeille, took her revenge since her regular allowance had ceased to come. She wrote to Mr Deacon several times. He became anxious. Having had no news of his wife, he telegraphed her, demanding that she break with Abeille or divorce. He promised to be the most loving of husbands. After two weeks Mrs Deacon replied that he was a tyrant and, knowing he had business there, urged him to go to America and leave her alone. She added that it would be better if they communicated through their solicitors in future. Mr Deacon's reaction to this was to announce that she would be receiving a visit from him in St Moritz. Mrs Deacon cabled at once that she was leaving the next day and proceeding to the Italian lakes with her friends, the de Gramonts.

Mr Deacon went to Geneva to consult a specialist. There he learnt from a friend, Mr Scheffer, that Abeille had been ensconced in St Moritz. He then established that the de Gramonts had left a fortnight before Mrs Deacon. Knowing that she would stop at the Hôtel Promontório in Grisons, Switzerland, he sent an ingenious despatch enquiring whether or not 'Monsieur et Madame Abeille' had left yet. The reply came back: 'Left for Bellagio'. Years of suspicion were vindicated. According to Mrs Deacon, though hotly denied by her husband, she received an ironic telegram from him: 'Have fun with your Abeille.'

Mr Scheffer told Mr Deacon that it was ridiculous to suggest that Abeille was having an affair with his wife. They were both too well known in society. In the general confusion, Mr Deacon vacillated between fury and contrition. He wrote to his wife, apologising for his actions. Some days later Mrs Deacon came down to Geneva from the Villa Serbelloni at Bellagio and explained that a series of coincidences had led to misunderstandings. There was something of a reconciliation and the family spent some days together in Aix-en-Provence.

Soon it was time for Mr Deacon to depart for the United States. As he embarked in a steamer at Le Havre, he clutched a friendly telegram from his wife signed 'Love from All'. In the middle of October 1891 he returned to Paris. Once more he found Abeille a regular visitor to his house. The question of divorce reared its head again. He employed detectives to try to catch Mrs Deacon at 12 rue de Penthièvre, where Abeille had a small apartment, but his plan was rumbled by an agent in the pay of Mrs Deacon. He never secured enough evidence for legal action, despite discovering that, hot from Abeille's love nest, she had dined with a young man in a *cabinet particulier* of a Champs-Élysées restaurant. In the circumstances, he let Mrs Deacon and the children set off for the South of France for the winter season of 1891/2, while he remained in Paris deciding what to do next.

2

MURDER IN THE SOUTH OF FRANCE

Mrs Deacon began her stay in the South of France at the Hôtel de Noailles in Marseille, but early in February she moved to Cannes where she expected to spend the rest of the winter. Travelling with her were her four daughters, her stepmother and a small retinue of servants. A few paces behind came Émile Abeille.

It is no surprise to find Florence Deacon in Cannes, which had been transformed from a simple fishing village into a fashionable winter resort by Lord Brougham, not so much for the favourable climate found there but for the inclement weather avoided elsewhere.

French and Germans, but most of all English, flocked to Cannes in the late nineteenth century and spent their time playing bridge, flirting or having tea at Rumpelmayer's on the boulevard de la Croisette. Next door, easily spotted due to a profusion of multi-coloured flags, stood the Cercle Nautique, a favourite haunt of Mr Deacon. Here the Prince of Wales played baccarat, here his younger brother, the Duke of Albany, a haemophiliac, fell down the club stairs with fatal results, and here the barman once counted seven Russian grand dukes in the club at the same time.

Mrs Deacon engaged rooms for her family at the Hôtel Windsor, one of eight good hotels on the eastern side of the boulevard du Cannet. It was a highly suspicious Mr Deacon who arrived there suddenly on Monday, 15 February. He wasted no time in examining the hotel register and was not altogether surprised to spot the name of Abeille among the guests. He demanded that the family move elsewhere. Rooms were therefore taken at the Hôtel Splendide opposite the yachting harbour, one of Cannes's oldest hotels and still flourishing today. Gladys's friend, Élisabeth (Lily) de Gramont, recalled later that the hotel was flanked by palms and was a suitable theatre for a drama of jealousy 'because of its air of Italian opera'.[1] Mrs Deacon chose a salon and bedroom for herself on the first floor but told her husband that there were no other rooms available there. So Mr Deacon, Marraine Baldwin and the children were lodged on the floor above.

Their affair being long-standing, Mrs Deacon was becoming lax in her precautions. Even so, it is astonishing that Abeille had the temerity to install himself in Mrs Deacon's hotel. It was not long before the bright eyes and dark brow of Edward Parker Deacon were poised intently over that hotel register. Again the name of Abeille leapt from the page. Mr Deacon went directly to the hotel office where the management, obeying instructions, informed him that Abeille had departed. This was not the case. Abeille was hiding in a room on the other side of Mrs Deacon's salon. He would soon find more reasons than one for regretting the absence of a communicating door.

A low profile was maintained for the next two days while Mr Deacon prowled about, his mind alert to any clue leading to Abeille. Nothing happened on Tuesday night, and on Wednesday Mrs Deacon paid a visit to the Comtesse (Mélanie) de Pourtalès, one of the beautiful ladies-in-waiting to Empress Eugénie of France, herself painted by Winterhalter. Mrs Deacon returned home tired, only to find her husband poised to discuss divorce. He wanted his wife not to contest the action, thereby avoiding much scandal. But divorce meant ostracism from society and, apart from her children, society was Florence Deacon's dominant interest in life.

When Gladys and her sisters were safely in bed, both Deacons called on Marraine Baldwin. At ten o'clock Mr Deacon excused himself and left the hotel to attend a ball at the Cercle Nautique. A clear half an hour later Abeille, attired in a smoking jacket, called on Mrs Deacon. At 10.45 p.m. Irma Deodat helped Mrs Deacon to undress and left her in a white dressing-gown.

Mr Deacon returned at about midnight and observed a light shining under his wife's door. He approached with stealth and recognised 'the rough voice of Abeille' within. He went up to his room, collected his revolver and went in search of Paul Baumann, the hotel secretary, who was at work in his office. Mr Deacon ordered Baumann to accompany him and they proceeded in silence to Mrs Deacon's bedroom door. Baumann carried a lighted candle. Exhorting the secretary to 'follow me with the light as soon as the door is opened', Mr Deacon knocked loudly. The response was a quick shuffling sound.

In the next two or three minutes Abeille considered his options. He could not get through to his own room, but he could leave by the salon door into the passage, but would come face to face with Mr Deacon. Another possibility was to leave by the window, putting his trust in a cornice of about twenty centimetres, which ran round the outside of the building. In the haste of the moment, his nerves on edge, that idea was discarded as too risky. Mrs Deacon claimed later that Abeille 'was reclining against the mantelpiece', as any innocent visitor might do, but knowing Mr Deacon's fiery temper, it is small wonder that what he actually did was to take sanctuary behind the sofa in the salon.

'Open the door at once!' cried Mr Deacon. 'If you do not open the door, I will burst it in.' Mrs Deacon opened the door, dressed in her night clothes. As soon as she saw that her husband was armed, she blew out the dressing-table candle, rushed back and knocked the secretary's candle from his hand. Mr Deacon noticed that the salon door was open and when a new light had been struck, he forced his way in. He saw 'the shadow of a head' behind the sofa. He jumped onto the sofa, put his hand on the lurking figure's shoulder and fired three shots. One bullet lodged itself in the wall, another hit Abeille in the breast and the third entered his leg. Mr Deacon then pushed aside the sofa, seized Abeille, and addressed him in French: 'There you are! I have you!'

Abeille, who had been trying to adjust his trousers, did not reply but just managed to get up and stagger into the passage, where he collapsed in a pool of blood. Mr Deacon, who remained exceptionally cool throughout, asked him if he was badly wounded. Abeille responded with a droop of the head.

Then Florence seized her husband's hands, threw herself at his feet and implored him to spare her, to leave Abeille alone and to make no scandal for the children's sake. It was too late because the shots had aroused the servants and other guests on the first floor. They all came running out until they saw Mr Deacon whereupon they retreated quicker than they had come. Mr Deacon pushed his wife away and replied: 'I will not shoot you for the sake of our children. I have caught you at last, and now leave you to give myself up.' Simultaneously, he told Baumann to take note of the impression of two heads on the pillows and ordered him to summon the police. He spent the remaining hours of the night at the Mairie.

Meanwhile the partially dressed victim, his clothes soaked in blood, was carried to his room and attended to by Irma. A local doctor, Dr Escarra, and Dr Vaudremer, a physician from Paris, came to examine him and pronounced his condition to be very serious. Both Montesquiou and Prince Poniatowski wrote that Abeille was fit enough to make a new will in favour of Mrs Deacon, and the sum of half a million francs was mentioned. Montesquiou also recalled that Abeille constantly cried out somewhat unnecessarily: 'I am finished!' Though everything possible was done to help him, Abeille, never strong, lost consciousness at about eight o'clock in the morning and died soon afterwards.

Mr Deacon remained in custody. That afternoon he made a statement to Dr de Valcourt, the American vice-consul. He was given the chance to prosecute his wife for adultery but, when told this would mean she would be taken into custody, he replied: 'No, I shall not lay a complaint for the sake of my children, nor did I intend to kill Mr Abeille. I only wished to mark him.' At all times he expressed consideration for his children to whom he was deeply attached, and his main concern was to obtain custody of them. Mr Deacon spent the night of the eighteenth at Dr de Valcourt's house. The next morning he was conducted to Grasse by the chief commissaire where he was put in prison.

Florence Deacon began the day after the crime rather differently. She cancelled a luncheon engagement with the Princesse de Sagan. She was generally criticised for this, though Montesquiou, after parodying the incident in his poem 'Déa' in *Les Quarante Bergères*, enquired: 'Does disaster preclude politeness?' He concluded that at this moment of social ruin, such a gesture was not in bad taste. Boni de Castellane, that most debonair of society figures, recalled that when a society hostess heard that Abeille had not even attempted to jump out of the window, she turned to a young man and told him: 'Now, my dear friend, you must learn to do gymnastics.'[2]

A few days after the murder, Mrs Deacon was given permission to go to Paris to consult friends. The children remained with Marraine

Baldwin. In her apartment at the rue de Grenelle, Mrs Deacon made a statement to the *Daily Telegraph* reporter:

> When I am at home I am accustomed to relinquish ceremony, and while I went into my bedroom to put on a dressing gown M. Abeille remained in the salon . . . The best proof that we had nothing to be ashamed of is that he remained where he was, and his appearance, as well as mine, shows that we were simply conversing together when he was attacked in such a cowardly manner. I am aware that it has been said that I took a great deal too long to open the door of my room but you must remember that I was in the salon, and it took me some little time to light the candle.[3]

This was a somewhat distilled version of events. Though she was given to exaggeration and no doubt altered the story to suit the situation, Mrs Baldwin told a different version to Mary Berenson in March 1901, who passed it on to her own mother. The gist was that she had married 'a dissolute madman', who had soon tired of her, had been taken up in Paris society, and that her husband had advised her to take a lover. She had 'fallen madly in love' with Abeille. She was 'tormented to death by her conscience, but her worldliness prevented her getting a divorce'. On the night in question, Mr Deacon was reading in her salon when Abeille was announced. Mr Deacon went out and got his pistol. She thought Abeille hid behind the sofa to make divorce inevitable:

> At any rate he died without a word. *No one* stood by her . . . This pretty, silly lady, whose whole life was bound up in society, and who was desperately in love, found herself deprived of lover and society together. Whenever she speaks of love she weeps. She has had lots of chances to marry again, but refuses them as she still loves this man.[4]

News of the tragedy received widespread coverage in France, England and the United States. Mr Deacon came under hostile attack in the French papers. That an American had shot a Frenchman engaged in the national sport was considered outrageous. Mr Deacon was described as a 'cowardly assassin', and a change in the law relating to husbands who take lives in such circumstances was demanded. On the other hand, the large American colony in Cannes tended to be supportive of him, their code of conduct in such matters being different from that of the French. The *New York Times* correspondent in Cannes reported that 'Many of the quieter class of people here considered the style of Mrs Deacon too pronounced, though she was popular on account of her great beauty.'[5] In Newport, where Peter Parker had been well known, the activities of his grandson caused 'quite a sensation'.

The tragedy fired the imagination of Henry James, who had not forgotten that one summer afternoon shortly after their marriage the Deacons had visited him at his home in Bolton Street, London. Now he reached for his notebook:

> A very good little subject (for a short tale) would be the idea – suggested to me in a round-about way by the dreadful E.D. 'tragedy' in the South of France. – of a frivolous young ass or snob of a man, rather rich, and withal rather proper and prim, who marries a very pretty girl and is pleased with the idea of getting her into society – I mean the world smart and fast, *où l'on s'amuse* – the sort of people whom it most flatters his vanity to be able to live with.[6]

James then outlined a characteristically complicated plot. Though he returned to the subject as late as 1901 and urged himself not to 'lose sight, by the way of the subject that I know – I've marked it somewhere, as the E. Deacon subject',[7] he never made use of it.

The long, slow process of French law ground inexorably into action. Witnesses were examined, including the hotel secretary, M. Baumann. On 27 February the Deacons were confronted in 'an exceedingly painful scene'. Mr Deacon was so affected that he had to go to bed immediately afterwards. Mrs Deacon persisted in denying any impropriety between herself and Abeille. On 4 May Mr Deacon altered his will to exclude his wife and established a trust for his four daughters, which provided Gladys with an income all her life and was only wound up when she died.

The murder trial took place on a day of stifling heat in the Assize Court of the Alpes Maritimes in Nice on 20 May. The day before the case was due to be heard Alexandre Dumas *fils* advocated that, since the divorce law now existed in France, the days of crimes of passion

were over. He maintained that husbands 'have only the right to repu-
diate wives, and that if they shed blood they are liable to be dealt with
as common assassins'.[*8]

The courtroom was filled to capacity, the end gallery with fashionable ladies, colourfully dressed, and in elegant bonnets eager to see
justice done. Mrs Deacon was not in court, pleading ill-health, but a
statement from her was read. She asserted that her husband was 'a
madman and a drunkard' but claimed that she hoped he would be
acquitted 'on account of her children.'[9]

Mr Deacon was described as 'tall, slim, with close-cropped hair,
tinged with the silver of his forty-five years and his domestic woes,
around the temples . . .'[10] He soon won the sympathy of the onlook-
ers. He attempted to defend himself in French, but he was no linguist
and the jury struggled to understand him. He reverted to English.
The lengthy proceedings had the occasional light moment as when
he spoke of Abeille: 'When I saw this little man wounded, I felt
poignant regrets for a man having some conscience must always regret
killing another man.' A storm of applause rose from the spectators. M.
Baumann confirmed the imprint of the two heads on the pillows.
Irma, a lady of the most professional silence, stated she had never seen
any impropriety between her mistress and Abeille. Lombard, a
manservant, employed by the Deacons, was more forthcoming. He
confirmed Mrs Deacon's visits to Abeille's entre-sol.

The prosecution accepted various points but concluded that Mr
Deacon had killed Abeille 'to satisfy the hatred that had rankled for
four years'. Maître Demange rose at 6.30 p.m. to defend Mr Deacon,
stating that Mrs Deacon had been drawn to Abeille through vanity,
and that Abeille's cowering was proof enough of his guilt. He spoke
of 'the legitimate anger of an irreproachable husband who sees the
honor of his children being torn to shreds'.[11] Despite an address in
which Demange 'justified his reputation for forensic eloquence', and
elicited applause from the spectators, the jury's verdict was that
Deacon was guilty of unlawfully wounding Abeille, though without

* In November it was asserted that the Abeille family had paid Dumas 20,000 francs
to write this article; also that Mrs Deacon paid 300,000 francs to make sure that her
husband was convicted, 120,000 of which were to newspapers [*Dubuque Daily
Herald, NY,* 23 November 1902].

intent to cause death. The sentence of one year's imprisonment was followed by a barrage of hisses, groans and hootings.

Mr Deacon's brother, Harleston, shook him by the hand and pronounced it 'a most unjust verdict and sentence'. Meanwhile Mr Deacon 'moped the while in a somewhat grim style, repressing his feelings like a veritable stoic, yet really looking very near breaking down'.[12]

Thus Edward Parker Deacon left the court for a prison cell in Nice. His last words were addressed to his brother: 'Take care of the children.'

3

AMERICA

Gladys and her sisters remained with their mother until, on 10 March, the public prosecutor transferred custody of the girls to Mr Deacon, who promptly sent representatives to take them away. Mrs Deacon opposed this decision and the girls left after an emotional scene. Audrey and Edith went to Mr Deacon's brother, Harleston, while Gladys and the baby Dorothy travelled to Genoa with Marraine Baldwin. A few weeks later Gladys and Dorothy were sent to the Convent de l'Assomption at Auteuil in Paris. Dorothy became 'the pet of the community', living in the care of the sisters, while Gladys began her lessons.

'I so often think of you and wish you were here with me,' wrote her father, as he awaited trial at the Hôtel Richemont in Cannes, but he explained that she was now a young lady and must be 'where you may learn all that will go towards making you a good intelligent honest woman'.[1] He hoped she would not take after her mother.

On 2 April Gladys sent news of herself to her mother: 'One little line from Gladys to give you a thousand loves and kisses and tell you that I am very good and busy preparing for the examins [which] begin on Wednesday.'[2] A sister sat beside Gladys as she wrote. She was 'trying hard to be very good, her health and spirits are excellent'. Before the letter was finished, Gladys's spirits got the better of her, the poor sister concluding: 'Have you ever had Gladys by you when you and she were occupied in correspondence? Not a sinecure – is it?'[3]

In June T. Jefferson Coolidge, the United States Ambassador to France, responded to requests for Mr Deacon's release by asking the French foreign secretary to set him free.[4] In July Mrs Deacon applied in the courts to regain legal possession of her children. She failed, but it stirred Mr Deacon into prosecuting her for adultery to ensure that he always kept them. On 22 September President Carnot granted him a pardon in celebration of the centenary of the establishment of the first French Republic.

On leaving prison in September, Mr Deacon's sole aim was to take his children to America and devote himself to their education. He wrote to Gladys, who had been on holiday at the Hôtel des Réservoirs in Versailles, declaring: 'I will do everything in my power that you shall be happy and not stay at the convent this winter but have a good home. I will see you very soon.'[5] He sent Audrey and Edith to America with Marraine Baldwin, thus removing them from the jurisdiction of the French courts.

Mr Deacon was granted custody of his children before the Tribunal of the Seine in Paris on 3 November. Immediately, he made haste to the Convent de l'Assomption to find Gladys, but when he arrived the lady superior told him that Gladys was not there. The day before had been a holiday and Mrs Deacon had taken Gladys out. Neither had returned. Mr Deacon summoned the police, who searched the convent and the Deacon home in the rue de Grenelle, but the mother and the kidnapped child had disappeared to 'some place beyond the reach of Mr Deacon'.

Mrs Deacon was hoping that if she obtained the guardianship of her children she would maintain some footing in society. She threatened that if her husband did not stop his criminal action against her he would never see Gladys again. The tribunal sat on 16 and 17 November and decreed that Gladys should be returned to the convent, where both parents would be allowed to visit her. But the case had been making headlines in the press, with the result that the abashed nuns refused to take her back.

A considerable number of lawsuits were now pending. In Grasse, Mr Deacon had sued his wife for criminal adultery. This case, if proved, could land Mrs Deacon in prison. Mrs Deacon had appealed in Aix, filed a divorce suit in Paris on the grounds of cruelty and demanded custody of the children. Finally, Mr Deacon had filed a divorce suit in New York, where they had been married. He accused his wife of having had affairs with the Prince de Poix, the Comte de La Rochefoucauld and the lawyer Senator Léon Renault. He announced: 'The French judges have as scant regard for morals as they do for law and order.'[6]

The moment a decree absolute was granted in February 1893 and custody of the three eldest children was confirmed to Mr Deacon, all the other suits were dropped. Florence Deacon reverted to being Florence Baldwin and remained in Paris with her youngest daughter, Dorothy.*

Mr Deacon and Gladys, now aged twelve, crossed the Channel to England, Gladys writing to her mother: 'I cannot tell you how much I feel to leave you altho' I am sure it will be but for a time, as Papa tells me you are coming to see us all in America.'7

In London Gladys and her father stayed at the Burlington Hotel in Cork Street and explored the shops together. Mr Deacon bought Gladys a dress, an ulster and a hat for their forthcoming voyage. On their return to the hotel soldiers and police were keeping the crowd back because the Prince of Wales was holding a levée. 'How big and clean the English soldiers look,' reported the twelve-year-old. Presently they set sail from Southampton on the steamship *Trave*. Gladys was delighted to have a huge cabin all to herself.

They arrived in New York on 23 March where a *New York Times* reporter was lying in wait for the man who had caused so much sensation during the past year. Mr Deacon began by saying he was very tired:

> And what a crowd the Abeilles are! One of the progeny of brothers produced in court a forged letter, purporting to come from me, which said that it was my intention to kill Cocoa Abeille as soon as I was released. I have come to America to stay, but if I hear of that man Cocoa defaming my character, I will cross the ocean again to have an interview with him.8

He described his divorced wife as a woman destitute of moral sense. He tapped his forehead and added: 'She has something wrong here.' Mr Deacon was visibly aged by his great ordeal, his brow furrowed, and his hair streaked with grey. Gladys and her father went

---

* Some years later Mrs Deacon explained to Mary Berenson that the reason Mr Deacon allowed her to keep Dorothy was that he 'repudiated her as not his own'. [Mary Berenson to Hannah Whitall Smith, I Tatti, 2 March 1901, Lilly Library; Strachey & Samuels (eds), *Mary Berenson – A Self Portrait from her Letters & Diaries* (Victor Gollancz, 1993) p. 95.].

to the Buckingham Hotel on East 50th Street and 5th Avenue, where she was reunited with her two sisters, who came running up to her, screaming: 'Gladys, Gladys.'

'Then,' noted Gladys, 'I received Edith's bear-hugs.'

The three girls remained in their father's custody for the next three years. They settled in Newport, Rhode Island, the fashionable resort, where they had already spent several summers. Marraine Baldwin still occupied the admiral's cottage, Snug Harbor, on Bellevue Avenue and, despite the family difficulties, maintained good relations with Mr Deacon. He would go to Newport because, as Gladys put it, he liked to hear the news.

Their first home was a small cottage at 83 Rhode Island Avenue. Several servants were employed, and the food was excellent. All her life Gladys loved animals, mainly dogs but also cats and horses, finding them easier to love than humans. Another resident of the house was her dog, Eden, which had travelled with her from New York. In May domesticity was further assured when all the girls became the proud owners of kittens. During these days, Gladys rode in a dog-cart, took picnics in a steam launch, caught fish, heard Jean de Reszke as Faust at the Metropolitan Opera in New York, and went for a driving tour in the White Mountains.

Gladys began her schooling in Newport with her sisters and secured excellent exam results. But at twelve she was considered too old for the local school, so in November she began a three-year stint at the Howard Seminary for Women, West Bridgewater, Massachusetts. The school was an impressive building, opened in 1875, offering parents 'an institution where their daughters could learn good manners and good teaching.' She pronounced it 'much nicer than I thought it would be':

> Each girl has her own room and they hang pretty pictures up and other things so that some of them have quite lovely rooms. The school building is built of red brick. It has two 'tourelles'. I really think it looks like a museum. The letters here are not read.[9]

Gladys had hoped that Audrey would join her at the school but, despite being on her own, entered wholeheartedly into school activities.

Gladys's father passed his time between Narragansett Pier, Newport, and the Hotel Bellevue in Boston. One night he was in the Somerset Club when the assembled company fell to discussing crimes of passion. A callow young man gave it as his opinion that they never happened any more. Whereupon Mr Deacon looked at him darkly and enquired: 'Young man, do you know who I am?'[10] William James, brother of Henry, was shocked that Mr Deacon talked about the Abeille murder in front of Gladys: 'He is vain to the last degree, I fancy, of his conjugal exploit, and I have no doubt it constitutes a distinction for him in the eyes of fashionable New Yorkers – not in mine however.'[11] Gladys dreaded her occasional visits to New York because 'those frivolous gossips . . . will clump around me to see the talked-about "daughter of those Deacons"'. She consoled herself that she was 'wise in worldly knowledge', and she told her mother: 'I can face those warriors of society armed with their gossip-loving tongues and well coated with rouge and powder.'[12]

Her mother was living in Paris with her great-aunt, Mrs Michler*, looking after Dorothy. She was irritated by an unfounded rumour that she was about to marry Comte Louis de Turenne,† a witty old-school diplomat.[13] Her main preoccupation was to gain custody of her daughters to which end she came several times to America, but Mr Deacon made it clear to Gladys: 'As long as I have a penny and life, no one shall part us.'[14] One such visit was in October 1893, when Mrs Baldwin took a house at East Orange. Gladys tried to cheer her mother up, quoting to her, 'after the rain, the good weather', but could almost see her mother shaking her head forlornly and replying: 'After the rain the good weather for everyone else, but the good weather of my life is over and after the fine days of winter the April rains must come.'[15]

---

* Sarah Archer Michler (1836-1919), Florence's great-aunt by marriage (an aunt of Admiral Baldwin's first wife, Pamelia Tolfree). As Sallie Hollingsworth, she had been a great belle in her day. In 1861, she married, as his second wife, Brigadier-General Nathaniel Michler (1827-81), who had served in the US Engineers during the Civil War. She lived at 1563 Madison Street, Oakland, Alameda, California, surrounded by fine pictures and a large collection of books, was well read and widely travelled.
† Comte Gabriel Louis de Turenne d'Aynac (1843-1907), a man wearing a monocle, the model for Babal de Bréauté in Proust's great novel, who described himself as a connoisseur of *objets d'art*, though everything he chose ended in disaster.

On the day after her thirteenth birthday in 1894, Gladys wished she could have been in Paris with her mother and had the kind of birthday party she enjoyed when she was little. The headmaster's wife tried to console her by telling her that everything in this world was 'but an introduction to the beauties of the next':

> I wonder if I really am worldly! I wonder if it's nice to be so. If I could only have someone to tell me, someone who would not preach to me, for I always feel as though I want to be bad and to shock the ones who preach so much.[16]

Gladys did not hesitate to ask her mother for things she needed - a guitar from Paris, which her father would pay for, books to help her form a good library, by good authors and well bound, and a new gown:

> I would like to have it made of pale green silk with a sort of '*reflet*' in it. I do not care how it is trimmed as long as it is very pretty. I feel as if I were asking too much but I feel I know you would like to see your little Gladys well dressed.[17]

She played the mandolin and sang with a voice that developed from a 'high, clear soprano' into a 'very deep contralto'. She learnt German and enjoyed the opera and the theatre, longing to see Sarah Bernhardt on stage. Then it was painting that became 'the only thing' she cared for. Among the best in her class, she was given a prize – *Masterpieces of American Literature*.

Mrs Baldwin made a further custody attempt in June 1895, taking a house on Dram Island, Sorrento Harbour, Maine, where Gladys was hailed as 'quite a belle in the young set'.[18] Gladys was determined to be released and urged her mother to keep pressing the lawyers. But her father's line was that he would only hand Gladys over if Mrs Baldwin let him keep Edith and Audrey.[19]

★ ★ ★ ★ ★

In October 1895, when she was fourteen, Gladys spotted an item in the newspapers that changed her life. She wrote to her mother:

I suppose you have read about the engagement of the Duke of Marlborough.

O dear me if I was only a little older I might 'catch' him yet! But Hélas! I am too young though mature in the ways of women's witch-craft and what is the use of the one without the other? And I will have to give up all chance to ever get Marlborough.

But when he comes he'll dress in blue, what a sign his love is true!' You see what consolation there are in those simple lines!'[20]

To Gladys, as to many American girls, Consuelo Vanderbilt's engagement to the Duke of Marlborough appeared to be the ultimate in success. The union of her wealth and beauty with his dukedom and Blenheim Palace conferred sudden respectability on the Vanderbilts, whose fortune of $200 million had been acquired by means more foul than fair. The Duke of Marlborough was portrayed in the press as the most eligible bachelor ever to arrive on the east coast of the United States.

This fired an ambition in Gladys – to outdo Consuelo. She did not know her, although both were often in Newport, and neither was she her bridesmaid, as was often suggested later. Gladys was safely tucked away at Howard Seminary, dreaming of the impossibility of it all. Her ambition was evidently fuelled by a visit to a fortune-teller, though what he said is unclear. However, years later, her friend, Mrs Agnes Grylls, wrote to her:

Do you know I believe that all your life you have been subconsciously influenced by that wretched fortune-teller & that if it had not been for his wickedness in telling you all the things he did you would be a different woman – living a normal life in a normal way. Don't be furi-ous with me for writing this – it is not meant to be impertinent – I just feel that this man is responsible for the ruin of your life – it makes me simply mad.[21]

On her fifteenth birthday in 1896, Gladys received a letter from a friend of hers, who had been in the same hotel as the Marlboroughs in Cairo, reporting the duchess had worn 'the most beautiful gowns imaginable'.

★ ★ ★ ★ ★

In her last year at school, Gladys became a member of its dramatic and social club, of a dinner club that met every Saturday, and was president of a five-girl tea and chocolate party group, which met regularly in her room:

> The care of dishwashing falls to the lot of both president and secretary. I have to wash all the tea cups while my unfortunate secretary has to wash the spoons and saucers.
>
> I always make the tea or chocolate whichever it may be and I assure you it is no small labor.[22]

In the spring Mr Deacon informed Gladys that she and Audrey could go to Mrs Baldwin for the Easter vacation. 'I know you will be pleased to hear this,' he wrote. But Mrs Baldwin pressed for total custody. So Mr Deacon arrived at the seminary one day and laid his terms before Gladys. If Mrs Baldwin did not accept his proposal of the Easter vacation, then he would surrender her to her mother. But in exchange Mrs Baldwin would have to relinquish all claims to the other children. Gladys would have to become a Baldwin and renounce him as her father. Gladys was in a desperate dilemma and appealed to her mother:

> I feel my brain power giving way under this awful weight. Everything is a blur. I don't seem to realise. I can't understand, comprehend my position. I am not fit to decide anything either for myself or for the others . . . I am crazy. I don't know what to do. My poor little sisters, I may never see them again! That is for long years to come.

Soon after this, Mr Deacon's long-suffering lawyer, W. P. Blake,* resolved the situation, for fear, according to Gladys, that if Mrs Baldwin came to Boston to do battle with 'this peculiar man (Papa)' she would influence him to give her more than he intended. In March 1896 Mr Deacon wrote to his former wife releasing Gladys and Audrey: 'Giving you the children is the greatest proof that I can give of my faith and confidence in you.'[23]

* William P. Blake (1846–1922), Harvard-educated lawyer. He dealt with family matters for some years to come.

And so Gladys left the Howard Seminary with the gift of *Virgil's Bucolics & Six Books of Aeneid* (1891), Virgil being her favourite author at that time, and returned to live with her mother. Audrey and Edith stayed in the United States in order not to interrupt their education, Audrey sailing to Europe on 9 November 1898, and Edith staying longer.

Gladys almost certainly never saw her father again, though she sent him regular presents. On receipt of a pair of braces, he replied: 'Of course anything worked by the hands of my handsome daughter would be prized by me.' Gladys also urged Audrey to write to him.

In the winter of 1896/7 Mr Deacon contacted Henry James, who professed himself interested in the 'drama' that had restored him to America, and to the part played in his life by his daughters: 'by what you can do for them, and by all that they, I take it for granted, are able to do for you'.[24] James's brother, William, was less sympathetic: 'I think the cuss is ½ insane – at any rate not worth wasting paper on – he is always bombarding me with incoherent notes to which I rarely make reply.'[25] Henry James wrote that he hoped to meet Mr Deacon's daughters: 'I wish I could see your girls. But I shall be sure to – the future is theirs and I shall hang on to it hard enough and long enough to be brushed by their wing.'[26] Sadly Henry James and Gladys never met, though she admired him: 'He was the English Flaubert . . . a rare product of America . . . He was thoroughly honest. He had a brain as fine as silk.'[27]

Henry James's hope that Mr Deacon was bearing 'the burden of flesh' in 'some place of cool Atlantic airs' was soon confounded. In July 1897 he stood as Mayor of Newport, but was seen removing not only his shoes but also his false teeth in his hotel. On Independence Day he dressed as a veteran of the Grand Army of the Republic, and rode alone on a horse for many hours, carrying umbrellas of exaggerated colours.[28] Two days later, he was expelled from the Newport Reading Room, America's oldest surviving club, 'because he persisted in taking ice from a water pitcher to cool his head'.[29]

His doctor diagnosed 'a form of insanity known as confusional mania; an exhaustion insanity'. He advised that Mr Deacon should go to a quiet place where he could be watched, but still continue riding, walking and fishing. He warned that he had a naturally unstable nervous system, with an inherited taint, would eventually go insane, and that if he did not get proper rest, he could become dangerous.[30]

The worst happened on 22 August 1897 at the Hotel Bellevue in Boston. Mr Deacon had a fit and became almost uncontrollable. His lawyer, Mr Blake, arranged for him to be sent to the McLean Hospital in nearby Belmont. Mr Deacon calmed down when he arrived there, though he realised it was an asylum for the insane. A newspaper report described him as looking 'haggard, worn and emaciated', having lost 'that commanding and dignified air for which he was once noted'. He seemed 'but a shadow of his former self, and to be worn with troubles and age'.[31]

A fortnight later, the medical superintendent of the hospital forwarded to Mr Blake a letter Mr Deacon had written to Gladys: 'I send it to you because knowing the circumstances so well, you can tell better than I whether it should go as addressed.'[32] Mr Deacon was more relaxed than had been anticipated, though the other patients annoyed him so he was moved to a suite of rooms in Upham House, at fifty dollars a week. The hospital assessed him:

It seems to us extremely probable that he has had a disease of the spinal cord for several years, that more recently the same disease has appeared in the brain, constituting what is known as general paralysis, and that he will never recover.[33]

They considered that he might have periods of remission, and could even live outside a hospital, but that he would soon grow worse again, was unlikely to live many years and was best kept under medical supervision.

In December Mrs Baldwin came to see him at Upham House, accompanied by his brother Harleston, and her brother Charley. They conversed together quietly and it was hoped that the visit might improve his mental state.

In his last years Mr Deacon took comfort from Florence Baldwin's letters, giving news of their children. In March 1898 he was delighted to hear that she intended to visit him again. He retained a sense of humour, as when speculating to her about his brother's wife: 'I wonder Mrs Harleston has no babies. Harl is too serious for that!!!'*

---

* Harleston Deacon died without children in 1926. He had married Susanne Parker Knox (1861–1954) in 1893.

And the man who had insisted so vehemently that his wife should renounce his name now addressed his envelope to 'Mrs Florence Deacon', and began his letter: 'My dearest Florence'. But at five o'clock one Saturday morning in April 1898, he sawed through his bars and escaped by jumping from the second floor of the hospital. Despite twisting his ankle, he pressed on for ten miles, finally spotting a young woman on the veranda of her house and suggesting he work for her as a seamster. She summoned help and a car came for him. When he recognised a hospital attendant he bade a polite farewell to the lady, got into the vehicle, and returned calmly to the hospital.[34]

In March 1901 Mrs Baldwin was reporting that her former husband 'believed himself to be a nephew of Moses'.[35] Edward Parker Deacon suffered a brain seizure at the hospital and died of pneumonia on 5 July. All four Deacon girls inherited $200,000 (including $120,000 of personal property and real estate in trust).[36]

Three days later a brief funeral service was held at the Trinity Church, Newport, attended by Marraine Baldwin, and a few local figures. Then his brother, Harleston, and Mr Blake accompanied his body and he was buried next to his sister Ida in the Island Cemetery, high above Newport.[37]

PART TWO

The Pursuit of Pleasure

Villa Farnese, Caprarola

Gladys in 1913

4

PARIS IN THE BELLE ÉPOQUE

I was a miracle.
Differential Calculus was too low for me.
                    Gladys, Duchess of Marlborough, May 1976

Gladys returned to Europe in 1896 or early 1897, and that October she continued her education in Bonn. In old age she recalled her dislike of it: 'I was at school in Bonn in a small house near the university. I had to learn by listening and that was no good . . . It was a stupid place. I learnt nothing there.'[1] Gladys was more or less a beginner in German, though she had taken lessons in America and continued her studies in Paris with a German governess. Mrs Baldwin accompanied her to Bonn and was delighted to find that she was to be living with German girls. What she did not appreciate was that those girls were enthusiastically trying to learn English and French so little German was spoken. It was not long before Gladys was dismissing Bonn as 'this weary hole'.

She went to the Frölich School to attend all the German classes in the hope of hearing good German spoken. She explained to her mother:

> I am going to give this place a fair trial until Xmas and study hard, but if I don't speak then, I don't think it would be worthwhile to come back. I am in hope that the course at Frölich will help me, if they don't, then I 'hang up the hat' as the saying goes.[2]

Despite frequent supplications to be taken away, Gladys stayed in Bonn until December 1898. She lodged at 10 Baumschulen-Allee, a house in a wide street in the centre of the town, from where she wrote in February 1898: 'The heating is so elementary that my hands are perishing with cold.' One delight was a regular painting lesson with an artist who spoke no French or English, so that while Gladys could understand his German, he could not understand any of her questions. In due course a German lodger who spoke French was found. The teacher 'came back literally dragging the poor frightened creature behind him who nevertheless served very well as interpreter'. Gladys also took Italian lessons; and by April she could play a waltz 'quite finely' at the piano. Her studies at the keyboard came to an end for two reasons. One day she sat beside an open window and heard someone else playing so beautifully that she knew she could never aspire to that standard. Also one of her sisters played at home, and she concluded that one person practising in a house was quite enough. Other recreations included taking photographs with a Kodak and working a tapestry.

Now aged seventeen, Gladys paid frequent visits to friends at Darmstadt, a place of which she became particularly fond. For a while her life was 'nothing but parties, coaching trips, etc., with some very charming people'. Gladys and Audrey, who joined her at school in Dresden in 1898, were naturally concerned as to how they would be received in society after the publicity the family had suffered over the years. There was no adverse effect. In Italy, Gladys went to a ball with her friend, Lily Kirk, and made a court bow to the King and Queen. She reassured Audrey that she was full of confidence about her position in the world: 'I have had enough success to ensure it, so don't worry about yours.'[3]

Not every girl of her time studied the classics, but Gladys attended a course on Homer at the end of 1898 and was overjoyed that she could understand every word. She took up Latin by herself and dived enthusiastically into a book of Pliny, which she described as 'a wonder of elegance in its style'. Blessed with great application she relished her work: 'This studying mania is getting stronger and stronger and I shall end as a professor before long.'

In her last term Gladys was the ring-leader in a school revolution, brought on by the 'ridiculous severity' of the teachers. They tried to win her over, but she proved more than a match for them: 'I did not give way at all but I let them think I was on the point of coming to their side, bringing with me the other ten girls and re-establishing peace at Baumschulen 10.' From that day on she held the whip. The teachers were all too aware that at a sign from her, hostilities would be resumed. 'It is a delightful comedy,' wrote Gladys, 'and I begin to enjoy the sweets of Divine right!'[4]

★ ★ ★ ★ ★

In 1899 Gladys returned to Paris where she studied mathematics with a tutor at Sacré Coeur, a method of learning that held more appeal to her than 'listening' at Bonn. She was able to make rapid progress. 'We discussed,' she recalled. 'I worked and he corrected . . . Sometimes he saw it my way!'[5]

Gladys was fortunate to have a brain that could digest new information accurately at first reading. She also knew how to dispense to others what she had just learnt, to maximum advantage. A report in 1902, which concerned itself more with her beauty than her brains, had this to say of her:

She is a bright, lively girl, thoroughly well-bred and intelligent, and up-to-date both in literature and art, but full of fun, even witty at times . . . She is quite at home in conversing either with young or old, and with the latter evinces a pretty deference which wins her golden opinions.[6]

Her tutor called her 'a brain genius' and Gladys suggested that this was why she was able to spend so much time totally alone. She did not attend university, but was a keen advocate of a university education: 'It smooths life.' And she recommended it strongly to a young person, enquiring: 'Have all your talents been brought out of you?'[7] She continued to study on her own or with tutors for some years to come and emerged with seven languages, a wide general knowledge, a fascination for mythology and a lifelong love of art, literature and poetry. 'When I read poetry, I am up in Heaven!'[8] she said.

Gladys's power of conversation, her extraordinary use of the written word and her intriguing personality had an astonishing effect on nearly everyone she met in her long life. Combined with this was another gift, that of a quite remarkable beauty, a radiant manner and smile, 'the embodiment of sunshine . . . a bright winsomeness of manner which immediately takes you by storm. Her chief beauty, perhaps, lies in her large [bright blue] eyes, and the perfect moulding of her brow, and although by no means of a classical cast of feature, yet she attracts more than many with a perfect profile.'⁹ She possessed a good Hellenic profile, of which she wrote obliquely in 1927: 'If God has been good, if He has given you a Greek nose, a perfect mouth, and wide set eyes, so much the better.'¹⁰

Great beauties often believe themselves flawed. Gladys came to notice a small dip between her nose and forehead, which came to play on her mind. Her enormous staring eyes she used to advantage, fixing them directly on the person she was talking to, and seeming to look right into their soul. Many found this an alarming experience. Nor did she ever lose her flair for rolling those eyes provocatively.

As early as 1899, and again in 1901, Gladys was sketched by Giovanni Boldini, a lasting friend despite numerous quarrels. He came from Ferrara in northern Italy and made his name as a fashionable society portrait painter in Paris. A dashing figure, he frequented cafés, was a splendid raconteur, rode elegantly and danced well. He played the piano and sang. He was one of the first in Paris to ride a huge bicycle and to own an automobile. Bernard Berenson described him as a 'disagreeable, rather dandaical personality, looked as if he had a nasty taste in his mouth. As artist, ultra-chic, particularly when portraying elongated society ladies as if with translucent glass, very taking and with a certain dash and pep even.'¹¹ Among his most famous works were portraits of Count Robert de Montesquiou, the Marchesa Casati, and Consuelo Vanderbilt with her son Ivor.

Boldini had what Consuelo Vanderbilt described as 'a salacious reputation with women' at an early age, finding it hard to resist plucking a fruit that came within his grasp. In his later years, when a female head shared his pillow, he instructed his maid to rouse him at seven with an appropriate excuse. His companion then departed and he repaired cheerfully to his work. In October 1901 Consuelo felt obliged to advise Gladys not to see too much of him. Lily de Gramont also sat for a portrait but gave up the sittings realising that she would have to pay 'one way or another'.

Jacques-Émile Blanche tried to persuade Gladys to come to Offranville to be painted by him, but that had no appeal. In December 1901 she was sketched by Paul César Helleu who was delighted at the prospect and asked his patron, Montesquiou, to let him know the moment she returned to Paris. He had to contain himself until Gladys recovered from a bout of 'flu', but at last his time came. He expressed his joy to Montesquiou's faithful secretary, Gabriel Yturri:

> You are fortunate to possess that one thing that I have adored for so many years! What a queen you have! I saw Miss Deacon last night and she told me that she can come and pose here. You know I would be delighted to lunch with you and Montesquiou but there's not a minute to lose. And as she is happy about it, I prefer that she should come here and pose. You have no idea what a bore it is to leave after lunch, with a cardboard under one's arm after the first sitting. For 1,000 francs I will do many drawings of the adorable creature. What a nuisance that she is leaving! There are so many things I could have done of her this winter . . .[12]

Gladys kept Montesquiou informed of the progress of the portrait: 'The sittings continue every afternoon, but it was only yesterday after numerous tries that the master believed he had grasped the runaway spirit in the pose.'[13]

★ ★ ★ ★ ★

In 1899 Mrs Baldwin took Gladys on a three-month visit to Charley Baldwin, at Beaulieu, in California. Having sailed from Le Havre to New York, they then took the long rail journey to California, arriving eight hours later in New Orleans on account of a sandstorm in Arizona. Gladys wrote to Bernard Berenson:

> Then on the way through the swamps of Georgia, our train was nearly wrecked, the rails having been tampered with by some brigands.
>
> As it was our two engines were thrown right over, and the baggage car followed them with all our belongings.
>
> And there we remained all night on a tressel some thirty feet high with water at the average of ninety foot deep all around us. It was simply awful hanging between life and death for what seemed like all eternity. Some of the men were killed, and mortally wounded but the passengers were all saved, the horrid things. I went to see the wounded firemen the next morning and hearing of their miserable pecuniary condition started out to wring some money out of my fellow passengers. Oh my dear friend, the awful time I had with these creatures for

give they would not though these men had saved their lives in sacrific-
ing their own.

However, I made some three hundred francs by my tenacity but the
disgust I felt had left a deep scar in my breast.[14]

Florence Baldwin and Gladys arrived at Charley Baldwin's ranch in
Santa Clara County in December 1899. Hardly had Florence appeared
than local society became suspicious, fearing that Charley was intend-
ing to re-launch his scandalous sister into strait-laced San Francisco
society. It was one thing when he took her to lunch at the University
Club, another when he took her to a play at the Columbia Theatre,
but too much when he tried the final test - lunch at the prestigious
Burlinghame Country Club, a considerable draw for prominent locals
since its foundation in 1893. The 145 members did not care for this
and Charley was invited to resign, which he did on 11 February 1900.

A cryptic note in the local paper stated:

Since the Sunday in June 1896, shortly before he married Miss Ella
Hobart, when he had trouble on the polo grounds with Louis Du
Plessis Beylard,* and a duel seemed imminent, Baldwin has not been
popular in the Burlinghame set. His former troubles with his brother-
in-law [Edward Parker Deacon] and his contact with individuals
outside the club, left him many opportunities to enjoy his own
company.[15]

On 20 February 1900, Mrs Baldwin and Gladys left America,
accompanied by Florence's aunt, Mrs Michler, and their staff. Gladys
never crossed the Atlantic again.

★ ★ ★ ★ ★

Gladys launched herself enthusiastically into the belle époque of Paris.
Her Svengali was that most flamboyant of aesthetes, Count Robert de
Montesquiou-Fézensac (to give him his full title), a society friend of
her mother's for more than a decade. He presented himself as a nobleman and poet, or, as Gladys described him: 'a poet of sorts'. Proust

---

* Louis Du Plessis Beylard (1852-1904), a troublesome character, one-time consul
in Jamaica.

drew on him for the Baron de Charlus, and Oscar Wilde, possibly, for Dorian Gray. When he went to New York in 1903, he was hailed as 'a reigning divinity . . . due to his good looks and good clothes'.[16] Reflecting on the matter in 1977, Gladys pronounced: 'Well, he was not evil and he was elegant. One could dress like that today!'[17]

He lived in style, owned a jewel-encrusted tortoise, and entertained lavishly, though for every party he gave, there were two lists – one for those to be invited and another for those to be excluded. The count derived more pleasure from the latter. Angular, affected, striking poses, tall and with hair perked high, it is said that he hid notoriously black teeth behind gloved hands. He was mocked and derided by his contemporaries – Gustave Schlumberger,* historian of the Byzantine Empire, was not unique in hating him. He nurtured 'a violent antipathy' to the count for his 'extraordinary infatuation, his incredible pride, almost childish, his jealous wickedness'.[18]

Montesquiou's secretary Yturri had been raised in Buenos Aires, emigrated to Paris at the age of fifteen and served Montesquiou from 1885 until his own early death. Gladys thought that Yturri secretly hated Montesquiou, and remembered that people speculated that he composed his master's poems. Yturri made great friends with Gladys and one day she sent him a small present. She was thrilled with the success of her gift, which inspired in return 'such delicious verse'.

Montesquiou had sided with Gladys's mother over the Abeille affair. She amused him by wearing a hat festooned with ivy, and announcing: 'I'm already wearing the head-dress of a ruin.' She also told him plaintively: 'I was not born to be ignored.' The count was no less impressed by Gladys, nicknaming her 'The Marvel'. At dinner at one of his celebrated fêtes at Versailles he exclaimed: 'And Gladys Deacon was truly beautiful. She had the absolute appearance of an archangel.'[19]

Soon after their first meeting, Montesquiou sent Gladys his photograph with a flattering note. She was 'very, very touched' by what he said about her 'little head' and promised him her photograph in due

---

* Gustave Schlumberger (1844-1929), an extravagantly moustached figure, and an admirer of Gladys's mother, having found her 'very likeable, very hospitable, having retained numerous friends, despite her misfortunes'. In 1908 he would accompany the Berensons on a visit to Caprarola, her home north of Rome.

course. Later he offered her some poetry: 'I am in delicious anticipa-
tion of the verse you are going to dedicate to me,' she wrote. 'Nothing
could go to my heart more than such an honour and I thank you with
true feeling.' The poem, '*L'Éventail*' ('The Fan'), eventually published
in *Les Paons* (*The Peacocks*) in 1908,[*] described the gentle waving of a
fan held in a pale hand, which sent out imperceptible ripples of air
that reached the stars and the ocean and the forest and Heaven and
far-off universes beyond. Gladys read the poem at Versailles in 'a
silence where battles are bemoaned' and was enchanted. They also
bonded over fascination for what she called 'the externalized soul of
Aubrey Beardsley', the artist, who had recently died, and a fascination
for Whistler and his litigation with Sir William Eden.[†] Her strong
friendship with Montesquiou was forged through such shared
adventures.

★ ★ ★ ★ ★

Gladys loved the 'omnipotent charm' of springtime in Paris and was
glad when the overseas visitors arrived – 'such a relief to talk to other
than those odious Frenchmen'.[20] It also steered her into the world
of the Marchioness of Anglesey,[‡] who became her self-appointed
chaperone. She was an American with fine porcelain features, who
entertained at her villa, L'Hermitage, at Versailles. Gladys referred to
Minna Anglesey as 'Aunt Min', while the artist Romaine Brooks
wrote of her conversation: 'With each slight puff of breath, feathery
thoughts were wafted from place to place . . . A vocabulary was not
necessary; mere chirping and twittering answered just as well.'[21]
Gladys enjoyed her receptions where she met a mixture of bohemians
and worldly people:

---

[*] Robert de Montesquiou, *Les Paons* (Édition Définitive, 1908), p. 119.
[†] Sir William Eden, Bt (1849–1915), father of the future prime minister, Anthony
Eden, had commissioned a portrait of his wife but only paid 100 guineas for it.
Whistler then painted out Lady Eden's face and refused to hand over either the
portrait or the 100 guineas. The story was told in *The Baronet and the Butterfly*, put
out by Whistler in a small edition of 250 copies. Montesquiou urged Gladys to find
a copy, and eventually she secured copy number 10 of the Paris edition.
[‡] Mary ('Minna') Livingstone King (1843–1931), born in Georgia, USA, married
first to the Hon. Henry Wodehouse. She then became the third wife of the 4th
Marquess of Anglesey.

This combination is a most happy one. The ones bring out their various talents to dazzle the others and these in turn make great show of '*grandes façons*' so as to show these good people that a man with tradition shows off to a better advantage in a salon than any other, however clever.[22]

In November 1901 Mrs Baldwin was worrying that Gladys was refusing every offer of marriage, appeared 'to demand the impossible from life, and wears herself out with reading at night & excitement in the day'.[23] Gladys was twenty years old and, like many who lead full and adventurous lives most of the year, she found the Christmas season oppressive, but thought: 'It is so delicious to gallop in the deserted woods and fancy all the sprites, ghouls, leprechauns, manes, fays and elves, hiding in the underbush.' She went shopping in the boulevards, but Paris was full of crowds. She found it a strain and concluded that her respect for political institutions was growing: 'I could not but wonder how it was that so many people could live in one town, under one law and with comparative unison and contentment.'[24]

Gladys often spent part of the season at Versailles. In 1902 Montesquiou rented a house there to give parties. On 10 September Comte Bertrand de Fénelon, an intimate of Proust, entertained guests at the Hôtel des Réservoirs. Gladys attended together with Montesquiou, Comte Georges de Lauris, and his lesbian friends, Anne Morgan, Elsie de Wolfe and Bessie Marbury, who shared a house on the boulevard de la Reine at Versailles and were particular purveyors of Parisian gossip to Bernard Berenson in Florence.

In Paris, Gladys was welcomed into the salon of the Comtesse (Thérèse) Murat, along with Abel Bonnard. It was here that she caught the eye of Lily de Gramont, who, like Montesquiou, hailed her as 'a blazing archangel. Her intellect was heavenly, fascinating, astounding.'[25]Another consistent friend and supporter was Thérèse Murat's intellectual sister, the Marquise (Solange) de Ludre, who shared a similar circle to her sister and that of the Comtesse (Rosa) de Fitz-James. She preferred to entertain at home, and eschewed public forms of entertainment. Gladys greatly preferred the intellectual world of Paris to the Season she had lately experienced in London.

Mrs Baldwin and her daughters moved about Europe according to the time of year. In the summer, they invariably went to Sils-Maria, an Alpine resort in the Engadine, not far from St Moritz. Here Gladys met the most powerful intellectual influence in her young life.

5

THE BERENSONS

The weird Gladys, with her soft elixir ways,
Like Sphinx, like Medusa . . .

Carlo Placci on Gladys

She is perfectly natural, and is a frightening mixture
of extreme youth and very dangerous womanhood.

Mary Berenson on Gladys

It was traditional to take to the mountains in the summer season. Gladys arrived in Sils Maria in August 1897. They went frequently to St Moritz and it was almost certainly Carlo Placci, a recurring figure in their lives, who introduced them to the art critic Bernard Berenson. Placci was Berenson's greatest friend and a key figure in Florentine society – a cultured man, a well-off dilettante and an aesthete, who wrote the occasional undistinguished novel or short story. He, too, was staying at the Hôtel Caspar Badrutt.

Gladys was only sixteen when they met and Bernard Berenson was twice her age at thirty-two. He fell in love with her and in December 1901, a year after marrying, he told his wife, that he would dearly have liked to marry her. Mary Berenson was surprised, having had no idea of the intensity of his feelings: 'I think thee* did wrong not to follow that strong feeling, and try to marry her. There would have been some chance for thee to have at least a little real, satisfying joy, instead of the frugal fare of duty. However, thee did what thee thought right, and if it was a mistake, all we can do is to make the best of it.'[1]

Deeply distressed, Mary wrote the following day to say she felt she was going to die and quite wished she could. She pursued the Gladys

---

* Mary Berenson used the Quaker style of 'thee'.

theme: 'But even if thee had had the bliss of marrying Gladys by now I am sure thee would be in Hell. And could thee be sure of making a good third choice?'[2]

Bernard Berenson – Bernhard until 1914 – was a Lithuanian, born in Russia in 1865. His parents had emigrated to Boston when he was ten, and after school, he pursued intense personal studies in the Boston Public Library, where he soon became a self-confessed pest, drawing out more books than the attendants thought he could possibly read. His first plan was to become a critic and literary historian. But some members of the Harvard community and the immensely rich Mrs Isabella Stewart Gardner, of Fenway Court, a great patron of artists, sent him on a three-year educational tour of Europe. By concentrating on art as the field in which he considered himself the weakest, he followed in the footsteps of Giovanni Morelli and became a considerable connoisseur, identifying Renaissance paintings, exposing misattributions and spotting forgotten masterpieces in obscure collections and in the corners of dimly lit churches. He repaid Mrs Gardner by helping her form one of the finest art collections in the United States. He grew into a legendary figure himself, revered by the world for his recondite knowledge.

Later he went into business with Joseph (later Lord) Duveen, the famous art dealer. Looking back, Gladys explained: 'Duveen couldn't sell a picture without Berenson's endorsement, even if it was worth ten million dollars!'[3] Berenson was not averse to taking commission, though it was something he did not care to discuss. He introduced expressions such as 'life-enhancing' into the world of art, and extended the metaphor to his friends, who were invariably judged either 'life-enhancing' or 'life-diminishing'.

In the late 1890s he was at work on *The Drawings of the Florentine Painters*, which was published in two volumes in 1903. He had met his future wife, Mary Costelloe, in 1890 and presently she had left her husband for him. Originally a Quaker from Philadelphia, the daughter of Robert Pearsall Smith, and his wife, Hannah Whitall Smith, she had married Frank Costelloe in 1885 and had two daughters. She would not divorce as she had converted to Roman Catholicism and only married Berenson in December 1900 after her husband Frank's death at the age of forty-four. Meanwhile she travelled with him as his 'pupil and secretary'. Theirs was no easy relationship, since she had the habit of falling in love elsewhere, and in time he, too, broke away from his initial monogamy to embark on a series of love affairs, some of which Mary, rightly or wrongly, encouraged. In later life he confessed that he never met a woman without wondering if he wished to sleep with her.

Gladys was soon corresponding with him, building up a relationship steeped in mythology. She saw herself as a maenad – a wild creature frenzied with wine. And Berenson was a faun, a rustic god, a kind of Roman Pan, a prophet who spoke to men in their dreams, the guardian of herds and the patron of wild pursuits. From time to time the maenad warned the faun that her thyrsus was getting hot and she would soon be pursuing him over Florentine hills. At one point she sent Berenson a thistle from Paris as 'a tiny souvenir of my pleasant character'. She explained: 'I fear alas that even the thistle is not enough to adequately express my prickly disposition. But search and you will find that within the spiky exterior there lies a heart capable of feelings of fondness and serenity.'

When Gladys was in Paris, she missed him and longed to see him. 'You are not a person to me,' she declared, 'you are a burst of soul and spirit.' She found one of his publications in a local bookshop and made friends with the owner so as to be able to dip into it from time to time. Then occasionally Mrs Baldwin would announce that they were going to Florence, and Gladys would be thrilled:

> B.B. We will make long walks, you will tell me everything. In the late afternoon we will come home bringing to your comfortable arm-chairs that slight weariness so exquisite at twilight and it will be a year before dinner is served.

Before her 1899 California visit, Gladys was sad to be leaving, not only because it meant separation from Berenson but on account of the endless visits to couturiers and milliners, parasites whose exist-ence depended on a woman's vanity. She wrote to Berenson:

> Every day until now I would ride in the enchanted forests, full of memories and ghosts. It's Marly, it's Versailles, it's Garches; but now I'm left with Paquin, with Doucet and with Worth.

She would have preferred to remain in Paris, gathering cherries and weaving garlands. She regretted being condemned to a life of perpetual emigration. Her notions were more romantic:

> I wish I could die so as to be buried in the earth and return in the shape of a beautiful tree with a slender and glorious silhouette, or rather to emerge from its branch as a delicate and beautiful flower which, no sooner picked, would wilt in order to return the next year more beautiful still. Why can't it be so?

She was concerned that Berenson might be lured away by other beautiful women, but hoped he would come to Paris to celebrate her eighteenth birthday the following February. Meanwhile, she begged him to accept the gift of her feelings as 'a discreet offering from the Maenad to the Faun, who without a thought tramples on the wailing and burning hearts of mortals'. On her return from America, she was relieved to hear that he had not forgotten her and that she had not been 'relegated with the herd of past conquests'.[4]

* * * * *

Despite describing herself as a conquest, Gladys had known since April 1900 that Berenson intended to marry Mary Costelloe (whose husband, Frank, had died in 1899). For a while, she told him, the whole family had been furious. Only when Carlo Placci assured them that the future Mrs Berenson was a charmer did they decide to forgive him. But change was inescapable:

> I am afraid your faun days are over and all that remains for your only Maenad is to follow your illustrious example . . . And so dear friend, goodbye. Forgive such a long silence from a beautiful woman who has a true and deep friendship for you.[5]

Gladys signed her letter 'a poor deserted Maenad'.

The newly married Berensons had moved into Villa I Tatti, in the hills above Florence, and gradually turned it into a haven of culture where Berenson held court for nearly sixty years. On 27 February 1901 Mrs Baldwin and Gladys arrived to stay there, which gave Mary Berenson the chance to scrutinise her guests. Almost every day she wrote to her mother, Hannah Whitall Smith, an ardent Quaker, then living in England. The mother was hardly a gentle person. She had whipped her baby son, Logan Pearsall Smith, black and blue at four months to try to stop him crying. When her husband died, she had sold his false teeth. She was to be the recipient of a lot of information on Gladys.

Mary summed up Mrs Baldwin as a famous beauty, now fading, 'and she resents bitterly being eclipsed – as she certainly is by her brilliant & beautiful daughter'.[6] Mrs Baldwin was becoming increasingly formidable, her fine features o'er-topped by an immaculate pile of mahogany-coloured hair, well captured in Boldini's 1906 portrait of her. Lady Grey of Fallodon told her lyrical son Stephen Tennant, who developed the description, that 'Nothing compared with this leech and squid mama, dominating the social sea like a Dreadnought! Empty ballrooms yawned & lulled – drowsy footmen, butlers nodded over forsaken caviar . . . She was really 80 women!! . . . She was Warwick Castle, the Grand Canyon on legs.'[7]

Mary Berenson preferred Gladys:

> The girl is rather wonderful, but she is, it seems to me, considerably spoiled by living in that milieu. They are dreadfully rich, the sort of people who change all their clothes, nightgowns and sheets, *every day* (a mother and 4 daughters!) and have some famous actress or singer or musician at five hundred or a thousand francs two or three nights a week, when they give dinner parties. *Why* they came here is a mystery to me, but I suppose it is always better than staying at a hotel.[8]

Mary speculated that 'underneath those gorgeous dresses are all the marvellous lace petticoats and underclothes & stockings which come in the next pages of a fashion magazine, & finally that they are clients (as they are) of all the doctors for the hair, complexion, nails, eyebrows, etc., all the swell masseuses, all the perfumery, glove – jewel – cosmetic shops advertized in the back pages of such a magazine'. She soon concluded that Mrs Baldwin was 'a lovable but an excessively silly woman, who has ruined her life, and is trying to ruin her daughter's'. Gladys, she thought 'naturally gifted to an unusual degree, but erratic, whimsical, incredibly extravagant and undisciplined, and happy only in virtue of that blessed possession, *Youth*!'[9]

Mrs Baldwin suffered from her questionable past. Mary was furious that, for this reason, their friend, Miss Blood,* would not receive Gladys and her mother. When Berenson took them off to Siena, she concluded that it had been a strain trying to relate to their world.[10]

In Siena Berenson took Mrs Baldwin for a tour around a picture gallery and came back impressed that such an apparently superficial woman should have so much taste and natural feeling for art. Alas, he had been taken in, for Gladys revealed that her mother had returned from the expedition and collapsed exhausted on her bed, exclaiming: 'What a delightful man he could be if only he would stop caring for those old *croûtes!*'[11] But the friendship forged between Mrs Baldwin, Gladys and both Berensons would survive all manner of complications in the years to come. When Mary was passing through Paris, Berenson urged her to stay with Mrs Baldwin: 'I do want to keep hold of Gladys,' he wrote, 'even at the expense of her mother and I am really fond of her on her own account.'[12]

★ ★ ★ ★ ★

Nearly a year later, the residents of I Tatti were once again stirred out of lethargy by Gladys's sudden arrival. Mary recorded:

> Suddenly Gladys came . . . and she has been filling our time & thoughts. She is radiant and sphinx-like. Strange likenesses to her mother flit across her face. Placci has come to adore. She has been marvellous.[13]

Gladys had been staying in Florence with Lady Paget,† and very much fêted. During the coming weeks Mary was transfixed with admiration: 'She is a radiant wonderful creature, so amusing, so entertaining, so beautiful – I never get tired watching her.'[14] Gladys played a game called 'Lamb', which involved her running round the older members of the group, gambolling round them 'with freakish jumps & leaps,

---

* Florence Blood (1866–1925), lesbian companion to Princess Jeanne Ghika at Villa Gamberaia.

† Walburga, Lady Paget (1839–1929), born Countess von Hohenthal, widow of Sir Augustus Paget (1823–96), a British ambassador. She lived at Torre di Bellosguardo, south of Florence.

peering up into our eyes with her wide open blue orbs, looking both innocent & mischievous'.[15]

Despite her success in Paris and London, Gladys purported to be sick of the fashionable set encountered in those cities and wanted the Berensons to believe she was happier with them than anywhere else.[16] When she left with Berenson, Mary assessed her guest:

Gladys – 'the weird Gladys, with her soft elixir ways, like Sphinx, like Medusa, like a lot of innocent and poisonous things mixed up', as Placci says – has gone, and things tend to seem a little flat. She is certainly the most fascinating sphinx I have ever encountered. She wants awfully to come back and go with us on our little *giro,* and we hope she will be 'let', by her mamma and her chaperone – Lady Anglesey. What a girl!

Mary was anxious for Gladys's future. Still virtually a child, her mother would force her into a rich marriage, whereas she needed six or seven years to mature:

And if she marries fashionably, all her fine powers will run to seed (unless by miracle), and I dare say she will become one of the most famous and infamous Beauties the world has ever known. What may, however, preserve her from that fate, is her frailty of health. Of course her silly mamma never told her anything, gave her any ideas of taking care of herself. Since a small child, she has never slept more than 4 or 5 hours at night and her eating has been simply preposterous – years of sweets and pickles. She says – that their mother has *always* failed them, whenever they were in any need, physical or moral. The younger children hate her, but Gladys is now able to take her humorously, as a general thing.[17]

Gladys's tour with Berenson included Pisa, Cometo, Viterbo, Orvieto and Siena. Mary joined them later, finding everyone in good spirits and the weather fine. She thought that Gladys turned 'one's head with her beauty & her vivid personality', leaving her feeling plodding:

So even the most serious person shoots out butterfly wings at the touch of her wand, but they are alas too frail to carry the heavy body.

Or else the serious man simply 'falls in love' and then becomes whatever sort of animal he really is. Thus, she has no chance of knowing people, and she passes like a brilliant, terrifying vision. Circe was lonely too I daresay, & this frightening child finds men 'so stupid'. B.B. is oppressed, as I am, by the sense of the irrelevance of all the things we care about for such a creature, so he remains either dumb or silly. Fortunately she is a hundred people in one, and entertains herself by her own rapid changes of mood.[18]

At Viterbo they ran into Lady Ottoline Morrell* and her husband, Philip. Gladys called out: 'Goodness me! There's a Soul!' They observed Lady Ottoline, 'a tall drooping figure in a fur coat & low neck hung all over with jewels & crowned by an immense poke-bonnet, on which nodded & trembled an immense array of ribbons & funereal feathers & ends of lace'.[19] The Morrells joined them in their carriage, Ottoline engaging Berenson in a culture conversation, while divesting herself of her poke-bonnet and tying a lace shawl over her head.

Mary also wrote the first of several perceptive descriptions of Gladys in her diary, giving the best impression of her at this time. She found her radiant and beautiful, daring, enchanting and tiring:

A wonderful creature, but too young to talk to as an equal, and so much of a born actress to take quite seriously. But so beautiful, so graceful, so changeful in a hundred moods, so brilliant that it is enough to turn anybody's head. Part of her mysteriousness comes from her being, as it were, sexless. She has never changed physically from a child to a woman, and her doctor said she probably never will. She calls herself a 'hermaphrodite', but she isn't that. Brought up by a mamma who thinks of nothing but Dress & Sex, her mind plays around all the problems of sex in a most alarming manner with an audacity and outspokenness that make your hair stand on end. She is positively impish. But she has never felt anything, so she dares.

Her defects are bad form – for she is distinctly in bad form – and lying; but as Bernhard says, she is so wonderful she can afford the first, and she may outgrow the second.[20]

* Lady Ottoline Morrell (1873-1938), half-sister of 6th Duke of Portland.

Gladys told Mary she had not felt so well for months. She was in high, even boisterous spirits. On 1 April they found themselves in a little village and soon she had a train of about two hundred children and a number of grown-ups following her two miles down the road, like the Pied Piper of Hamelin. Mary wrote,

> It was one of the most enchanting sights I ever saw. She snatched one little boy's red scarf and danced ahead waving it (she knows every dance ever invented in every country – she learnt this at the Paris Exposition), leaping high and singing, looking wonderfully beautiful; and then came this humbling, shocking mass of children, all looking at her, & running to catch her, with by-plays of boys wrestling along the side of the path. The road wound down for several miles, zigzagging from the little town, and at each turn, the whole crowd stopped & shouted & waved to the grown-up inhabitants of the village, who came out in a crowd onto the ramparts to watch.[21]

Berenson joined in, running, shouting, leaping, and playing with the children.

Mary worried that he was inviting trouble by caring so much for Gladys and, despite her undoubted brains and powers of observation and description, she concluded that a month in her company was disagreeable since Gladys thought only of herself: 'I never heard her say anything that indicated that the happiness of a single other human being was an object to her.'[22]

The group was back at I Tatti at the beginning of April. Mary was surprised that Gladys appeared to be enjoying herself at the villa, 'for a greater set of Frumps from Frumpignano were certainly never assembled together'.

Gladys now seemed to abhor Paris and London despite her success in both capitals: 'She is a wonderful Vision – teasing, annoying, tiresome, selfish at times.'[23]

Interlude

CECILIA

1902

The first time Gladys appeared in a novel was in 1902, when, at the age of twenty-one, she inspired the American novelist F. Marion Crawford to base his heroine on her. He was a prolific author, well-known in social circles in Paris and Rome, the nephew of Julia Ward Howe, the brother of Mrs Hugh Fraser, and the half-brother of Mrs Winthrop Chanler, all of whom wrote books.

He saw Mrs Baldwin on her American visit in 1902, and in the same year, he published *Cecilia – A Story of Modern Rome*. There is evidence that he had Gladys in mind, since he knew her well, saw her often, and told Vittoria Colonna, Duchess of Sermoneta, one-time reigning beauty in Rome, that he was contemplating 'a queer novel', though adding: 'My heroine only resembles Miss Deacon in looks.'[1]

Cecilia bore many similarities to Gladys:

> Some people said she was perfectly beautiful, others declared that she was a freak of nature and would soon be hideous, but, meanwhile, was an interesting study; one young gentleman, addicted to art, said that her face belonged to the type seen in the Elgin Marbles; a Sicilian lady said that her head was even more archaic than that, and resembled a fragment from the temples of Selinute, preserved in the museum at Palermo; and the Russian ambassador, who was of unknown age, said that she was the perfect Psyche of Naples, brought to life, and that he wished he were Eros.[2]

Marion Crawford's descriptions of Cecilia suggest that not only her beauty but also her character was inspired by Gladys. 'Exceptional gifts, exceptional surroundings, and exceptional opportunities had made Cecilia Palladio an exception to all types, and as unlike the average modern Italian young girl as could be imagined.'[3] Furthermore she had an appreciation of art, had attended lectures at the Sorbonne, and read Nietzsche.

In preparation for this, Crawford asked the Duchess of Sermoneta what she thought about Gladys, and gave his view:

> . . . though we talked much, and she talks well, I never got anywhere near to understanding her. My friend and I agreed she would make a marvellous Beatrice, but what character may really be under that strange archaic type of beauty, goodness only knows. I like to think that the one may suit the other. She is like the Archaic Minerva in the Naples Museum.[4]

The duchess replied that she thought Gladys's beauty was 'weird'. Crawford continued:

> Yes, she inherits what one might call 'natural publicity', she cannot help attracting attention, and people will always talk about her . . . She interests me very much, her gifts of mind seem to be extraordinary, and I cannot help believing that she has a generous and enthusiastic nature.

He also commented: 'She is clever and has read a mass of stuff without quite understanding it, but always meaning to understand and judge fairly of the value of things and people.'[5]

6

THE MARLBOROUGHS

She prefers death to life without you & yet she cd burn your eyes
from their sockets.

She is your gardien, your right arm against all the world & yet
when you & she are face to face, she cd sell you for a brass farthing.

She wants your good before her own & yet she longs to make
you suffer in an instant of this hideous perversity which is the
other half of love.

Gladys to the duke (undated)

Gladys had focused on the Duke of Marlborough and his wife, Consuelo, since their wedding in 1895. Her girlhood wish to marry him had been written with humour to her mother, but was nevertheless well set in her, and enforced by the predictions of a fortune-teller. She cannot have dreamt that she would ever meet them, but when she did, it was a powerful turning-point in her life.

The meeting took place almost certainly soon after the birth of Lord Ivor Spencer-Churchill in October 1898, but it could have been as late as 1900. She knew Consuelo well by the beginning of 1901. The duke and duchess were immediately and powerfully drawn to her. Their lives would never be the same again.

According to Consuelo's misleading memoirs, *The Glitter and the Gold*, in which she painted herself as victim and saintly heroine, the meeting took place in London, where Mrs Baldwin had taken Gladys to introduce her into English society. To each daughter she gave the advice: 'Hold the prize high' – make the dog jump for the biscuit. Men must learn to jump to the tune of Mrs Baldwin's beautiful daughters. Consuelo left a generous description of her:

Gladys Deacon was a beautiful girl endowed with a brilliant intellect. Possessed of exceptional powers of conversation, she could enlarge on any subject in an interesting and amusing manner. I was soon subjugated by the charm of her companionship and we began a friendship which only ended years later.[1]

Gladys appeared at a time when neither of them was happy. Charles Richard John Spencer-Churchill, 9th Duke of Marlborough, had survived a gruelling childhood. Born in Simla, India, on 13 November 1871, he was nicknamed 'Sunny', not for his sunny disposition but for his courtesy title, Earl of Sunderland.

His parents had divorced in 1883 following the sensational elopement of his father (then Lord Blandford) with the Countess of Aylesford, a notorious *cause célèbre* with many unfortunate ripples, not least the attempted blackmail of the Prince of Wales by Lord Randolph Churchill. In 1881 Lady Aylesford bore Lord Blandford a son, known as 'Guy Bertrand Spencer' or 'Bill Spencer', who spent much of his youth at Blenheim.*

Marlborough used to complain that he had been bullied by his father. Gladys judged that he had been 'wounded as a child'.[2] His aunt, Maud, Marchioness of Lansdowne, explained to Gladys:

> He has always to my mind been misunderstood. Up to ten years old he was one of the most charming boys I ever met, & most joyous; after that his spirits seemed to have vanished & he quite changed, but I have always remained very fond of him, & I think he has been cruelly wronged during the last 12 years.[3]

On the other hand, years later, Ethel Boileau, the popular novelist, wrote to Gladys: 'A man told me the other day that when "he" was a little boy, he used to pull wings off flies and whip dogs with a sparkle in his eyes.'[4]

Duty had been instilled in him by his formidable grandmother, Frances (Anne), Duchess of Marlborough. The Marquess of Londonderry (one of Consuelo's lovers) thought that his childhood had been so badly handled that he had become a pessimist,

---

* Guy Bertrand Spencer (1881–1950). He became a brewer.

developing from the sadness of his early life, and that he imagined the whole world was against him.[5]

In December 1891 Albertha, Lady Blandford, Sunny's mother, had to petition her former husband for the upkeep of her son, but the court decided that no provision should be made. Nevertheless, he completed his education at Winchester and Trinity College, Cambridge, before his father died 'somewhat suddenly' at Blenheim on 9 November 1892, at the age of forty-eight. Thus, four days before his twenty-first birthday, Sunny became 9th Duke of Marlborough and master of Blenheim.

When he married Consuelo Vanderbilt in 1895, some $2.5 million of capital stock of the Beech Creek Railway Company was transferred to two trustees for his benefit, and an annual income of four per cent was guaranteed by the New York Central Railroad Company until the day he died. In order to achieve this, he had to relinquish a girl he loved, almost certainly Muriel Wilson,[*] in favour of the Vanderbilt fortune, so badly needed to maintain Blenheim.

Much has been written of Consuelo's reluctance to marry the duke. She had considered herself engaged to Winthrop Rutherfurd,[†] a debonair New York socialite. But her mother threatened to have a heart attack if they married, deciding that Marlborough would be a better catch. Then she threatened to shoot Rutherfurd if they eloped. Consuelo was young. She gave in. In her memoirs, Consuelo made clear how little she and the duke had in common, and presented a depressing picture of silent meals, a frosty atmosphere, and of social activities generally dismissed as 'tiring'.

The marriage took a turn for the worse as early as 1898. In January 1901 the duke confided in the lawyer, Richard Haldane,[‡] the

---

[*] Muriel Wilson (1875-1964), later also a possible wife for Winston Churchill. She was the youngest daughter of Arthur Wilson, of Tranby Croft (where, in 1890, Lt-Col. Sir William Gordon-Cumming, Bt, was caught cheating at cards in the presence of the Prince of Wales). Only as late as 1917 did she marry Lt-Col. Richard Warde, MC, Scots Guards (1885-1932). She remained a friend of Marlborough all his life. She was not in sympathy with Gladys. In relation to Muriel, Gladys told the duke: 'Dark women are unlucky to you.' [Gladys to the Duke, 18 June 1918].

[†] Winthrop Rutherfurd (1862-1944), a well-connected American, whose mother was a Stuyvesant.

[‡] Richard Haldane (1856-1928), QC and successful lawyer, later lord chancellor. Created 1st Viscount Haldane, KT, OM.

circumstances of his 'domestic troubles'. He told him that in 1898 Rutherfurd had stayed with them at Melton. Consuelo had then gone to Paris for two weeks with Mrs Henry White,* a fellow American, who happened to be Rutherfurd's sister. In Paris she had spent two weeks with Rutherfurd. The duke had permitted this visit with some reluctance, greatly disapproving of the association.

Consuelo admitted 'intimate relations' with Rutherfurd since the spring of 1898 when they had met in Paris, that he was 'the one man to whom she had been attached in her life'. She told the duke that Rutherfurd had frequently promised to elope with her if she so wished. This had placed him 'in the most painful and trying position'. In November 1899 the duke objected to another 'gentleman' in Consuelo's life.

When Rutherfurd appeared in London in January 1900, the duke allowed Consuelo to have a meeting with him. But Rutherfurd declined to elope with her 'on the plea that he was too attached to her'. She returned to Marlborough in despair, declaring that she had been grievously deceived but now had no choice but to stay with him. She realised she had ruined any chance of a happy home life. As a result of this debacle, the duke was only too pleased to accompany his cousin, Winston Churchill, to the South African War, serving with the Yeomanry Volunteers.

When he returned some months later, he hoped that time spent with her mother would have calmed Consuelo down. Instead he learnt that she had lived with Frederick Guest† for six weeks in Paris, while staying with her father. She told the duke that any further 'close intimacy' with him was now 'somewhat distasteful to her'. Haldane advised him as to how he should now conduct himself. The duke accepted that he should offer the mother of his children 'every equitable opportunity of repairing the error of the past' and should strive 'in spite of the shattered home to save her from herself, from

---

* Margaret 'Daisy' Stuyvesant Rutherfurd (1854–1916), a striking beauty, who made a great impression on Edith Wharton and Henry James, and had been famously painted by Sargent in 1883. She lived at Wilton Park in London.

† (Rt Hon.) Frederick Guest (1875–1937), third son of 1st Lord Wimborne. A keen polo player, then in the Life Guards. He rose to be chief whip under Lloyd George, and secretary of state for air. In 1905 he married Amy Phipps, an American from Pittsburgh. He was the father of Winston Guest, husband of C. Z. Guest (Lucy Douglas).

these terrible issues to which her manner of life would inevitably lead her'.[6]

★ ★ ★ ★ ★

Gladys paid her first visit to Blenheim in 1901, at the age of twenty, arriving in advance of the large Unionist rally on 10 August at which the duke, Joseph Chamberlain, Arthur Balfour and Winston Churchill addressed some three thousand delegates from the front steps of the palace, celebrating the union of the two parties and the resolution of the South Africa question.

Her arrival relieved the tedium of the Marlboroughs' doomed marriage, which the duke would describe as a 'false and sordid story'.[7] Not only was he dazzled by Gladys, but so, too, was Consuelo. She adored talking to her late into the night, discussing art and books with her. Once again Gladys inspired love from both husband and wife.

The duke disappeared for a few days after the rally, taking a cure at Harrogate. From there he wrote the first of many letters to Gladys, hoping that she and Consuelo were having 'an enjoyable time' in his absence, sending her his 'fond remembrances' and quoting La Rochefoucauld: 'Absence diminishes mediocre passions and enflames the big ones, as the wind extinguishes candles but lights fires.' He cherished 'the fond illusion that the candle has not been blown out', and lingered on 'the possibility of its burning'.[8] Reluctantly, he was pessimistic about his chances.

The duke had to return to Blenheim on Saturday, 31 August because the Kaiser had so enjoyed his stay at Blenheim in 1899 that he had asked the Marlboroughs to receive his son for a few days. As Consuelo put it: 'We could but agree.'[9] The duke was back in time to greet the crown prince and 'his Teutonic retinue'.[10] On that day an open landau drawn by four horses and with outriders swept through the gates of the palace and out stepped a shy young man, Crown Prince Wilhelm of Prussia.

He was nineteen, just a year younger than Gladys, and had come to England from the austere German court, still in mourning for his grandmother, Empress Frederick. 'The Crown Prince,' wrote Consuelo, 'was tall and slight, and gave one an impression of shyness and indecision. Very fair, with prominent blue eyes, and a silly expression that accentuated the degeneracy of his appearance he nevertheless had charming manners and took infinite pains to please.'[11] The crown prince was known to be susceptible to a pretty face, but it never amounted to much. This time he fell badly.

It was a small house party. Besides Gladys, the duke invited Viscount Churchill and his wife, Verena (later a great ally to Gladys), to join the German suite, Count Wolff-Metternich (the German ambassador), Count Mensdorff, Count August zu Eulenburg and Colonel von Pritzelwitz.

According to a serial in *Le Matin* in August 1902, love burgeoned between Gladys and the crown prince as a game of tennis drew to its close on a perfect summer evening. The crown prince pledged his love with the ring his mother had given him for his first communion, and Gladys gave him her bracelet. He also inscribed a book to her, *Deutsche Liebe* – 'To his dear Miss Deacon in friendly memory – Your Wilhelm C. P. [Crown Prince].'[12]

Meanwhile Count Wolff-Metternich did his best to monitor the flirtation, while Consuelo tried in vain to restrain Gladys. The ambassador thought his trouble was over when the crown prince leant over the visitors' book on the Monday and inscribed: 'I felt very much at home here',[13] but worse was to follow.

The prince insisted on personally driving the Marlborough coach to Oxford. Wolff-Metternich shook his head anxiously and protested that the lovelorn youth had never driven a coach in his life. Consuelo sat next to him ready to seize the reins in an emergency. Gladys was sandwiched in the back between Marlborough and Metternich, with the crown prince continually turning round to gaze at her, to the consternation of the other passengers and the near apoplexy of the ambassador. After a tour of Oxford, the prince left by train. Consuelo heaved a sigh of relief as she watched 'his silly face protruding from the window to catch a forlorn and parting glimpse of the lady he was leaving'.[14]

But that was not the end. Back in Germany, the Kaiser noticed that his son's ring was missing and sent a furious message via his chamberlain to Consuelo, demanding its return. Gladys surrendered it somewhat reluctantly, and Colonel von Pritzelwitz sent the bracelet back.

Consuelo protected Gladys as best she could, reporting to her: 'I also hear there was much gossip at Newmarket about the Crown

Prince; I simply told a very great talker that there was no truth in it; but that you had returned the ring as you thought it childish nonsense. Really society is not only indiscreet but drivelling.'[15] Naturally the Berensons quizzed her about the romance next time they saw her. She told them the crown prince had given her a ring, 'was very devoted to her, but all the rest is newspaper rubbish. She says he is a *perfectly charming Boy*, absolutely unspoilt & simple & transparent.'[16]

In another version, Tina Whitaker*, a Sicilian heiress who entertained grandly at her home, Villa Malfitano in Palermo, related that the crown prince was driving in a dog-cart at Blenheim and complained that his ring cut into his fingers. Gladys offered to pull off his glove and remove the ring while he held the reins: 'On their return from the drive, she said she would keep the ring as a souvenir; at this he demurred, saying it had belonged to the Queen, his grandmother [Queen Victoria], and that he could not give it to her. But she was obdurate and kept it . . .'[17]

Later the same month, Gladys and Consuelo travelled to Germany to do some sightseeing. The visit panicked the German court, and the moment they arrived at their hotel in Berlin, an imperial ADC presented himself, on the Emperor's instructions, to show them round. It soon transpired that his real mission was to make certain there was no tryst between the crown prince and Gladys. In contrast to Consuelo and Gladys, who revelled in exploring Sans Souci and the galleries, the ADC looked dour throughout. The Kaiser had taken no chances. Not only was the crown prince banished from Berlin, but the officer selected proved to be 'a man impervious to woman's charm', as Consuelo euphemistically described him. In Dresden they were released from his company and free to converse again about life, art and philosophy. They took steamers down the Elbe and went to the opera in the evenings. Their only point of dissent was the Germans, whom Gladys liked and Consuelo detested. It was a trip that Consuelo remembered as a happy break from the tedium of Oxfordshire and she was especially pleased to find Gladys in a positive mood, aware that she could be satirical and cynical.

* Caterina (Tina) Scalia (1858–1957), married Joseph Whitaker, of the Marsala family.

Gladys's romance with the crown prince left her unscathed. Shortly before the German trip, Mrs Baldwin reported her as still at Blenheim and 'perfectly happy'. But for the hapless crown prince there were unfortunate repercussions. He was forbidden to attend the Coronation of Edward VII due to his flirting.[18] And shortly before his death in 1951 he revealed that there had once been a charming American he would much have liked to marry. The Kaiser had forbidden the match because, according to the rules of the German Imperial Family, his son could marry only a princess. On 6 June 1905 the crown prince did his bit and married Princess Cécilie of Mecklenburg-Schwerin.

By the end of September, Kate Moore, a well-known purveyor of gossip, had told Carlo Placci, who in turn told Bernard Berenson, that Ivor Guest, Lord Wimborne's heir and a first cousin of Marlborough, had fallen in love with Gladys, to no avail. Berenson imparted the news to Mary, who was disappointed:

I almost wish Gladys would marry some nice Englishman, but I have heard that the Wimbornes are rather social climbers, and I suppose if she marries there, she will be lost to us. Well she was a radiant vision & with entrancing possibilities in her. The pity is that they will probably come to very little – from our point of view . . . And it must be very hard to say farewell to her.[19]

Not long after Gladys had returned to Paris from Dresden, the Duke of Marlborough came to see her. He found her in good spirits and went home bearing gifts from her for his two sons. Consuelo was enchanted with them: 'Blandford & Ivor send you kisses and many thanks. They remember you quite well.'[20] The next time Gladys returned to 'the fog of London', she did so in an atmosphere heavy with gossip about her and the Marlboroughs. She complained to Berenson:

I am so tired of those complacent English, of their talk of never-coming victory,* of the new beauty & perhaps of a possible scandal of an impossible kind!
  I had so much of it last summer I nearly had an attack of hydrophobia![21]

---

* The Boer War lasted from 11 October 1899 until 31 May 1902.

She was not disappointed in her expectations of London: 'It is cold. The inkstand is full of icicles and my head of blue devils. I wait in patience for a brilliant epistle from "the lady-killer of Settignano".'[22]

★ ★ ★ ★ ★

Early in the New Year, Consuelo told Gladys that the other guests had said charming things about her, and 'Lady de Grey, Consuelo Manchester etc are not particularly sweet spoken as a rule'. Growing closer to Gladys, her letters were almost those of a lover. From the loneliness of Blenheim, Consuelo begged her not to pass too many exams and get beyond 'your poor old Coon'. She defined Marlborough's relationship with Churchill: 'Sunny is still devoutly attentive to Winston's every remark – a great sign of friendship.' She was less enthusiastic: 'Winston still on the talk – never stops and really it becomes tiring.' She added:

> Whenever I am depressed I imagine myself in Italy with you – not with the Italians – just reading, contemplating everything beautiful and breathing in the spirit of the universe in great deep breaths – uplifting and refreshing. Don't laugh at me! I think I should have liked to be a Vestal Virgin & forever nourished the fire of life & rejoiced in enforced virtue, recognized as such! or else Cleopatra – I hate the middle course.[23]

Gladys asked Consuelo for a lock of hair and Consuelo promised to send her 'a Coon ringlet'. By 1902 it is fair to say that both duke and duchess were enthralled by Gladys.

7

THE LONDON SEASON – 1902

Before leaving I Tatti for Bologna in April 1902, Gladys took Mary aside and told her that Consuelo was 'nearly broken-hearted because the Duke would make such wild love to her'. Mary became more anxious about the fate of the 'brilliant, beautiful, cruel, selfish, untrained' Gladys. Nor could she be sure whether or not to believe her: 'All in all I never knew a person who told so many lies as that beautiful radiant creature.'[1]

There had been an afternoon when Gladys found the duke's mother and sister Norah in Florence and went to spend time with them. Lady Norah had four pet frogs with her and had trained one of them to jump into her mouth from her hand when she called: 'Hoo! Hoo!'

During these years, there had been many suitors. In 1911, W. T. Stead, the famous and controversial journalist, greatly admired and befriended by Gladys, wrote that American newspapers had forever been linking her name to some prince or duke: 'She has become a legendary figure in the mythology of Anglo-American journalism.'[2] Among those mentioned were the Marquis de Lubersac, lover of the famous courtesan, La Belle Otéro, and of Gladys's mother, and Prince Karl of Liechtenstein,* another suitor of Gladys's mother, who had turned his attentions to the daughter in 1899. Paris buzzed with the story.

Claude Lowther, connoisseur of art, presently an MP, and later the owner of Herstmonceux Castle, came home to his family,

---

* Prince Karl Aloys of Liechtenstein (1878–1955), cavalry master, and briefly prime minister of Liechtenstein from 1918 to 1920. He was closely related to both the Emperor of Austria and the Kaiser. In 1921 he married Princess Elisabeth of Urach (1894–1962).

announcing that he had discovered 'the most beautiful family in the world, mother & daughters all equally wonderful'.[3] A more serious candidate was Lord Francis Hope, brother of Princess Doria*, and destined to be Duke of Newcastle. He was a hopeless character who spent his life dissipating his fortune (which included the infamous Hope diamond). In late 1901 he was a genuine suitor, but lost his foot in a shooting accident and, perhaps on that account, also lost his chance with Gladys.

In April 1902 Gladys was pursued by the Count of Turin,[†] described by Mary as 'the Royal Personage of Florence'. The count sent her flowers but to the wrong address. Mary commented: 'She does well in avoiding him, for he is a rather compromising person.'[4] At that point Gladys appeared to prefer Leo Stein, Gertrude's brother, a tall, balding man with an undernourished red beard, full of bizarre gestures and eccentric ideas. Of him she said: 'He is too nice really, quite elemental, by which I mean partaking of the irrepressible nature of the wind & sea etc.'[5] But he never had a hope. Again Mary noted: 'As to Gladys taking Stein seriously, it is out of the question. She refused Ivor Guest with £120,000 a year! She has a morbid horror of marriage.'[6]

For June and July 1902, Mrs Baldwin rented 3 Hyde Park Place, the Bayswater home of Lady Henry Somerset, in order to launch Gladys into London society in the summer of 1902. A brilliant season it was to be, with England preparing for the Coronation of Edward VII on 26 June.

Consuelo did not prove as broken-hearted as suggested. She escorted Gladys all over London. Gladys floated from party to party, like a goddess, dressed in vestal white. She was never far from the apex of high society and everywhere she went heads turned to gaze at her. On 8 May she sat in the stalls at Covent Garden with the Marlboroughs for the opening night of the opera season, attended by

---

* Lady Emily Pelham-Clinton-Hope (1863-1919), married 1882, Prince Alfonso Doria (1851-1912), later prominent in the life of Florence Baldwin. Mother of Filippo (1886-1958), Orietta Borromeo (1887-1969), and Giovanni (1890-95).

† Vittorio Emanuele, Count of Turin (1870-1946), general in the army, son of King Amadeo (briefly King of Spain and the Indies), and cousin of King Victor Emmanuel III of Italy. If famous for anything, it was for fighting a duel in 1897.

King Edward and Queen Alexandra. A fortnight later she was there to hear Melba, Caruso, Scotti and others sing in a night of Italian opera. *The Lady* reported that 'Two of the most beautiful girls in London, or indeed, anywhere' were to be seen side by side in Madame von André's* box – Muriel Wilson, the girl Marlborough would have married, and Gladys, 'the lovely American with her fair, golden hair and exquisite pale damask complexion'.[7] Both girls wore white and Gladys carried pink roses.

Gladys stayed at Blenheim from 16 to 18 May, in the company of Jennie Cornwallis-West (the former Lady Randolph Churchill), her husband, and Claude Lowther. On 10 June Madame von André took her to an Austro-Hungarian concert at the Royal Institute of Painters in Watercolours in Piccadilly, and then Gladys retreated for another week at Blenheim.

Two days later the Berensons arrived in England and drove to Oxford with Roger Fry. They were to have seen Gladys but their work cataloguing the drawings at Christ Church Library was so engrossing that they wired her not to come. She was livid and, not being one to be put down easily, dashed off a furious note to Berenson. They did see her at a dinner Mrs Baldwin gave for them with the actor Norman Forbes and the Scottish poet Douglas Ainslie[†]. According to Mary, Mrs Baldwin was 'radiantly beautiful in a head-dress of golden and purple' in contrast to Gladys, who was 'pale and worn-out in a huddled up black dress, and could talk of nothing but the "Beauty Ball" she was getting up'. The décor was good, but the conversation 'pitiable'.[8]

Mrs Baldwin and Gladys were eagerly awaiting the Coronation, but two days before the great event, the news spread that the King was ill (he had fallen victim to appendicitis, then known as perityph-litis) and the Coronation was postponed. The stunned nation waited anxiously for news of his operation. It was successful, and Mrs Baldwin, in black velvet with tiny diamond tassels, took Gladys to the magnificent Crystal Palace Ball on 2 July, which became a celebration for the King's miraculous recovery. The season continued with the Imperial Coronation Bazaar at the Royal Botanical Gardens in

---

* Alice Palmer (1859–1941), American-born wife of a rich financier.
† Douglas Ainslie (1865–1948), poet, critic and diplomat.

Regent's Park on 11 July. Gladys was a stall-holder, along with twenty duchesses, sixteen marchionesses, and sixty-two countesses. This proved a tragic occasion, with gales tearing through the awnings and thunderous rain drenching the guests. A Canadian lady was killed when a piece of coping-stone fell on her head as she waited to see Queen Alexandra arrive.

So hectic was her life at this time that it was not unusual for Gladys to attend several events on the same night. She looked 'very lovely' at Blanche, Lady Howard de Walden's reception for colonials and Indians at Seaford House, and not long afterwards had her son proposing to her. Although she had meant to accept him, she later regretted that she had bitten his head off in anger.[*9] Then she went to Claridge's for a dinner dance given by Princess Hatzfeldt and Lady Cunard, sitting at a table with Lady Marjorie Manners.

It did not suit Mrs Baldwin to remain in London for the postponed Coronation, now fixed for 9 August, but Gladys was determined not to miss it. She stayed on in the capital, but in something of a quandary as all her friends departed for a break in the country. The Duke of Marlborough was at Blenheim; Consuelo and Verena Churchill were away. Lady Blandford was staying with her sister; Lady Norah Churchill had gone to Norway; and the Leslies[†] were at Portsmouth. To her fury, an invitation from Mrs Cornwallis-West was suddenly cancelled.

Not wanting to have to ask to be taken in, she stayed at 3 Hyde Park Place, quite alone for four days. 'I am going to tell no one I am alone & shall receive nobody,' she told her mother. 'Like that it will be all right.' It would have invited the most disparaging comment for a girl of twenty-one to be discovered unchaperoned in London. She was well aware of this and urged her mother not to tell Minna Anglesey, 'who might write it to some of her cat friends and make mischief'. Meanwhile she lunched one day with Lady (Arthur) Paget and spent a day at Cliveden with the Crown Princess of Romania, who was enjoying a stay of 'absolute happiness' with her new friends, the Astors.[10]

---

[*] 8th Lord Howard de Walden (1880-1946). In 1912 he married Margherita van Raalte.

[†] Sir John Leslie, Bt (1857-1944) and his wife, Leonie Jerome (1859-1943), sister of Jennie Cornwallis-West.

On Saturday, 9 August King Edward VII was crowned. The ceremony was curtailed somewhat in order to preserve his strength. The Duke of Marlborough, who had recently been given the Order of the Garter, acted as Lord High Steward, while Consuelo was one of the four duchesses holding the canopy during the anointing of Queen Alexandra. Gladys watched the procession from a vantage point in the Mall. The Queen smiled in her direction with such grace that the image remained with her vividly all her life. Gladys was impressed by the elegance of her bearing and the way she could wear a vast quantity of jewels and still look relaxed and natural.

After the Coronation Gladys went to Hillington Hall, King's Lynn, the home of Sir William and Lady ffolkes, and the neighbouring estate to Sandringham, to enjoy the peace of an English summer. But her peace was shattered when *Le Matin* in Paris began to serialise the story of Gladys and the crown prince under the title: '*Les Deux Aigles*'.[11] Instantly Gladys became world news as the story was flashed from Paris to New York and from there to London. The *Daily Telegraph* described it as 'romantic' and related that details of the romance had caused much amusement in Berlin. It caused none to Mrs Baldwin who wrote to *Le Matin* on 13 August:

> My daughter has no other protector but me . . . I know better than anyone the true nature of the short relations that a meeting of forty-eight hours at Blenheim, the home of the Duke and Duchess of Marlborough, has caused between the Crown Prince and my daughter, both of whom are mere children.
>
> A lot of imagination is needed to transform them into an affair of state.[12]

Gladys protested to the *Daily Telegraph* that the statements were 'absolutely false' and demanded their emphatic contradiction. Yet *Le Matin*'s account, though written in romantic vein, tallies surprisingly well with the later version told by Consuelo in *The Glitter and the Gold*. Considering how few people there were at Blenheim that weekend, it would be interesting to know exactly how this story emerged, and in such detail. Following Mrs Baldwin's letter, the editors of *Le Matin* dropped the serial, explaining with belated piety that 'The intervention of a mother is something we hold sacred.'[13]

There were further rumours that Mrs Baldwin had paid a large sum to have the story dropped.

The article had far-reaching results. Those people Gladys had as yet failed to dazzle now became acutely aware of her existence. She reached the dizziest heights of fame. She became so celebrated that a manufacturer even produced a cardboard doll, with clothes that slotted onto it, named 'Miss Deacon'. Contemporary writers talk of her having 'burst into society'. Her friend Albert Flament wrote that she 'traversed Europe like a meteor in a flash of dazzling beauty and of conversation no less exceptional'.[14]

It would be nice to freeze the frame there, the meteor burning brightly at the end of a long London season, with Gladys caught at the zenith of her beauty at the age of twenty-one. But a meteor flares up and fades away, and this was to be Gladys's fate. She would flare up again to dazzle further in the course of her extraordinary life. But never would it be so perfect in the future.

In the meantime, as Gladys left London for Paris, she was sure in the knowledge that she had taken the city by storm.

8

'DEATH OR PERMANENT DISFIGUREMENT'

Society all over the continent has heard the news with a great horror, in which there is mingled a deep and sincere pity.[1]

In August 1903 Neith Boyce, the American writer, recorded that Gladys had been 'off her head' twice in her short life. As early as 1900 she had alarmed her mother by exhausting herself 'in contemplation of the wonders of the English Section' at the Louvre, and then dressing up as a Hoppner* in the evening, with powdered hair and flowing robes, to attend a ball. As she prepared to spend the winter in Rome, Mrs Baldwin noted her excitement – 'She can talk of nothing else' – while detecting a hint of instability: 'She is much improved to my thinking, more *assise* and less *éballetine*.'[2]

The second incident occurred in the autumn of 1902 when Gladys was depressed and highly strung. At the beginning of October she was sent to Biarritz to rest. She then went to England to stay with Lord and Lady Clifford of Chudleigh at Ugbrooke Park. In the peace of Devon she read the works of Gibbon, which inspired her to write to Bernard Berenson: 'I am filled with giant ambition when I think of the vast stores of bravery, learning, [and] virtue which have been amassed by passing generations for us poor minions.' At the same time Gladys was happy to reassure the art critic that she was moving in more sober circles than hitherto: 'I am divinely happy here, no longer "wound" with those awful people of the racing set, whose tongues do "kiss one into madness". I now understand why Jupiter was a drunkard and Venus so fast and giddy. They lived on the fats of the land and had to pay for their godhead & comfortable living in hundreds.'[3]

---

* John Hoppner (1758-1810), an English portrait painter in the style of Reynolds.

Back in Paris, Gladys regretted the departure of Montesquiou to New York and the Marlboroughs to the great Delhi Durbar in India. Her mother was also in New York, and in her absence, Gladys committed a grave folly, described by Marthe Bibesco as 'her obedience to a barbarous conception of Greek beauty'.[4] Mabel Dodge Luhan observed that Gladys 'was content to lie for hours on her bed, happy in loving her own beauty, contemplating it'.[5] As she gazed, she wondered how she might correct the slight hollow between her forehead and her nose, which denied her the true classical beauty she had so often admired in museums and galleries.

This might never have happened had she not been ill. Montesquiou was intensely upset when he learnt about it, the more so because he saw great danger in the temporary success she was having with the experiment. He wrote Gladys a long letter in which he quoted Madame de Sévigné: 'Look after your health, my girl. It will help you in all things.'[6] He warned her that decisions taken in a state of nervous debility might have dark and ominous consequences that could last as long as life. Gladys would have done well to heed his words.

In 1830 the German chemist, Baron Karl von Reichenbach, had discovered the creation of paraffin by the distillation of beech-wood tar. This soon became popular with doctors, Theodor Billroth using it to lubricate resected joints. Gladys may have heard of the experimental work of Dr Robert Gersuny,* a distinguished Austrian surgeon, who first employed it for cosmetic use. He injected paraffin and Vaseline beneath the epidermis at a temperature of 104 degrees to fill cavities and build up tissues. In 1899 he had injected liquid paraffin to create a testicular prosthesis in a castrated patient. He went on to experiment with Vaseline (created in 1875) sometimes combined with olive oil. In Vienna he cured a man of intense nervous pains by attaching the corresponding nerve of a rabbit to the diseased nerve. Gersuny used his injections in early examples of breast augmentation with, in many cases, disastrous results.

The operations caused inflammation, infection, embolism and yellowish skin at the point of injection. Nodules formed, the paraffin migrating through fatty tissue, especially if the patient spent time in

---

* Dr Robert Gersuny (1849-1924), director of the Rudolfinerhaus Hospital in Vienna.

the sun. There were incidents of wax cancer, while removing the paraffin proved hard and often left scars.[7]

Gersuny never employed his methods on faces, but this method of injecting paraffin was popular in the first twenty years of the twentieth century. Gladys's first step was to explore the Museo delle Terme in Rome, where she found many fine Grecian heads and measured the distance between the eyes and noses. Returning to Paris she took advice from a professor at the Institut de Beauté, who gave her instructions. Then she had paraffin wax injected into the small depression above the bridge of her nose to build it up and form a straight line from the forehead to the tip. Evidently this was a simple operation with a needle, the doctor then moulding the wax to the new shape and letting it harden. At first the endeavour had a measure of success, but in the long term it was a disaster. It has been suggested that Gladys pulled and twisted at her nose before the operation healed. Her nose became red and sore and she could not go out. Paraffinomas appeared in her chin. She called a surgeon and was told that she had necrosis* of the nose, a progressive disease that could lead to permanent disfigurement or even death.

Word soon spread. Mary Berenson heard people talking about it in Gazzada, north of Milan:

> They said her unfortunate nose was so swollen that she has shut herself in her room at Biarritz and won't see anyone. Sure enough, comes a letter from her today from Biarritz saying the world is hollow, and that she is bored with balls & dinners & flirting, & means to be a hermit. She does not allude to her nose, however.[8]

In February 1903, news of Gladys's operation was telegraphed from Biarritz across the globe. She was described as being ill 'as the result of the unsuccessful subcutaneous injection of paraffine last fall in an effort to improve the lines of her nose'. It was stated that this was a not uncommon operation in France, but in Gladys's case, necrosis of the nose bones had set in. This was a progressive disease, which, unless instantly checked, could result in permanent disfigurement or at worst

---

* Necrosis is defined as death of a bone or portion of a bone in mass, as opposed to death by molecular disintegration.

in death: 'Society all over the continent has heard the news with a great horror, in which there is mingled a deep and sincere pity.'[9]

★ ★ ★ ★ ★

Fortunately, the worst prognostications of the surgeons did not occur. While her mother was still in New York, Gladys returned to Paris, spending quiet days with her sisters at the rue Jean-Goujon. Her days seldom varied. She rode for three hours in the morning, enjoyed having a friend such as Leo Stein to lunch, read all afternoon, dined at six thirty and retired to bed at nine. She wrote to Berenson: 'I melt into sleep with a voluptuousness so delicious that I am content never to go to a party again.'[10]

Despite the relaxed picture she painted, Gladys was not content for long. The pace of her brain quickened and she bubbled over with questions for Berenson:

Does Mme de Montebello* still dazzle you with a bird's eye view of continental politics?

Does she tell you that war-fare is become a spiritual process because the combatants now see each other across Shrupp-swept plains, with the eyes of faith? Does she still magnetize very young men sitting in electrified circles about her throne? Does Carlino [Carlo Placci] count himself among them? Has the Grazioli† at last laid her bones to rest?

Speak upon all these things O Belial & come with me to Spain whither I would go.

P.S. How are Mr Botticelli's feet? Less swollen I hope. Give my love to all the invalided virgins even though there be 11,000 & quickly write another book to point out the beauty of their putty faces . . .'[11]

When Mrs Baldwin returned to Paris she was alarmed to find her daughter in a bad state. The beautiful Gladys of the previous season,

---

* Albertine, Comtesse Jean de Montebello (1855–1930), a keen anti-Dreyfusist, with whom Carlo Placci was besotted. Described by Princess Catherine Radziwill as 'one of the loveliest, most charming women Paris could boast', Berenson called her 'an Egeria of international relations' [Rumour & Reflection, p. 32].

† Nicoletta, Duchess of Grazioli, with whom Berenson had been infatuated until he met Gladys, lived until 1938.

now aged twenty-two, had declined into a nervous wreck. She was diagnosed as suffering from 'nervous disorders' and was placed in Dr Paul Sollier's sanatorium at Boulogne-Billancourt, on the outskirts of Paris.* Visited only by her mother, she remained there until April. Gladys explained her plight to Berenson on 11 February:

> One line before I am imprisoned for 6 weeks or 2 months. After having been in bed for 5 weeks it has been decided that I am to go to a Sanatorium to be under treatment for some sort of nervous trouble!!!
>
> I am to be there in company with morphinomanes, ether drinkers and goodness knows what not!
>
> I have grown much taller, thinner and all my hair has been cut off! Audrey says I look like a consumptive collegien . . .
>
> Give my love to Mary cold as ice & take care of yourself or they will send you to some aquarium or other.[12]

Fortunately, Mary Berenson passed through Paris on her way to Haslemere in Surrey and took the chance to pay Gladys a visit. So alarmed was she by Gladys's condition that she did not return to I Tatti until May, making Berenson angry at her prolonged absence. The first news she heard was that Gladys was in 'such a frightful pressure that it amounted to madness. She was threatening to kill some people who had offended her. Poor child.'[13]

On 3 April Mary lunched with Mrs Baldwin, who gave a 'frightening account' of Gladys and showed her 'a frightfully depressed letter'. Mary called on Gladys the next day and found her 'well and jolly, and getting fat – awfully affectionate'. Gladys fell on Mary and could not stop hugging her, so delighted was she to see her. Mary gave this report to Berenson:

> Her attention is a little wandering & hard to fix, she jumps inconsequently from one subject to another, but I made her get out of bed and stand with her right hand upraised and scream: 'black and blue,

---

* Paul Sollier (1861–1933) was a psychologist dealing with the memory, and a believer in isolation therapy; a pupil of Dr Jean-Martin Charcot. Marcel Proust was to spend four weeks at his clinic in 1905–6.

cut me in two' that she would let me bring her back to I Tatti with me.[14]

Mary also found that Gladys's memory was impaired and that the lying was getting worse. She told Mary half a dozen contradictory things during the visit. Mary again lunched with Mrs Baldwin – 'as *hopelessly* foolish & lying and indiscreet as ever' – and met Audrey who, she thought, 'hasn't a quarter of Gladys's bewildering charm'.

In her haste to write to her husband, Mary forgot to give her impressions of Gladys's nose, which had been swollen but was now somewhat better. She had great difficulty in extracting a remotely plausible version of what had happened from Gladys herself:

> She said that she must have knocked it, she couldn't remember where. One doctor after another asked her if she was *sure* she hadn't been monkeying with it and she always vowed she hadn't. It got worse & worse, swelled up & became an open sore. At last, when she came to the Maison de Santé, the doctor threw her into a hypnotic sleep, and, as she said, 'got the truth out of me, so that he was able to cure me'. 'What *was* the truth, Gladys?' 'I don't know. I can't remember any more, but he got it out all right.'
>   Strange tale.[15]

On Wednesday, 8 April, a few days after this encounter, Gladys suddenly arrived at the rue Jean-Goujon to the astonishment of her mother. She was accompanied by an attendant from Sollier's and announced that she was on her way to the Louvre to buy Easter eggs. On Saturday she intended to leave for a hotel in Versailles. 'I suppose I must let her have her way,' was Mrs Baldwin's feeble comment.[16]

★ ★ ★ ★ ★

Though Gladys needed peace and quiet, it soon became clear that she was unlikely to get it. Lord Francis Hope was still pressing his suit and had just broken his engagement for her sake. Then the Duke of Marlborough excited Gladys by arriving in Paris for a few days, having recently returned from the Delhi Durbar. Mrs Baldwin was worried that Gladys might elope with him, merely to spite Consuelo. 'What a hateful silly muddle it is,' wrote Mary to Berenson, 'and poor

Gladys with her excited brain drifting about in it with no one to guide her. I haven't told you how silly and hopeless the mother was. She is *worse than useless* to her children.'[17] Berenson was puzzled: 'Poor dear Gladys. I'd give anything to have her well and happy. I feel so much more fatherly than lover-like to her.'[18]

Gladys went alone to the Hôtel Vatel in the rue des Réservoirs, at Versailles, while her mother took Audrey on an automobile trip. While the Berensons hoped to lure Gladys to Italy, another duke arrived in Paris. Mrs Baldwin conceived the idea that Gladys should marry him and she warmed to the notion.

The new suitor was the fifty-nine-year-old Duke of Norfolk, who had lived like a monk since being widowed in 1877. He was a grave, stooping figure with a shaggy black beard, generally deemed uninterested in young girls, and not easily turned by Paris frocks or sharp American humour. It was said of him: 'His best friend could scarcely call him good looking.'[19]

He had lost his son and heir, the Earl of Arundel,* the previous summer, so was in quest of a new wife and a male heir, and since Gladys was ostensibly a Roman Catholic, she became a candidate. It was suggested that Edward VII encouraged the plan. Gladys stayed at Arundel Castle, with the duke's unmarried sister, Lady Mary Fitzalan-Howard, as chaperone. There she rode his horses, played golf on his course and rode about Sussex in a little car.

So hypnotised was the duke that he allowed himself to be subjected to a ridiculous charade at a dinner party in Paris. Gladys addressed him as 'Marie', put an antimacassar on his head and made him pretend he was the Pope. Meanwhile she dressed another guest as the King and the two acted a long interview between King and Pope. Then Gladys said to him: 'Marie has another game he loves to play – play your game, Marie.' Promptly, the Duke of Norfolk, Earl Marshal of England and Premier Duke of Great Britain, left the room, removed his coat and returned on all fours, with a large green cushion on his back, and trotted around the room like a dog.[20]

'What absurdities about Gladys and "Marie" de Norfolk!!' Mary wrote to her mother. 'But she is enough to turn anybody's head – a

---

* Philip, Earl of Arundel and Surrey (1879-1902), was born deaf, dumb, blind and of weak intellect, 'a travesty upon a human being'. Trips to Lourdes were of no avail.

mixture of Circe and Aspasia and (alas) American Girl that attracts, repels, delights, charms and annoys.'[21] In the end nothing came of the romance, and in February 1904 the duke married the heiress to the Barony of Herries, a union that produced the 16th Duke of Norfolk (who arranged the Coronations of George VI and Elizabeth II, and Sir Winston Churchill's State Funeral) and three daughters. In 1907 Gladys amused Berenson by telling him that the duke's highest ambition was to be 'in society'.

There followed another London season in the summer of 1903. Gladys was evidently fully restored to health. She reported to Berenson: 'I feel so well and cheerful that I long to make you adopt my cure and go to Sollier's. He is a fraud of course, but then his method is so good that even incomplete application is telling.'[22] And to Montesquiou she wrote: 'Restored to health, thanks to my rest, I am enjoying myself smugly and stupidly.'[23]

The purpose of this season was for Mrs Baldwin to launch Audrey into society, repeating for her Gladys's undoubted success of the previous summer. She took a house in London. Audrey accompanied Gladys to Blenheim one weekend (where young Lord Brooke was also a guest), and the two sisters were frequently seen out together. But neither of them did so well. Gladys had various social problems, despite attending events such as the Covent Garden gala, given by the King and Queen for President Loubet of France.

A witness to this season was Jean Hamilton, wife of the General, Sir Ian Hamilton, a close friend of the Marlboroughs. By the summer of 1902 she had worked out that the Marlboroughs were not happy together. In May 1903, the young Duchess of Manchester told her of Gladys's 'disloyalty' to Consuelo, while at the Blenheim weekend in July, she observed the Russian Ambassador, Count Benckendorf, 'sighing' with love for Gladys, and Jennie Cornwallis-West, 'condescending to be amused by Miss Deacon's American stories, she told them very cleverly.'[24]

According to the ever-fanciful American press, there was a falling-out between Gladys and the Duchess of Westminster when she was staying with the Cornwallis-Wests* and the duchess refused to have her in her stand for Chester Races. Later in the summer Daisy,

---

* Jennie and her young husband, Major George Cornwallis-West.

Princess of Pless invited Gladys to sail with them at Cowes, and they were invited aboard *Meteor III*, the Kaiser's yacht. Just as they pushed off, Daisy was handed a note from Admiral von Eisendecher, informing them that *Meteor* would not be sailing that day because the lack of a breeze threatened the yacht's racing record. Only later did it dawn on Prince Hans, Daisy's husband, that the real reason was the presence of Gladys, the episode of the crown prince still weighing on the Kaiser's mind.[25]

Worse still, according to Douglas Ainslie, Gladys appeared determined to ruin Audrey's season, and despite claiming to help her, she 'simply overpowered her'.[26] This was confirmed by Elsie de Wolfe, who maintained that Gladys did everything in her power to make her sister's season a failure.

There was a serious incident inspired by Gladys's irritation that Mr Widener, the 'squillionaire Philadelphia butcher', had singled out Audrey for special attention. Mrs Baldwin went away for a few days, leaving the two sisters alone in the London house. Audrey decided to give a lunch party for Mr Widener and Lady Cunard, to which Gladys objected, saying it was not proper, in the absence of their mother. But Audrey went ahead and arranged food and flowers. Behind her sister's back, Gladys wrote secretly to the guests to say that Audrey had another engagement and the lunch was cancelled. On the day, Audrey waited for her guests in increasing despair. Later that afternoon she saw Mr Widener in the park and was further upset when he bowed coldly to her. Finally she extracted the truth from him, as Mary Berenson related:

> She went straight back home, found Gladys, knocked her down, pummelled & kicked her black & blue, & finally said 'This time I've only bruised you. If you ever play me such a trick again, I'll *wound* you, & give you a scar you'll wear the rest of your life!'[27]

In September Gladys retreated to Blenheim. There she rose at ten, read, continued to read or talk throughout the day and retired to bed at midnight. Meanwhile Mrs Baldwin took Audrey to a hotel in Maloja, Switzerland, which amused Gladys: 'For some weeks past Mamma complained that Dorothy (picture of health) was looking pale and needed Engadine air. In due time Mamma left with

– Audrey!'[28] Mary Berenson put it differently: 'I daresay Mrs Baldwin's stupidity has been penetrated with the idea that those two wild-cats are better apart.'[29]

Gladys came and went between France and England, visited Venice with Consuelo in October, and in November was spotted at a private view at the New Gallery in the company of her actor friend, Norman Forbes, who himself owned a gallery in Bond Street.[30] At about this time, Consuelo included her in a dinner for the Prince and Princess of Wales. One of the guests was Lady Desborough, who reported to A. J. Balfour that Gladys, 'a horrible and hideous American girl', had bored the prince by insisting on 'shrieking' French songs at them after dinner 'with a twang like a banjo'.[31]

Meanwhile in Majola Audrey forged a deep and loving friendship with Catherine Pozzi.* Where Gladys had been unpleasant to Audrey, Catherine was the opposite, later describing her as 'a kind of angel, absolutely pure, with astounding beauty'.[32] Their friendship was founded on a mutual love of Faust and Goethe and soon became the union of two lonely souls, defying what Catherine called the normal conventions. Catherine then left for Paris while Audrey set off to the Castello di Urio on Lake Como. The two met only once more for a few intense days in Paris, but kept up an intimate correspondence, discussing their feelings and response to literature – the novels of Anatole France. Audrey locked Catherine's letters away for safety.

By the end of September Audrey was at 1 rue de Celle, Versailles, where, on 4 October, the sculptor Auguste Rodin, an old friend of

---

* Catherine Pozzi (1882-1934), poet, daughter of Dr Samuel-Jean Pozzi (1846-1918), one-time lover of Sarah Bernhardt, who declined to amputate her leg lest he get the operation wrong. He was the subject of a famous Sargent portrait in 1881. He was murdered by a deranged patient, who had become impotent as the result of having his leg amputated by Pozzi. Gladys decried his death. Julian Barnes has told his story in *The Man in the Red Coat* (2019). Catherine was raised in intellectual and artistic circles, alongside men such as Paul Bourget. In 1907 she became the first wife of the popular dramatist Édouard Bourdet, later administrator of the Comédie Française, by whom she had a son, Claude, later a member of the French Resistance. In 1912 she developed symptoms of tuberculosis. She studied history, philosophy and religion, became a friend of Anna de Noailles and Rilke, and in 1920 she entered into a passionate eight-year affair with Paul Valéry. She died in Paris from TB, aggravated by the use of morphine and laudanum. Six of her poems were published as *Mésures* in 1935.

her mother, came to lunch and impressed Audrey with his air of tranquillity. They discussed Japanese theatre and the painter Jean-Louis Forain, in whom Rodin detected considerable talent. Audrey then went hunting in the Touraine. Returning to Paris she found that her mother had tired of Paris life.

In some distress, Audrey wrote to Catherine: 'We are heading for Rome on the 1st of Nov for the whole winter. Mama has let the house. Oh I am so sorry! I had so hoped for this winter and our days in the Quartier Latin.'[33] There was one final meeting before the Deacon entourage directed their steps to Italy or, as Catherine Pozzi put it, Audrey 'followed her alarming mother to Italy.'[34]

9

THE DEATH OF AUDREY

In later life, Gladys frequently noted the date of 22 May with the sad words: 'My sister Audrey. Dear, dear Audrey.'[1] Yet as late as 1976, in New York, Boston and London, there was a far-fetched rumour that Gladys might have killed her sister. Perhaps such a rumour was inevitable, given the considerable attention Gladys attracted wherever she went, the contrary effect she had on people, who either loved or hated her, combined with the recent memories of how her father had meted out justice to her mother's lover.

Of course Gladys did not kill her sister, but in 1903 Mary Berenson had recorded that in her confused state Gladys 'was threatening to kill some people who had offended her'. More worryingly, in 1907, the Comtesse Greffulhe recorded Gladys saying: 'Yes, I have killed someone. Yes, I forced him to die. I knew afterwards that he had died in the way that I had wished him to die.'*[2] This might simply have been provocative talk, but given the antipathy between the two sisters and the recent incident in London, it is concerning. From such talk, rumours grow.

Gladys's mother had arrived in Rome in December 1903. The principal reason for this move was Mrs Baldwin's involvement with Prince Alfonso Doria Pamphili, her constant companion. Gladys was soon surrounded by admirers – in particular Prince Roffredo Caetani, though there were plenty more, of varying ages and suitability. Mrs Baldwin and her daughters began their stay at 143A via delle Quattro Fontane.

Scarcely had the family arrived than Audrey fell seriously ill. By the end of January she felt better, telling Catherine Pozzi: 'It is almost

---

* The Comtesse Greffulhe often used the masculine pronoun when sometimes she meant the feminine.

worthwhile being ill to feel the glorious coming back to health – I feel like a lizard with a new green skin. It's a nice feeling.'[3] But Audrey did not get well. She and Catherine continued to write to each other, while in March Audrey was taken to the Grand Hotel, Porto d'Anzio, south of Rome, near where Pontius Pilate had once had a villa, to take the sea air.

In order to recover from influenza and trouble with her heart, Audrey was moved to Florence on 5 April, to the Casa di Cura, a clinic found for them by Prince Doria's daughter, Orietta Borromeo. Audrey's condition was not considered serious so Mrs Baldwin asked Gladys's friend, Lily Kirk, to accompany her there, fearing to miss her train back to Rome. However, the doctor soon became concerned, detecting that Audrey was suffering from infectious endocarditis, exacerbated by brain trouble and violent fevers. This had developed from the influenza and meant that she must rest for three months and avoid any exertion or excitement. She found it hard to rest, as the matron described on 9 April: 'She has a really brilliant mind and a very erratic one too, I find, on nearer acquaintance. It is difficult to follow her always, so quickly does she pass from jest to earnest.'[4] The matron feared 'some little mental taint' inherited from her father, but concluded: 'I should describe her as unusually balanced in mind – or rather in soul, for the soul, the real Audrey is extraordinarily clear and forceful - but the mind is at times, strange, erratic, melancholy.'[5]

Audrey languished in Florence for several weeks as her condition gradually deteriorated. She was on a regime of digitalis, but it did no good. In May she became excited and delirious and was frequently given morphine to calm her heart.

Before this became a serious crisis, Gladys arrived to stay with the Berensons, bringing her customary contradictions with her. Mary Berenson noted: 'It is hard to keep on the one hand from falling completely victim to her extraordinary charm, & on the other to being quite angry & disgusted with her.'[6] She was soon regaling them with lurid stories of Parisian and Roman society. Gladys had not seen Berenson for two years. She arrived, 'weary of the merry-go-round of Roman festivities',[7] as Mary put it. Berenson found her considerably altered: 'Mentally and morally she is greatly improved. One can now talk to her quite seriously, and there is very little her mind does not grasp, and penetrate. Happily too she is quite unspoiled, and in many respects as simple a child as when she was 16.'[8]

One afternoon J. P. Morgan's[*] artistic agent, Mr Fitzhenry,[†] 'a swell-looking old man', though something of a bore,[9] hopped out of his carriage and rushed up to kiss Gladys's hand. Countess (Hortense) Serristori then appeared, but Gladys was rude to her, being jealous of 'every attractive woman in her own set'.[10] Despite this, the countess was determined to befriend her, feeling she might need support in Rome. However, such was Mrs Baldwin's reputation that her husband forbade her to meet her.

On 15 May Mrs Baldwin arrived from Rome, summoned by a telegram saying that Audrey was now seriously ill with meningitis. Mary Berenson deduced that Gladys hated Audrey: 'I think she would be really glad to hear of her death. And yet she is naturally very much afraid about it.'[11]

Gladys lunched with her mother, which resulted in an awful quarrel after which they would hardly speak. Mary Berenson painted the scene:

> As she [Mrs Baldwin] drove away, Gladys's heart misgave her, she felt a sudden desolation, & she cried out after her 'Mamma! Mamma!' in a tone of real childish distress. And that miserable, heartless woman never turned her feathered head to her child's cry. It was awful. Poor Gladys ran back under the trees & sank down into a chair quite pale. 'That's my *Mother!*' she said. And indeed anything more revolting than Mrs Baldwin I never saw. She came up all painted & costumed to talk appalling gossip, while her daughter Audrey is lying in the hospital apparently dying. All she seemed to think of was 'How trying for me – just as I was beginning to have a good time in Rome. O what a bore it is to have children!'
>
> Audrey's illness turns out to be rather an acute attack of madness than meningitis. She has been trying to kill herself and she requires four nurses to hold her. The immediate danger is not her heart, which

---

[*] John Pierpont Morgan (1837–1913), American financier, art collector and philanthropist.

[†] Joseph Henry Fitzhenry (1836–1913), a generous donor to the Victoria & Albert Museum, an illegitimate son of Count Henri de Chambord (1820–83), grandson and last legitimate heir of King Charles X of France.

is weak from influenza, may go to pieces under the strain, for she has not slept for three days & nights, & has not taken any nourishment except by injections. Gladys says it is clear to her that the only thing to do is to take her to that asylum in Paris where she herself was cured of a similar '*accès de folie*' [time of instability]. But the mother is determined to take an automobile trip with Prince Torlonia.

The evening at I Tatti proved unusual. A friend from Milan, Don Guido Cagnola,* came specially to meet Gladys, describing her as 'the eighth wonder of the world'. The Berensons, Emily Dawson and Don Guido had a tiring dinner until at ten thirty Gladys sprang to life, as Mary relayed to her mother:

> Gladys awoke and began to say such awful and yet amusing things that we were electrified. Don Guido simply couldn't tear himself away. She talked in such a fashion that with almost any other Italian alive she would certainly have lost every shred of reputation. To us, it was evident that she was merely inventing & exaggerating from sentence to sentence, as the ideas grew up in her mind, but, except for her wit & extreme beauty & a sort of utter childishness there is about her, it would not have been *possible* to say such things. She pretended to give us a chapter from a book she imagined she was writing on 'Attractiveness in Men'. As a matter of fact, she does not care much about men – or women either – being absorbed in her own dream. She said such awful things that I felt it necessary to go out with Guido to explain it all. But he saved me the trouble by saying 'You know I don't believe a word she said. It was merely a play of daring imagination,' which was very clever of him, for that is what it was.[12]

In the late afternoon Mrs Baldwin came up to I Tatti, looking very pretty, and wept becomingly over Audrey's state:

> The girl is better, but Mrs. Baldwin says she knows she will die, and really I believe she and Gladys would be immensely relieved. Gladys

---

* Don Guido Cagnola (1864–1952), an entertaining if worldly Italian art collector, who owned the 'dreamlike' Villa Gazzada, near Varese, enriched its collections and gave it to the Holy See in 1946. He founded the journal *Rassegna d'Arte*.

hates her, always has, and Mrs. Baldwin doesn't know what to do with a girl who can't make her own way. *She* has no social advantages to offer her, and Gladys has only got on by her own efforts. Audrey, though beautiful, is not fascinating, and has no 'go', so she has been a dreadful burden to her mother ever since she came out. And of course the silly woman has *no other* ideal in her but society life.[13]

Next evening Gladys returned after a visit to the German sculptor, Hildebrand* with Hortense Serristori, and declared that her sister's fever had diminished, but Mrs Baldwin summoned a Roman doctor who changed the treatment, then arranged for two famous Parisian doctors to come. Gladys chided her mother: 'How are you going to pay for them, you who are so much in debt already?' Mrs Baldwin laughed and said: 'Well I shouldn't have telegraphed if I had thought they would take it seriously!'[14] But the Parisian doctors did come, causing Gladys to say she hoped they would charge her mother exorbitant fees. Gladys then became lethargic, tired after the Roman winter.

Matters deteriorated fast. Irma Deodat, Gladys's nurse, arrived to say that one of the Parisian doctors had pronounced Audrey's case as absolutely hopeless: 'The Bacilli of influenza have settled around her heart, and are busy forming clots there, any one of which, if not instantly dispersed, would kill her.'[15] There were now four day nurses and four night nurses in attendance because, in her over-excited state, Audrey struggled so much.

Mary Berenson called at Mrs Baldwin's hotel and had a heart-to-heart talk with Irma, who told her she thought Mrs Baldwin was going crazy, had a mania for over-spending, but no money, cried and complained when bills came in and cabled wildly to America for funds. She would then think nothing of going out and ordering six new dresses with hats and veils to match. Edith and Dorothy lived at an expensive hotel, attending a convent as day school, another costly arrangement. Mrs Baldwin had spent two hundred pounds on hats the previous year, and taught her daughters never to go anywhere but Doucet, Worth or Paquin for their dresses.

* Adolf von Hildebrand (1847-1921), a neo-classical sculptor in the Florentine tradition.

Only Gladys had occasional flashes of common sense and would employ a small, cheap but good dressmaker, only to have these creations derided by her mother. Irma also said that Audrey had inherited her mother's obstinacy and her father's temper, and was terribly difficult. She was so jealous of Gladys's success that she had become impossible to live with.[16]

As Audrey's mind wandered further, Mrs Baldwin kept telling her to 'Leave your dreams alone, darling, they are not true.'[17] Gladys went down to stay at the nursing home, wishing to 'will her to sleep', and Prince Doria hovered about. Audrey seemed to recognise Gladys for a moment, drawing her down and putting her arms round her neck. As the nurse put it:

> Audrey knew her, kissed her, & laid her head on her shoulder. Gladys held her, and Audrey liked the scent of her (she has always been very sensitive to scent as to sound) going off after a little into a quiet sleep.[18]

On 21 May Audrey suffered a final terrible convulsive fit. She was given a hypodermic of caffeine and ether to inhale. She made one last agitated struggle, even holding out her hand to say, 'Goodbye Mamma.'[19] She sank slowly into long hours of shallow breathing, realising, it was thought, the presence of those around her, until at two thirty the following day, as the matron wrote, 'She simply stopped breathing; the exact moment one hardly knew.'[20]

Edmund Houghton went to photograph Audrey in her coffin, worried that he would find her much changed. The matron described her: 'Her glorious eyes are slightly open, looking into the beyond; the lips parted, just bordering on a smile. "Audrey with the lilies" she talked of in her delirium, and Audrey amongst lilies, peaceful and beautiful, will remain with all who loved her, a memory of purity, steadfastness, charm and loyalty, and of the goodness which she declared was "the one thing that mattered".'[21]

Mrs Baldwin sent a distraught Gladys out to buy black belts, gloves and fans, while she waited to receive Prince Doria in a beautiful négligée, her hair 'in a well calculated disorder'. She considered having Audrey embalmed but Mary Berenson persuaded her to do no such thing.

A funeral service took place at the nursing home, which was Protestant, and Carlo Placci announced that everyone in Florence was taking against Mrs Baldwin because neither she nor Gladys had been kind to Audrey. Mary Berenson went to the Casa, and noted: 'Audrey looked most unspeakably beautiful, and the whole house was absolutely filled with flowers.' Mourners included Prince Doria, Roffredo Caetani, Charles Loeser,* the Berensons (Bernard attending his first ever funeral) and the disreputable Lady Claud Hamilton.† They then drove over to the Evangelical Cemetery (Cimitero degli Allori),‡ on the outskirts of Florence, where Carlo Placci joined them.

> Audrey's grave was made in the grass under an ivied wall & some cypresses, a lovely place, and it was quite lined with flowers. There was a little service at the graveside, after the coffin had been lowered. Mrs Baldwin then went to her carriage, and the few people who were there came to say a few words to her . . . Presently Prince Doria came, and they drove away together, leaving Gladys, who was very deeply moved, kneeling at the grave, attended by Caetani. All the rest had been so touching and well carried out conventionally that the end seemed a little comic . . . Placci was perfectly disgusted.[22]

The next day Gladys and her mother left for Rome, Mrs Baldwin beautifully made up even to the painting of her ears, dabbing her lace handkerchief to her eye from time to time, yet perfectly composed. Gladys did not think her mother felt Audrey's loss while she was completely desperate, all broken up, with red eyes, her hair rough, and wearing an old dress badly. In her grief, she was 'ferociously bad-tempered with all their suite of princely & ducal adorers who came in from Rome'.

Gladys had never experienced such grief before and had to contemplate the 'mysteries of existence'. She discussed with Mary her

* Charles Loeser (1864–1928), American art connoisseur and collector. He bequeathed thirty works of art to the Palazzo Vecchio in Florence. Florence Baldwin preferred him to Berenson, whom she dismissed as an 'arriviste'.

† Carolina Chandos-Pole (1857–1911), married Lord Claud Hamilton (1843–1925). Mary Berenson wrote that she 'enjoyed one of the worst reputations in Europe' (24 May).

‡ Sir Harold Acton and his brother, William, Alice Keppel, Sir Osbert Sitwell, Sir John Pope-Hennessy and Charles Loeser are among those buried there.

disbelief in a future life, and did not know what to do. She wanted to find something comforting to read to her little sisters. She left Mary with a little white kitten that she had bought for Audrey, which went on to produce generations of I Tatti cats.

As Prince Doria settled all the bills for hotels and the private car to Rome, Mary Berenson confessed she was glad to see them go, as she could take no more of Mrs Baldwin.[23] Her husband was convinced that Gladys would be 'eaten up with remorse for not having got on better with her sister', while he judged her mother 'about as fit to cope with any serious moment of existence as any other bird of paradise'.[24] Worse than that, Gladys began to voice her worry that she had been in some way responsible for Audrey's death. The matron reassured her to the contrary:

> You must never feel that Audrey said anything unkind or untrue – if I have heard such things it has never been from her. That you did not understand how ill she felt, & tired her – yes – but never anything more. It was the cook evidently she had mentioned as causing that scene so bad for the heart . . .[25]

In Paris Catherine Pozzi was bereft. She had wanted to come to Audrey's bedside but had been discouraged by her own mother, the doctor and by Mrs Baldwin. Thus ended a brief but intense loving friendship, one of vital importance to Catherine: 'She has never left me. I have been inhumanly faithful to her. She is what I possess of purity and truly the only one,' she told Paul Valéry years later.[26] She kept a photo of Audrey lying in her coffin with her and never let go of shared memories.*

Gladys's pain can be felt in her reply to a loving and sympathetic letter from Consuelo:

---

* Early the following year, Gladys sent Catherine Pozzi Audrey's copy of *Faust*, which she had been reluctant to part with. 'Still you were her friend,' she wrote, 'she loved you, would have given it to you herself probably – so here it is.' [Gladys to Catherine Pozzi, Rome, 27 January 1905 – BNP, Fonds Catherine Pozzi, NAF 28072, Boîte 17-1]. For a full account of the passionate friendship between Audrey and Catherine, see Nicolas Cavaillès, *L'Élegance et le Chaos – Correspondance de Catherine Pozzi* (Non Lieu, Paris, 2011) pp. 181-247. Catherine dedicated her memoirs, *Agnès*, to Audrey's memory.

My numb heart cries unceasingly. The pain in me has burned away all but what is the nucleus of immortality in us and I feel as much in death as I do in life, now that I see how close bound they are – the one pathway to the other . . . If this living be of importance, why should she have been withdrawn?[27]

And a year later, at the time of Yturri's death, Gladys wrote to Montesquiou in Paris:

You have many friends and they will all share your sorrow; but none more than I, who have, since last year, lived on happy and sad memories, which open the heart to the sharing of grief.[28]

Interlude

THE ETERNAL SPRING

She was lonely of soul; she slept within a circle of fire, or a high wall
of thorns. One did not approach her by a door politely opened.[1]

In 1906 Gladys became the heroine of another novel, *The Eternal*
Spring, by the American author Neith Boyce. The story involved an
honourable American, Barry Carleton, coming to a fictionalised Villa
I Tatti, ostensibly in love with Elizabeth (based on Mary Berenson),
then falling in love with Clara Langham (partly based on Gladys).
Much of this was inspired by what Mary told Neith about Gladys's
father, and the shooting in 1892, in turn derived from what Mrs
Baldwin had told Mary, when they first met in 1901.

The fictional Clara has some of Gladys's qualities and remoteness:
'It was evident that she was quite undisciplined; part of her discom-
fort, no doubt, came from this unchartered [sic] freedom. There
ought to be a strong hand over her whims and caprices.'[2] Gladys was
portrayed as dark, not blonde, with a slender figure and beautiful
hands, 'long and delicate, yet strong'.[3]

'Her profile was that of a Lippo Lippi *Madonna*; and when she again
turned toward him he saw that she really carried out a marvellous
degree that same type – the rounded forehead, the thin, arched
eyebrows, the eyes half-covered by drooping lids, the full and pensive
mouth.'[4] The portrayal of her character could have been more sharply
drawn, though, as in life so in the novel, Clara inspires great love and
there are a number of rejected suitors. She converses well. She is, by
turn, gregarious, flirtatious and then reclusive: 'She was near, her sweetness had the power of something that might be possessed – and at the
same time she was inexpressibly remote.'[5] Clara Langham's qualities
were beauty and intelligence, flawed by her volubility, dependence on
her mother, and the mixed values of intellect and materialism.

The issue of inherited insanity was at the heart of the portrayal: 'Clara, I am told, is exactly like her father . . . The same excitable and melancholy temperament, the same sensitiveness . . .'[6] Whether the real-life Gladys was as concerned by the fear of inherited insanity is questionable. It was certainly a fear in society, and when, years later, Dorothy was about to marry Prince Antoni Albrecht 'Aba' Radziwill, his wicked mother, 'Bichette'*, used it against her, even though the general line was that she was an Abeille not a Deacon.

Mary Berenson believed that Miss Cracroft was also part inspiration for Clara in the novel. She was an unlikely figure to have been merged with Gladys, but Clara is frequently to be heard playing the piano in the novel – and Miss Cracroft was a weary spinster Mary had found to play for the guests at I Tatti.

The portrayal of Mrs Langham, on the other hand, was a completely convincing portrait of Gladys's mother, with her great beauty, her disdainful attitude to all and sundry, and her constant need for funds to finance a pointlessly extravagant lifestyle. If Mrs Baldwin ever read *The Eternal Spring*, it would have greatly displeased her.

Neith Boyce was the long-suffering wife of a devoted if relentlessly unfaithful husband, Hutchins ('Hutch') Hapgood. In November 1907 her book came to Mary Berenson's attention. She reported to her mother: 'Neith's book, *The Eternal Spring*, is about the villa (more or less) & Gladys & Miss Cracroft rolled into one, & me. It is pretty poor, I am sorry to say: but we might get it out of the library.'[7]

Neith Boyce had observed Gladys and her mother when they visited the Berensons at I Tatti in 1903, and picked up something of their troubled past. In June that year Mary told her that she was not in love with Berenson, but that he had been with Gladys and 'was, a little, yet'.[8] Hutch suggested that she develop the story following an article he had written on 'The Dignity of Madness', inspired by a woman referred to as Mrs P. Neith developed this, incorporating Gladys's situation as she understood it. From Mary she gleaned:

Her father died insane, after having shot her mother's lover, a young Frenchman. The mother, a great beauty, has been discredited and

---

* Prince Antoni Albrecht Radziwill (1885-1935), and his mother, Princess 'Bichette' Radziwill (1863-1941), née Countess Maria-Rosa Branicka.

shady ever since. Gladys, very beautiful and talented, has been taken up by English society, and it is said her ambition is to marry the premier Duke of England, Norfolk. She is, as B.B., who is in love with her, describes her, fascinating because of the brilliance of her mind – a hectic brilliance – 'a rapid consumption' as he put it. She has been 'off her head' twice, Brunnhilde [Mary] said. Ecco a heroine and a sensational psychological plot![9]

In the same year Neith had visited the formidable Janet Ross*, at Poggio Gherardo, who was, not surprisingly, less than impressed by the precocious American girl taken up by the Berensons. They had brought her to see Mrs Ross, who reported that Gladys had announced: 'I always like to be the tallest and handsomest and cleverest person wherever I go.' To this she riposted: 'Well, if you'll show me your heels, I'll tell you how much shorter you are than Mary.' Gladys then said: 'I tell you what I'm going to do – I'm going to come here in my automobile and run Mary and BB into the ditch – I think it would be so funny to see BB dead.' Mrs Ross concluded that Gladys's manners were dreadful, her beauty exaggerated, her eyes 'tête-fleurant', her hair dyed, but conceded that her mother was a real beauty, though 'tremendously made up'.[10]

Inevitably, the novel is dated when read in the twenty-first century.

---

* Janet Duff-Gordon (1842-1927), biographer and historian, befriended by Dickens and Thackeray as a child. Married, 1860, Henry Ross. Lived in Villa di Poggio Gherardi from 1888.

IO

ROMAN DAYS

In the early 1900s Rome still had a king, the 'Black Nobility'* held sway, and the palaces were occupied by their princes; there were court balls, dances, and equestrian events. Gladys had conquered Paris and created a sensational impression in London. In Rome she kept two horses and rode in the park of the Villa Borghese. From the end of 1904, for nine years, the family rented a magnificent apartment in the Palazzo Borghese, a sumptuous building shaped like a harpsichord near Ponte Cavour.

At times she was watched by Gabriele d'Annunzio, who challenged her to jump a large gate on a borrowed horse, hoping she would fall off. This singular, undersized man had not yet become a romantic legend as novelist, poet, and founding father of Fascism, yet the great Eleanora Duse had been prepared to surrender her stage career for this latterday Casanova. Chips Channon recalled 'the story that d'Annunzio fainted when he saw [Gladys] such was her beauty'.[1] It seems exaggerated, yet Edith later suggested the pair had been 'engaged'. Pressed about him in later life, Gladys was aware of his immorality and dismissed him as 'someone the nobles did not accept'. Neither did she think him a great man. 'He had spark but not fire,' she declared.[2]

Central to the lives of Mrs Baldwin and her daughters was Prince Alfonso Doria, Mrs Baldwin's admirer for at least three years and often with them in Paris and St Moritz. Prince Doria was the owner of one of the city's most magnificent palaces, covering an entire block, overlooking the Corso. It was so packed with art treasures that the Kaiser confessed he had nothing to match it in Berlin. Doria was an old Harrovian, devoted to fox-hunting and a successful breeder of

---

* The 'Black Nobility' referred to Roman aristocratic families who had sided with Pope Pius IX in 1870.

racehorses. His wife, the former Lady Emily Pelham–Clinton, daughter of the 6th Duke of Newcastle, was a significant figure in Roman society, though she had retreated somewhat after the death of her younger son in 1895, paying daily visits to the family mausoleum. The arrival of Mrs Baldwin obliged Roman society to take sides.

In January 1904 Carlo Placci had spotted Mrs Baldwin at a party given by Lady Anglesey with 'the Dorias and other people whom it is chic to meet'.³ It was widely felt that had Gladys's mother been more tactful in her relations with Prince Doria life would have been easier for the family. Laura Chanler, daughter of the famous Mrs Winthrop Chanler (a half-sister of F. Marion Crawford), was a friend of Edith and Dorothy, and though they were allowed to come to her apartment in the Palazzo Bonaparte, Laura's mother considered it too shocking to allow her to accept hospitality from a woman as infamous as Mrs Baldwin. Edith once asked Laura why they never came. She knew the reason, but declined to explain. Mabel Dodge Luhan observed Gladys: 'She was beautiful, as Judith was beautiful, or like Salome and she loved only herself so she was not bothered about lovers,' she wrote, but pointed out that on account of her mother, Gladys was considered 'a free lance'.⁴

The precise relations between Prince Doria and Mrs Baldwin were never clearly established, but since he paid 300,000 francs towards the opulent decoration of her new apartment, it is safe to assume they were lovers. But Edith was surprised to hear that when Princess Doria had left for London, her son Filippo had failed to say goodbye to her. Prince Doria kept saying 'how badly Emily must have felt' and how 'That boy has nothing of me' and 'Why should I have such a son?' to the point that Edith wrote to Gladys: 'If Old D is not in love with Pcesse D why should he care? You know I think he does like her after all.'⁵

The family spent the early months of 1905 in their new apartment. When the Berensons came to stay in March, Carlo Placci warned them that they would find themselves unpopular because of the Doria relationship. The Dorias were not getting on,⁶ Princess Doria had turned Rome against Mrs Baldwin, and she hated Gladys.⁷

Mrs Baldwin's position was further damaged when she was befriended by Princess 'Bichette' Radziwill, a somewhat dubious figure, who decided that here was a maligned figure, who needed her support. Little did she know how her generosity would later rebound on her.

Born as Countess Maria-Rosa Branicka in 1863, Bichette had married Prince George Radziwill in 1883 and was the mother of six legitimate children. By 1904 she was so fat that Daniele Varé wrote: 'She could not get into a railway carriage (unless it were a cattle truck),' and she was so extravagant, that money was a problem: 'She put her trust in money, but not her money in trust.'[8] Countess (Hortense) Serristori told Mary Berenson that the Princess hated her six children and was only interested in her lovers. Bichette claimed that she had had only three or four: 'The rest is pure exaggeration.' As Mary Berenson said, you might mix up sixty or sixty-one, but not three or four.

Gladys was adopted as the Princess's constant companion in that first winter in 1904 (before Audrey died). The Princess liked to surround herself with pretty girls, and took Gladys up, so as to have her adoring admirers, Roffredo Caetani and Prince Torlonia,* at her house – though eventually twenty-three-year-old Gladys proved 'too much of a handful'.[9] Mary Berenson was horrified. This was 'the *worst* milieu morally or socially that Gladys could have fallen into . . . Poor Gladys!'[10] Countess Serristori stated that no one would dream of marrying a girl who moved in such company.

Another observer of all this was Dom Pedro de Carvalho e Vasconcellos, a young Portuguese with a tubercular condition, who was frequently in Rome and a friend of the famous Comtesse (Élisabeth) Greffulhe. She was one of the inspirations for Proust's Duchesse de Guermantes and had a celebrated salon at her house in the rue d'Astorg in Paris, where she entertained musicians, savants, physicists, chemists and doctors. They talked to her, as Lily de Gramont noted, 'on subjects that she could not possibly understand'.[11] She took a particular interest in Gladys on account of her own romantic friendship with Roffredo Caetani.

Pedro moved in the Doria set and was disparaging about 'la petite Deacon', without knowing her personally. He found her mother so stupid that she had become the heroine of her own tragedy, while fearing that Gladys would do the same or worse 'but only by

---

* Don Marino, 4th Prince Torlonia (1861–1933). He introduced the first motor-car to Rome in 1892, to the annoyance of those in carriages. In 1905 he met (Mary) Elsie Moore (1889–1941), daughter of the celebrated and rich American socialite, Mrs Kate Moore, on a visit to Venice. They married in 1907 and divorced in 1928.

ambition and with all her intelligence which is great, it is perhaps better from the social point of view and for the future Abeille, to hold her responsible as finally it is the same thing'.[12]

Mrs Baldwin was keen that Gladys should marry Prince Torlonia because he was immensely rich. Gladys had mulled over the idea, wishing he would postpone his proposal until she was ready. By December 1904 Pedro de Carvalho was reporting that there was no prospect of such a marriage, and that she was so put out by her mother's relationship with Prince Doria that she was contemplating disappearing to Greece. He dismissed her as incapable of inspiring genuine passion in the heart of a man.[13]

★ ★ ★ ★ ★

Roffredo Caetani, Principe de Bassiano, an eligible and handsome bachelor of thirty-two, was a more serious suitor. Edith's friend, Julia Meyer,* daughter of the American ambassador to Rome, thought Gladys made a serious mistake in not marrying him.[14]

Roffredo was the second son of the 15th Duke of Sermoneta, a one-time minister of foreign affairs in Italy, and his English wife, Ada Bootle-Wilbraham. He was a godson (some hinted biological son) of the composer, Franz Liszt. The Caetanis were 'Black Nobility', descending from a brother of Pope Boniface VIII. They lived in Palazzo Caetani and had a highly cultured background. Roffredo himself was a gifted composer and was considered very attractive to women. 'Roffredo only had to smile at a girl,' his sister said, 'and he was always very nice to them – and she thought she had been chosen.'[15]

The Comtesse Greffulhe had met Roffredo at a Wagner celebration at Bayreuth in 1902, and fallen for him, but being caught in a loveless marriage, she could do no more than live out a tortured and unconsummated relationship. For nearly ten years they met when they could, wrote to each other, while she promoted his career as a composer, encouraged him and consoled him when he was depressed. Their relationship remained secret to all but a few.

The comtesse was resigned to him marrying one day and hoped it would be to someone who would make him happy. She did not want

---

* Julia Meyer, later Donna Brambilla (1886-1979). She and her husband later lived at Caprarola. Author of *Jottings from Julia's Journals* (1965).

him to marry an American. When it looked as if he might marry Gladys, she wrote disparagingly of creatures with noses reconstructed by Vaseline and bulging eyes.[16] Her view was that a girl like Gladys did not engage her heart, was only interested in making a show for the world, and would willingly exchange her 'skin' for untold millions in front of a mayor and a priest.[17] To the comtesse, Roffredo referred to Gladys as '*Le Joujou*' (the toy).

For the next four years the possibility of Gladys marrying Roffredo was a topic of conversation in Italian society. The romance was forever changing direction. In July 1904 Bernard Berenson chatted to Count Rembrelinski, who told him that Gladys got on Roffredo's nerves and had ruined her chances. Roffredo would certainly have married her, but instead she had set her cap at Prince Torlonia. Yet a month later, Rembrelinski reported that it was Mrs Baldwin who was ruining Gladys's chances in Rome, and that Roffredo was keener than ever to marry her.

In September Berenson and Montesquiou, who were together in St Moritz, visited Roffredo in Pontresina. Roffredo told Berenson that he had never been in love, but was ready to sacrifice everything to the experience. He did not mention Gladys but soon afterwards indicated to Carlo Placci 'nothing less than a desire to marry her'.[18]

In 1905 a rumour spread that Gladys had claimed to have refused a proposal of marriage from him. Roffredo was furious and told Berenson that Gladys knew perfectly well that his family would never allow him to marry her, that 'no one in his sense would dare to marry her', and that if she had really said that, he would never speak to her again. The proposal story gave Princess Doria the chance to rouse the Sermonetas against Gladys and her family.

In May 1906, when Gladys was in Florence, Berenson took it on himself to impress on her what an ardent admirer she had in the young composer. He cited the instance of Roffredo discussing the proposal rumours circulating in Rome to show how sincere Roffredo felt. Gladys took it the wrong way. Roffredo then accused Berenson of harming the relationship by interfering. Berenson riposted that he had merely tried to help. Gladys heard about this in Roncegno:

Much amused dearest B.B. at the exchange of letters between you and another great friend. Cupid's messengers must not be a year late. Now you know I was amused at your – forgive me if I say it – rather silly words. The intention was probably good but a little ill timed and ill clothed.[19]

The public verdict on the Roffredo romance was that his ardour cooled when he realised that Gladys 'was not opposed to the admiration she excited everywhere'.[20] Gladys's reputation was damaged. Whereas in the winter of 1903 a particular social set in Rome had talked of nothing but her, by the spring of 1905 she was scarcely mentioned. Mary Berenson feared that if the Sermonetas and Torlonias turned on her, she would be ostracised by Roman society altogether.[21]

★ ★ ★ ★ ★

Completely broken by Audrey's death, Gladys had taken to her bed immediately after the family returned to Rome in 1904. She felt isolated because Dorothy was too young to be an intimate friend and she often quarrelled with Edith, who was already spending more time with Marraine Baldwin in the United States.

In this spirit of loneliness, Gladys contacted her old friend Montesquiou, in Paris: 'I am very frightened of you because like all the angels your power is fearsome and, above all, like petrol, an unknown quantity. I am afraid to draw your attention to me . . .'[22] Gladys bemoaned the fact that Montesquiou never came to Rome and begged him to record his voice on a wax spool so that she could play it on her gramophone. 'I will even take the liberty of making you repeat yourself, which alas never happens,' she wrote. Shortly afterwards she and the count embarked on a project to get an article of his published in an English review.

A year later, on 6 July, Yturri died, ravaged by diabetes, after twenty years with the count. She hastened to console Montesquiou: 'I loved this poor Yturri so much. He was so good, so understanding to those who loved him, so entirely devoted to you . . .'[23] Her mother heard the news from Maurice Lobre, the painter of Versailles. She wrote that she was sad that Yturri 'had left for the great voyage without a word of remembrance from me'.[24]

★ ★ ★ ★ ★

In June 1904 Gladys and her mother made a pilgrimage to Audrey's grave in Florence. Berenson invited them to dinner, an occasion that left him with an indefinable bad taste in his mouth, as he explained to Mary: 'Perhaps it was my nerves climbing up their noses.'[25]

Gladys was still in an emotional state and promptly invited herself to stay at I Tatti, while her mother returned to Rome. But at the last minute she got cold feet and sent Berenson a note via his driver, telling him she was in the train, sitting between two bandboxes – 'But I'll come back whenever you wish.'[26] Berenson was relieved that she did not come.

A week later she joined the Marlboroughs in Paris. Then she fell ill again, suffering, like Audrey, from a racing heart. Prince Doria drove the family to Vallombrosa in his motor-car, on the orders of her doctor – 'Less likely to agitate the bell clapper in my chest,' she explained.

In Vallombrosa, Gladys was meant to rest, but could not resist exploring every new town they visited. She confessed in a letter to Berenson that, since Audrey's death, the wonder had gone out of her soul, but seeing some Giottos had startled her back into consciousness. She wrote:

> Then in a rush came back the whole world and with it the love of things (because I felt sure of their existence again) and changed, for now I know of something higher and deeper and aweful which is the very core of them all.[27]

Berenson hoped she might now 'become a real person, with deep humanity & keen mind . . .'[28]

Vallombrosa had a soothing effect on Gladys. She enjoyed the 'great rivers of mist' that poured into the valleys, the clouds 'gathering at the same time, clustering mysteriously about the mountain tops (one of them a huge purple-black one like an island lingers in the sky each day, overlooking the show)' and sat wondering at it late into the night.[29] And yet in the haunting atmosphere of night gloom: 'The thought of Audrey, ever lying deep in me, rose to great distress.'[30]

At the Grand Hotel, Vallombrosa, Gladys lived quietly, finding even the most trifling conversation with her sisters exhausting. Nearby there was another suitor, who recalled to her years later:

I do not forget Vallombrosa, the Tyrol, Versailles . . .! all of which reminds me of a delicious and very often cruel child, wearing an old black boater any old way, over her golden hair, at whose feet – so badly shod, with black soles with holes in them – I so often longed to lay myself down . . . but only Frantz [Gladys's dog] was extended the privilege.[31]

It was Octave, Duke of Camastra, a bachelor of forty, who had fallen in love with her. The duke pressed his young friend with invitations to take walks or donkey rides deep into the forest and allow him to escort her to the picnic of the day. He needed her company – 'It is like a *bath of light*, sovereign treatment for rheumatism and my soul is terribly rheumatic . . .'[32] There were frequent delays and postponements, for Gladys was no respecter of punctuality. Camastra was patient. He regretted not seeing Gladys before midday:

Rhenish legend relates that the hotel-keepers die in the whirls of the great river when *La Lorelei* combs her golden hair on its banks. Being neither hotel-keeper nor the Rhine, and not being admitted to contemplate the charming spectacle of which you speak – oh! how much more fortunate is Octave *Le Lançon!* – I shall not die, but I suffer most cruelly for having to wait so long to see you . . .[33]

After Vallombrosa, the group went to the Dolomites and to Innsbruck, and then the faithful duke drove Gladys and Dorothy to Achensee Tyrol. Camastra was at the wheel of his car for two weeks. Berenson wondered how Gladys tolerated him: 'Camastra is a beautiful creature but I could not stand a fortnight of him.'[34] A little over a year later, the rejected duke married Rose Ney d'Elchingen in Paris. Both the Camastras remained lifelong friends of Gladys.

At Achensee, Gladys began to feel more spiritually whole, telling Berenson: 'Have I lived part blinded in some enchanted forest? I now live out of the world seen, or rather living more in it see through the "appearance" into a part of the reality.'[35] Mary hoped that Gladys would 'fall into the right hands' without being sure 'whose hands those would be'. She wished she was not mixed up with her friends in Rome and could read better books: 'The revelation will fade unless it is strengthened from outside. But her letter makes me feel as if there was less chance of her becoming a Satey Fairchild* than sometimes we feared – she is capable of sailing into seas that the other [Audrey] at her most radiant moment of flowering never imagined the existence of.'[36]

There were glimmers of humour too, as when Gladys contemplated the Germans who flocked to Achensee for their holidays:

Germans, nothing absolutely but Germans seen, slow, heavy laden immensely fat folk who walk for pleasure or instruction or perhaps appetite. To me they seem stomachs. But such stomachs! Imagine the stomach so sovereign in the man that every part of him slaves and endures for it contentedly. At all hours they are ordering, admiring, comparing, discussing, sharing, devouring mountain and valley herds, whole fields and vegetable gardens, faces greasy with satisfiable desire and pleasure.[37]

★ ★ ★ ★ ★

When Berenson arrived in Rome in January 1905, the Duchess Grazioli told him that Gladys 'was making herself thoroughly disliked with her flightiness and insolence'.[38] Her three principal suitors – Roffredo Caetani, the Duke of Camastra and Prince Torlonia – had all broken off relations with her, while Mrs Baldwin and Gladys were 'at such daggers drawn that they have become almost *impossible* in society'.[39]

Berenson tried to see Gladys but she had gone into one of her early reclusive phases, hiding at the Hotel Minerva, having been ill since the beginning of the year. The Berensons came to visit in March 1905, finding Mrs Baldwin away in Paris visiting couturiers and Gladys alone with Dorothy.

On the one hand, Mary found Gladys enchanting and endearing, claiming that her illness had given her 'the leisure to become acquainted with herself and to notice and enjoy the difference of things'. She appeared to have rejected society; she was by turns silly and unforeseeing, wildly extravagant and reckless and 'so much more beautiful than ever before – she is startling!'[40]

---

* Sally Fairchild (1869–1960), painted by Sargent, friend of Henry James and Robert Louis Stevenson, who rejected numerous suitors in order to look after her mother.

It transpired that the illness was both serious and unusual. Gladys had had her first period only the previous autumn and they had stopped in January. They had been artificially induced by dilation and this would happen again as the period was fourteen days late. The retention gave Gladys nausea and fever. She underwent a secret operation, though the doctors said they could do little for her. Mary noted:

> Her womb has turned way back, a congenital malformation, so as to close the neck; hence, except when she is exuberantly well she can't have her monthly relief, & all that had to be absorbed by her system. In fact, ever since she was 14 she has had 'morning sickness' – during the last three months it has been nearly constant, her nausea. But they say nothing can be done surgically . . .[41]

Mary was afraid that Gladys would be delicate for evermore. But she saw advantages:

> She is becoming much more real – although she still tells stupendous lies – and far more consistently thoughtful. She says she feels disgusted with the wild extravagant society life she led, except for the youthful 'fun' & animal high spirits of it. But she says there is not a person in that mad whirl she ever cares to see again, & she doesn't care a bit to get well. Bed & books & thoughts are far more entertaining, she says, than changing your dresses a dozen times a day & rushing about in search of expensive pleasures.[42]

Roman society was full of speculation, especially as Gladys was in the hands of a 'female doctor', some people suggesting she was crazy or had consumption of the intestines. Before they left, Mary concluded that it was impossible to tell how serious Gladys's illness was and that Gladys was 'still an awful liar, and she won't face her situation or live on any plan'.[43]

★ ★ ★ ★ ★

Gladys recuperated in Roncegno, Mrs Baldwin convinced that she was 'not really very ill' but just wished to be alone. When Berenson met Mrs Baldwin and Prince Doria in St Moritz, the prince complained that Gladys was causing terrible family rows: 'Ah if only Gladys were not so cruel. I tell you, she is a real thorn in her side.' Berenson detected that Doria had nearly said 'our side'.[44]

By the end of 1905 Gladys was back in Rome, 'exceedingly well in all ways' and enjoying 'the luminous immobility' of her life. She still disliked Christmas: 'Only I find Xmas more a day of sad recording of changes come than a day of satisfied banter.'[45] Despite Princess Doria's professed dislike of Mrs Baldwin and her daughter, they both cele-brated New Year's Eve at the Palazzo Doria. Tina Whitaker observed them there, Mrs Baldwin with a 'hard, determined face, handsome still', being openly courted by the prince, and Gladys 'handsome, but her eyes are too wide apart, and although she has a beautiful figure, there is want of grace in her movements'.[46]

Gladys, aged 14.

Gladys with her mother,
Florence Baldwin.

Gladys and Audrey
on the boat 1889.

Edward Parker Deacon at Sturtevant Farm, New Hampshire in June 1895.
Left to right in descending size – Gladys, Audrey and Edith (seated).

Count Robert de Montesquiou.

The Duke of Marlborough.

Crown Prince William of Prussia.

Bernard Berenson with
Florence Baldwin.

Gladys with her dogs.

Audrey during her London season.

Prince Roffredo Caetani.

Gladys with her dog,
reclusive at Caprarola.

The Casino in the
Garden at Caprarola.

Florence Baldwin by Boldini, 1906.

Gladys – a passport photo.

Consuelo Vanderbilt, Duchess of
Marlborough, by Helleu.

Count Hermann von Keyserling.

HRH The Duke of Connaught, 1919.

Gladys's portrait by Boldini, 1916.

Interlude

MARCEL PROUST

In his two-volume biography of Marcel Proust (the celebrated novelist whose longest sentence was 394 words), George Painter identified Gladys as Miss Foster, a character mentioned in passing, the third heiress in the café in the fog, proposed as a bride for the Prince de Foix.[*] Inevitably, Gladys was of great fascination to Proust. He took considerable interest in her between 1906 and his death in 1922.

In August 1906, Proust was staying at the Hôtel des Réservoirs, where he had incarcerated himself for five months. During the last three he never left the hotel at all. 'I haven't left my bed, I haven't seen the palace, the Trianons, or anything,' he wrote to Madame de Caillavet. 'When I open my eyes it's already the dead of night, and I often wonder whether the room I lie in, lit by electricity and hermetically sealed, isn't anywhere in the world rather than at Versailles . . .'[1] Instead of going to St Moritz that year, Gladys and her mother occupied the rooms above his, spending their time with friends.

One such was Hans Schlesinger, a French painter and brother-in-law of Hugo von Hofmannsthal, the librettist and poet, who was seldom far from Mrs Baldwin's entourage. It was not long before Proust became aware of the fascinating presence in the room above his. He informed Reynaldo Hahn of Gladys's arrival, but exhorted him on no account to discuss her with Schlesinger. He became exceedingly sensitive on the subject and related the full circumstances of his knowledge of Gladys to Madame Émile Straus[†].

[*] See C. K. Scott Moncrieff (translator), Marcel Proust, *The Guermantes Way, Part 2 (Remembrance of Things Past)* (Chatto & Windus, 1949), p. 132.
[†] Geneviève Halévy (1849-1926), married first to the composer, Georges Bizet, and later to the banker, Émile Straus. She was another part model for Proust's Duchesse de Guermantes.

One day he was on his bed and observed the twenty-five-year-old Gladys from his window, heavily veiled, stepping into an automobile. But during the time she was at the hotel, he never met her. One evening he attempted to do so, mounting the stairs to her room. Unfortunately for him, Gladys had gone to bed and he was obliged to talk to her mother, their only encounter. He urged Madame Straus to inform Robert Dreyfus that this was his sole experience with Gladys: 'I was never once well enough to see her, neither with me, nor with her.'[2] Later he took the trouble to write to Hahn, urging him to tell Montesquiou that he was not interested in meeting Gladys: 'I am beginning to prefer objects,'[3] he wrote, in reference to a poem in *Les Hortensias Bleus*, which the count had lately sent him.

This was far from the case. Proust yearned to make Gladys's acquaintance, but he had to wait until the following year to achieve his wish. He never forgot his first attempt, and when Mrs Baldwin died in 1918, he wrote to Gladys:

> I remember your mother so well at Versailles, her beauty and her goodness. I had gone upstairs to make your acquaintance but you were in another room, you were ill. I felt that just a very thin wall prevented me from seeing you and kept us apart. Alas it was a real wall and a symbolic one which was to extend endlessly in the plain of time. Very often I have thought of this evening . . .[4]

In July 1907 he invited Gladys to attend a splendid dinner party he was giving at the Ritz, but as she explained to the Comtesse Greffulhe:

> I cannot go to Monsieur Proust because Mademoiselle Reisdorf [her former governess] *forbids* it. She has care of me and Maman would be most unhappy to hear from her that I had gone to the Hôtel Ritz without a chaperone.
>
> I am sorry but force is holding me here.[5]

One of his guests was the Duchesse de Clermont-Tonnerre (Lily de Gramont). It was she who finally brought Proust and Gladys together. He was delighted by the meeting and confessed he was 'bewildered by so much charm'. Lily quoted his opinion of Gladys: 'I never saw a girl with so much beauty, such magnificent intelligence, such goodness and charm.'[6]

With Lily, Proust hatched a plan to get Gladys married either to Prince Léon (Loche) Radziwill, the prototype for his 'Prince de Foix' in his novel, who had a 'high idea' of her, or to his cousin, 'Aba' Radziwill, evidently also 'very taken' with her. Loche Radziwill had been married briefly, between 1905 and 1906, to Claude de Gramont. Gladys did well to avoid him. He went on to have relationships with dubious women, including Liane Louvain, a 'bar butterfly' on a mahogany stool, described as one of 'the professional sirens who roost up there to be seen and invited to adventure by rich men',[7] and Marthe Dalbane, the 'Dead Flower', many of whose male lovers came to grief.* Proust conceded that along with her 'beauty, superior intelligence and a nature both good and delicious', he could hardly advise Gladys to marry 'to please her friends'. He was ecstatic about Gladys, again declaring that he had never seen a girl 'of such beauty and such magnificent intelligence'. And yet he was concerned about her future, and furthermore wondered if Aba was not more interested in her sister Dorothy, as proved to be the case.[8]

At a time when Proust thought Gladys was preparing to return to Rome, he wrote further to Lily that, considering a law in Rome forbade the removal of beautiful works of art and antique statues from the country, it was absurd to suppose that the authorities would allow 'this marvellous person who gives the impression of having been engraved on a Greek or Sicilian medal to immortalise the beauty of a goddess or the glory of a city'[9] to leave Italy for long. As it happened, on 7 July Gladys left Paris for the Engadine.

In turn Gladys considered Proust 'incomparably the best of all those writers at that time'[10]. She read the volumes of À la Recherche du Temps Perdu as they were published, and believed that he was not as ill as he liked to make out, but needed the enforced solitude in which to write.

They met again during the Peace Conference of 1919, and Proust attended a dinner just before Gladys's wedding in 1921.

---

* Loche Radziwill ran the casino in Monte Carlo, and controlled gambling concessions in the principality. He was found dead on 2 March 1927. At first it was said he had died of a heart attack, but it later emerged that he had been murdered by an opiate overdose. It was said that the 'Dead Flower' had been with him on his last night.

SEPARATION

Gladys has nothing to do with the impending separation of Marlborough and his wife!!! Who knows Gladys may be Duchess of M. yet – but on what?
　　　　　　　　Bernard Berenson to Mary, 23 October 1906

Many thought Gladys was responsible for the break-up of the Duke of Marlborough's marriage to Consuelo, but they were wrong. It was Consuelo, not the duke, who first strayed from the marital path. In 1910 Sir George Lewis confirmed to the journalist W. T. Stead what Gladys had herself told him – that she had nothing to do with the separation; nor was her name introduced in any way.[1]

She had, however, played a significant role in the lives of both Marlboroughs since 1901. The duke had become intimate that August; Consuelo had been close to her. There exist what are virtually love letters from her to Gladys. After Audrey's death, Consuelo had written: 'Dear little Gladischen, my heart is very full of tenderness for you.'[2] She longed for her 'clever & dear thoughts' and announced: 'I have never cared for any other woman like you,' and told her she loved her.[3] By 1906 that friendship had cooled, after which Consuelo and her circle became vengeful towards Gladys. Having steered Marlborough towards Gladys, it suited Consuelo to take the line that Gladys had stolen her husband. Gladys was well placed to know the duke's sorry version of his marriage to Consuelo, her infidelities and his despair.

For some years the duke and duchess had wanted a divorce, but to obtain one meant proving infidelity in Consuelo, and she proving physical cruelty and infidelity, or desertion and non-support on his part. In October 1906 matters came to a head and the duke asked for a legal separation. He wrote to Consuelo when she was staying in Paris with her father:

It is painful for me to dwell in detail on those immoral actions on your part which began in the early years of our married life. Your attachments to Mr. R. and to Mr G.* The recollection of those terrible periods can never be effaced from my memory.

I have felt that throughout those periods I showed you loyalty and interested actions. I effaced myself and I set on one side my own feeling of bitter humiliation. I tried to be a help and a comrade to you in distress. I remembered that you belonged to a great family in America for whom I entertained sentiments of affection and respect. It was for your sake in particular and for those who were dear to you in general that I obliterated my own feelings in order that I may know in my heart of hearts that no consideration of personal pride or outraged honour should allow me to be unmindful of all those manifold obligations and consideration which the Head of one family should display in consequence to the daughter of another.

I suffered much in consequence ... I forgave and I tried to forget ...

Since those days others have come into your life, with whom your relations have been of an immoral character. In this last case I have done all in my power to prevent your intimacy with my cousin L. C.†
If I had done nothing, said nothing, but simply spied on your movements, you would have had cause to make comment. This is a course some people adopt.[4]

The duke had waited until she was with her father in Paris before writing. William K. Vanderbilt, Consuelo's father responded angrily:

You dwell upon the impropriety of my daughter's conduct, but do not mention the fact that you have never been faithful to her either in mind or body since the beginning of your married life (I mention no names but am aware of facts).

Consuelo was fully prepared to make you a loving and faithful wife, but has never received one word of affection or encouragement from you, so that if any impropriety has been committed, you have yourself and only yourself to blame.[5]

* Winthrop Rutherfurd and Frederick Guest.
† Lord Castlereagh, later 7th Marquess of Londonderry, KG (1878-1949).

It was made clear by the duke's lawyers that the duchess had had 'various intrigues' and had 'committed adultery'. She had twice been forgiven, though she had confessed her adultery to a third party whose name would be given in court (possibly by Gladys). She was now accused of adultery with Lord Castlereagh. Evidence was gathered from detectives and from the butler, William George Fletcher, at Sunderland House: 'The fact of Lord Castlereagh going to the Boudoir with Her Grace was rather noticeable,'[6] he volunteered.

As noted, Consuelo had committed adultery with Winthrop Rutherfurd in 1898. In old age, Gladys went so far as to state that Consuelo's second son, Ivor, was 'the result of two nights in Paris with an American',[7] and she was in a position to know. Even years before, in 1918, she had joked with the duke when her former boyfriend, Lord Brooke, produced yet another son:* 'Shame upon you, father of one & upon me, mother of none.'[8]

Daisy, Princess of Pless accused Consuelo of involvement with a certain Prince Z, in Vienna in 1902, and in March 1907 Tina Whitaker heard from Marchesa Lea Rudini of Consuelo's visit to Paris with Lord Castlereagh.[9] The duke wired that he did not want his wife back, but she chose to ignore him. Lady Castlereagh, the political hostess whose 'shrewd worldly wisdom', Consuelo wrote, 'proved a wholesome antidote to any sentimental tendencies on my part',[10] intervened to rescue a dangerous situation, and finally King Edward VII and Queen Alexandra made it clear that divorce between the Marlboroughs would be met with disapproval.

Winston Churchill tried to effect a reconciliation. He judged that matters would be calmer if Marlborough swallowed his pride, was less influenced by the fools to whom he listened, and relinquished the evident pleasure he took in blackguarding his wife's name. But the duke had come to the end of what he called the 'false and sordid history'[11] of his marriage. He threatened never to speak to Jennie Cornwallis-West again if she repeated the mischievous accusations floating about. He was convinced that Consuelo

---

* The Hon. John Greville (1918-42), third son of the Earl of Warwick, born on 2 February 1918, a painter and writer, served as a flight lieutenant, RAF, killed in action in the Second World War.

would malign him, something that became a paranoid obsession of his for years to come, and he was right – there were many who took her part.

In January 1907 a legal separation was granted. One of the effects was that the King instructed Lord Knollys to write to Churchill, asking him to notify the duke and duchess that they 'should not come to any dinner or evening party, or private entertainment at which either of Their Majesties are expected to be present'.[12] The duke was a Knight of the Garter and there were occasions when he attended the Chapter of the Order at Windsor, but on these occasions his carriage was called before the other Knights sat down to feast with their Sovereign.* Another effect was that Theodore Roosevelt wrote to Whitelaw Reid, describing the business: 'The lowest note of infamy is reached by such a creature as this Marlborough . . . surely you don't object to my considering the Duke of Marlborough a cad!'[13]

A difficult phase began, the duke protesting when Consuelo proposed taking their sons to Biarritz. He suggested Brighton instead, which Consuelo interpreted as being 'tiresomely worded just to annoy and worry her'. In May the duke telegraphed to Gladys to say he was coming to Paris to tell her that he was divorcing Consuelo. According to the Comtesse Greffulhe, Gladys had possession of Consuelo's (presumably incriminating) letters and could have given them to him, but instead she burnt them.

Mrs Baldwin was delighted. She went about Paris boasting that Gladys could marry Marlborough whenever she liked.

★ ★ ★ ★ ★

It was by no means certain that that would happen. There were several occasions when Gladys might have married another. After Roffredo Caetani, the most pressing suitor was Lord Brooke, son of the Earl of Warwick and his famous wife, Daisy. He had run away

---

* The duke was present at the Garter Investiture of King Manoel II of Portugal on 16 November 1909, and of the Prince of Wales on 10 June 1911, and attended Garter ceremonies in June 1912 and June 1914. He was also present at the Accession Council on 7 May 1910, following the death of Edward VII. The ostracism continued into the next reign, George V still sidelining the duke in the 1930s.

from school to fight in the Boer War and returned something of a hero. He soon fell at Gladys's feet, and in 1903 he had given her a toy Japanese dog.

In St Moritz in 1905, Mrs Baldwin told Berenson that Gladys was 'all but engaged' to him. She then lowered her voice dramatically and enquired whether or not he thought Gladys was fit for matrimony. Berenson could not work out what answer was expected of him, so he parried the question. Mary remarked that it was unlikely Gladys would ever marry, and nor should she 'at any rate without a full explanation such as would put most people off'.[14] Prince Doria assured Berenson that Lord Brooke was broken-hearted, but that Gladys would marry nobody who would not give her sway over Consuelo.

A year later, in May 1906, at I Tatti, Mrs Baldwin announced proudly that the Brooke engagement was on. Yet when Mary Berenson found Gladys in Florence, there was no mention of Lord Brooke, Berenson despairing: 'for she pays no heed to her future, & she is spoiling all her chances. We hear her universal reputation is just as bad as it can be. And she is laying no mental treasures, no interests, no pursuits, not even any friendships.'[15]

However, Gladys was soon with her mother and Lord Brooke at the Hôtel de l'Europe in Venice. Edmund Houghton, the photographer friend of the Berensons, saw them there, noting that Gladys was quiet, appeared to be engaged to Brooke, though nothing was said. As ever, Mary's comment was double-edged: 'She is certainly radiant & brilliant enough to turn any man's head – but that is her danger.'[16]

In August 1906 Gladys herself confirmed the engagement, but then all of a sudden Brooke broke it off. It appeared that no less a figure than Edward VII had intervened to advise against the match. And since the King had an understanding of some duration with the young man's mother, Lady Warwick, his words carried weight. In 1907 Mrs Baldwin had been to London to remonstrate with Brooke, and now Gladys was threatening to cross the Channel to attempt to swing the King to her side. Mary Berenson's verdict was: 'She has inflicted herself rather seriously with the Duke of Marlborough I am afraid.'[17]

★ ★ ★ ★ ★

Spending the spring of 1907 in Rome, the Comtesse Greffulhe surprised her confidant, Dom Pedro de Carvalho, by taking an interest in Gladys. He wondered if she might find 'a profoundly true side'[18] in her, but remained doubtful. Ruefully he quoted Victor Hugo: it was possible to find a pearl in a dustbin. In Rome, the comtesse presented Gladys with a beautiful scarf, prompting Gladys to reply: 'You will be the goddess in her mysterious palace and I a Sylvaine charged with discovering the true secrets of your wild subjects.'[19] She offered her a mirror made specially in Naples and the comtesse accepted it with a suitably flattering reply.

The friendship became closer in Paris. What Gladys did not know was that the comtesse was seeking doctors' opinions about her character and having her handwriting analysed. The verdict was negative. Dr Henri Favre, an astrologer and alchemist (a friend of George Sand and Alexandre Dumas *fils*, then aged eighty), found her deceptive, capable of moving others to sympathy with her eyes, and prepared to go to prolonged lengths to obtain what she wanted. He found her detached and thought she had never loved anyone. He suggested that she had the habit of doing malicious things, and a completely black spirit, the hands of a reptile with a long lifeline, revolving around instinct, a sensual mouth, a 'voluntary' chin, and seraphic eyes, and that her stated mission was: 'I want to dominate, I want to drive, I dominate. I don't care.' She had no strong moral current.[20]

The handwriting analyst detected singularity of spirit, anxiety in her allure and in the manifestations of her mental state, both mysterious and cryptic. There was stability of thought, with both the need to express herself and equally to hold herself in. She had a feminine spirit, without the least masculinity in her instinct. She wanted to elevate herself in life, but lacked the necessary drive, so she tended to retreat into vague spaces. She sought grandeur without the means to obtain it.[21]

Gladys's many letters to the comtesse were admiring and invariably expressed a longing to see her. They began 'Dear Goddess' or 'Dear Fairy', and she signed herself 'obedient', 'ardent' or 'devoted' Sylvaine. 'I love you for all that is in you which is noble, enthusiastic, intelligent, beautiful and gracious,' she wrote in July 1907,[22] and in October (after the visit to Venice): 'I love you with all my heart.'[23] In old age, Gladys recalled the comtesse as 'vain' and 'dashing'.

One day in Paris Gladys cancelled a meeting with the Comtesse Greffulhe because Lord Brooke had arrived. She told the comtesse that she had liked her fiancé, but he had made no headway with her. Whenever there was a row, she had hugged her pillow and cried. She claimed to have been engaged at the age of fifteen, but that when she was kissed, she had been so disgusted that she threw the ring back and no longer wanted to marry the man. Then there had been a suitor with a considerable fortune, (Lord Howard de Walden or Prince Torlonia*), and another who had thought her disloyal (Roffredo Caetani) and had gone away. She said she found it odious if a man was in love with her and she could not give him what he wanted as she did not love him. She warned her suitors accordingly. And so her life involved studying, visits from friends, and talking most days to the comtesse. She had been to Naples in April, was going to paint and declared that she considered she would make an 'ideal mistress', rather than a legally wed wife. The comtesse concluded: 'In her analysis of matters, she sees artistic detail rather than deep feelings.'[24]

★ ★ ★ ★ ★

Lily de Clermont-Tonnerre, a known lesbian, had first met Gladys at the salon of the Comtesse (Thérèse) Murat. The Comtesse Greffulhe suggested that Lily bring Gladys to a polo match. Lily collected her at her hotel, expecting to hear no more than banal expressions of gratitude. Instead Gladys told her that she had just finished reading Thomas Hardy's *The Well-Beloved*, and launched into an eloquent comparison of the novels of Hardy and George Meredith and the difference between the English and the French spirit. Lily listened with rapt interest and observed Gladys, in a light dress, which hung loosely about her in the English style. 'She seemed to be a young Greek warrior with a perfect profile. Were not her eyes too large and too blue?' In due course they arrived at

---

* Thomas (Tommy), 8th Lord Howard de Walden (1880-1946), an immensely rich peer and power boat racer who was sculpted by Rodin. She liked him in 1903, but he had proposed to her too soon and, though she had meant to accept him, she later regretted that she had bitten his head off in anger. He married Margarita Van Raalte in 1912.

the polo match and sat down at a tea table beside the green lawn. Gladys changed, like a chameleon, becoming 'a dazzling young girl with a worldly laugh, having captured instantly the tone and atmosphere of her surroundings'.[25] Gladys carried a parasol attached to a harness of jewels. She brought her bull terrier, Jack, with her and he, too, had his own parasol.

When she attended a race meeting or football match, she dressed in the colours of her favourite team or racehorse. Lily took her to a lunch-party at which Anatole France was present. Giotto was the sole topic of conversation, and Lily felt uncomfortable as she knew so little about him. Gladys, on the other hand, was an expert, thanks to her travels in Italy. 'With her habitual impetuosity,' wrote Lily, 'she contradicted France, who riposted with successful passes so that everybody listened and watched enchanted.'[26]

Lily was one of the girlfriends of the American writer Natalie Barney and often visited her house in the rue Jacob. However, she did not want Gladys to meet Miss Barney, telling her young friend: 'I shall not take you to Miss Barney. She can't teach you anything.'[27] In old age, Gladys invariably became irritated if women such as Natalie Barney or Romaine Brooks were introduced into the conversation. She dismissed them quickly: 'We are getting onto dangerous ground here.' She took pains to point out: 'Lily's love for me was *absolutely* pure.'[28]

But she was of interest to such women. Her developing friendship with the Comtesse Greffulhe was close. Another who took a strong interest in her was Baronne (Madeleine) Deslandes, another well-known lesbian, who had inspired Oscar Wilde to commission her portrait by Sir Edward Burne-Jones. The diarist and writer, Edmond de Goncourt, described her as having 'a supple body and an animal elasticity',[29] and d'Annunzio told her he would ravish her when she was in her coffin. She entered a relationship with Colette. Madeleine wrote to Gladys: 'You make me think of a diamond. You are, I believe, cold, pure and white, and cutting like that admirable stone. The diamond has something cruel about it too, don't you think?'[30]

She made a less positive impression on Gertrude Stein and Alice B. Toklas, whom she saw in Florence in the early summer of 1906. Gertrude dismissed her as 'too easily shocked to be interesting'.[31] She remembered that at a dinner in Paris, Gladys had suddenly declared: 'Stein and I are the only two people who have had enough courage to put the manners they were born and bred with completely aside and have therefore been able to live an unencumbered life.'[32] In 1976 Gladys remembered Gertrude:

> I hated Gertrude. I disliked her. She was hard and ugly, and a hard man or woman isn't worth bothering about. No, never! . . . She was absolutely round . . . hideous she was! She wore hideous clothes in a disgusting way. But she was clever.[33]

Some years later, in 1909, Bessie Marbury, the American theatrical and literary agent, expressed her view that Gladys was a lesbian. Mary Berenson was horrified: 'It turned me quite sick to read of Bessie Marbury accusing Gladys of being a lesbian (she is accused of it herself,* shd be more gentle . . .).'[34] Gladys, unmarried until the age of forty, was easy prey for such gossip. She was attractive to these women and, being a solitary figure and self-sufficient, did not rely on men as some women did. But Gladys was so obsessed with her childhood dream of marrying the Duke of Marlborough that no other suitors, male or female, stood a chance. Besides, the gift of her great beauty had an isolating effect. Forever surrounded by admirers, Gladys was forever playing one off against another.

If Gladys's relationship with the Marlboroughs was strange and involved both of them, so too did her relationship with the Berensons. Few of Gladys's letters to Mary survive, but she sometimes added precocious messages for her in letters to Berenson: 'My love in honeyed streams to that sweetest of white mice cooked in gooseberry jam, Mary . . . Kiss Mary cold as ice for me . . . And please give my love to Isolde . . . Kiss Mary ever contrary for me.'

In Sils in the summer of 1907, Gladys succeeded in shocking Countess Serristori by announcing that she was 'all for pure love,

---

* Bessie Marbury shared her life with Elsie de Wolfe, and to some extent with Anne Morgan – 'Anne Morgan still on the organ' as one of Cole Porter's unpublished lyrics went [Dickie Fellowes-Gordon to author, 1991]. They lived together at Versailles.

independence, no ties but of the heart, all for living with the man she would love no matter how poor or undistinguished'.[35] Though these views were never tested, she remained a lifelong advocate of the importance of physical love. 'One is changed by ecstasy,' she said in old age. 'Physical love is the creator of all things. It is a recreation. And when I say a recreation, I don't mean a recreation, but a re-creation!' Marriage, on the other hand, was 'something very different'. And as for children, she said cryptically: 'One hopes something stops them from coming.'[36]

During this holiday, Berenson was drawn once more into the mysterious web that the twenty-six-year-old Gladys spun, but he was concerned about her face. Three years after the wax injections, the damage was beginning to show: 'She is fatter, puffy-cheeked and her mouth has taken a curious twist,' he informed Mary, 'but still dazzlingly radiant.'[37] Two days later he remarked: 'She has been monkeying with her face, as hitherto with her nose. Consequently, she has lost her beautiful oval and her mouth is queer. But she retains all her radiance.'[38] In artificial light she looked worse:

> She looked like a porcelain doll, wh. had got a swelling of the cheeks, and the red patch of which had run into the face. Today she swore she was not painted – but she looked, with her huge pupils, like something mannequin-like and repellent.[39]

After spending seven hours with Gladys one day, he concluded: 'I must confess that at her very best as today she beats even the Serristori at an all around talk.' But though 'entirely captivated' when with her, he was 'rather sceptical' and distrustful when away. Then Gladys retreated again into solitude, busy baptising some puppies.

★ ★ ★ ★ ★

The Berensons and Mabel Dodge Luhan were anxious when Gladys left for Venice with her mother and Douglas Ainslie. There, they found the Duke of Marlborough and Winston Churchill breaking their journey to Vienna.

Churchill was delighted to have Marlborough's company, though the embittered duke scarcely dared go out for fear of gossip and was accordingly much on his own. On 20 September Churchill was due for a gondola ride with Gladys at ten thirty and then to climb the tower of San Giorgio Maggiore. They would visit Torcello. His day was to be shared with other female company, but in the end he dismissed Gladys and the others as 'these strange glittering beings with whom I have little or nothing in common . . .'[40]

In old age, Gladys did not have a good word for Churchill. 'He was in love with his own image – his reflection in the mirror.' At Blenheim he always had to be in the centre of everything that happened. 'I watched him all the time,' said Gladys. 'He took an instant dislike to me . . . I knew him from top to bottom . . . He was entirely out for Winston.'[41]

Interlude

CAPRAROLA

'There is nothing in all Italy like Caprarola,' wrote Edith Wharton, after her first sight of the Villa Farnese in the early 1900s. In 1908 Prince Doria established Mrs Baldwin in this Renaissance villa. It remained her home for the rest of her life, even after Doria's death in 1914.

Caprarola stands in a splendid position. Built by Vignola in about 1547 on the orders of Cardinal Alessandro Farnese, it lies about thirty miles north of Rome. Palatial and pentagonal, it dominates a small town of stone houses perched along narrow streets, and has a fine view over the Italian countryside towards Monte Soratte.

Built around an inner court, the first-floor rooms are reached by a spiral staircase wide enough and shallow enough to climb on horseback. The rooms are vast and magnificent; over the centuries they have witnessed much pageantry with grand receptions for popes and princes. The Sala dei Fatti in particular caught the imagination of visitors from Queen Christina of Sweden in the seventeenth century to Gabriele d'Annunzio in 1913.* It had at least four hundred bedrooms, most of them unused in Mrs Baldwin's time.

The villa is surrounded by a deep moat, crossed at the back by a small bridge, which leads into extensive gardens, as fine as the edifice itself. When Queen Christina saw them, she was so overcome that she gasped: 'I dare not speak the name of Jesus lest I break the spell.' The gardens are divided into two parts, separated by trees and ornamented with a plethora of terraces, walks, cascading fountains and grottoes. There is a secret garden and an exquisite casino. Of

---

* The title of d'Annunzio's novel, *Forse che sì forse che no*, is picked out in mosaic on one of the bathroom ceilings.

particular note are the huge sylvan figures with varying expressions of solemnity, ferocity and rustic laughter.

Mrs Baldwin loved the place for its grandeur and beauty, for the nightingales that sang through the night, for the wood that was 'a green carpet' and for the air that was fresh and clean. 'It is one of the most beautiful places in the world,' she wrote to Rodin, 'with a marvellous horizon, solitude, waters and birds, and sufficiently far from humans to know nothing more of them than one wishes . . . It is a setting worthy of a grand master.'[1] She paid rent of 5,000 francs a year, recouping 2,000 from the sale of chestnuts.

The rooms were so immense that they were always cool, despite the heat of an Italian summer. Though often alone, Mrs Baldwin was happier here than anywhere else. After a long winter of travelling, she loved the 'quiet nights in my soft sheets' and revelled in the coming of spring:

> Days follow each other in increasing loveliness; today and yesterday have been like summer, and the wisteria has covered the walk in a glow of purple, while the irises stand in great masses of odorous purple.[2]

Sometimes white peacocks and blue peacocks promenaded side by side, a white gentleman with a blue lady and vice versa.[3] There were crocuses and tulips and 'all sorts of lovely things . . . peeping out in the Bosco'. Gladys loved especially the 'beautiful and subtle movement' of the staircase and found amid the cascading fountains and the statues of river gods the perfect setting for her classical beauty. Edith Wharton searched France for a pocket Caprarola and was always cheered by the prospect of a visit to Mrs Baldwin's haven. 'The thought shines through *les brumes septentrionales* [the northern mists],'[4] she wrote to Berenson. So too was Mary Berenson in awe of Caprarola. Once she arrived in a downpour with lightning 'flashing across the campagna, & the thunder rolling among the Ciminian Hills as if Trotan & Zeus were contending on the Monte Venere'. She thought it magnificent: 'It is more than an occupation, it is a career.'[5]

Lunching there in 1910, they could not believe they could know someone who lived in such a gorgeous place. They judged the gardens 'the grandest . . . ever made (outside of Versailles)' and were in awe of

Mrs Baldwin's 'nearly perfect taste' and daunted by thinking of the money she must have spent on it.[6]

By 1911 Mrs Baldwin had made a high terrace with a park, shut in by a pergola. In the evenings she lit the paths with Chinese lanterns, and local workers came to sing field songs, music heard from Russia to the Sudan.[7]

When he saw it, Berenson wrote: 'It is a sight to make the Gods envious.'[8]

12

THE CHINAMAN

Als Gottes Atem leise ging
Dann schuf er Graf Keyserling

(As God's Breath was running thin
Created he Count Keyserling)

Emil Preetorious

At the age of twenty-seven, Gladys surprised everyone by embarking on an unlikely five-month romance with a then relatively unknown Baltic philosopher, Count Hermann von Keyserling. This was a relief from the tedium of the early months of 1908, which found her at the Palazzo Borghese, fending off reports that she was going to marry Antoine de Charette.* Keyserling materialised in Rome in the spring of 1908, fell violently in love with Gladys and asked her to marry him. His letters are filled with passionate imprecations: 'I am so intensely happy with the fact of having found you – happy, I say, with the mere fact of your existence . . . For a long time I have searched, through many lands, for a woman with lively energy such as yours . . . I love you. I am longing for you, will always think of you.'[1] He drafted many letters, some of which he sent:

---

* Marquis Antoine (Tony) de Charette (1880-1947), a French marquis descended from Charles X of France, and great-nephew of President James K. Polk of America. From his father's family he was heir to some of the greatest art treasures in France, from his mother's to impressive plantations in Tennessee. Though French, his family spent time in Rome. Presently he eloped with Susanne Henning, daughter of a banker from Louisville, Kentucky, against her parents' wishes and married her in 1909. Later they divorced. The Comtesse Greffulhe saved an article about this romance, but none of the others who monitored Gladys's activities referred to it.

I am free . . . You too are made for freedom – but you are a woman . . .
You guess that I love you. You know I am not just toying with you.
My desires are as sincere as our first kiss. You know me well enough
to know that there is nothing vile or pernicious (in my character) . . .
I know that if we see a lot of one another, if I'm not mistaken, your
feelings will only grow and the flame become irresistible. Love does
not cease at this point. It will become an inferno . . . Your luminous
presence has not left my house. I still see you in the clarity of the big
room . . . I hear your sweet, sweet voice - and now and again I am
overcome with the need, the ardent desire to kiss you roughly, indel-
ibly, to kiss you to death, to breathe in your beautiful soul. I think I
could love you until the end of time . . . my desire for you is almost
killing me.[2]

There were excursions to Lake Albano, Gladys offering a drive
beyond: 'I have memories of bridges spanning green chasms of rocks
& trees & of a road cleaving up a mountain side.'[3] She would send her
carriage to take him to a meeting at the Villa Doria Pamphili, or to
Caprarola.

He told her that he had long searched for 'a form of living energy
such as yours'.[4] He had been sick with dysentery, but he rose from his
bed to attend a dinner on condition that she was present, and on a
later day, not only did he look forward to dining with her in the evening, but he declared he would wait in a restaurant at two o'clock in
the fleeting hope that she might pass by. After an afternoon in her
company, he felt relaxed and happy: 'Beauty all around and harmony
within; the perfect music of silence.'[5]

Hermann von Keyserling was the scion of a Baltic family, involved
in intellectual and spiritual matters for seven generations. Caesarian
Keyserling had been Voltaire's most valued intellectual friend; Johann
Sebastian Bach had dedicated a work to one Keyserling; Immanuel
Kant was tutor to the family of another. Hermann's grandfather,
Alexander, was the founder of Russian geology, an adviser to Emperor
Alexander II and a friend of Bismarck, who said he was the only man
whose intellect might have intimidated him. His cousin, Eduard von
Keyserling, was a yet more famous writer and poet.

Keyserling was born in 1880 on the family estate at Köhno in
Russian Livonia (Estonia), the son of a politician and orator. He

described himself as a mixture, sensitive and impressionable on one hand, a man of 'volcanic violence, of primitive vitality, with the instincts of the conqueror and ruler'[6] on the other. He had wanted to be an explorer. As a student he was contented, if somewhat rough – 'a paragon of primitive health and brute strength'. Physically, he was a giant of a man. His friend Don Salvador de Madariaga* wrote that he was like a heavy lorry propelled by a Rolls-Royce engine. He drank heavily – Madariaga called him 'a huge tankard on legs' – but never got drunk 'because the stuff had to travel too long to get to his head'.

Keyserling's days as a man of action ended when he was badly wounded in a duel, after which he turned to natural sciences, completing his doctorate in geology in 1902. Philosophy meant little to him until he read Houston Stewart Chamberlain's *Foundation of the Nineteenth Century*. He went to Vienna determined to meet Chamberlain, and made friends with the mystic Rudolf Kassner, whom he judged as one of the deepest – though perhaps least easily understood – thinkers of his time.

In 1903 he went to Paris and was welcomed into the intellectual and worldly salon of the Comtesse (Rosa) de Fitz-James. She was known as Rosa Malheur because her husband was consistently rude to her, entertained every Tuesday, gave endless lunches and dinners and made celebrated gaffes. Of her it was said, 'She wanted a salon, but all she got was a *salle à manger*.'[7] At that time Keyserling was 'a bushy-haired' young man.[8] Rosa helped him get his early works published.

In 1905 the Russian Revolution temporarily deprived Keyserling of his lands and his fortune, which meant that for nearly three years he was impoverished. Meanwhile he worked in Berlin, producing treatises and two books, *Prolegomena to Nature* and *Philosophy and Immortality*. By 1908, although still only twenty-seven, nearly a year older than Gladys, he was a respected figure in German scientific circles.

The mere fact of Gladys's existence gave him joy: 'I can't help loving what is really great and perfect and beautiful – loving it just for

* Don Salvador de Madariaga (1886–1978), Spanish statesman, writer and scholar, who lived in exile after 1936.

its own sake, apart from all personal considerations.'[9] In her absence, he found his realisation of her grew stronger. 'I never understand reality better than in those states where everything seems to fade away, like inconsistent dreams,' he wrote, 'shapeless, formless & yet so wonderfully definitive.'[10] After lunching with the poet Anna de Noailles, whom he described as Gladys's rival, he hastened to reassure her: 'This delicate butterfly cannot make me forget the powerful tigress,' and he added, 'You make me think like nobody else did.'[11]

On 11 May 1908, Keyserling asked Gladys to be his wife. She could give him no immediate answer and they parted in a state of uncertainty. Yet he was optimistic, thinking of the future. He sent her a chapter of his latest manuscript with a letter:

> I love you. I am longing for you, will always think of you. But I won't write any more ere I hear from you. I could not.
>
> Will we ever meet again? God knows . . . But if we do at all, it will be forever.[12]

Gladys stayed in Rome while Keyserling made his way to Vienna. 'Repetition is the one thing really unpardonable,' he wrote to Gladys, 'everything has to be unique. That's why death is so necessary – & that's why love is so beautiful. Love is nothing but an everlasting creation, an ever surprising transformation.' He found waiting for Gladys to resolve her mind hard to endure, though he promised to wait in silence and to deluge her neither with protestations of love nor with passionate entreaties. As a philosopher, but more as 'a man of the world', Keyserling confessed himself gravely in awe of her.[13]

Keyserling bore the burden of a 'dread silence' on Gladys's part for twelve long days, but she never left his thoughts; nor did he doubt her. At last, on 23 May, a letter arrived saying she was still unable to make a decision. He replied that he was ready to wait as long as was required, but wanted to know her feelings. 'Being a woman you cannot realise what uncertainty means to a man, & especially a man like me.' He told her that she was the one thing in the world he cared for: '. . . more than ever I am longing to have you in my arms, to be close to you. But will I see you again?' The world about him and 'heaps of people' he saw meant nothing to him in comparison with her.

The following day Keyserling became anxious about this 'most idiotic waste' of time. A new world 'of hope, of longing, of unmeasured trust' had awakened in him feelings of which he had previously thought himself incapable. Gladys was the only person upon whom he had ever depended. In his agony, he was fortified by optimism: 'Threads of feeling spin from one star to another & everything is bright with the fragrance of youthful confidence.'[14]

Keyserling left Vienna for Munich and Gladys headed briefly to Paris. He told Rosa de Fitz-James his hopes in respect of Gladys, and she was soon on the case. She reported that Gladys had told the Comtesse Potocka that in the year before she had failed to marry 'an English lord' (Lord Brooke).[15] Rosa finally met Gladys who told her that she had seen Keyserling during ten days in Rome, that he had then written her charming letters – 'He writes wonderfully, then he stopped writing, I don't know why.'[16]

On 3 June Keyserling received a devastating letter from Gladys. She asked him to cool down and not to write any more. He tried to agree, but found no clear message in the letter, nothing to build on and nothing from which to form any conclusions or decisions. He asked her to answer him more specifically in ten days' time. After that, if need be, he would break with her. He wrote: 'This is too much for me. The life of a floating jelly-fish is not mine, of all the many methods of dying this is the one I object to most.'[17]

Yet he could not be cross with her. It was, rather, the woman in her emerging, '& minding a woman is as foolish as minding the weather'. He also suggested that they should have six months of silence and then review the situation. Presumably on account of the shape of his eyes, Gladys indulged the fantasy that Keyserling looked like a Chinaman. He objected strongly to this epithet: 'Don't call me Chinaman, please.'[18] Gladys replied:

Upon my word dear Keyserling – since you'll not consent to the more descriptive name – you do rush rash & raging words upon me!

What gall have you licked? Surely it was not off my letter!

You kill courtesy & I, on the moment, wrote you a fearful letter which I since calmly tore up.

You are no doubt right for yourself but I think I am for myself.

Well, since you must calendar, then let 3 months stand & see what happens . . .

Do be kind & intelligent. Men make themselves objectionable in every instance, place or moment. They hedge a woman's walk with thorns.

They accost one rudely everywhere. Be different, for Heaven's sake!

You tell me I'm a dwarf & one with a bee in his bonnet. Well, if this be, bear with me, think to have found a rarity, a jewel in his cap. I hate harsh words. My hand finds a parthion shot, my legs grow long to run away.

Stay, tarry a while longer, majestic Nord-Deutches Lloyd, near this island of ungrown man & over grown bramble-bush!

G.D.[19]

Matters did not improve. On 12 June, still in Munich, Keyserling complained about the 'insouciant fashion' in which Gladys amused herself by keeping him dangling in space. He was exasperated, launching into an eloquent peroration, which shows how clearly he understood Gladys's enigmatic character:

Let us rather speak of the haughty Amazon as nubile to the pen as to the javelin? Where are you now? Which mortals are you making happy by your presence? O visionary woman, incarnate dream of a God above the laws of nature, reveal to me the voice which follows your destiny. Your eye though open is blind. Like a sleepwalker you tramp through life. The wisdom of your letters seems unconscious of your soul. You speak of ignorance, yet you have understood everything. Both supremely wise and unthinking little girl, you rule worlds and roar with laughter. Your cold anguish is unbelieving but you sob with the little cries of a bird. Who can hold you? You are a comet, a capricious comet, of whom even God does not know the path. You escape me now – there, you are gone: will you ever return? Astronomy is silent. Silence and darkness, I cannot rejoin you, but in my thoughts I clasp you in my arms.[20]

Mrs Baldwin travelled by train to join Gladys, who was briefly in Paris, and found herself in the same carriage as Mary Berenson.

Evidently Mrs Baldwin was under the belief that the engagement was on, though Mary commented that Keyserling didn't have a penny and 'no one thinks she will really marry him':

> The mother pretends to be in despair, but she tells so many lies you can't form the faintest idea what she thinks. She told us that she was going to spend July in St Moritz; a few minutes after she said she & Gladys were going to spend July travelling in Norway; in half an hour she was going to spend that elastic month at Therapia, & when we said goodbye, she was going to remain in Paris. This gives an idea of the state of her mind, if mind it can be called![21]

On 20 July Mary was in Rome, to which Mrs Baldwin and Gladys had returned. She described Gladys as looking 'like a beautiful cocotte. She makes me feel alive.' But when she visited Mrs Baldwin a few days later, finding her ill in bed, Gladys peered into the room once or twice 'with hostile eyes'.[22]

Meanwhile Rosa de Fitz-James told Keyserling how delighted she was that he might marry Gladys. However, she warned him that Gladys did not possess a fortune, that two kind hearts were not enough, that no one could live on a sonnet and that happiness would be matched by great worry. She heard that Gladys had spoken of Keyserling to Berenson and to Olivier Taigny, who quoted her as saying: 'I would like to marry the only person who I consider my equal and even superior to me – the Count Hermann von Keyserling.'[23]

In her European travels Rosa consulted Prince Franz of Liechtenstein, a former Austro-Hungarian ambassador to St Petersburg, who had made some enquiries about Gladys without mentioning Keyserling. 'He was hard on her and did not believe her good.' She worried that 'the character of this young girl was complicated and difficult'.[24]

Keyserling continued to adore Gladys, clinging vainly to straws throughout the months of August and September. In the meantime, unruffled by his persistence, Gladys went dutifully to the Hotel Barblau in Sils-Maria with her mother, Edith and Dorothy. She described it in a letter to Winston Churchill: 'This place holds us for some time more. I am happy, joyous, amused. Mountains, snow-capped, rain unceasing, a great many splendid people in fine clothes but here & there in the fields, a soaked haystack cutting a figure of more rural dash.'[25]

The St Moritz holiday brought the librettist Hugo von Hofmannsthal into her life and resurrected Berenson's interest in her. Despite finding her 'morose & furious', he was determined to spend an evening with her, having enjoyed one tea at which she 'really buckled down to think & say what she meant'.[26] She was still beautiful and playful, though her deteriorating face was a worry, her mother passing this off as lupus, an ulcerous disease of the skin.

Gladys then quarrelled so badly with her mother about the route they would take back to Italy that she moved into a room in the town. Here Berenson found her and they spent most of the day together. He tried to remonstrate with her: 'She feebly tried to bluff & pass it all off on my innocence, ignorance & unfashionableness,' he wrote to Mary, adding that finally he had persuaded her to return to her mother. In the course of the conversation she told him that she had written 'a very good novel' – which never subsequently materialised. Another issue was a serious quarrel between Gladys and Montesquiou. Despite Berenson's attempts to reconcile them, they never regained their early shared admiring friendship.

She left the hotel at one in the morning. Her visit caused considerable talk among the domestic staff, Princess Soutzo's* chambermaid remarking that 'a very smart cocotte had come for the Englishman upstairs'. Berenson was amused. The following day Gladys returned to Mrs Baldwin.

★ ★ ★ ★ ★

Gladys spent ten to fifteen days in Venice in September, where she mused to Keyserling on the meaning of love and how it was possible ever to leave such a much-loved place as Venice: 'Perhaps because one must leave everything always, for fear of dying of the grief of becoming its prisoner. Old people are almost always sad, have you noticed? I recall having long asked myself what the sadness could be which is at the bottom of all joy. Poor friend, this is a strange letter to write to a fiancé.'[27]

* Princess Hélène Soutzo (1879–1975), Romanian wife of the writer, Paul Morand (1888–1976).

Keyserling's Russian estates had been restored to him, and in August he had crossed the Russian frontier to discuss the business of running them with his mother. This completed, he would be totally free and independent:

> If then you will be mine, I will come to you as soon as I'm free; but should it come to a break-up of our relationship – it should have to come to some conclusion by then – then I shall stay at Rayküll for an indefinite period, perhaps for ever. I feel that my way of life has become obsolete and I yearn for a new tune, a new tempo.[28]

To one such letter she replied: 'Accidente! dear Keyserling, no I've no idea whatever of marrying. I use to say eloquent things at this junction but by oft repeating them, I first got them crocked then forgot them altogether. Now 'tis a strait-locked subject.'[29]

By 20 September the philosopher had despaired of Gladys and wrote to ask for the return of his manuscript. He begged for a photograph of her as a material reminder of the past. 'And the five months you participated of my life have been interesting enough, well worth remembering.' It was to be his last letter, he wrote, though 'as our planet is of limited size', he predicted – correctly – that one day they would meet again. He ended firmly, but optimistically:

> I will be much interested then to see what has become of you, whether you will have learnt by that time the discipline of feeling & character, without which, even with transcendent gifts, nothing really great can be performed. But what has been between you & me is over now, dead and buried – How wonderful it is to hear the voice of Death, of the absolute End, join in the exuberant Fuga of ever-growing Life! . . .[30]

He was, he said: 'Ever alive though dead for you.'

Gladys might have believed that the affair was over, but Keyserling continued to preoccupy himself with her. At the end of the year, he wrote to Countess Marguerite Bismarck, ironically his future mother-in-law, about 'everything that I have gained through the loss of what I wanted for five eternal months'. He declared himself frighteningly happy:

Am I not finally, unconsciously, helping the course of destiny? For instance, it is thus teaching us the possibility that my behaviour towards G. D., which she condemned so stupidly at Föhr [North Frisian island near Sylt], was, from a higher standpoint, very wise. I might have anticipated that *only then* would a civil marriage be possible, when she would comply with certain conditions – but as she did not, I was stuck from the start. Under no circumstances would I have made a further step, and besides, stupid obstinacy is certainly my cardinal fault.[31]

In December 1908 Gladys quarrelled with her mother because she abhorred her sister Edith. She set off to live alone in Paris, installing herself in the Hôtel la Pérouse, near the avenue d'Iéna. Rosa de Fitz-James told Keyserling that Gladys had been to see her, 'very beautiful, *ganz verschroben* [quite cranky], saying things that were exalted, impossible, genial and stupid', and then Gladys wrote to say that she had read his latest article on women, found it 'remarkable' as 'all which comes from our dear Keyserling'. She offered to translate it.[32] In April 1909 Rosa reported that Gladys was there again without her mother, going out a great deal in society, where some people fell for her, but the general view of her was malicious. One evening Gladys invited Keyserling to come and see her. At other times she took him to see Thérèse Murat and the Comtesse Greffulhe.

Keyserling remained unmarried throughout the Great War, and then married (Maria) Gödela von Bismarck-Schönhausen, granddaughter of the Iron Chancellor, in 1919.

Interlude

THE MARRIAGE OF ZOBEÏDE

In 1908 Gladys found herself inspiring the lead character in a new version of Hugo von Hofmannsthal's play, *The Marriage of Zobeïde*. This had been written in 1899, a weird tragedy about a woman committing suicide after a brief foray into marriage and an unrequited love affair, played out in the kingdom of Persia.

In July 1908 Hofmannsthal, best known as the collaborator of Richard Strauss, was in Bad Fusch, Austria, and wrote to his wife that he found Gladys entertaining: 'I can very well use her as a character for the play that I will write shortly after this.'[1] He also confided in Hélène von Nostitz that Gladys was one of the few people who inspired in him 'a mysterious and sometimes very painful feeling of needing'.[2] He was working on three plays simultaneously, all on the theme of the happiness of marriage.

Gladys was in St Moritz with her mother in August 1908, 'morose & furious', and soon ran into Bernard Berenson. A day or so later she met Hofmannsthal by chance at a tea party, given by his brother-in-law, Hans Schlesinger, for the Viennese soprano Selma Kurz. Hofmannsthal described her as 'in certain sense the most brilliant person that I have ever seen. Her eyes like blue fire. Her daring, occasionally amounting to insolence in her talk, has possibly even increased.' He was fascinated, as others had been before him, by her power of dominating a large party with her conversation. 'She flatters, insults, penetrates. The speed and elasticity of her mind is astounding,' he wrote. 'She often has something of a lascivious young god in girl's clothes.'[3]

Hofmannsthal was amused when her mother interrupted one of her stories. She riposted: 'Mamma! One muffles a new-born, but one doesn't muffle an adolescent.'[4] He thought it Shakespearean.

Hofmannsthal had first met her in Rome in March 1906, telling his wife, Gerty, that she was Schlesinger's 'greatest angel'.[5] On 2 April 1906 he wrote:

Yesterday we visited Miss Deacon. She really is the most beautiful creature that I have ever seen in my life. I don't believe that Helena or any other Greek goddess could have been more beautiful. She also converses very understandingly and entertainingly, but I think if you are not used to her, such a degree of beauty could really be disturbing. I managed to talk to her quite well, because the light was dim and her face was in shadows. She is even said to be very funny and frisky, imitating people etc.[6]

This was during the phase when Roffredo Caetani might have married her. Hofmannsthal hoped he would: 'It would be nice if she got married. She would become even more beautiful (she is a bit too skinny) and more pleasant.'[7] He was also aware that the German crown prince had been willing to sacrifice his empire to marry her. When he met her at Rodaun, near Vienna, he presented her with a signed copy of *Das Kleine Weltheater*, and wrote to her:

This afternoon walking through our fields and our hills which at the moment have such a sweet, rich and pastoral beauty, I suddenly found you again within me. But what pleasure! What joy: your profile, some of your gestures, the sound of your voice. What a nuisance it was, what a really sad thing to have lost almost entirely until now one of the most beautiful things of this world, and how I had hoped to keep it alive.[8]

But instead of using Gladys in a new play in 1908, he proposed using her in a reworking of *The Marriage of Zobeïde*, suggesting that in one scene Zobeïde should be 'ready for anything, courageous as a drunkard, quick-witted; and what about Gladys Deacon?'[9]

Sadly, he never completed this version.

13

THE COMTESSE GREFFULHE
AND THE SISTERS

Gladys was never likely to marry Keyserling, despite her mother's concerns, not least because of her continued if intermittent involvement with the Duke of Marlborough. While Keyserling was still pressing her, Gladys was writing to the duke from Palazzo Borghese: 'Why these slapping allegations that I do not write? Wd you have me rush on you with nothing but breath? – I've nothing to say!' She was alone at home in an apartment where everything was covered with paper, even the chandeliers. She was reading poetry and eating moderately: 'One can compose one's life with next to no comforts . . .' she stated, saying she realised she led a 'peculiar life' but had nothing in common with those who did not understand this. Calling the duke 'a lazy beggar', she asked for more books and declared: 'I have been very happy these days by myself. Oh how I sd like to live alone! Not the most beloved could give such blessedness.' She signed off, heading to bed 'ere some exasperated yawn doth cause my jaw to break.'[1]

It was generally considered that, while she had conquered London and Paris, Gladys had failed in Roman society. Pedro de Carvalho finally met her and described her as very intelligent, and interesting to look at, 'like the Indian idols', but he worried that her superficial qualities of beauty hid a fragile nervous system, and were not backed up by 'solid substance.'[2]

At that point Gladys left for Paris, maintaining that she was happy there and that nothing would induce her to marry.

★ ★ ★ ★ ★

At the end of May 1909 Gladys turned up unexpectedly for a visit to I Tatti, Mary Berenson finding, 'She is rather heart-breaking now, when you think what she once was.'[3] Mary thought her 'impossible in manner & conversation' and 'gone off terribly in looks'. Her nose had become thick, her cheeks somewhat swollen, and her complexion and hair were not good: 'Her radiance has become chorus-girl vulgarity, she speaks of very *risqué* things all the time, her voice is hoarse & her laugh ugly. Furthermore, you simply cannot believe one word she says. She is undisguisedly fake and lying. Yet with all this there is something so thrilling, so exhilarating, so unusual about her that you feel as if you cannot live away from her.'[4]

Gladys performed her usual tricks at I Tatti, making Cecil Pinsent, the architect, gasp by tweaking Berenson's beard and calling him 'Bibbins'. At lunch she had them all laughing, and then in the evening appeared at dinner with her dress torn and her long yellow-dyed hair in a ponytail. The Berensons were looking forward to a good talk with an eminent brain surgeon, Dr Donaldson from Philadelphia, but Gladys spoiled that. Mary was alarmed that Gladys might spend the whole of June with them.

At tea the next day Gladys shocked and fascinated the guests, including Leo and Gertrude Stein. And so it continued, Gladys alternately fascinating or shocking those with whom she came in contact. Next, Mary had to give her a bran bath because she was suffering an attack of nettle-rash. Gladys dined at the Villa Gamberaia in the moonlight, 'let down her long hair & glided around the trees and cypresses like a real hamadryad',[5] went away, reappearing with a white dog she had bought, and dominated a tea party being, by degrees, boring, disgusting and teasing, while eating mounds of chocolate. Her appearance shocked Mary to the point that she and the Countess Serristori chided her about it. Gladys's existence in Florence was no better:

> She was in bed in a room of a disorder that even a College girl could not surpass, eating hundreds of cherries & smoking endless cigarettes.*
> The nightgown was dirty, her hair uncombed, her whole aspect piggish! She was, however, as gay as a cricket & said she was perfectly happy. I told her we were all horrified with her dress & hat, & she said they were quite good enough for Florence, that she didn't care a

---

* In those days, smoking was not quite usual, even among young women.

d— how she looked, & only felt happy in very old clothes. I looked in her wardrobe, & there were three very nice dresses. She was going to dine with the Corsinis tonight, & I begged her to wear one of these, but she said she wouldn't. The dress she does wear isn't well decent – all the hooks are off the back, and it shows her *skin*! Besides, it is stained & frayed & torn & burned in a perfectly disgusting way. But she said 'Why shouldn't I be comfortable?' & called us horrible snobs for objecting to her looks. She says she has found out exactly what she likes, & she never means to do anything but amuse herself. Night before last she went out with [Charles] Loeser to see the eclipse & never came home till 5 o'clock. It is no wonder that people say all kinds of things about her. She only laughs. She *says* she has £2,500 a year to live on, but I doubt it, & I think she is probably eating up her capital, & will soon get to a dreadful point. But no one can do anything for her, that is clear. She said again she loved no one except herself, & in fact hardly noticed them, except as faces in an audience. She is never convinced, utterly incapable of falling in love, and she has no kindness in her nature.[6]

Two days later Gladys was with her mother, Edith and Prince Doria at the Caffè Giacosa in Florence and announced they were going to Caprarola, 'but I dare say this means they are really going to Paris,'[7] commented Mary. She may have been right since in the same month, Berenson heard that Gladys spoke of Mary and himself as 'her only real friends',[8] and yet when he was in Paris he did not see her.

After the summer of 1909, by which time she was twenty-eight, Gladys drifted out of the Berensons' orbit, and from then on news of her was largely second-hand. There were contradictory rumours about her relationship with the Duke of Marlborough. Some said she had not spoken to him for three years, whereas he had stayed at Caprarola that year. Others said that Gladys was his mistress, and that when Consuelo was considering divorce, 'the private police evidence was overwhelming'.[9]

The American newspapers took the line that Gladys was content living in Paris: 'I can live my own life, have my own friends and not be criticised by every English woman who owns a husband, a house and a pair of eyes.' As the *Washington Post* commented: 'She is . . .

more beautiful than ever. What will happen? Surely we shall hear some new chapter in her astonishing sentimental history?'[10]

In July 1909 Gladys was back in Paris, pleading for meetings with the Comtesse Greffulhe. In contrast to the comtesse's other friendships, Gladys was the one forever asking to be taken to exhibitions, or if she could call on her, or to borrow some of her fine clothes to have them copied. Earlier in the year in Paris, the friendship had deepened as the comtesse tried to make Gladys paint, without noticeably good results. She sent Gladys flowers, creams, delicious strawberries and eggs. 'I remain an obedient Sylvaine,' wrote Gladys.

At one point Gladys joined her mother, as she told Madame Greffulhe, 'to play policeman to my family for a while'. She wished her mother would marry – 'It wd be a comfort to me!'[11] Despite her protestations she spent five months at Caprarola, sometimes alone, having sent all the servants away on a prolonged holiday, other than a cook suffering from heartbreak: 'You cannot imagine the solitude given by these enormous empty rooms, and the 400 uninhabited bedrooms.'[12] Her only companions were two little Chinese dogs.

Gladys was back in Paris by the end of 1909, again alone and again relying closely on the comtesse. In February she suggested they attend the Reynaldo Hahn ballet *La Fête de Thérèse* but, as so often, she was unwell and unable to go. In February her spirits rose, but when ill in bed, she begged the comtesse to visit her. One day in April she spent five hours with her, later returning to her bed, tired but happy. In May she asked if her friend Mrs Schuyler Van Rensselaer could come and see the comtesse's Houdon sculpture of Diana. Gladys went to see the Ballets Russes, and was enthusiastic about Ida Rubinstein – 'Yesterday in costume she was in extraordinary beauty.'[13] But she was unimpressed by Régina Badet, the dancer, whom she thought 'frightful, common and unsightly'.[14]

It was to the comtesse that she turned in moments of depression, telling her she wished she could be away 'where beasts wd roam under flowering bushes & where alone an archangel wd sometimes stoop to converse with me'. She could forget everything – even her name:

I am sure this intense desire which eats at my heart to be away & to forget is a desire to die. Sometimes I think I was too unhappy until a year ago when I fled fr. Rome, & that that great change alone is now necessary to me.

All true life is hidden but not enough. One sd be able to cut oneself off from everything at least every 24 hours.[15]

Given the amount they saw each other, she was then horrified to be told in August that Élisabeth Greffulhe had thrown her over, 'as she always does'. Gladys riposted: 'I was left with my mouth open, furious and wounded. I do not want to be left. No one has ever done that. Please don't.'[16] The two remained in touch, though after 1912, the correspondence ceased.*

Meanwhile the rumours abounded. It was said that Gladys was under the auspices of the Duke of Marlborough when in London, while in Paris she was being kept by Roffredo Caetani (which was not the case). Mary Berenson commented: 'She *has* made a mess of things. Think what she started with!'[17]

★ ★ ★ ★ ★

DOROTHY

In June that year Prince Doria told Berenson that Gladys's youngest sister Dorothy was about to marry and that Gladys was being as nasty as possible about it. The groom was Prince Aba Radziwill, born in Berlin in 1885 and son of 'Bichette', who had befriended Gladys and her mother in 1903. In the winter of 1909 Bichette had turned to Dorothy, inviting her to stay. Dorothy proved correct if flirtatious.

Bichette was the only person taken by surprise when Aba fell for Dorothy and proposed. He had an 'inflammable' nature, had already tried to marry various housemaids and governesses,[18] and had been a suitor of Gladys's in 1907, frustrating the plan of Lily de

---

★ The Comtesse Greffulhe wrote to Gladys when her mother died in 1918. She sent a present when she married in 1921, but did not attend the wedding. No further contact is recorded.

Clermont-Tonnerre and Proust to marry Gladys to his cousin, Léon 'Loche' Radziwill. It had been unwise to have a pretty girl like Dorothy in the house. Mrs Baldwin was equally blamed for having Aba to stay at Caprarola when his mother thought he was in Venice.

On the surface, this was a prestigious match for Dorothy since the Radziwills were one of the richest and most distinguished families in Europe. But Mrs Baldwin judged him 'weak in his intellect', and Mary Berenson, seeing his photograph, thought he looked 'very silly'.[19]

On hearing of her son's engagement, Bichette descended to open warfare. She turned numerous Radziwills against the couple and threatened to depose Aba in favour of his younger brother, Karol, effectively leaving him penniless. She turned Roman society against Dorothy. She put it about that her own husband, Prince George Radziwill, was in a mad-house[*] and that Dorothy's father had died insane. This fooled nobody because, as Mary Berenson put it, 'no one ever pretended Dorothy was the child of Mr Deacon'.[20]

When Mary met Dorothy at Caprarola in April 1910, the bride-to-be announced that she was determined to marry at the end of June, despite feeling too young and with concerns about the immorality and many crimes committed by the Radziwills and Branickas over the centuries. One motive was that neither Gladys nor Edith had married and she wanted to avoid their fate.

In the ensuing unpleasantness, Aba consulted lawyers as to the legality of being removed as head of the Radziwill family. Bichette raked up Mrs Baldwin's past, at which point Mrs Baldwin discovered that the princess had had an illegitimate baby in Naples. Carlo Placci was full of it: 'It is all over Rome. What a silly woman to throw stones out of her very fragile glass house!!'[21]

In the end the Tsar of Russia did not depose Aba, so he was able to turn eighteen-year-old Dorothy into one of the 'swellest' princesses in Europe, as Mary Berenson described her, commenting: 'It is really enough to upset women trying more reasonable industries when such rewards fall to blue eyes skilfully used! However, there is a young man thrown in, who would be too high a price for most people to pay.'[22]

* Prince George (1860-1914) had 'lost his reason' seven years before.

On 20 June Comte Alexandre de Gabriac, who wrote about society in *Le Figaro*, reported to Montesquiou that he was on his way to London to attend the wedding. 'Meanwhile,' he added, 'Gladys is making the necessary subtraction from the list of her numerous admirers.'[23] Furious, Gladys made it clear that she would not be attending the wedding, and remained in Paris. She was enraged that Aba's aunt, Princess Strozzi (now Madame de Halpert), 'the ugly sperm whale', as Gladys called her, had proved the villain of the piece by allying herself with 'disgusting old Doria' to support the young couple.[24]

Dorothy was married quietly in London on 5 July, in the Roman Catholic St Mary's, Cadogan Place, at a time when Bichette was in Austria for the wedding of her younger son. Gladys was horrified to read an article stating that Ivor Wimborne (then Lord Ashby) had been among the guests and that she, too, had been present. Her dress was described, and it was a dress that she did indeed own. Neither had been there. As she told the Comtesse Greffulhe, this proved that her 'crafty' mother was 'the Machiavellian author of the article'.[25] She resolved to see neither her mother nor Dorothy again.

Bichette responded to the wedding by informing the *Almanach de Gotha* that this marriage was not recognised by the Radziwill family. But when Dorothy declared herself pregnant in February 1911 (wrongly), the Radziwills relented. Mrs Baldwin and Prince Doria were considerably relieved. However, Mrs Baldwin's reputation suffered a further decline, her manipulation of the wedding being deemed: 'the work of a cruel & unscrupulous adventuress'.[26]

By October Mary Berenson was aware that Dorothy was 'working herself up to being one of the very *Grandes Dames* of European society'.[27] And Mrs Baldwin was delighted at having 'made one of the great matches in Europe for Dorothy' to the point that she was 'now immensely cowtowed to by all.'[28] Matters improved when Aba's father died in an asylum in Berlin in January 1914 and Aba became head of the family. Dorothy was given equal status as a serene highness alongside her husband in the *Almanach de Gotha*, although problems with Bichette over money and family estates rumbled on.

★ ★ ★ ★ ★

EDITH

Mrs Baldwin now turned her attention to Edith. Her third daughter was living mainly in America, and had been formally adopted by her step-grandmother, Marraine Baldwin. While she was Marraine's favourite, she was no favourite of Gladys. Marraine had brought her out in Newport, where she had been courted by Robert Walton Goelet, a financier with a fortune estimated at $40 million. Florence Baldwin had a millionaire duke in mind for her, but that depended on Edith returning to Europe. Horrified by her mother, Edith stayed away. At the time of Dorothy's wedding, Mrs Baldwin had talked of Edith 'with great bitterness'.[29]

Edith became engaged to George Lee Peabody shortly after Dorothy's wedding. He was a banker with Lee, Higginson, and the scion of a well-known and rich family. Born in 1869, he was eighteen years her senior. In 1891 he had married Elizabeth Copley Crowninshield, but had divorced her for desertion in 1907. Edith looked forward to marrying, despite a fortune-teller's warning that a tall, dark woman would bring them unhappiness. Peabody assumed this was his former wife. In advance of the wedding, Mrs Baldwin gave Edith sumptuous presents, on the understanding that she would repay them after her marriage. Mrs Baldwin was back in France in January 1911, boosted by funds from her brother, to the point that the Deacon family lawyer, William P. Blake, reported that she was 'flourishing again' and living at 'the very expensive Hôtel Liverpool' in Paris. 'She is a wonderful woman & not easily subdued,' wrote Blake, though he hoped with little confidence that she might now live within her means.[30]

Not long before the wedding, Peabody was playing tennis with Edith in Newport. The temperature was 101°F. He suffered serious sunstroke and was rushed to hospital in Boston.

The wedding was postponed; there were relapses, and a brain tumour was diagnosed. Edith remained at his side. Peabody was desperately in love with her, but she was nervous about allying herself to a man who looked as though he was broken for life. A new will was drawn up in Edith's favour, but he was too ill to sign it. Peabody underwent three operations for the growth in his head, during which a tumour the size of a hen's egg was removed, but on 9 February 1911 he died, leaving Edith distraught. Florence Baldwin's response was brutally materialistic:

> I have not heard from Edith since poor Peabody's death. How unfortunate and sad his dying after such [a] great struggle for life. He had a tumor of the brain. It is unfortunate too for Edith not to have married as I begged her to months ago. She might not have been less unhappy, but she could have cried in greater comfort. He had 625,000 frs a year.[31]

Since Peabody's will had not been signed, Edith was not the major beneficiary, though she received a legacy of $25,000. But the Peabody family liked her and gave her $200,000.

Edith returned to Europe to study art and sculpture, but in due course her step-grandmother lured her back to the States. In 1916 she married Henry G. Gray, of New York City, son of Judge John Clinton Gray, of the Court of Appeals. She was also a major beneficiary in Marraine Baldwin's will, when she died in 1924.

The Peabody saga coincided with another of Florence Baldwin's financial crises. She pleaded with her brother to let her have the capital from the United States Trust Company of New York, while claiming to have been 'terribly victimised by Deacon & by my children'. She threatened to shoot herself, pointing out, 'but that also requires a great deal of courage & brings one's family disagreeably before the public'.[32]

She had confidently expected Edith to bail her out once she had married Peabody. No such marriage having taken place, no funds were forthcoming. Her brother considered her immensely extravagant, living in two palaces, while she bemoaned her plight in trying to subsist on $4,000 a year. Nor would her daughters help: 'All my children have thought it quite natural to despoil me & now that I have nothing more to give, to leave me alone.' She told him her only options were to emulate Elsie de Wolfe and become an interior decorator or to shoot herself 'at once'.[33]

★ ★ ★ ★ ★

As 1911 dawned, the American press noted that Dorothy had made a prestigious marriage and Edith appeared on the point of doing the same. They delighted in describing Gladys as the unhappiest of 'The Three American Graces':

> Gladys Deacon cannot marry the noble she loves. Unhappy, and cut off by many of the American colony abroad, she lives in Paris, not even coming to her own land.
> 'My beauty has been to me only a curse,' she said not long ago.

The Duke of Marlborough was identified as the 'noble', but he was not free to marry since his separation from Consuelo had not ended in divorce. So, 'the improbability of any marriage in the near future makes her quite the most miserable girl in Paris'.[34]

As it happens, Gladys had changed tack yet again and seemed to be becoming political, even about to write a book or give lectures on social issues. The controversial journalist W. T. Stead observed her. While in London in December 1910, she had thrown herself into the general-election campaign, supporting the Radicals. This involved attending a meeting to hear F. E. Smith, rising star of the Unionist Party. She found the speeches amusing and concluded that he was a self-conscious windbag, who 'could not even impress himself, much less his audience, with his sincerity'. She went to Trafalgar Square and alarmed her Unionist friends with her delight at Radical victories. She was shocked at how the nobles and pluto-crats abused their opponents, and weighed in so that lunches and dinners she attended came to resemble more 'cockpits than love feasts'. She then set off to explore 'the various social types of the common people'. Exquisitely dressed, she was to be found convers-ing with out-of-work men in the parks or serving girls and nurses. Stead wrote:

> She would pass from spending an hour in a palace of art erected by a millionaire to exchange views of life with penniless tramps or social outcasts. And she did it all not with the austere seriousness of a social student but with the gay insouciance of a laughing philosopher who loved to see men and things and to see them all.[35]

In January 1911 Gladys's mother complained that her daughter seemed to prefer living in a 'wretched pensione' (the Hôtel de la

Pérouse)* rather than with her at Caprarola.[36] Keyserling, likewise rejected, heard that she was 'living secretly in or near Paris, & sends her maid twice a week to a certain Hotel for letters. She has dropped all her old friends, or rather, turned most of them into enemies.'[37]

---

* The rue de la Pérouse is best known as the street where Proust's Odette de Crécy lived.

14

ENTER THE DUKE

Gladys's next reinvention was to move to London. By April 1911, at thirty years old, she was installed in rooms at 11 Savile Row, above Huntsman, the tailor's. This marked the next step in her relationship with the Duke of Marlborough, which culminated in their marriage ten years later. It was also the cause of renewed speculation among Paris gossips as to precisely what was going on between them.

There had been numerous gloomy and contradictory prognostications about Gladys. These were vigorously contradicted by W. T. Stead, by now somewhat of an ally to Gladys. He wrote:

> I saw a statement the other day that she was the most broken-hearted little girl in all Paris because of her hopeless affection for an English nobleman who was married and not divorced. The absurdity of the tale was evident to anyone who ever spent an hour in her company. A merrier maid never looked out of a more laughing pair of eyes upon an amusing world.[1]

Gladys spent the May bank holiday of 1911 with crowds of Cockney merrymakers and frolicked with costermongers on Hampstead Heath. She told Stead that she had never previously seen an English bank-holiday crowd: 'I never saw any one worse for drink. All were as merry as the day was long. Such simple, honest folk, dancing and skipping and singing in the blazing sun.' She was impressed at how easily and courteously the crowd greeted her when she stepped out of her motor-car. They were happy to instruct her in their dancing. Stead wrote:

> It is a pity there was no one there to snapshot the beautiful American as she practised the steps of the rustic dance with the costermongers.

In this, as everything else, Miss Gladys Deacon is as fearless as she is free, flitting from flower to flower with all the grace and swiftness of a butterfly.[2]

He was not sure where it was all going, but he was confident that it would be turned to good account.*

★ ★ ★ ★ ★

Gladys visited Norway in August 1911 and wrote to the Duke of Marlborough from the beach:

You devil! Why sd you think I am out of temper with you? It looks as if thy conscience pricked thee . . . Am I not the last of the Marlborough gems, Greek in temper with a more modern dash of Roman abt certain parts![3]

Anyone who fell in love with her – and several did – was now but a pleasant diversion, enjoyment of which she shared with the duke. Had Consuelo agreed to divorce earlier, then Gladys could have become Duchess of Marlborough sooner, but in 1911 there was no possible solution. Consuelo remained Duchess of Marlborough in name and title. She even attended George V's Coronation as a duchess, albeit separated.

Gladys had to be content with the role of mistress, occasionally accompanying the duke on holiday abroad or receiving him at her little London apartment. Her association with him was in the nature of a crusade; it was difficult at times and not without aspects of humiliation.

She never bothered with her sister, Edith, and was irritated by Dorothy. When the Berensons stayed at Caprarola in June 1911, they found Mrs Baldwin deserted by her daughters and heavily in debt,

---

* When Stead drowned in the *Titanic* disaster on 12 April 1912, Gladys wrote: 'He was not only the bravest man I have ever known, but the most clean-living one, a fact I only believed after reading the *Maiden Tribute* [*to Modern Babylon*]!!!' She was horrified that he had died while others less worthy had been saved: 'Fancy saving nothing but a lot of nasty women good for nought but shopping! Well, I hope no vote is given 'em now since they do not know how to accept life sacrifice when it is offered. Did you see those nasty maids were all saved too? I can imagine the way they howled, cannot you?' [Gladys to Mrs Baldwin.]

her beauty gone and her reputation worse than ever. Berenson wrote to Keyserling: 'Of Gladys she pretended to know nothing.'[4] Presently he did hear news, again relayed to Keyserling:

> Women tho' are unfathomable on account of their shallowness. We measure them by the meter, whereas it is the millimetre we should use. Of course that is not all I have to say about the adorable, fascinating, fomenting creativity of Gladys. I find it hard to get information. I believe I wrote to you of our visit to Caprarola & how Mrs Baldwin told us Gladys had said a year ago that she never wished to speak to her mother again.
>
> In Paris the only two persons who had a word to say about her were her cousin Winthrop* & the Marquise de Ludre. W. said he had little to say about her, but that little so bad that he would not say it. Mme de L. on the other hand reported that Gladys had written to enquire about d'Annunzio's *St Sebastian*,† & had announced she was returning to Paris *from* London July 3. In London nobody will speak of her – all rather ominous.[5]

In St Moritz, the news was that Gladys 'was crazy with hatred of her family'[6] and never saw them. And when Mrs Baldwin returned to Caprarola in October, she was upset by the cruelty of Gladys, 'who won't even write to her'.[7] Some months later, it was the same story: 'Of Gladys no one, apparently, knows anything, not even by hearsay,' Mary told Isabella Stewart Gardner.[8]

However, Gladys did respond to her mother when she heard that Roffredo Caetani was marrying. His bride was Marguerite Chapin, from New England.‡ Hearing the news on her arrival in Paris, Gladys reacted with generous amusement:

---

* Gerald Winthrop (1880-1938), one of three Winthrop cousins. His mother, Louise (who eloped with Count Biron when Gerald was six), was a granddaughter of Peter Parker and Elizabeth Allston Read, so he was Gladys's second cousin.

† D'Annunzio wrote *The Martyrdom of St Sebastian* and it was performed on stage to music by Debussy, and with Ida Rubinstein dancing, in a costume by Bakst. The Bishop of Paris forbade his flock to attend it.

‡ Marguerite Chapin (1880-1963). She met Roffredo when studying music in Paris with Jean de Rezke, and was later celebrated for editing *Commerce* and *Botteghe Oscure*.

Roff married!? Well that is too exciting! Don't tell me it's to that fat Radzi girl after all! . . . He is a brave man to fix his choice after so long a sojourn in this world of mis-mating & - eh - re-mating. Isn't all this marrying, giving in marriage, taking in marriage a gorgeous sight? There is something so healthy & cattle like abt it.[9]

Two years later Gladys congratulated Roffredo on the birth of a child, by which time they were almost strangers. 'You wandering spirit, will I ever see you again?' asked Roffredo. 'You seem to have become as restless as a cloud.'[10]

Meanwhile Gladys's difficulties with her mother impinged on her life when she was in Paris. Living now on the quai Voltaire, she went to get a cigarette box engraved, and the shopkeeper pointed out that her mother had left bills unpaid for eight years. 'I received . . . a visitation from quite the most appalling person I have ever seen, who smelt very badly and informed me in shrieks that you owed bills,' she informed her mother. She referred the woman to their family lawyer, Léon Renault, at which point 'she once more broke into smelly yelps & announced that I (!!!) never paid my bills, etc, etc. Fancy that. I who have never owed 5 centimes to a living cat for 5 minutes.'[11]

In 1912 Mrs Baldwin recognised the complications of Gladys's long wait for the Duke of Marlborough: 'I understand you,' she wrote, '& appreciate all that make the joy & hardship of your life.'[12] Her own existence continued to haunt her. On Christmas Day 1912, she wrote from Caprarola:

> This is certainly an unhappy world and yr poor Mammah is one of its most wretched inhabitants, my pecuniary situation is a standing worry, so grievous that life is an incessant torment. If I could only finish these wretched debts in peace, but I am of necessity doomed to everlasting worry, for 20,000 frs a year means but bread & *niente altro*. Clothes, doctors, the thousand incidentals can't find a place in such a restrictive figure.[13]

Mrs Baldwin pleaded for money from Gladys and her sisters, and from her own brother. Her step-mother was unsympathetic. 'I feel so deeply what you write about Florence Baldwin,' she wrote to Charley.

'How can she go on leading such a life? I am glad dear little Audrey died, she felt what was going on so much.'[14] Gladys took a firm line with her mother: 'I have never asked you, nor you given me any "bread of life". That does not concern me and is not my business.'[15]

★ ★ ★ ★ ★

In Paris Gladys had her only ever encounter with Princess Marthe Bibesco, who recorded in some detail her impressions of what she called Gladys's 'Gorgon face'. The Romanian princess and Gladys disliked each other since both were beauties who were lionised in intellectual circles. Marthe Bibesco never saw Gladys before the wax had taken its toll, but regretted this 'real crime against beauty'. The princess noted that the wax had run under her skin into her neck, leaving blotches, which obliged Gladys, at least during this encounter, to disguise the deformity with a cloud of tulle. Another guest muttered: 'I thought she was a marvel, but she is nothing but a curiosity.'[16]

Contemporary photographs show a thickening at the bridge of Gladys's nose and a swelling around the mouth, combined with a general deterioration in her skin. Further comparisons can be made by studying the two heads by Epstein, the first sculpted in 1917, the second in 1923. By the later date, Gladys's lower jaw had begun to protrude somewhat. The wax had loosened the epidermis so that the lower part of the face slipped, the skin from the jaw forming a second chin. There is a legend that Gladys received a visitor while sitting by the fireside. She refused to look him full in the face, but gently massaged the wax, melted by the heat, back into the bridge of her nose.

The majority of stories about Gladys's face suggest that she was self-conscious about it, and several that it caused her withdrawal into the life of a recluse. But all that happened as early as 1903, and while the operation failed, she did not allow this to destroy her life. She continued to mix in society and to pose for artists. She may have tampered further with it, but later damage came as the natural deterioration of ageing.

The Abbé Mugnier – judged so worldly a prelate that Forain said of him: 'He will be buried in a table-napkin' – was at the Bibesco encounter. Gladys discovered a new friend. He caught her attention by interrupting a long and argumentative discussion about the classics and the Romantics by announcing: 'Romantic! Classic! What is all that? Take me for example! Every day I wake up in the morning classical and I go to bed at night romantic!' The room dissolved into laughter.

Gladys launched into a diatribe against French poetry, comparing it unfavourably with English poetry. Marthe Bibesco remained silent for a long time and then cried out: 'How lucky that we have both!' Gladys and the princess then joined battle. Provocatively, Gladys declared that there had been no poets in France since Villon (who lived in the fifteenth century). Marthe then conducted Gladys on a voyage through the world of poets, finally arriving at Alfred de Musset. 'Musset?' said Gladys, scornfully. 'But he's a poet for my maid.' Princess Bibesco reckoned that she won the day by replying: 'How lucky for a poet to be liked at the same time by your maid who is no doubt French and by me who am not!'

In her memoirs Marthe Bibesco described Gladys as 'Medusa'. She quoted a friend who had known Gladys in Italy, young, unhappy and adorned with aquatic flowers from the Pontine marshes: 'She was Ophelia.'

'Yes,' said Forain. 'An Ophelia who knew how to swim.'[17]

★ ★ ★ ★ ★

In the summer of 1912 the Duke of Marlborough and Gladys spent a fortnight together at Mont-Dore, the fashionable spa in the Auvergne. The duke enjoyed it and believed that Gladys was also happy. Afterwards they returned to their respective palaces, he to Blenheim and she to Caprarola. He missed her and became depressed. Without her 'bright presence and light chatter', he stayed alone, shunning other company, which he pronounced 'dull, commonplace and utterly uninterested except in the ordinary banalities of life'.[18]

The historian, A. L. Rowse, wrote that of the previous seven Dukes of Marlborough, five had suffered from melancholia. Sunny was one of these, the burdens of the world resting heavily on his shoulders. Blenheim needed his constant care and he was greatly concerned with the welfare and education of his two boys. Lady Grey of Fallodon thought he was unappealing: 'He looks like an ostler smelling a bad smell.'[19]

He was continually aggravated by the way in which Consuelo was written up in the radical press. To a flattering reference in the *Daily Chronicle,* he commented: 'The P. [*Pater*] looks wicked; C a tart about to say the Lord's Prayer',[20] adding, 'Philanthropist, Beauty, the used wife, Patriotic Yank, what else!!!'[21] He was relieved when the Duke of Westminster evicted his wife* at twenty-four hours' notice and became the press's latest target. Marlborough's bitterness towards Consuelo caused him to hate Americans and mistrust them. Both he and Gladys wrote disparagingly of 'the Yanks'.

It is from letters between the duke and Gladys that we can follow their story. Of the two, Gladys was the more spirited and articulate. Even the duke commended her as an 'admirable correspondent', her letters being 'admirably expressed' and 'pregnant with varied and charming ideas',[22] while he confessed, correctly, that his letters were 'terribly boring'.[23] While ideas spilt from Gladys entertainingly and sometimes mischievously, the written word was not his forte. She was original while he was buttoned up, anxious and reserved, even while trying to express affection: 'You have been a good Gladys to your Sunny. And he loves you for all your goodness to him.'[24] She expressed this rather more succinctly: 'I have known you practically all my life & I have always been able to do you good. My enormous vitality alone is a tonic – even my doctor says.'[25]

They had their own nicknames for each other and for the characters who peopled their correspondence. 'MG . . . YS' was often his greeting: 'My Gladys . . . Your Sunny'. She would reply: 'MS . . . YG'. Then 'OB' stood for 'Old Bird' and sometimes the duke addressed her as 'Bird Darling'. Mr Asquith was known as 'Squiff', King George V as 'King Log', and Lord Lansdowne 'Little L'. Consuelo was 'OT' – presumably 'Old Tart'. The closeness of their involvement can be judged by Marlborough's declaration that he was visiting his lawyers to ensure that she would be properly cared for in the event of his death.

In September 1912 Gladys suggested that he should come to Caprarola, but he declined on the grounds that he accepted an

---

* 'Shelagh' Cornwallis-West (1877-1970), who gave the ball which Gladys attended at Grosvenor House in the summer of 1902.

invitation only if he was sure to be welcome and he feared that her mother would create rows. Gladys spent much of 1913 in London. To her annoyance the duke went to Beaulieu-sur-Mer in March for a stay that he professed was of considerable boredom to him. When Gladys announced that she was ill, he panicked and nearly came home, but on hearing that she had recovered, he prolonged his stay by several days in order to enjoy the tennis at Cannes. Gladys was livid and wrote him a scathing letter, which made him considerably anxious as to his reception on his return in April.

While in Beaulieu, besides being involved in three motor accidents in four days, the duke caught up on news about 'a dark, swarthy looking mulatto'[26] - Consuelo's latest lover, the young Reginald Fellowes,* in her service since at least the previous summer. The duke resolved to have Fellowes watched by detectives when he returned to London. Meanwhile the young man's parents, Lord and Lady de Ramsey, were annoyed because Consuelo would not let their son get married. According to Marlborough, there was 'a girl cut and dry for him, anxious to ally herself with his dusky loins'.[27] It was possibly all to the good when in August 1919 Fellowes married Princess Jean de Broglie – the immensely rich Daisy Fellowes.

In May and June 1913 Gladys stayed at Caprarola. She was in Paris in July on her way there again when a friend told Berenson that she was 'looking well & beautifully dressed in the latest Callot, & not speaking evil of anyone, but all sweetness & amiability'.[28] She had apparently made it up with her mother but persisted in loathing her sister Edith. Once as she came out of the Ritz, she cut Edith dead as though she was a total stranger. She even left Rome for Florence in December 1913 because Edith was there. During that winter Gladys was in London.

In the spring of 1914 she paid a visit to Lausanne and then to Paris, where Berenson heard she was 'as electrifying as ever', now aged thirty-three. She stayed at her tiny new apartment, 23 quai Voltaire on the left bank with a view across the Seine towards the Louvre. Mrs Baldwin's apartment was on the first floor and quite small, decorated

---

* The Hon. Reginald Fellowes (1884-1953), second son of the 2nd Lord de Ramsey and his wife, Lady Rosamond Spencer-Churchill – therefore a first cousin of the Duke of Marlborough.

by Elsie de Wolfe between 1912 and 1913. Mary Berenson described the result as 'a little jewel of an apartment'[29] and was convinced that Mrs Baldwin had lavished thousands on its decoration.

Then in August war broke out in Europe. The belle époque was over.

Interlude

RODIN AND MONET

Many of the friendships Gladys made with the great artists of Paris were at her instigation. Time and time again she 'hesitated' before a great man, 'trembled' at the thought of approaching him, and then all of a sudden she was a regular visitor, his most ardent admirer and keenest correspondent. Montesquiou had been one such person; Rodin was another. Writing from Savile Row, Gladys approached the sculptor with courtesy and reserve:

> Dear Sir, I don't know if you will remember me, but I recall that when I had lunch with you at the house of my mother, Mrs Baldwin, you said you were at Meudon on Sundays and that I could find you there . . .[1]

Rodin did indeed remember. They had met as early as 1904. They met again, and presently he fell victim to her charm. Rodin was in his seventies during the years that Gladys knew him. 'My last years,' he once said, 'are crowned with roses: I am surrounded by devoted women and nothing is so sweet.'

Rodin's life, his background and his approach to art fascinated Gladys. She said that he fell into that group of artists who were from humble origins, with noisy homes, fathers who came home drunk. Thus they were driven on by poverty. Invariably they had strong and determined mothers – not the kind of women who preened themselves, asking, '*Est-ce que ce n'est pas un joli chapeau?*' (Isn't this a pretty hat?), but women who, though they did not necessarily understand what the man was doing, appreciated the importance of his doing it, and were behind him crying: '*Avance, avance, avance!*' (Advance . . .) Rodin, she said, never talked about his family. His background was that of a French peasant. He gave her a white marble sculpture of a nude girl, signed and dedicated, and said: 'Don't look too much at my other work. Life has taught me what will sell.' She added: 'He didn't like giving things away. Like all French peasants, his fists were tightly closed.'[2]

Rodin had a passion for Greek marble and often ran up debts because he could not resist buying it. He loved women and liked to caress them. Gladys said: 'He precipitated himself on every woman he met. You know . . . hands all over you!' What she called 'the drive of the semen' was important to him and quite separate from 'the drive of the brain'. He surprised her by saying: 'My business is sex and I'm sick of it.'[3]

In her letters Gladys heaped praise on him: 'Dear and truly divine master, thank you for being the artist that you are. You are a blessing to me for which I thank Heaven.'[4] He replied: 'Most respected friend, You know how to carry me away before my very eyes and praise from a woman such as you takes me in as if you were victory personified . . .'[5] Gladys congratulated the sculptor, but Rodin thought the praise should go to God himself: 'For it is he who guides and unveils the ancient and ever-renewed grace of woman.'[6]

Mrs Baldwin and Gladys shared the deep wish that Rodin would visit Caprarola. 'Why aren't you at Caprarola!' wrote Gladys in June 1912. 'If only you knew how beautiful everything is here.' Mrs Baldwin suggested that he and Madame Rodin should come in March 1914 and stay as long as they liked. But though Rodin visited Italy in January 1912, and again in 1914 and 1915, time never permitted a visit to Caprarola.

During the Great War, Gladys expressed concern for Rodin's safety. She was much relieved to hear that the German advance on Paris had been arrested. 'I hope,' she wrote from London, 'that you are quite well and that your genius gives you the necessary wings to rise above all the clamour of this war.'[7] His principal preoccupation was to bequeath the Hôtel Biron as a museum so that his work might not be forgotten, a possibility that terrified him. In the autumn he was in England, at Epping, worrying about a future German advance on Paris: 'The Germans can always come back, and that upsets me very much,' he wrote to Gladys.[8]

Rodin held an exhibition of bronzes at South Kensington and suggested that Gladys might go and inspect them. She was enthusiastic and offered to drive him back in her car to where he was staying

– Mary Hunter's home, Hill Hall, Theydon Mount, in Epping. The expedition took place, with Rose Beuret and Miss Grigsby.*

In 1916 Gladys reminded Rodin that she was 'amongst the most fervent of his disciples',[9] and proposed a cup of tea with him before he caught his train to Meudon. The following January, Mrs Baldwin announced gleefully: 'Rodin has married his old wife!'[10] The sculptor finally made an honest woman of Rose Beuret on 29 January at Meudon after a shared life of fifty-three years. Two weeks later she died of bronchial pneumonia in their cold, half-empty house, leaving the confused old man alone in a world of miserable dreams. Gladys responded quickly by offering her condolences on Rodin's loss:

> Madame Rodin's very sweet charm and her exquisite simplicity struck me greatly, and I realise what the loss of a life-long companion must be to you, Dear Master.'[11]

She hoped that Rodin's strength would return with the spring, and that when she came back to Paris she would find him in his garden, restored to perfect health. But Rodin did not linger long. On 17 November 1917, a few days after his seventy-seventh birthday, he died and was buried with Rose in the shadow of *The Thinker* at Meudon.

★ ★ ★ ★ ★

In May 1914 and again in October Claude Monet welcomed Gladys at his large house at Giverny in the Seine valley, where he was spending his twilight years. He lived there with his second wife, surrounded by the garden he had created. In July 1916 Gladys went to Giverny, as she reported to the Duke of Marlborough:

---

* Emilie Busbey Grigsby (1876-1964), whose mother educated her on the proceeds from a brothel in Cincinnati, reputed to be the mistress of Robber Baron, Charles T. Yerkes (1837-1905), who left her a fortune. She lived in New York and sold her considerable collection of art and books in 1912. George Meredith said that in her he had finally met the heroine of his first novel, *The Ordeal of Richard Feverel* (1859). Henry James was displeased to find his name linked romantically with hers. She entertained Rodin and W. B. Yeats at her home, 80 Brook Street, London, in 1913. Gladys saw them all together at that time. Gladys told me that Miss Grigsby was 'a woman of bad reputation'. 'With men?' I asked. 'No, with women,' she replied. [Gladys to author, 11 March 1977.]

We found Monet looking like a divinity of gardens, but in beautifully cut tweeds! with a rustic straw hat on his splendid head, waiting for us with his daughter in law in his garden, which was not at its best, too many colours clashing.

He looks absolutely magnificent with health, his eyes are all right since he has been doing what he wanted to do – i.e. – decorative work. (And you chide me that I am ill when bored!!)

He breathed health & power & how nice & simple he is! His 35 years of life in the country between work & nature have prevented the contamination of city artificiality, wit & all ill nature.

I never saw an artist with as little envy in him.

We found tea beautifully set out in the lovely, fresh yellow dining-room, we walked in the garden & we saw the new décor on which he has been working 2 years. It is still incomplete but incomparable.

But I doubt that he will let it go out of France. I do so wish you had been with us. I positively needed you yesterday, looking at it.

Mme M. never stopped talking, they were dead tired when we left & I was sea-sick from untellable fatigue when I got home.[12]

Fortunately, Monet lived on and Gladys was able to take the duke to see him in the 1920s. Gladys photographed Monet. In her album she had a photograph of the poet laureate, John Masefield. The captions were significant – 'John Masefield. He became Poet Laureate & a pompous man.' As for the artist, he was captioned: 'This was Claude Monet, a great painter and he remained a simple man.'[13]

15

THE GREAT WAR, 1914-16

The outbreak of war found Mrs Baldwin and Prince Doria in a chalet in St Moritz. On 4 August Ralph Curtis informed Isabella Stewart Gardner in Boston: 'Her daughter Gladys is there also which people think makes it *much* wickeder. No women see her.'[1]

While Mrs Baldwin returned to Italy, Gladys hastened to Paris to help the war effort. The capital was emptying of men, all bound for the front. At the Gare de l'Est Proust bade farewell to his brother, while at the Gare du Nord the worldly Abbé Mugnier heard as many quick confessions as possible in a smoky café. Within three weeks German troops were within thirty miles of Paris and on 29 August the disturbing sound of distant gunfire could be heard from the city. The government left Paris for Bordeaux on 2 September, and an esti- mated one million people departed in their wake. Proust headed for Cabourg on 4 September, while Montesquiou retreated to Trouville.

At the end of August Gladys hastened to the British Embassy to obtain a visa from Sir Francis Bertie, and broke down and wept. On 3 September she left Paris for London, taking £3,728 with her. Before leaving, she made an unsuccessful attempt to persuade her childhood nurse, Irma Deodat, to come with her. The least Gladys could do was to arm her with two letters of commendation in the hope that they would protect her. One was written to the American ambassador and the other to her suitor of thirteen years earlier, the Crown Prince of Prussia. In the letter Gladys implored his mercy for the people of Paris, and hoped it might extend to Irma 'in the memory of the time of your early youth and mine'.[2] The letter was never needed.

From London Gladys reported to her mother that, whereas Paris was 'tomblike', the bourgeois in England were 'very much on the bustle'. Society ladies had retired to the country, men had gone to war. London was unlit at night, and dangerous. The King was still shooting pheasants, and Winston Churchill had had his brother Jack transferred to headquarters from his regiment. Gladys concluded: 'I believe as I did at the beginning, that this is going to be an endless war – years of it, & peace will come not from victory but from general lack of – everything.'[3]

The Duke of Marlborough rejoined the army as a temporary lieutenant-colonel and served as a general staff officer in 1914 and 1915. Gladys threw herself into distributing food and clothes to the old and young. An ardent animal lover since childhood, with dogs, cats and horses, she made efforts to raise money for the Horses Relief Society. On 30 November she wrote to her mother:

We will all be grey-beards before it ends. The prisoners of war will return to us looking like the Prisoner of Chillon, but from the natural cause of advanced years. Perhaps they will have become respected citizens of Döberitz and other concentration camps with large & flourishing mongrel families . . .

I don't believe in an English invasion, a successful one. How cd it be done? They say Zeppelins have already passed over London & other places to reconnoitre & these may throw fire bombs & burn this town – Well that may be, but the Germans actually seizing this island I don't believe for a moment.[4]

It was not long before Gladys was reporting: 'There's not a family in society not in mourning.'[5]

Before the year was out, Mrs Baldwin suffered a blow with the death of her companion, Prince Doria. On 5 December Tina Whitaker noted that he had been seized with a sudden fit and was supposed to be dying.[6] The next day he felt unwell when he got up, returned to bed at noon, lost consciousness and died at twenty past six in the evening. His death took from Gladys's mother her most loyal friend, a great gentleman, 'with a heart and soul as sinless as a child'.[7] Mrs Baldwin was disgusted that his unmarried son, Filippo, failed to read any wires sent him and stayed away with the Scottish nurse* he later married, thus failing to attend his father's funeral, an act she

---

* Mrs Baldwin later heard that the nurse was attempting to cure Prince Filippo of a fondness for self-abuse. She wondered if she tied him up.

described as 'this last blow to his dear & suffering heart'.[8] Doria's death also removed the last vestige of financial security, for Mrs Baldwin's name was not mentioned in his will, and to her distress even the proceeds of an insurance policy went to Filippo. Nevertheless, her life tenancy of Caprarola was secure. Mrs Baldwin summed up her feelings:

> Poor Doria I miss dreadfully – I used to think him sometimes a terrible bore yet he was very sweet and always very helpful and sympathetic and now all is a wilderness and my voice is heard by no answering one.[9]

Italy joined the war in May 1915. 'Well,' wrote Mrs Baldwin to Gladys, 'the great event has at last taken place. Italy has declared war and vindicated herself but to my astonishment the Austrian Ambassadors are still in Rome.' In the agony of it, she wrote disconsolately: 'I wonder if we will ever meet again.'

When Bernard Berenson and his secretary, Geoffrey Scott, stayed at Caprarola in August 1915, Mrs Baldwin told him that Gladys had been in Belgium and was busy taking the Belgian Army, Navy and Royal Family under her charge. She had spent a great deal of time with the intellectual set of the British Museum and South Kensington. Mrs Baldwin also said that she had converted a loan of £400 into £16,000 on the Stock Exchange and that 'she would marry no one but M[arlborough] & perhaps not even him'.

Mrs Baldwin was ageing. Her eyelids had dropped and her hands and throat were covered with brown spots. While she remained as superficial as ever, she was also one of the most useful women in that part of Italy. She had opened a workroom and by September six thousand sterilised masks against poison-gas fumes had been sent to the trenches. She employed local women to turn raw material into garments for the Red Cross and paid them better than the average wage. She was forever appealing for funds to keep the process going, stating that she had long ago run out of private resources.[10]

She was on the point of converting Caprarola into a hospital for the wounded. 'It is an inconceivable mixture. One admires her & one is horrified with her at the same moment,'[11] wrote Mary Berenson. Mrs Baldwin admitted having spent £6,000 on the palace. Mary reckoned it was more like £20,000: 'There are huge traits in her that are simply appalling – so appalling that it is almost a miracle that one *can* like her. Only Dostoiewsky could do justice to her . . . Solitude & old age if they weren't accompanied by decay might liberate a very remarkable character.'[12]

★ ★ ★ ★ ★

Gladys spent most of 1915 in London, and that May she became a naturalised British citizen, a step towards her eventual marriage. The Duke of Marlborough made appointments to see her, promising her flowers (usually orchids), perhaps an aquamarine brooch or some game from Blenheim. They dined together when he was in London and sometimes he would send his chauffeur, Troubridge, to pick her up at Burlington Gardens, near Savile Row, and bring her to the station to meet him. He worried about her loneliness and was consistently overjoyed to see her. Not that everything ran smoothly. After one particular letter from Gladys, he replied: 'Beloved, your spiteful letter I expected. I felt that OB was beginning to get her hackles up, and that I was to get a scratch or two . . .'[13]

When he visited his sons at Eton, Gladys would lunch at a hotel in Windsor, and they would meet surreptitiously 'in the usual place' on the Long Walk. Gladys was the only light that shone in Marlborough's life and he often wrote rather shyly and formally thanking her for her kindness and 'affectionate solicitude' towards him. She provided a striking contrast to Consuelo who, as ever, caused him distant misery: 'Now I do not often complain – but few men have been plagued with such a woman as C – truly her life is spent doing harm to the family whose name she bears.'[14]

The duke had evidence of her wickedness when the 7th Earl of Jersey died and he believed himself the earl's rightful successor as lord lieutenant of Oxfordshire. Consuelo pressured Lord Lansdowne, in the Conservative cabinet, to have the new Lord Jersey, then aged forty-two, appointed. Marlborough marshalled allies such as F. E. Smith, Winston Churchill, Sir Edward Carson, Bonar Law and Max Aitken to support his cause and even stormed round to Lansdowne House in Berkeley Square to beard Lansdowne in his lair. 'Never has he had such a plain spoken statement as I made to him!' he reported to Gladys.[15]

Churchill influenced Lord Lansdowne in Marlborough's favour, pointing out what an injurious blow it would be if he were passed over, stressing that Lansdowne was his uncle and recalling the duke's twenty-two years of military experience with the Yeomanry. He reckoned the separation from Consuelo was so long ago as no longer to be an issue.[16] Reeling from Marlborough's visit, Lansdowne replied that he was open on the question and, if anything, prejudiced in the duke's favour, though he pointed out: 'But he is sometimes his worst enemy and he was so violent and abusive when he came to see me yesterday that anyone listening to his language would have doubted whether he was fit for any appointment requiring the possession of good manners and an even temper.'[17] In the end the duke got the post, despite all the machinations 'from the C gang'.[18] He thanked Winston for his and F. E.'s intervention, writing somewhat intemperately: 'The dirty dogs have been downed and may they now come and lick their chops in rage and annoyance.'[19] From France Gladys wrote that he would know on whom he could rely in the future.

Most of this time Gladys was in Paris, going to receptions, concerts, musing about the antics of Dorothy (the Radziwill estates had been taken over by the Germans), lunching with Marius Michel, and tackling investments. In October she went to Lausanne for eleven days for throat treatment following bronchitis. She and the duke swapped political news, and she told the doctor: 'To think that I have been taking all this trouble & expense abt my throat, probably to end under a bomb.'[20] She loved being back in Paris, where she felt at home.

In the New Year of 1916 Mary Berenson saw Gladys with her mother at the quai Voltaire. Having not seen her for some years, Mary was distressed at the deterioration of her face: 'Isn't it awful? Her face is grown very full and heavy-jawed, and all her colours jar – hair too yellow, lips too red, eyes too blue . . . She looked deplorable not a lady. It made me v. sad.'[21] Mrs Baldwin worried about the face and recommended electric massage. On the other hand, Sir Francis Bertie (now Lord Bertie of Thame) saw Gladys for the first time since the outbreak of war at a lunch given by the Marquise de Ludre, and observed: 'She still has fine eyes and good features.'[22] She was now thirty-five.

Her next adventure was to be painted by Boldini. The duke was delighted that Gladys had agreed to sit, aware that she hated the process, but hoped that he would not make her look like a tart – 'He can't help it, the brute'[23] – or fill the background with cushions.

The sittings were prolonged and the duke was soon annoyed that Gladys would not come to see him in England: 'Oh that Picture. Of course it will never be completed; that pig B. likes your company and will in a day or two rub out the head for the third time. I don't know when to expect you . . .'[24]

After further delays, the picture was ready. It portrayed Gladys seated facing to her left on one of Boldini's traditional Empire sofas, wearing a low-cut evening dress and with an ostrich-plume fan in her hand. Mrs Baldwin was not impressed: 'It doesn't do you justice, there's that tooth effect I don't like, which in you is certainly not apparent. I, too, think the dress *un peu décolleté* [somewhat low-cut].'[25]

Gladys brought the portrait over to England, unframed. The duke was pleased with the result and told her: 'I have found an excellent place for your picture which pleases me.'[26] She remained in London during May for a throat operation, then retreated to Brighton. But after a row with the duke, she swept up to his London home, 15 Great College Street, and seized the picture back. She took it to Brighton, explaining:

Since you dislike me enough to say the things you have said, you cannot want my picture for the motive for which it was painted, & you like it only because it is a fine painting . . .

You hurt my heart so much that I was carried away by sore & indignant rage & did things which I regret & ask you to forget & forgive.

But the foundations of that quarrel are very deep, none realize it better than I do.

Putting various things you have said, & what you said Ivor said to you, makes me see very clearly what your own meaning is.

Well Sunny, I have loved you against my family, the world & my conscience & I have loved you in fair days & foul. Perhaps I have given up too much in my desire to remain so clean & true to you. You never used to talk to me so two years ago. I don't know what has been the matter with you. Perhaps you have found a better friend, a better councillor, one less self-seeking – perhaps a friend of yours desires to make you adopt his view of life – what do I know? – you are no longer my Sunny, but another.

I am sure that I am not changed but to you who are soured towards me . . .

As you hate me, it will please you to hear that my throat is one suppurating mess. My mouth all foul.[27]

The duke apologised and expounded some of his woes and worries, which included the fear that he might have to close Blenheim:

I realise quite that you cannot appreciate my position. You have few responsibilities and my own are tremendous – the effect of responsibilities on my character is a source of annoyance to you, because possessing none yourself you *cannot* understand how anyone else can have thought for the morrow . . .

I liked your picture because I realise that in the days to come it will be the sole object which I shall possess to remind me that I passed some happy days with a fond heart – in a life which has otherwise been one of exceptional chagrin. But since you distrust my motive I must not stand in your way. I have the little photograph. Perhaps that should suffice.[28]

Gladys was mollified and wrote that she would return the picture: 'It was a true love gift costing me unbearable posing for a month, & nameless qualms, lest you wd not like it, & since you do love your poor bird still, it is yours. Take it to B. [Blenheim] & keep it.'[29]

The duke always feared that Gladys would debunk to Paris, and pressed by Boldini, who promised he would keep his hands in his pockets, she crossed the Channel in July, settling once more into her apartment on the quai Voltaire. 'I ask no questions about yourself,' wrote her mother, 'since you evidently desire me to remain in ignorance of all that concerns you.'[30]

On 17 July she wrote to the duke to say that she was seeing Boldini, who was happy to have with him a woman, gay, pretty and young. She asked him how Degas was, and he replied: 'Bah, he thinks only of his age!'[31] The war raged on, Gladys reporting:

The savagery has become unimaginable & at Verdun a man swore to me that on 304 there were rivulets of blood after some fight, running down the slopes. The men who have been in it since the beginning say that those who saw the early fighting alone have no conception what it has now become.[32]

At Blenheim the duke fell off his horse, suffering a compound fracture to his foot. For weeks he was immobile and depressed, worried that he might be permanently lame, and yet more so how Gladys would react since she had dropped Lord Francis Hope when he had lost his foot. Nervously he wrote: 'I expect to have a limp for all time. It is as well to tell you this for if you hate that – you will have an excuse for leaving me.'[33]

Gladys saw many of the wounded in Paris, and heard of the slaughter on the field of war, yet the social life continued around her. But she was depressed:

I cannot beat up any *joie de vivre*. My soul is like a stone at the bottom of a well. I cannot cure myself of the feeling born of all my solitary reflections in England that life is finished for me. My vanity no longer buoys me up & flattery gives no uplift. I simply don't care abt anything on earth. I think I feel this spiritual decease more here among these gay people than when I have no point of comparison. There is a gulf of ice between their tremendous enjoyment & my barren detachment. I put up a desperate defence & fight to hide it, & therefore come home so exhausted that I dissolve in tears when alone. To be really unhappy is a most extraordinary thing. It ravages all the luxuriance of one's inner forces like some deadly pest in a populous city . . .

Soon I will go away very far, either to some eastern convent where I can find serenity, or out of life altogether which will soon be the merest simulacrum.

I don't know why I say these things to you who have never been sympathetic with the great ills not born of actual fleshpots especially when mine was the voice to speak them, especially again as here I have some to whom I can speak & who wd understand.[34]

Gladys's problems with her mother's debts reached a crisis point when Mrs Baldwin tried to force her to part with $8,000 of capital in the United States Trust Company of New York. Mrs Baldwin was about to be evicted from Caprarola for owing about $500. She argued that Gladys would never marry or have children, was used to living on £40 a month, whereas she could not be expected to. She threatened to go to court to break Mr Deacon's trust, and 'yelled' that she would kill herself. Gladys was considerably vexed, aware her mother had turned to her as the 'weakest' of the three daughters, even though, through their marriages, her two sisters were now much richer. She consulted Léon Renault, the family lawyer, who told her it would be 'like a drop of water dropped on a red hot plague'. He said he had never met anyone 'as utterly hungry to spend on herself as she!'[35] Gladys did not relent. Mrs Baldwin also pressed her brother, Charley. In July she again threatened suicide, pointing out that Lady Sackville's brother, Henry, had killed himself because she turned a 'deaf ear' to his misfortunes: 'If a definite catastrophe happens to me I like to feel you too would regret not having been more helpful.'[36]

Marraine Baldwin warned the Baldwins: 'She composes those heartbroken letters and she has *no heart to break.*'[37] Edith tackled her uncle Charley: 'I can't believe that you are now so entirely out of sympathy with Mamma that her trouble doesn't find some echo in your heart.'*[38]

In September Gladys had two run-ins with Consuelo at Colombin's in Paris. They had not spoken for years. Gladys was buying a plum cake, turned and found Consuelo's eyes fixed on her, a mere foot away. Gladys 'looked blank' and went on with her purchase:

C is a phantom, an absolute wraith of thinness – quite half of what she used to be. She looks extremely delicate, whether from that slightly sagged look women get who are past early youth, or from bad health, I cannot say. Her hideous clinging dress made her look thinner still. She is no longer pretty at all & so appallingly thin that it is painful. She seemed when I glanced at her, very depressed & subdued but seeing her again later, she seemed to have recovered & have an *effronté* expression (This second time she did not see me).[39]

The second meeting, nose to nose, was a day or two later, again at Colombin's, where she went with the Marquise de Ludre: 'I was in tearing spirits for some reason or other & was rather annoyed she sd see me

---

* As usual, Charles Baldwin obliged.

so "on the bounce". I sd have looked what I am – i.e. a victim. I looked like a pig & overflowing with animal spirits, most annoying.'[40]

Gladys's power to fascinate was by no means lost. Abbé Mugnier told Berenson that he had witnessed an occasion at which she had been 'as brilliant as he could conceive'.[41] On the other hand, the philosopher Henri Bergson, to whom Keyserling had once recommended her, was unimpressed. In 1916 Jean Giraudoux was still able to describe the thirty-five-year-old as the most beautiful woman in the world and to observe the effect she had on passers-by as they walked together to lunch. Gladys was an hour and a half late for her appointment, but he felt that for someone of her beauty, an hour and a half was 'the minimum' time to wait. She ran towards him 'with the speed of light' and the Parisians, emerging from the restaurants, gazed in wonderment:

> They all looked at Gladys, she reminded them of someone they had once seen, but they could not recall exactly where. It is not true, she reminded them of someone they had not seen and who is the most beautiful woman in the world. A hoop passes before her, she runs and catches it in flight. She becomes the most beautiful girl in the world. All that is free is married to Gladys. I see her marriage with the Sunday sun, with the pigeons, with a little boy of the hoop, with an exacting husband who doesn't want to leave her. I take her away. Gladys must be married to the Arc de Triomphe which one can see sparkling above the arch of the merry-go-round.[42]

Gladys sat opposite Giraudoux with her head resting on her crossed hands. 'I am being listened to by the most beautiful grown-up child in the world,' he wrote.

Marlborough visited Gladys in Paris, and went back to London in a melancholy state:

> The world for me is growing grey – and since without you it would be hardly worth the effort to go on living – you must bear with me when I attach importance to your arrival. The time for us to be together may indeed be short – for who can foresee the requirements of the year 1917?[43]

Interlude

EPSTEIN

In contrast to the august, white-bearded figures of Rodin, Monet, Degas and Anatole France, and to the elder statesmen Gladys knew, such as Clemenceau and Aristide Briand, it was a refreshing delight for her to meet the young and talented sculptor Jacob Epstein in London. On so doing, she threw up her hands and exclaimed: 'A genius who is young!'[1] Epstein joined the ranks of Gladys's circle when he was thirty-six, through a new friend of Mrs Baldwin called Gladys Fletcher Robinson.* She had an unfurnished apartment in Cheyne Walk, which she was prepared to let Gladys have for £100. Mrs Baldwin reported that 'She said a Mr Epstein was in it and that if you wanted it please hurry.' Gladys did not take up the offer but she made friends with the tenant.

Epstein had already achieved success with works such as the Strand statues, the tomb of Oscar Wilde at Père Lachaise cemetery in Paris, and portraits of Admiral of the Fleet Lord Fisher, Augustus John and the Countess of Drogheda. In April 1917 Gladys paid him £150 towards a marble clock she commissioned, which was never made. In the same year she sat for the first of two sculptures. Epstein sculpted the straight nose, the lips already more naturally open than closed, the lower part of the eye more exposed than is natural and the chin grown heavy.

Through it shines the striking quality of her beauty. Epstein saw it as something eternal, and the finished bust was different from anything

---

* Gladys Fletcher Robinson, a controversial woman, the widow of Bertram Fletcher Robinson, editor of the *Daily Express*, who had given Sir Arthur Conan Doyle the idea for *The Hound of the Baskervilles*. Some said that Conan Doyle and Mrs Fletcher Robinson had conspired to kill Mr Fletcher Robinson in order to take possession of the plot line.

else he ever did; neither did it belong to any period. While Epstein pronounced it 'somewhat stylised', his second wife called it *The Etruscan Bust*. Richard Buckle wrote that Gladys's 'striking looks' were 'rendered with a grand archaic simplicity which recalls nothing so much as the Delphic charioteer'.[2]

Gladys loved the bust and Epstein was duly appreciative of her judgement. She was, he wrote, 'a woman of great discrimination in Art . . . and thoroughly understood what an artist was aiming at'.[3] However, when the bust was exhibited it caused 'great uneasiness' among the English ladies who patronise artists. When a photograph of it appeared in the *Chicago Evening Post*, a friend of Gladys wrote furiously: 'An artist (?) ought to be severely punished for a work like this.' Epstein wrote angrily of critics such as these:

> They expect a work to be entirely lacking in character and would rather have a portrait lacking all distinction than one which possessed psychological or plastic qualities, and a combination of these qualities is abhorrent to those ill-educated snobs who run about London airing their money-bag opinions and who dominate with their loud-voiced arrogance the exhibiting world.[4]

Having discovered Epstein's talent, Gladys worried that he might enlist in the army and be sent to an early death in the war. She prevailed upon Marlborough to approach Sir Edward Carson to ensure that this did not happen. Eventually the duke dined with Max Aitken (by then Lord Beaverbrook), who promised to do his best. On 4 March 1918 the duke reported the outcome:

> Well I have fixed up Epstein for you. He is to join the Canadian forces as an artist to mould figures and make sketches in the manner he thinks best. He will therefore not get killed and one day no doubt in recognition of your efforts he will present you with something from his chisel. Beaverbrook has been most painstaking in the matter. Never again say I do not get things done for you according to your liking.[5]

Epstein would reappear in Gladys's life in 1920 and later at Blenheim.

16

ARMISTICE, 1917-18

Over Christmas 1916 Marlborough took stock of his situation. He decided it was time to break his last bond to Consuelo. Gladys was nearly thirty-six and had waited patiently for many years, and he real-ised that if he did not take a definite step she might make up her mind to settle without him, and this was the last thing he wanted. He was relying heavily on the provisions of the new divorce reforms, which had been discussed since 1909, and which would make desertion for more than three years one of the grounds for divorce. But the war had delayed the Bill and nothing constructive happened until as late as 1923 when Lord Buckmaster's Matrimonial Causes Act was passed. In March 1918 the duke made another unsuccessful attempt to get divorced. He and Gladys were forced to remain in their present unsatisfactory state.

Ill-health dogged Gladys during much of 1917. In March the duke was appalled to hear that she was in London with not even a nurse to look after her. As sympathy did not come easily to him he relied on a letter to express his anxiety. Gladys was livid: 'Why did you write me this? So as to draw my attention that you wd not even telephone to me? Ah, my friend, how strange, how little human you are!'[1]

She retreated to Brighton until September, first in the Bedford Hotel and later in the Norfolk. Marlborough wondered if her move was a belated tribute to 'the lately defunct nobleman', her former friend the 15th Duke of Norfolk, who had died on 11 February. He worried about her safety and both were convinced that the war had at least two more years to run. On 16 June he wrote to her: 'I note you think the war will last as long as we continue to kill the wrong men in battle. It will cease the day we could be certain of killing all the right ones.'[2]

Gladys returned to Paris in September and stayed in her little apartment until the end of the year. Meanwhile Marlborough again contemplated closing Blenheim and wondered if he could find a seminary in Spain where the monks would be kind to him and he could find sunshine and silence. He was annoyed when Lord Beaverbrook suggested that he should give Blenheim to the nation, and worried about Lord Blandford who was about to go to war. Then he quarrelled with Winston Churchill over the 12½ per cent increase in wages for skilled workers. Gladys warned him: 'WSC is the nucleus of Bolchevism [sic]. He will try to be the Marat of the future. As I've told you over & over again, he is dangerous to your interests.'[3]

On 23 March 1918 the first of the German shells hit Paris, fired from huge naval guns seventy miles away that were of the kind nicknamed 'Big Bertha' (after Bertha Krupp of the German industrialist fame). The shelling persevered for many months and the quai Voltaire became a danger zone. 'For nearly a fortnight one had to offer large tips to taxis to come to this quarter,'[4] reported Gladys.

Gladys had a narrow escape when a shell landed thirty yards in front of her, as she was ambling back from the house of the Comtesse (Édith) de Beaumont one Sunday. Her skirt was blown almost over her head, while she was thrown onto the pavement, and a piece of iron wastepipe, dislodged by the explosion, fell on her shoulder. She was saved by a fur shawl collar she was wearing, but suffered a badly bruised arm and pain in her side and back. Gladys related what happened: 'Four people were blown to atoms. For ten days I was constantly seasick from the memory of the sight I saw when I was helped to my feet by those who came up.'[5]

Marlborough was alarmed to hear of her misadventure and urged her in vain to leave Paris. His anxiety increased when she told him of a visit she had made to see the damage done by the German guns.

★ ★ ★ ★ ★

Edgar Degas died in Paris at the age of eighty-three on 27 September 1917. Gladys soon became interested in the various sales that then took place. On 21 March 1918 she went to the first at Durand-Ruel's, as she reported to Marlborough:

I went with a charming man [Walter Berry] to the Degas sale. Pictures (not by him but by various artists & collected by him) went for colossal prices. £40,000* changed hands in 1¾ hours. A Gauguin I sd have liked in spite of my bad financial position & wd have bought for £40 went to £700 etc. . . . I think I'll go to the end of Degas Coll. Sale. I don't know what to do with myself otherwise.[6]

A further cache of pictures, by other artists, that Degas owned took place on 26 March at the gallery of Durand-Ruel's rival, Georges Petit, at 8 rue de Sèze. Walter Berry bought a painting by Gauguin, then entitled *Paysage de la Martinique*, which he later bequeathed to Gladys.[†]

The first sale of Degas's own work took place in his studio on 6 May, to which Gladys went along with Walter Berry and Madame Hennessy. She purchased two signed pastels of dancers from the 1890s. She found the atmosphere at the sale 'fearfully exciting'. A particular source of amusement was Mrs Robert Woods Bliss of Dumbarton Oaks in Washington, who steadily climbed 'the ladder of prices' in her attempt to secure one of Degas's pictures. Gladys informed her mother:

> Hers is a very good one though & as her purse is castor oil, I sd think it must be fat enough to draw upon. She has a pretty, extraordinarily mean little face, & her expression became so rapacious during the bidding that it stirred even Mr B. into laughter.[7]

The duke had been worried when he heard that Gladys was going to the sale, convinced that she would pay too much. She informed him:

> I actually bought another 'Three Dancers' in various yellows, oranges & yellow greens. I've spent £1,040 for the two. I feel like some sort of criminal. I can't buy. It goes against my grain. I've worked so hard to make money [by shrewd investing] that I've lost the art of spending it.

---

* She later noted that the papers stated £60,000.

† Numéro 45, *Paysage de la Martinique*, signed and dated 1887, 26 et 27 mars 1918, one of ten Gauguins on sale. It was bought by Degas in the 1891 Gauguin sale and is now called *Allées et Venues* and, after various adventures, currently resides in the Carmen Thyssen-Bornemisza collection in Madrid.

Everyone said I'd made a bargain. I got this one against Vollard who got the better one of the 2 for 18,600. There again I didn't dare & yet it was stupid not to. He will sell in 7 or 8 years at 50,000. He bought for at least 600,000 frs worth, all for himself. His sale will be wonderful! He has cancer, I hear.

Well so the Bs [she & the Duke] now have two groups of dancers, one purples & dark greens, the other light oranges, green & yellows, each a good foil for the other.

And now I will not buy 'arrivé' great masters again. I won't have it that a dentist can get the best, right under my nose.[8]

The duke was persuaded that Gladys's sound knowledge of art had ensured that her purchases were good examples of Degas's work. She explained:

In youth, they [minor artists] are still obedient to the rules & carefully model their slender idea but later the idea never grows or changes, or reaches any greater interest & alas le métier becomes lax & poor. Men full of genius like Degas, Cézanne especially, Gauguin, Van Gogh & Renoir begin with an adopted métier, careful, exacting, shy. Their personal idea is something which has not yet been expressed in classical drawing & which ill fits it. One feels a tightness, which is a lack of care, a lack of harmony between the vision & the portrait. Then as years pass, bringing with continuous application & hard work, the complete mastery of draughtsmanship, the Idea becomes more & more impelling, & finally forces a new technique wherewith to express itself more frequently, as in the extraordinary brushwork of Van Gogh's middle period . . .

Well, I've looked at pictures a long time & yet every day, I feel more convinced that to understand fully what the artist's meaning really is, is impossible in its entirety. As in everything, each can only see according to his power of comprehension, of sympathy, of knowledge, of difficulties overcome or rounded. It's more easy to converse with a deaf & dumb person on his or her intimate state of mind, than to take in the mystic & sensuous passion with which great pictures have been painted, for they are trying to express the most intimate sensations & imaginings of creatures unlike the rest of humans in that they possess that incomprehensible thing which is genius . . .

It's such a pity *perhaps* that the French art should be tainted with bourgeoisie & it certainly is. Only their genius makes it endurable. English 'art' is suburban, born in villadom, & has at present no recovering genius.[9]

Her companion at the sales, Walter Berry, struck up a close friendship with Gladys who discovered in him a thoroughly honest and highly cultured man. She called him 'an inspiration to people's lives'.[10] Like her, he was an American, born in Paris, then hovering round the age of sixty. A brilliant lawyer with a fine literary mind, his tall, thin form of six foot three inches cut an imposing and elegant figure in the streets of Paris. He was of aristocratic appearance, with a long, straight nose and piercing blue eyes. In Paris he held the important appointment of chairman of the American Chamber of Commerce. As such he was a useful ally to fellow Americans living in France, since he could arrange special banking facilities during wartime.

He had been a vociferous campaigner in bringing America into the war. In October 1918, Berenson wrote to Mary: 'He seems to live altogether with Gladys, Proust and Cocteau.'[11] Proust attributed the German defeat to the arrival of the Americans and the arrival of the Americans to the efforts of Walter Berry so he dedicated his *Pastiches et Mélanges* to him. He is best remembered as what Mrs Winthrop Chanler called the 'dominant seventh chord' in the life of Edith Wharton.

Berry loved women, especially intelligent ones. This inspired someone to ask, in a New York club, how he was able to 'seduce the minds of our women', to which Frank Crowninshield, celebrated editor of *Vanity Fair*, replied: 'If only he left them in an interesting condition.'[12]

Walter Berry's friendship with Gladys developed from the rather formal 'Dear Miss Deacon . . . Yours sincerely, Walter Berry' to his calling her 'Gardenia' or 'Gladyssima' and signing himself with a solitary 'A', short for 'Anaconda'. Their friendship revolved around lunches, teas, theatres and dealing in stocks and shares. The invitations with which he regaled her were always entertaining. When the actor Firmin Gemier sent him two tickets for *Antony and Cleopatra*, he wrote to Gladys:

Shakespeare in French is always a peculiar joy!

Don't you want to go?

Do.

They are terribly serious about it and close the doors during the acts
– and it begins at 1.15. Would you mind – if you can go, and I do so
hope you can – having a *casse-croûte* with me somewhere *en route*?[13]

★ ★ ★ ★ ★

Since 1914 Mrs Baldwin had been the driving force behind the
Farnese Relief Fund at Caprarola: sixty-five women working away
to send 4,000 flannel shirts and 7,000 cravats, woollen helmets,
gloves and more to the men at the front. In January 1918 she went
to the United States to do canteen work and to raise funds. She
returned to Europe, 'prosperous & jolly',[14] spending a few days with
Gladys before returning to Caprarola. The contrast between Italy
and America disheartened her enormously, as she explained to Mary
Berenson:

> I came back here with great plans, but how difficult it is to move
> anyone or anything in this country. One beats one's wings against the
> iron hand of ancient laziness & lethargy & there's hardly an appreciable
> result, try as we may. I am trying to organise a class for knitting socks
> for the front with knitting machines that I have brought back & also
> 40,000 flyswatters for the Italian hospitals . . .[15]

She complained that she had received 'a stiff cold note' from
Dorothy and nothing from Gladys since they had parted in Paris. 'I
am disgusted with both. They really carry indifference to its ultimate limit.' Mrs Baldwin was 'disenchanted & weary'. She felt she
had given too much of her soul to the war effort and was consequently exhausted and depressed. Her last words to Mary were: 'I
feel it cruelly there's not a human being in this land that I can call
friend.'[16]

Gladys was staying with her friends, the Ménians, in the Loire
when, three weeks later, Dr Lombardi telegraphed her at the quai
Voltaire to say that her mother was gravely ill. Chester Aldrich, later
director of the American Academy in Rome, then with the American
Red Cross Commission, telegraphed the next day, again in vain,

beseeching her to come. It was too late. Mrs Baldwin died peacefully at Caprarola on 15 July, aged a mere fifty-nine.

Many odd stories grew about this death. She was said to have died of malnutrition – to have been found in the well of the grand spiral staircase at Caprarola; she might even have been murdered. The staff were rumoured to have fled from the palace, and pillaging to have followed in the wake of her death. For none of these stories is there the remotest evidence. Prince Maffeo Sciarra, a nobleman living in Rome, moved into Caprarola and remained at the palace until Gladys was traced and finally arrived there. Thus nothing was lost. There was, however, a disturbing account of Mrs Baldwin lying in state at the palace. As one mourner approached the bier, a cloud of flies dispersed from the corpse.[17]

As soon as possible Gladys came to Rome and stayed at the Grand Hotel. Her mother was laid to rest in the Protestant Cemetery (where the poets Keats and Shelley are buried).* Presently, Harleston Deacon, Gladys's uncle (and guardian during her father's imprisonment in 1892), came over from America to help sort out her affairs. An auction of furniture and other possessions was held at Caprarola to pay off Mrs Baldwin's copious debts.

As ever there were contradictions. A year after her death, Mrs Baldwin's war efforts were recognised by the posthumous award of the Italian Red Cross. And one of those who wrote to Gladys saw her death rather differently from those concerned with debts and pillaging. It was Marcel Proust:

> The war has not accustomed me to death. The death of young people does not appear to me to lessen the sadness of the death of those who were not so young where it sweeps away less hopes but destroys more memories. I remember your mother so well at Versailles, her beauty, her kindness . . . I hope that the phase will not last too long for you until this terrible illness which is grief and the suffering of the loss is soothed so that you can appreciate the divine sorrow of remembering.[18]

---

* Mrs Baldwin's tomb is a handsome one, with the word 'PAX' engraved at the top, space for another name, which was never filled, and the inscription: 'Thou has made us for thee Oh Lord! – And our heart is restless until it rests in thee. – St Augustin.'

Though Gladys had had a difficult time with her mother, she mourned her greatly, often referring to her death. When Churchill's mother died in 1921, she wrote to him:

You know my own poor dear Mamma died 2½ years ago & time has not softened the dreadful blow it was to me. The breaking of that first heartbond of one's life, the disappearance of the witness of childhood's fair hours is so awful that only those who have felt it can at all realize the grief, the heartbreak of it.[19]

Gladys's mother died a few months before the Armistice on 11 November. As the end of the war approached, so the social world revived itself. The Ritz in London was filled with every type of society, and the social war horses put on their harnesses once more. Lloyd George went to Versailles and was heard to announce that he had won the war. Marlborough was aghast to consider the empires that had fallen – the Slavs, the Teutons, the Mohammedans. Now power would rest with the Rockefellers and the Carnegies.

When peace came, London filled with drunken crowds and ten thousand bottles of champagne were consumed at the Royal Automobile Club. Yet at this moment Gladys found everything black. Her spirit was crushed and she felt she had failed in life. Well used to such depression, Marlborough tried to cheer her up, believing she would do well to spend forty-eight hours laughing with a buffoon. She concluded that the best remedy was to leave Paris for the South of France.

17

THE IRISH DUKE

Shortly before her thirty-eighth birthday, Gladys went to Nice to look for a cottage. In January 1919 she found Tells Cottage in the chemin de Fabron, a secluded and pretty neighbourhood just behind the main town and stayed there for two years. It was high in the hills, and when it rained, the hills were hidden and the sea disappeared in a dense mist. She was soon planning what to plant in her 'handkerchief garden', while working in the 'swell' garden of her mother's American friend, Marie Taylor, at Clairefontaine, chemin St Antoine, to learn when to graft and so forth. She found that this new adventure interested her 'immensely.'[1] Besides Marie Taylor, she would see the nineteen-year-old great-niece of Henry Labouchère, sweet-natured Catherine Thorold, whose dog once dug up the plants in Gladys's garden.

Friends wondered why she had gone to the Riviera. 'What are you doing in Nice? You will freeze!'[2] wrote Boldini. Gladys went there partly for the climate. Having been in close contact with the Duke of Marlborough, there seem to have been no meetings at this time, and few surviving letters. This may have been a strategic retreat, since in the complicated business of obtaining a divorce from Consuelo Vanderbilt, he might have had to appear to have no contact with Gladys. But there might have been a cooling between the two. In June 1919, the duke was to be found staying at Berenson's Villa I Tatti, rented by Ivor Wimborne, his companion of the moment being Phyllis Boyd.* With them, on their honeymoon, were Duff and Diana Cooper.

---

* Phyllis Boyd, later de Janzé (1894–1943), daughter of Captain William Boyd and his wife, Lady Lillian FitzClarence, daughter of the 2nd Earl of Munster, thus descending from William IV. She married Vicomte Henri de Janzé in 1922, and had been, variously, the mistress of Lord Moyne, and Hubert Duggan, stepson of Lady Curzon. Gladys noted in 1916 that Phyllis was being pursued by Ralph Lambton, who bought her a house, and had set her cap at the Duke of Westminster. She was also involved with the well-known stud Tommy McDougal, master of the West Berkshire Hounds. Cecil Beaton wrote that she had 'the strange and tragic beauty of a tamed wild animal'.

During her first months in the South of France, Gladys formed an unlikely new attachment – with the old Duke of Connaught, who had gravitated to the Hôtel des Réserves at Beaulieu, shortly after the wedding of his daughter, Princess Patricia to Captain Alexander Ramsay at Westminster Abbey. He would presently buy a villa on Cap Ferrat but, meanwhile, he was often to be found at Maryland, the villa of Muriel Warde's mother, Mrs Arthur Wilson, or lunching or dining with the attractive American-born widow Adèle, Countess of Essex, at Villa Loo Mas.

Gladys wrote to the royal duke inviting him to her cottage, to renew an acquaintance of some years ago. The duke had been to Blenheim shooting over the years, and Gladys had noted his presence, along with A. J. Balfour and Lloyd George, in Paris the previous July – 'the Connaught (who is thought so extremely *grand seigneur!!*)' as she described him to Marlborough – 'dining out which seems to be the usual occupation of men in office. Feeding rationlessly must occupy 7/8 of their time. The old things are delighted with themselves.'[3] She and Marlborough nicknamed him 'The Irish Duke'.

Arthur, Duke of Connaught was the last surviving son of Queen Victoria. Born in 1850, he had been a godson of the great Duke of Wellington, his christening immortalised in Winterhalter's picture *The First of May*. By 1919 he was sixty-nine and had lived at the centre of the nation's life. He had been a soldier since his earliest days, was a field marshal, had served as governor-general of the Dominion of Canada and held the senior grade of all the British orders of chivalry. His Prussian-born duchess had died, to his sorrow, in 1917. That and his daughter's marriage had left him feeling lonely.

The duke was a ponderous, well-meaning man, not averse to a pretty face. One of his long-term lady friends was Lady (Leonie) Leslie (sister of Jennie Cornwallis-West). If there were concerns that a particular lady had designs on him, she would be dispatched to the rescue. In the Leslie family, they said: 'We send you out like the Fire Brigade.'[4]

The duke accepted Gladys's invitation to Tells Cottage with alacrity, expressing the hope that she would not go to the trouble of inviting any other guests, preferring to see her on her own. The first rendezvous took place on 19 March at three thirty and was a success.

Afterwards he sent her some photographs of his daughter's wedding, hoping she wouldn't be 'too bored with so many pictures of the damn thing'.[5] He suggested another meeting, again just the two of them. Several such meetings followed, during which they discussed books and articles, and commiserated over the respective losses of his wife and her mother. The duke wrote after one meeting: 'I grieve to know how lonely and unhappy your mother's death has left you. Having so recently lost my wife I know what a blank the loss of a beloved one leaves in one's life.' He hoped to be able to comfort Gladys on his next visit and trusted that this would not 'grate against [her] lacerated feelings'.[6]

By the time the duke left for Paris on 11 April, less than a month after their first encounter, he was calling her 'Gladys', requesting a photograph of her – 'I am very anxious to have it'[7] – and glad that she had consigned her wristwatch to him for repair at Cartier. He put his feelings down on paper:

> Although you may not realise it, you have added a new joy and interest to my now rather lonely life – you know how I feel towards you; I have confided in you & trust you completely and I am sure that you will never disappoint me.[8]

Neither he nor Gladys was being completely straightforward. He later admitted that he had lost his heart to her, while flirting simultaneously with another American, Rhoda Doubleday, wife of a minor part-time diplomat and businessman, who was also to be found at Mrs Wilson's villa. Gladys still retained her mission to marry the Duke of Marlborough. As the Duke of Connaught's biographer, Noble Frankland, surmised: 'Friendship with the Duke of Connaught, she seems to have thought, would be a leg up in that direction. If so, this was neither a pure nor a good basis of friendship . . .'[9]

The friendship continued. When he arrived in Paris, the duke was elated to learn that Gladys was about to appear there in connection with her mother's estate. Her train was due in at 8.45 a.m. on 15 April, while he was due to leave, also by train, at 11 a.m. He left the Ritz and made his way to the quai Voltaire, only to see his letter of the previous day still in the concierge's rack. He was deeply disappointed, thoroughly depressed on the journey back to England, and tortured by the knowledge that Gladys must have been within half a mile of him for two hours.

Back home at Clarence House in London and at Bagshot Park, his country house near Ascot, Gladys was never far from his thoughts. He wrote to her that during the sermon and prayers at Matins his attention wandered to speculating as to what she was doing. He was insecure in his approaches to her, contrasting his lonely existence with her high bohemian life in the literary circles of Paris: 'You are so much more intelligent and cleverer than I am that I often feel that what I write is dull and perhaps too much about myself.'[10] He wrote soon afterwards that he commended Gladys for her frankness in saying what she thought and felt: 'I am afraid I dare not say what I feel. It is better & wiser that I should not put my thoughts on paper . . . although you know well enough what I do feel.'[11]

Life was certainly not dull in Paris. The Peace Conference was in full swing and Paris was awash with politicians and diplomats. President Wilson of the USA had long been a figure of controversy in Europe, and of close interest to Gladys. She soon surmised that his particular concept of the League of Nations was impossible.

Her visit to Paris was also the occasion of her last encounter with Bernard Berenson. He was walking near the Petit Palais in Paris when an old horse-drawn coupé stopped and a figure draped in widow's weeds got out. It was Gladys, who proceeded to approach him, almost poked a finger in his eye, and demanded: 'Horrible B.B. you mean you don't recognise me?' With her was Boldini, described by Berenson as 'an even more deplorable figure all bundled up in shawls'.[12]

Though he would live on until 1959, Berenson became embittered towards Gladys. In old age he told Umberto Morra:

I decided to stop seeing Gladys Deacon when I convinced myself that in human relationships she offered nothing but an offensive arbitrariness pursuing people in a flattering and ensnaring fashion only so as to be able to break off with them noisily when the fancy struck her.[13]

On 30 April Count Jean de Gaigneron, an intellectual and painter, invited Gladys to dine at the Ritz in a party consisting of Proust, Harold Nicolson, Marie Murat and Carlo Placci. Gladys sat between

Proust and Nicolson, the latter recording the conversation between them and judging Gladys 'very Attic' and Proust 'very Hebrew'. He ventured that a passion for detail was 'a sign of the literary temperament'. Proust was hurt by this and cried out '*Non pas!*' He then blew what Nicolson described as 'a sort of adulatory kiss' across the table in the direction of Gladys. The conversation turned to homosexuality – whether it was a matter of glands, nerves or habit. Proust was of the opinion that it was 'a matter of delicacy'.[14]

No such matters were discussed with the Duke of Connaught when he returned to Paris on royal duties in May. He relished teas with Gladys at the Loidan or Colombiers, once so much so that he inadvertently detained the Earl of Derby, the British ambassador, whom he found waiting for him at the Ritz. As ever the duke was grateful to Gladys for her kindness and assured her: 'Our friendship is so *close* and so *delightful* to me.'[15] On 14 May he returned to London, and two days later Gladys retreated to her cottage in Nice. She did not see the duke again until the end of the year, but received a stream of letters from him, filled with interesting news. He informed Gladys that the Dowager Empress of Russia refused to believe that the Tsar and his family had been murdered, that Sir John French, 'a vain little man & not quite a gentleman', hated Asquith, and he mused over the fate of the Kaiser, by then in exile in Holland:

> The question of the trial of the Kaiser in London is *causing* a *great* controversy; I think it would be an awful mistake, especially here in London. I don't see what good it is going to do, & I very much doubt whether an Allied Court would ever convict, & *how foolish* we should look if that happened!! I should let the wretched man disappear into oblivion – that would be an especially heavy punishment for the 'all highest' . . . The King is very worried about it; the Kaiser is such a near relation of his, he is also Queen Victoria's eldest gr:son & he has been entertained here in London as a *most honoured guest* by 3 successive sovereigns. I don't believe the Dutch will give him up & very much *hope* they won't.[16]

The letters continued throughout the year, the duke complaining that Gladys did not write often enough, though when she did, he found her 'always interesting, perhaps a little satirical'.[17]

In Nice Gladys tackled the weeds at her cottage and she became interested in the unravelling of Dorothy's marriage to the ineffectual Aba Radziwill, prompted by her wish to become what turned out to be the second of eight wives of the proactive Austrian Count 'Pali' Pálffy, a man who enjoyed the same success in seducing women as he did in hunting animals.

To Gladys's irritation, Dorothy had become her mother's favourite when she succeeded in becoming a serene highness. She had caused a sensation in Rome by driving a leopard through the ballroom at a fancy-dress party in 1913, part of a campaign to become the queen of Roman society in competition with Dora Rudini.* Throughout the war, Gladys had complained bitterly about her sister, that she had been too cowardly to come into her region of Paris, and of other exploits. There had been conflicting rumours of Dorothy's political affiliations – how she had worked for the Italian Red Cross, how she had entertained members of the Austrian and German legations at her villa in Berne, Switzerland, how she had been refused entry to Italy after her mother's death, while her husband was related to Hohenzollerns, Romanovs and Hapsburgs and her father-in-law had served in the Kaiser's army. During the war, Aba Radziwill lost his estates in Poland and Lithuania. Then in Paris she became close to Count Maurycy Zamoyski,† a great landowner and distinguished politician, who bankrolled the Polish free government during the war.

Her child, Elisabeth (Betka) Radziwill, was born in 1917. Dorothy then met Pali Pálffy in Switzerland, divorced Radziwill, and in November 1919 applied to have her marriage annulled in Rome. 'Those who know the American princess declare indignantly that she could never have been induced to separate from her husband by such

---

* Dora Labouchère (1884-1944), unhappily married, 1903, Marquese di Rudini, divorced in 1914. He committed suicide for gambling debts in 1917. Later married Prince Odescalchi, again divorced, in 1926. In 1922 he challenged Dorothy's second husband, Count Pali Pálffy to a duel, which he refused to fight. She died in Rome as a result of falling through a trapdoor damaged by bombs.

† Count Maurycy Zamoyski (1871-1939), Minister of Foreign Affairs in the Polish government in the 1920s. Nearly became Poland's first president in 1922, but withdrew from the election.

a base and selfless motive as his loss of property,'[18] mused an American newspaper.

★ ★ ★ ★ ★

The second and final phase of Gladys's friendship with the Duke of Connaught began in December 1919, when Gladys was still living in Nice. He arrived in Cannes at the end of December, and settled at the Hôtel California. Gladys had told him she was expecting some 'artist friends' to arrive who would not be to his taste. This confused him:

> What do you understand by 'artist friends', singers, actors or what? If they are good & are also nice I don't think we look down on them in England – I can't imagine who your 'English intellectuals' are who you refer to. I *know* some who are nice & others who are not – of course you are a regular Bohemian & may like some people who others again don't like.[19]

The duke was presently annoyed that Gladys would not make the journey from Nice to Cannes to see him and yet more so that she signed herself 'Yours respectfully':

> Surely 'Gladys' is enough. There is no other Gladys to my mind; you really must not do it again; I know you did it out of respect, but really it is unnecessary, our feelings of respect are I hope quite mutual & my feelings towards you are also of great affection; if you don't think it rude or impertinent of me to say so.[20]

While the duke continued to press Gladys for solitary encounters, she issued more unusual invitations, summoning him to the New Club to watch a teatime performance of black jazz performers (when he was more accustomed to the Band of the Grenadier Guards). The duke accepted.[21] At the end of December he called at Tells Cottage, but was not admitted. Gladys pleaded a bad attack of influenza. In his next letter he reported: 'Your friend the Duchess of Marlborough!! is building a villa near here.'*[22] When the duke settled in Beaulieu at the Hôtel Bristol, there were regular meetings, with friends such as Mrs

---

* Consuelo bought the land opposite Èze and built Villa Lou Seuil.

Keppel and Ethel Boileau* nearby, lunches and tennis matches, or Gladys might meet him for tea at the Café de Paris in Monte Carlo. On 9 April 1920 he left the South of France.

Gladys had little if any intention of marrying the Duke of Connaught, though some feared this might be her plan. But there was trouble ahead and the duke's protective lady friends moved in to make him feel that Gladys was making a fool of him. A little later on there were reports that he might be contemplating marriage with Lady Essex.† Nothing of that nature appears to have been published about Gladys in the press. But in January 1920, she was libelled in the *Daily Graphic* when, in an article about the collapse of Dorothy's marriage, the old story about Gladys and the Crown Prince of Prussia was resurrected. The paper stated that Gladys had been 'the centre of a great outcry in Germany in which her name and that of the ex-Crown Prince were so frequently coupled that she was banished from the country'.[23]

Represented by Lewis & Lewis, the Duke of Marlborough's solicitors, who briefed Sir Ellis Hume-Williams and St John Field as counsels, Gladys stated that 'she never saw the Crown Prince again, and never communicated with him, and anything she knew of him was what the world knew and humanity condemned'.[24] Gladys was awarded £500 damages with costs before the lord chief justice.

The publicity engendered by this may have been the spur to Lady Leslie or Lady Essex to poison the Duke of Connaught's mind. He fell into a trap and accused Gladys of making a fool of him. She replied in 'cruel and seething words', which led him to believe she hated him violently. On 17 April he wrote from the Ritz in Paris, begging forgiveness and accepting all the blame: 'I feel you are right in abusing me in the unmeasured terms you did, but I have felt none the less your terrible letter is I fear intended to show me that you cease your friendship which I have valued so much. It is hard at my

---

* Ethel Boileau (1881–1942), popular English novelist, wife of Colonel (later Sir Raymond) Boileau (Bt), living at Ketteringham, Norfolk. She first met Gladys in 1917 and became a perceptive friend.

† The reports about the Countess of Essex reached the United States in September 1920. Had the duke married her, he would have been widowed anew in 1922. She was found dead, mysteriously, evidently of a heart attack, in her bath, at her London home, a bottle of brandy at her side. She was sixty-three.

age to part with friends like you that I have liked & had up to that cruel letter trusted so completely.' Downcast, the duke resigned himself to losing her friendship and signed himself 'a grateful friend who prays for your health & happiness throughout life'.[25]

The Duke of Connaught's troubles were not over. On the day of his seventieth birthday his elder daughter, Daisy, Crown Princess of Sweden, died suddenly from erysipelas and blood-poisoning at the age of thirty-eight. The tragedy prompted an immediate response from Gladys:

> Sir,
> In the midst of my bitterness yet do I remember the agony of losing one near and dear to one – the sense of sudden emptiness, of collapse, of loneliness. This, therefore, is to tell you that I hope God's help be with you through these grievous hours.[26]

It was impossible for Gladys to avoid the Duke of Connaught for ever, especially after her marriage to the Duke of Marlborough. Yet she never forgave him. Normally invitations to Blenheim were marked 'A' if accepted and 'R' if refused, but any invitation to meet HRH The Duke of Connaught was firmly 'declined'. The friendship he had called 'so true and so pure'[27] was over.

Interlude

ROBERT TREVELYAN
1919 & 1921

In 1919 an infatuation got out of hand and set Bloomsbury alight. It had been brewing for two years. In the autumn of 1917 Gladys had met Robert Trevelyan in Paris, renewing an acquaintance first made at I Tatti in 1904. At that time Gladys had bewitched Bob and his wife with her extraordinary conversation. They found her irresistible, but were disapproving. Robert C. Trevelyan, often known as 'Trevy', was an elder brother of G. M. Trevelyan, the historian, and a lifelong friend of Berenson. Looking back in old age, David Garnett described him as 'a very good poet, now forgotten',[1] and Nicky Mariano, Berenson's secretary and amanuensis, remembered him as 'tall, lean, uncouth, with dishevelled grey hair, a long inquisitive nose, corduroy trousers, heavy boots, very poor table manners'.[2]

In 1917 Trevelyan suddenly fell violently in love with Gladys. There is a legend that she would lie on a bed behind a screen while he read his poems aloud to her. In the first months of 1918 he sent her several volumes of poetry. His love for her grew and he suffered. As his son wrote: 'He was very much changed by meeting Gladys.'[3]

In 1919 the matter got so out of hand that his friends intervened. One of them was Francis Birrell, a fringe member of the Bloomsbury group, who was proud to be artistic and bohemian. He was the son of Augustine Birrell, the distinguished Liberal statesman. His father thought him stupid, but Gladys thought him brilliant. 'There was this rift between them,' she recalled. 'He was not a genius, but his father was harsh on him.'[4] David Garnett remembered that Gladys entrusted to Frankie the delicate task of calming Trevelyan down. 'Frankie was given to exaggeration,' he wrote, 'but he made it sound hectic.'[5] In September Birrell gave Gladys a progress report. He apologised for meddling in her affairs and complained of the considerable inconvenience this was causing him. Trevelyan had 'more or less regained his equilibrium' in the three months since he had left England in June. But events had taken a turn for the worse. Birrell continued:

[I] discovered him shattered by a p.c. he had just received from you à propos of his visit to the Riviera, & have since been endeavouring to shepherd him off to Madrid, though I am not sure with what success.

Trevelyan was so stricken with love that he was unable to work or settle. He was 'rapidly becoming intolerable to himself & everyone else'. Birrell urged Gladys to 'summon up the brutality to say that you cannot bear seeing him regularly or something to that effect'.[6] Gladys replied, promising to send on to Trevelyan 'one or two abstracts from your letter'. He agreed with her that the situation was serious. 'Bob sometimes appears hardly sane – & is on the high road to worry himself into a mad house.'[7]

Nor did the matter rest there. In January 1920, the art critic Roger Fry intervened. He found Trevelyan in 'a very agitated situation'. He wanted to establish a relationship of pure friendship with Gladys, but doubted that he would be able to keep it on that level. Fry thought he would 'obsess' Gladys again. He was remaining silent only to speed his recovery. Fry mused on the condition of love:

It's a funny disease, isn't it, and very painful and worst of all tends to make one ridiculous though I may say that Bob has never appeared to better advantage than when recounting his woes – he's very simple and very honest and hasn't the ordinary share of *amour propre*.[8]

By June 1920, Trevelyan was more settled. Edmond Jaloux, literary editor of *Grasset*, was able to reassure Gladys: 'Did you know that I saw Trevelyan, a Trevelyan clipped, at ease, elegant, unrecognisable? He has a very melancholic expression when one talks of you in front of him!'[9]

★ ★ ★ ★ ★

The obsession was resurrected in 1921, after Gladys had married. Trevelyan was still wavering and unable to write. Gladys tried to help him, even taking him to the doctor. As Virginia Woolf wrote to Vanessa Bell:

> Poor Bob Trevelyan – poor Bob Trevelyan – Well if one meets Bessy [his wife] at the 1917 Club on a cold afternoon with her handbag and her great boots and her nice red Dutch nose, and her liberal sympathies – one does fall in love with the Duchess of Marlborough. I did at once.[10]

By January 1922, the infatuation was decreasing and Virginia Woolf was able to report to E. M. Forster that the poet was 'delicious . . . hungry, greedy – growling – and divine'. She explained: 'His love for the Duchess (this is Gordon Square gossip) has subdued and softened him, and he's having his arteries vivified in order to write more poetry, and out he pulls, as usual, manuscripts – in fact he was bustling off to see a new publisher.'[11]

Thereafter, Trevelyan, left with what Virginia Woolf called 'the legacy of Gladys Deacon', adopted a more general interest in the female sex. According to Nicky Mariano, he was forever 'infatuated in a schoolboyish manner with some young woman, usually repulsed because of his uncouth manners and ever yearning for an ideal fulfilment'.[12]

Gladys emerged unscathed from this obsession.

18

PARIS WEDDING

The wedding went off well.
The whole of Paris turned up and gave Gladys a good send-off.

The Duke of Marlborough

to

the ailing Jennie Cornwallis-West[1]

After years of obduracy, Consuelo finally agreed to a divorce from the Duke of Marlborough. She did so in order to marry Colonel Jacques Balsan.* Since nothing positive had come from the Divorce Commission, the Marlboroughs had to endure the charade of being seen to cohabit once more. The lawyers arranged that the various deeds of separation be revoked, and they returned to live under the same roof for a fortnight. The scene was Crowhurst, Consuelo's small Tudor manor house in the North Wolds. The duke's sister, Lady Lilian Grenfell, stayed with them as chaperone during this tiresome period. When Marlborough went home on 15 December 1919, he left a letter stating that they had grown too far apart to resume their union. Consuelo replied in kind. On 28 February 1920 Marlborough spent the requisite nocturnal hours 10.30 p.m. to 8.30 a.m. with an unnamed woman in room 193 at Claridge's, booking in under the name of Spencer.

Other family events occurred. His son, Lord Blandford, having outlived a fondness for stage-door petticoats, married Mary Cadogan, daughter of Viscount Chelsea, on 17 February 1920. Gladys was not present at the service. Then, on 22 July, Consuelo's father, W. K. Vanderbilt, died. After a visit to the United States, Consuelo put

---

* Jacques Balsan (1868-1956), aviator and balloonist.

Sunderland House in London, and Crowhurst, on the market and moved to Paris.

Marlborough was greatly relieved that the long saga of his marriage was over. On 10 November, the day the divorce petition was entered, he wrote:

> Thank Heavens it is all over – The last blow that woman could strike over a period of some 20 years has now fallen – Dear me what a wrecking existence she wd have imposed on anyone with whom she was associated.[2]

He launched himself into London society, attending as many parties as possible. He advised Gladys to keep in with her rich cousin Eugene Higgins* because everyone in England from the Royal Family downwards was greatly impressed by money. Gladys softened the French gossips and obtained approval for her marriage from her old family lawyer, Léon Renault. Meanwhile the duke dined with those in society he considered appropriate. His main concern about the forthcoming wedding was how 'King Log' and the court would react. 'That fortress one day will have to be raised [sic],' he noted. Fortunately, reports of the divorce coincided with the unveiling of the Tomb of the Unknown Warrior in Westminster Abbey, which took over as the main topic of conversation.

Throughout this time, Gladys remained in her cottage in Nice.

---

* Eugene Higgins (1858-1948), Gladys's first cousin, a lifelong bachelor, son of E. S. Higgins, of the power-loom New York company of the same name, and his wife, Emma, a sister of Admiral Baldwin. He inherited $50 million from his father, was described in 1898 as 'not only the richest but the handsomest unmarried New Yorker', and was much in demand in society in New York and Paris. He won the American fencing competition in 1890, owned the largest yacht of the New York Yacht Club, *Varuna*, and later another splendid yacht, *Thalassa*, and a stable of fine horses. He sold his father's carpet-manufacturing business and built up further riches by shrewd investments. At his death in a hotel suite in Torquay, where he had lived for the previous nine years, Higgins bequeathed $5,000 each to Gladys and her sister Dorothy, but nothing to Edith, while leaving the bulk of his fortune to the universities of Columbia, Harvard, Princeton and Yale. When asked by Dorothy (Gladys's sister) to help the impecunious Countess Marie Kleinmichel (1846-1931) in 1925, he sent but 100 francs.

Edmond Jaloux, a keen promoter of Proust, and a more intellectual companion than the Duke of Connaught, came to visit her. He tried to persuade her to translate Henry James into English for *Grasset*. He was flattering about her looks and her intelligence:

> I know few besides you with whom it is so pleasant and refreshing to pour out one's heart, confident of that quick and deep understanding which intelligence gives. Yours is extraordinary! It is vast and quite naturally acquired. You embody much of the archangel (whom you very much resemble physically), and of the erudite. And to discuss with a seraphim as if with a knowing spirit is a form of joy one rarely encounters, believe me![3]

But Gladys did no translations, for now the goal, first contemplated at the age of fourteen, and relentlessly pursued to the denial of greater happiness, came inexorably into view.

The Duke of Marlborough's decree became absolute on 17 May 1921 and he was free to marry Gladys. She was now aged forty and had waited so long to be Duchess of Marlborough that the sudden inevitability of the situation terrified her. When the duke put his proposal, she did not immediately accept. He was astonished: 'Haven't you had time to make up your mind?'[4]

★ ★ ★ ★ ★

Gladys prepared for her forthcoming wedding with foreboding. She dreaded the thought of having to behave like a duchess with the clear restrictions it would impose. On 21 April 1921 she closed her Nice bank account and settled her affairs. Before leaving the South of France she implored Epstein to come to stay and talk about art. The sculptor travelled to Nice for a week. Then Gladys braced herself to face the clamorous publicity her wedding would inevitably attract. Marlborough hoped she would be happy 'with all the rough edges of life knocked off' for her.[5] He decided to wait until he arrived in Paris before buying her an engagement ring.

On 1 June Gladys took up residence at 16 rue Auguste Vacquarie, the home of Lord Wimborne. The same day the engagement was briefly announced in *The Times*. From then until her wedding, Gladys was headline news. She was described as a well-known beauty and an intimate friend of Consuelo. The Deacon family dramas were resurrected, and lists of Gladys's former suitors were published. Reports stated that at one time or another she had been engaged to Lord Brooke and Antoine de Charette, and even to a Lieutenant Oliphant of the Royal Navy (though that was a different Gladys Deacon). Her father was described as a Boston millionaire and it was said that Whistler had painted her just before he died, for which no evidence exists. Inevitably the fable that she had been Consuelo's bridesmaid was circulated once more. A *Daily Telegraph* reporter attempted to interview the duke at his home in Great College Street, London, but the duke had nothing to say.

Privately Marlborough was delighted with the way the engagement was received. Posters in the street declared 'Romance of a Duke', and Lord and Lady Curzon appeared to agree that it was indeed a romance. Blandford and Ivor were charming to their father, Lady Sarah Wilson commented that Gladys was 'very beautiful', and his brother-in-law, Bob Gresley, that she was 'most agreeable to him'. The duke's mother, Albertha, Marchioness of Blandford, remained silent for the time being. Winston Churchill wrote with his congratulations and Marlborough replied:

> I think that Gladys and I will be happy in our lives together. She is a very remarkable woman and possesses the power of attracting all classes of individuals among the population of Paris to herself, a task by no means easy. Politicians, artists, May Fairies all stream along to see her. The round of social entertainment will soon become intolerable.[6]

The duke derived enjoyment from wondering how the 'Irish Duke' was taking the news. 'I hear old Connaught announced at his table the other day that OB would never think of marrying OM – I hope he has had a colic today.'[7] In Paris Marthe Bibesco was horrified at 'the conquest of an historic castle by one American over another, the latter very lovable and much loved'.[8] On the other hand, the historian Gustave Schlumberger, an old friend of the family, was delighted that Gladys, whom he considered 'certainly one of the most elegant charmers' he had ever met, with 'many trump cards in her hand', had given 'the most dazzling contradiction to the prophets of doom', who thought she had wasted her life, by becoming Marlborough's duchess.[9]

There was a flurry of pre-nuptial entertaining, notably the dinner given at 85 rue de la Faisanderie by Madame Hennessy, known, appropriately, in Proustian circles as '*la jeune Faisanderie*'. The Princesse de Polignac was there, and Marcel Proust emerged from darkness to attend the dinner, wearing the famous sealskin dressing-gown to his ankles. The Duke of Marlborough met him for the first time and, even though Gladys was among his ardent readers, had no idea who he was. But he and Proust got on so well together that the duke tried to persuade him to fulfil a long-held dream to visit England. 'You can go to bed immediately at the Gare du Nord,' he proposed. 'You can have a bed on the boat, and you can stay in bed while you are at Blenheim.'[10] Proust was touched by 'so much consideration from a man that I was seeing for the first time'.[11] They discussed illness and the duke expounded the theory that the moment one believed oneself well, one was well. He urged Proust to repeat to himself that he felt marvellous. Proust tried it but, as he wrote to Princess Soutzo, 'that made me go from bad to worse'.[12] He spent the next four months in bed.

After Gladys married, she drifted out of Proust's world, though when Edmond Jaloux congratulated Proust on *L'Ombre des Jeunes Filles* in June 1922, he reminded him that Gladys was 'one of the beings you most admire and who understands you the best'.[13]

The duke had told Churchill that they would get married at the British Consulate if Lord Curzon, then foreign secretary, would allow the consul general to celebrate it. On 22 June the *Daily Chronicle* revealed that complications had arisen over the wedding plans. While the duke would have settled happily for a civil wedding, Gladys was insisting on a religious service too. They encountered problems in finding a clergyman willing to officiate. Dr Chauncey Goodrich, pastor of the American Church in Paris, refused to bless the union, explaining: 'I have conscientious objections to remarrying anyone who has been divorced.' Then an English clergyman declined because the civil wedding at the British Consulate, though perfectly legal, was in no sense a French civil wedding, and no French religious service could take place without a French civil one.

Doubts hung over the couple until the eve of the wedding; the headlines got bigger and the press reports longer. On 23 June Gladys received a correspondent from the *Daily Express* and told him: 'All I know is that I am going to be married to the Duke of Marlborough on Saturday morning at twelve. I do not even know who is going to marry us.' She also told the reporter: 'You do not know what sort of time I have had the last two weeks. You do not know what it is to be married.' The reporter protested that he did know, indeed that he was married himself, but she brushed aside his remarks and told him that the destination of the honeymoon was being kept secret, even from her. The duke feared that otherwise the news would leak out.

Lavish presents poured into the rue Auguste Vacquarie, among them a piece of Persian embroidery that had been in one of the palaces of the sultans of Turkey for hundreds of years, the gift of the wife of Izzet Pasha, a daughter of Sultan Abdul Hamil II. Gladys had asked for feathered fans. Eighteen arrived in a variety of different colours. The press was invited to inspect her trousseau of summer dresses from Callot Soeurs, which were hailed as 'fit for a fairy Queen'. Journalists and public-relations officers pursued Gladys feverishly, right up to the day of the wedding, each one vying for an exclusive story.

The civil ceremony took place in the British Consulate at eleven o'clock. The Duke of Marlborough arrived from the Travellers' Club in the Champs-Élysées in a Rolls-Royce, wearing a grey suit with cut-away tails, but double-breasted and like a frock coat from the waist upwards. (The suit was thought to herald a new fashion in morning dress.) He swung a cane and smoked a cigarette. He asked waiting pressmen what the excitement was and they replied that they were waiting for the duke's wedding. 'Well, I'm Marlborough,' he said, and handed round cigarettes from a gold case. As he was photographed, he said: 'I have nothing to say – you chaps know more about my wedding than I do. Remember, the invitations are out for the religious wedding tomorrow noon. Be there and you'll see us married.'[14]

Gladys arrived in a navy-blue chemise dress of silk jersey, thickly embroidered down the front, and a large blue hat. The colour was chosen as an omen of good luck. She was accompanied by the beautiful Comtesse de Boisrouvray.* The duke kissed his betrothed's hand to the clicking of a battery of cameras. Gladys caught sight of a cine-camera, went up to it and touched it. She asked in French: 'Oh, is that a cinema? I didn't know. I shall come out frightful.'[15]

The bridal pair went inside the consulate to unite their lives in law in the presence of the consul general. Eugene Higgins, Walter Berry, J. T. B. Sewell and Gladys's old family lawyer, Léon Renault, were the witnesses. What thoughts could have passed through Renault's head? A former minister of the interior, he had known Gladys since she was a baby. On the very day of her birth in 1881, he was on his feet reporting to the committee on the Divorce Bill, the Bill that Dumas *fils* believed put an end to crimes of passion. He had numbered among his clients the Abeille family, and he had dealt delicately with Mrs Baldwin's creditors. Now, before he sank into deep retirement, he was playing a supportive role in a major society event, and he dearly loved talking about society in his sonorous old voice.

Gladys knocked five years off her age on the marriage certificate. After the ceremony she and the Comtesse de Boisrouvray smoked gold-tipped cigarettes and chatted to the consul general.† Then the duke took his new duchess to lunch with the Wimbornes and to Auteuil for an afternoon of racing.

The religious ceremony took place in the height of a fierce heat-wave and drought that had descended on Paris. A wave of bad temper was in the air, but as one overseas correspondent pointed out: 'Post-war Paris would indeed hardly be Paris without a few Saturday or Sunday volleys of revolver shots in the streets or parks.'[16] A number of startling incidents took place that weekend, but nothing matched the spectacle that unfolded in Eugene Higgins's drawing room at 7 place d'Iéna.

At the last minute the Reverend T. H. Wright, 'a tall, lanky Scot, in rusty clerical garb', rector of the Scottish Presbyterian Church in Paris, agreed to conduct the service. He stood at the end of a long drawing room under a bower of green branches and white flowers with a horseshoe of white gardenias above his head. Eugene Higgins

---

* The Comtesse du Boisrouvray (1882-1976), born Pépita de Polignac, with a Mexican mother. A bohemian, who had sung in aid of the French wounded in Switzerland during the war. Her husband, Amaury, was a war hero.
† The emergence of the couple can be seen on YouTube.

had a bizarre collection of oil paintings of nudes. Every year he scoured the salons for the biggest and best he could find. Not long before she died, Gladys's mother had paid a visit to this room and was surprised to be confronted by four huge pictures of naked women, 'enough to put you off sex for life'. Thus, as he pronounced the monotonous sentences, the poor rector was obliged to keep his head buried in his books.

Because of the stifling weather the drawing room became insufferably hot and a number of the guests took refuge in the garden. A diverse company was gathered, including Princess George of Greece, Edith Wharton, the Princesse de Polignac, Elsie de Wolfe, Mrs Robert Woods Bliss, Mr and Mrs Sheldon Whitehouse, Philippe Berthelot, Marshal Foch, Anatole France and the Comtesse (Anna) de Noailles. Gladys's sister Dorothy attended, but Edith refused and no members of the Churchill family were present. Walter Berry acted as groomsman and Gladys was attended by the Comtesse de Boisrouvray's twelve-year-old daughter, Christine.

Gladys wore a picture dress of gold and silver brocade tissue in a classical style with a veil off the face, lent to her by the Duchess of Camastra, wife of her erstwhile suitor, the veil a gift from Napoleon to his wife. There was a touching moment when Irma Deodat, Gladys's old nurse, now aged seventy-nine, was carried into the ceremony. Before it she arranged the veil and later declined wedding cake in favour of a piece of bread. Gladys made an early stand for the feminist cause by insisting that the word 'obey' be omitted from the responses. The buffet was held in the garden and Eugene Higgins became increasingly agitated as he watched high heels sinking into his lawn, while canes, umbrellas and parasols were speared into the grass to free eager hands for the ice-cold champagne.

'We are both awfully poor,' replied the duke, to questions about the wedding present he had given Gladys. 'Oh, don't mention anything about that in the newspapers. One should not mention those things now, especially in the English press, with the miners starving. What will the miners think, reading about wedding presents, jewellery costing £50,000? It makes them dissatisfied, it creates trouble. You can say I gave the bride a motor-car as a wedding present.'[17]

A long photographic session ensued on the tennis court. One brave cameraman asked the couple to 'adopt an affectionate pose'.

With some difficulty, Marlborough was prevailed upon to hold Gladys's hand. After standing motionless for a long exposure, she exclaimed: 'It's like a cow watching a train go past.'[18]

There were various reactions to this marriage. Marthe Bibesco wrote to Abbé Mugnier that for Marlborough it was 'a way, for him, to go to war, and for the beautiful Gladys to climb into his tower'.[19] Linda Lee Porter, Virginian-born socialite and wife of the as yet not so famous song-writer, Cole Porter, described it to Berenson as 'the most incredibly vulgar performance' she had ever witnessed:

> No clever person could have staged anything so utterly absurd – for stupid it was. I shall never forget the picture. Eugene Higgins's ugly house: Gladys dressed in gold brocade, *moyen-âge*, long lace veil lent by Rose Camastra, and literally covered from head to foot in orange blossoms, kneeling with Marlborough shrunk into his collar, in a bower of white roses at the end of the salon, the walls of which were alive with pictures of nude women. Nearest the wedding party sat the ambassador and his wife (he has none);* the minister, of what religion no one knows but himself, combined his own strange service with that of the Church of England, and was so confused he actually said 'John Charles Spencer-Churchill (or whatever his name is) wilt thou take this MAN to be thy wedded wife?' and Walter Berry, the immaculate, the only assistant. Hordes of strange people, the Harry Lehrs, Sertes, a few Duchesses and one conspicuous Englishman, Charles Montagu. During the whole service a babble of conversation. The wedding breakfast was served in the garden, and outside the house were at least 20 photographers snap-shooting the guests, and a cinema man unceasingly turning his machine. A huge tapestry and rug were arranged under the trees where Gladys and the Duke were 'taken' in every attitude, with and without the minister. It was funny – and horrible.[20]

At four o'clock the duke and duchess left for their secret honeymoon, which was correctly assumed to be in the South of France. Gladys wore a going-away costume of pearl grey crêpe-de-Chine, with a long skirt, a black hat with trailing feathers and a cape of

---

* Linda thought the ambassador was unmarried.

flowing black crêpe. As they drove away in their motor-car, Gladys bade farewell to her bohemian freedom, taking on a palace and a man of whom she would write but a year later:

> I feel again the thrill of terror which ran through me when I read it [the engagement] in the *D. Mail*. I loved him but was fearful of the marriage.[21]

PART THREE

The Pursuit of Profit and Possessions

Blenheim Palace

Gladys in 1921

19

BLENHEIM

The duke and his new duchess returned from their honeymoon on 28 July 1921. As their car swept up the long drive to Blenheim Palace, past what Lord Randolph Churchill called 'the finest view in England', Gladys must have recognised the contrast between this and earlier visits. Rarely had she signed the visitors' book. Now the beginning of a new brief era in the palace's long history was marked by the two rather formal names side by side, 'Marlborough' and 'G. Marlborough'. Sunny was the 9th Duke from its creation, but she was the twelfth Duchess of Marlborough. She was also mistress of Blenheim. Later she told Epstein, 'I married a house not a man.'[1]

Blenheim Palace had survived many vicissitudes since its construction between 1705 and 1733. The celebrated gift of Queen Anne to the victor of the Battle of Blenheim, its architects were Sir John Vanbrugh and Nicholas Hawksmoor, with embellishments from Grinling Gibbons and Sir William Chambers. The task of creating the gardens and the lake was entrusted to Capability Brown. The lake sprang into existence when Brown threw a dam across one of the outlets. The 4th Duke of Marlborough was astonished when he saw the result, and Brown is said to have replied: 'Yes, my Lord Duke, I think I have made the River Thames blush today.' The 9th Duke wrote of his palace:

> Blenheim is the most splendid relic of the age of Anne, and there is no building in Europe, except Versailles, which so perfectly preserves its original atmosphere.[2]

The 7th and 8th Dukes dispersed many of Blenheim's treasures, but the 9th was able to rectify much of the damage with the aid of Vanderbilt money. Capability Brown had surrounded the palace with grass, but in 1904 Marlborough brought in Achille Duchêne, the French architect and landscape designer, to repave the grand northern entrance court. On the east side of the palace, where the private apartments are, a sunken garden, known as the Italian Garden, was created and completed in June 1922.

The interior of the palace was imposing, and the state apartments were hung with portraits and the famous Blenheim tapestries. The dining room at Blenheim was a ludicrous distance from the kitchen, food travelling sixty yards along the stone-flagged passage, up a lift and then fifteen yards by hand before reaching the ducal table – plenty of opportunity to get cold. When Gladys was interviewed by the celebrated American novelist Djuna Barnes for *McCall's* magazine, she told Djuna: 'This may be a palace, but there isn't one decent bathroom in the whole bloody place.'[3] Another archaic feature was the absence of a telephone. Only after a protracted struggle was one installed in 1925. It was put in the gunroom with an extension to the office, and it was rumoured, falsely, that the duke never made use of it.

There were forty servants inside the palace and as many outside, though these numbers multiplied dramatically when guests came, bringing their own entourages. The footmen were all at least six feet tall and attired in maroon coats decorated with silver braid. Their hair was powdered daily with a mixture of violet powder and flour. A hunting establishment at Bladon, staffed by ten men, looked after the twenty thoroughbred hunters and the twenty carriage horses. There was a fire brigade, of which the duke was proud. Twenty gamekeepers took care of the shooting and Lord Carnarvon recalled how sternly they were treated. The head keeper was ill one day and sent the duke a message to say that he had entrusted the business of the day to his deputy. 'My compliments to my head keeper,' replied the duke. 'Will you please inform him that the lower orders are *never* ill.'[4]

Lord Birkenhead recorded that 6,943 rabbits were killed in one day at Blenheim, the greatest number in the annals of shooting. He also remembered that one afternoon the duke pointed out of the window and screeched: 'Look, the people!'[5] The other guests assumed that nothing less than a revolution could have occurred, but all they saw was a hunched old man making his solitary way across the lawn.

In the best landowners' tradition, the duke held a meeting in his farm office every Friday. Each bailiff was heard in turn, and reported how the cattle, sheep, pigs and poultry were faring. The meetings began at 10 a.m. and could last until 3 p.m., while the prospect of lunches getting cold was ignored. If the duke received unsatisfactory replies, he frequently broke into a rage.

Some years later, Gladys invited Lily de Clermont-Tonnerre to Blenheim. Lily noted that Blenheim was heated by £2,500 worth of coal each year. The staff worked quietly and invisibly and Lily found that the 'majestic silence' of the place got on her nerves:

> English servants and Chinese servants preserve the same silence, which is almost nerve-racking. I heard the fire crackling in my room without having seen it lighted, the curtains were drawn and breakfast was brought up without my being wakened, and at ten o'clock *The Times* was insinuated under my eyes. When I went down to the ground-floor, a groom of the chambers would murmur: 'Her Grace is in the Peter Lely Saloon' or in the 'Long Library'.
>
> By eight o'clock in the morning the lawn was rolled, the dead leaves removed and the flower stands filled with fresh flowers.[6]

But Blenheim was a cold world, peopled by Spencer-Churchills. Gladys had been acquainted with the duke's heir, Lord Blandford, and his brother, Lord Ivor, since they were little boys. She and Blandford only tolerated each other at the best of times. He wrote later: 'Mary and I both found her very difficult to get on with.' There was a dinner when the duke insisted they wore white tie out of respect for his new wife. Mary Blandford put on the Catherine of Russia necklace, prompting Gladys to claim that she had one just like it, which she dared not wear, so it was in the bank. 'This,' wrote the 10th Duke, 'was untrue, as were many of her statements.'[7] Gladys noted that her husband was deferential to his son and daughter-in-law: 'Poor thing, he is like a *pique-assiette* with them and so happy if the slightest attention is given him by them.'[8] With Ivor she got on better, in the early years of the marriage, due to a shared interest in art, he being a connoisseur and collector of French paintings.

Gladys had known Marlborough's American aunt, Jennie Cornwallis-West, for many years. Jennie died on 29 June, a few days after the wedding, so may have been too ill to read a letter from Grace Curzon, wife of Marquess Curzon of Kedleston: 'I do not like the new Duchess masquerading as tho' she were a young and innocent thing into the halls of Blenheim!'[9] Her sons, Winston and Jack, were frequently at the palace. Nothing could endear Gladys to Winston. If she tried to enlist his assistance on some project, his reaction was 'You go ahead and organise. I'll help.' Thereafter, she recalled: 'He'd leave you in the boiling-pot.'[10] Of Winston's wife, Clementine, Gladys said: 'You couldn't discuss a thing with her. She had no opinions, only convictions.'[11] His brother, Jack, was much in awe of Winston possibly, Gladys taking the line that they had different fathers. On the other hand, she liked Jack's wife, Lady Gwendoline, known as 'Goonie', who appeared resigned to live with the Churchills.

Gladys became a firm friend of Marlborough's intuitive mother, Albertha, Lady Blandford, who believed that Gladys understood her son's complicated character. And never far from the scene was another powerful Churchill in the shape of Marlborough's aunt, Lady Sarah Wilson. In her day Lady Sarah had taken part in the Relief of Mafeking and had been captured by the Boers. Proud, authoritative and very much a Churchill, it was said of her: 'She could never resist a pungent comment or a withering gibe.'

Soon after her arrival at Blenheim, Gladys accompanied the duke to a nearby fair. It was the first of many efforts Marlborough made to integrate his new wife into local society, but Oxfordshire was not keen to accept her. The county was stiff with conservatism and saw no reason to take this rather eccentric duchess to their hearts. Nor did the villagers or estate workers welcome Gladys with open arms, despite her joining in with the potato pickers and labouring with them for an hour. They had been fond of Consuelo, to whom, they felt, the duke had been unkind.

Some took it to the extreme of rudeness. One neighbour, Colonel John Eastwood, who lived at Woodstock, was invited to lunch at Blenheim, but declined saying he would be in London that day. Unfortunately, the duke rode by after lunch and spotted him in his garden. A row ensued. Marlborough strove hard to have Gladys presented at court. He approached his cousin, the Duchess of Devonshire, Mistress of the Robes to Queen Mary, but she declined somewhat disdainfully. Eventually he prevailed on Lady Birkenhead to make the presentation. Lady Birkenhead was somewhat surprised to see the Marlborough state coach and six horses draw up outside her London home on the evening of 13 June 1923. After dinner, they made their way to Buckingham Palace. Gladys wore a gown made from cloth of silver with a sixteenth-century train of Venetian lace. After her curtsy to 'King Log' and Queen Mary she sat in the front row, horrified by the debutantes. A few weeks later she noted in her diary:

> Garden Party at Buc Pal to which H.M. doesn't invite me because terrified of articles published re divorced men's wives going to court!!![12]

So the razing of the court fortress was not an unqualified success.

One person in Oxfordshire who did accept Gladys was Lady Ottoline Morrell, half-sister of the Duke of Portland. The legendary Lady Ottoline, who had met Gladys with Berenson many years before, was one of the most intelligent women of her day, married to the handsome Liberal MP, Philip Morrell. She was a friend of Augustus John (who painted a striking portrait of her), and of D. H. Lawrence, Henry Lamb, Aldous Huxley and many more. She was a lover of Bertrand Russell. She kept alive a real salon at Garsington Manor.

On her first visit to Blenheim for lunch on 25 September 1921, she was impressed to find it like an Italian palace, and was welcomed enthusiastically by 'the little Duke'. Gladys was waiting inside, dressed in a white cloth dress and dark fur:

> She has too heavy and full a face – and she has evidently doctored it
> – and had tucks taken in it. Her hair is too dyed – yellow straw colour
> – she has immense blue eyes – but her heavy jaw gives the impression
> of *une grande parleuse*. She is passionate and sensual – emotional but a
> remarkably redundant brain – obviously an adventuress who has had
> to exist by her wits and has plenty of wits to draw on.
>
> She is rather the type of Margot only saner – and has better taste –
> more humour and less conceit – tactful and flattering and more inter-
> ested in others . . .
>
> The Duchess of Marlborough said she has cast off all desires now
> for possessions – and that the Frenchmen who were at the war had
> done it – the extreme had been made and had left death behind it

now. That the acquisitive sense was much the same as immortality. I don't agree with that.

She wants to know and learn things that she would not be able to learn now – The Wisdom – one 'Fourth Dimension'. What is the 'Fourth Dimension's' task?

She did not feel she was living her life – only looking on at it – like reading a story book.[13]

Lady Ottoline told her daughter that Gladys was 'the only intelligent woman in Oxfordshire'.[14] The duke thought Lady Ottoline magnificent and she was a favourite with Gladys. She admired Lady Ottoline's individuality: 'She wore large floppy hats when everyone else wore neat little ones.' She used to drop things here and there as she walked about: 'Her friends were very good to her. They used to pick them up and give them back to her. You could follow Ottoline's path by the things she dropped everywhere.'[15] They shared an interest in cats and Gladys gave a Siamese to Lady Ottoline's daughter. Appropriately Julian Morrell named it Malbrouk after the French folk song about the first duke's rumoured death at the Battle of Malplaquet. In June 1922, Gladys asked Ottoline a favour:

Do you think I cd later on send you one of my cats to make Malbrouk's nearer acquaintance? The pasha of my Siamese harem has fled to the open country these 2 months & is evidently lost forever.[16]

Unfortunately Malbrouk proved 'too near a relation' and Gladys had to look elsewhere.

In December Marlborough became a grandfather when Blandford's wife, Mary, gave birth to Sarah. Less than a month later, Gladys was pregnant, writing:

Ill all day & every day & so depressed! This poor thing is unwanted & has a pretty bad outlook to face. Why does it want to come![17]

A few days later she wrote again:

I am so sorry I am going to have a baby. I have nothing to give it. Its father won't want to leave it anything. What is it coming for![18]

Gladys felt desperately ill: accidents happened and she feared that she was dying. Her condition deteriorated: 'So ill it seemed death was coming. If only it wd. Feel so afraid & so alone.'[19] On 15 January she suffered a miscarriage and was greatly relieved:

> Glad it's over. I don't want a child. I don't want to stay here, so what wd I have done with it. Very lonely but the nurse is company.[20]

While this was going on, the duke was in London, sending undemonstrative messages: 'I hope you like the nurse . . . I trust she is of service. Pray remain in bed now . . .'[21] He was in London for her birthday, and the best he could muster was: 'You have had a horrid time – and you have been so good not complaining.'[22]

Gladys's reluctance to have a baby is indicative of her general sense of unrest, and though her spirits returned in the summer, she was easily plunged into gloom. She and Marlborough lunched with Professor Lindemann, at Christ Church, attended the Ribblesdale dance in London, and Gladys distributed the prizes after a fête at Blenheim.

On 10 June 1922, there was a large party at Blenheim at which the Lansdownes, the Birkenheads, the Beaverbrooks, the Winston Churchills, Lady Irene Curzon, Lady Eleanor Smith and others were present. Another guest was the Christian Scientist Victor Cazalet, a frequent visitor to the palace. He suggested various Oxford undergraduates that Gladys might invite, among them Lady Ottoline's nephew, Lord Morven Cavendish-Bentinck, and Lord David Cecil. Both delayed replying for two weeks so that their refusals reached Gladys just two days before the dinner. Gladys wrote in despair to Ottoline:

> Entertaining is at all times fraught with discomfort, but not to be left time to find another man without evident rudeness to him by an eleventh hour invitation is really rather trying, don't you think so?[23]

The duke was equally indignant that David Cecil had replied to Gladys in the third person and given no more substantial excuse than that he was engaged elsewhere. Despite a bad start, Gladys danced until two in the morning.

Also staying at the palace that weekend was a friend from Gladys's Paris days, the artist Jean Marchand. Gladys owned two of his pictures, one of which was dedicated to her. She had often spoken of Blenheim and was keen that he should come and see it. Marchand was a vague and humble man. In the Great War he had served as a guard on the railways. He was shy at the prospect of the journey to Oxfordshire. He survived a chaotic journey to England and took the train to Bladon. When he arrived, a footman recognised him by his beard and asked him for his luggage. The artist handed over a small paper parcel and off they went.

When Marchand set eyes on Blenheim, it was, in the words of fellow artist Paul Maze, 'as if he had been dropped on the moon'.[24] The huge doors and the Great Hall bewildered and frightened him. His little parcel was taken to his room. In the evening he prepared to come down to dinner, but suddenly lost his nerve, ran for the lavatory and hid. Gongs sounded but he did not appear. Finally, at 10 p.m., Gladys had his dinner sent up to him. The next morning she asked: '*Où étiez-vous?*'

'*J'étais perdu,*' he replied.

The next day she looked after him and showed him round the palace, at which he gazed in awe and fascination. But he was not sad to escape. Gladys knew that Lady Ottoline wanted to meet him and took steps to arrange this. 'He looks very frail, poor man,' she warned, 'but gentle & delightful as ever.'[25]

After the guests left, Marlborough and Gladys went out on the lake for the first time. She was enchanted: 'The pond lilies are closed & their leaves curled at the edges. Beautiful ecstatic flowers! The acacias gleam all white among the green leaves.'[26] Gladys enjoyed riding in the park and was now well enough to take it up again. While the duke drove out in a buggy, she would gallop down the monument avenue or attempt the jumps in the riding school.

One of their favourite neighbours, Professor Lindemann, left his impressions of Gladys's 17 June party: 'The Blenheim dinner and dance was most amusing. They had got H. G. Wells of all people, and the Duchess made him dance, a most comic business.'[27] He was also surprised to find 'numerous weird people like Jimmy Rothschild'. At another such party he amused himself by putting a roll of Debussy onto the pianola back to front, and persuading the guests that it was one of the composer's more disturbed works.

On Sunday, 25 June, the Marlboroughs celebrated a year of marriage with a visit to Matins, but a picnic at Black Bourton proved below standard and put the duke into a grumpy mood. 'Sunny reads Napoleon before dinner, after dinner & in bed,'[28] observed Gladys. The next day they attended the Christ Church Ball, Gladys loving the blue-and-white-striped tent and the clusters of pink and white lights, which reminded her of Venice.

Their life was predominantly social, with occasional visits from the old life such as Rosa de Fitz-James. One night in London, she and Marlborough stayed up until 2.45 a.m. laughing at their own jokes. They attended the wedding of Lord Porchester to Catherine Wendell one day, and that of Lord Louis Mountbatten to Edwina Ashley the next. Gladys noted: 'Bad general presents. Royal crowds in the church & Royal crowds outside. Took ¾ of an hour from St Margaret's to Brook House. Never saw so many police.'[29]

At the end of the month, she prepared for a holiday with the duke in her beloved France, telling Lady Ottoline that it had been a strain living among foreigners, and always talking English.

> I am looking forward to going home – rapturously . . . I do hope that the '*intransigeant*' attitude of France won't make unpleasantness & that having married an Englishman I won't have to feel like an exile there too![30]

After a smooth crossing on 8 August, the Marlboroughs arrived in Paris. Gladys called on her old nurse, Irma Deodat, finding her 'looking very well, but only able to move miserably'.[31] They dined with Walter Berry at the Café de Paris, and next day lunched with him and Abbé Mugnier at the Plaza. They went on to Mont-Dore for a cure. At the cinema there Gladys observed 'lots of extraordinarily common, middle class people dancing.'[32] They decided to leave for Chillon at 10 a.m. on 2 September: 'We decide, or rather Sunny decides, for he does the deciding, that we are to leave at 3, instead.'[33]

At Clarens, Gladys hoped to find traces of Jean-Jacques Rousseau's descriptions of his youth there, but instead pronounced it ugly, 'like the new suburbs of Nice'.[34] But her diary burst into life when they reached Interlaken as she described the crashing waterfalls that fell a thousand feet from steep mountains to the valley below:

There like a vision of hell a huge swift shaft of water comes through the wall of rock, falls into a basin, from it into a narrow corridor at an indescribable speed & down another fall into a second basin where the water is churned into mighty eddies, then down into a long precipitous slide into yet another huge pocket & out of sight.[35]

Gladys was forever in awe of the wonderful feats of nature. At the Jungfrau, she and the duke walked to 'our first view of the terrors of an ice-mountain, a precipitous descent down a sheer cliff & a glacier yawning at our feet, immense, deadly, overhung by huge cones of ice.'[36]

Gladys's zest was matched by her husband's reserve. He was put out by a hearty Swiss chauffeur who insisted on shaking hands with him at Grindelwald, and declared that nothing would induce him to go near a glacier. Gladys succeeded in luring him into a grotto, where she left him while she crossed the glacier, roped to a guide:

We do it in half the ordinary time so as not to keep my old tyrant waiting too long & I get boiling hot. It's a fine sight & exhilarating feeling to go up 500 feet in abt 18 minutes, walking into the steps cut into the ice along the edge of yawning crevasses.[37]

From Interlaken they went to Bern where they had uncomfortable rooms, indifferent food and bad wine. 'We go out for a walk in the drizzle & hate everything we see. Even the bears in the pit look philosophically disgusted.'[38]

Back in Paris, Gladys had her side locks electrically curled, they lunched with friends at the Ritz, were joined by her uncle, Charley Baldwin, and his wife, inspected the Broglie Rembrandt at Duveen's gallery and had dinner with Walter Berry. Then, suddenly, Gladys caught 'the grippe' and so stayed on while the duke went home.

When she was a little better, Gladys briefly relived the life that used to make her happy. Her writer friends told her they were depressed and complained that the writings of their colleagues was '*de parti-pris*, thin and boring'. Edmond Jaloux said that he was editing a new Dada review since that at least amused him, and Paul Valéry announced that he was coming to Oxford to receive an honour. As for the painters, they had been at a loss to ascertain '*lequel est le vrai but*' ever since Cézanne had died in October 1906.[39]

On 25 September Gladys returned to London by the midday train: 'I felt no more emotion at leaving my dear France than if I'd been a trunk.' But at Charing Cross she fell into a deep depression. The footman came to meet her but did not have the carriage. She found that she was not expected at Great College Street, as her wire had not arrived. She was forced to dine off cold meat and salad, since the housekeeper informed her that the shops were closed. Her mind went back to a couple she had spotted at the station with whom she could compare her lot: 'Saw a woman at the station met by a man – she danced with joy & he seemed entranced.'

Gladys remained in a state of black boredom well into October. 'I wonder how long it is before I go,' she asked herself.[40]

20

THE USUAL LIFE

Long-lasting depression overcame Gladys on her return to London. She greatly preferred Paris, despite her complaints about the noise, dirt and, surprisingly, the cooking. Suffering from a bad cold, she stayed in London, dreading the return to Blenheim. 'The mere thought of those huge rooms makes my aching legs ache more,'[1] she wrote to Lady Ottoline Morrell. But on the following Saturday, Marlborough collected her and took her back by train.

Gladys was briefly cheered by the sight of a white frost, only to sink deeper into gloom. Her diary entries grew shorter until finally all she could write was 'Ah me!'[2] Blenheim in the autumn was 'almost murderous with heavy people & talk of guns, game etc.'[3] It was an intellectual wilderness. The little statue Rodin had given her sat on a low table in the first state room, but the palace guests passed it by, neither caring nor asking what it was.

Fortunately, Gladys made what she called 'a grand and useful discovery'.[4] By pruning roses she was able to keep out of everyone's way. One Saturday she succeeded in being alone from lunchtime until six thirty. When eventually every rose was pruned, she began to search for another line of escape.

On 13 November she lunched with Lady Ottoline, who recorded:

Gladys Marlborough came here today looking I thought really beautiful – like a Greek head – but she has a vulgar soul. She declaims – and is always rhetorical – a drawing room rhetorician – or a tub thumper. She never listens to anyone else – only to contradict – and to go on her own flood. Her talk is all in cascades – quite irrespective of who it tumbles on.

She is absurd in saying she does not mind being shut out of Conventional Society. I longed to say – but you are always trying to get back into it.[5]

The last months of 1922 confirmed this, with weekend visits and Blenheim house-parties. The Marlboroughs went to Yorkshire, and stayed at Wentworth Woodhouse with the Fitzwilliams and occupied rooms lately used by the King and Queen. Gladys felt 'too seedy to get up'.[6] On 23 November she took her seat on the duchesses' bench at the State Opening of Parliament, but her enjoyment of ducal status was somewhat marred by the scornful attitude of the other duchesses.

★ ★ ★ ★ ★

At Christmas Gladys trod the neighbourhood visiting the poor and the sick with little enthusiasm. The duke got a sore throat and a temper to match, and on Christmas Day, Gladys woke at six in the morning and wept. Marlborough gave her a foot muff and Lady Sarah Wilson a workbag, the only gifts she received. On 27 December she sat alone in the palace as rain torrented down and considered her two-year-old marriage:

> Most interesting to me is Sunny's rudeness to me. Not very marked in public yet – but that will come. I am glad because I am so sick of life here.
>
> Convention & commonplace & selfishness alone voice themselves over us. *Quelle vie*! But we will separate perhaps before long & I will then go away for good & ever.[7]

1923 dawned quietly and Gladys walked in the garden, discovering primroses and supervising the rose-planting. She was nearly forty-two, and remained at Blenheim feeling listless and bored. In February she accompanied her husband to London for the second Opening of Parliament in four months. 'It's becoming a bad habit,'[8] she noted. They took their places in the South Lantern of Westminster Abbey for the wedding of the Duke of York to Lady Elizabeth Bowes-Lyon in April 1923, at which Gladys was nearly frozen. A month later they were included in the house-party at Wentworth when the Prince of Wales came to stay. Royal occasions inevitably caused problems. When Queen Victoria's granddaughter, the Infanta Beatrix, and her aviator husband, Don Alfonso de Borbon, came to Blenheim, they insisted on departing at six in the morning. Their hosts had to be up and dressed to bid them farewell.

After a visit to Holland in June, which Gladys found 'as dirty as any other country',[9] she settled once more at Blenheim. There was a memorable house-party during the midst of a July heat-wave, when the temperature sometimes reached ninety degrees in the shade. Gladys gathered the Birkenheads, the Winston Churchills, the Merry del Vals, Prince Paul of Yugoslavia, Shelagh, Duchess of Westminster, and others, and invited a new literary friend, Lytton Strachey. She enjoyed talking to him or, rather, listening to him. 'He was a pontiff, so you listened and kept quiet,'[10] she explained. After his visit Strachey wrote that nobody except Gladys had been particularly interesting. But the palace captured his imagination:

> I wish it were mine. It is enormous, but one would not feel it too big. The grounds are beautiful too, and there is a bridge over a lake which positively gives one an erection. Most of the guests played tennis all day and bridge all night, so that (apart from eating and drinking) they might as well have been at Putney.[11]

When Gladys sent Strachey a photograph she had taken of the house-party, he was amused: 'The ladies' skirts look oddly long and the tip of Winston's nose comes out beautifully.'[12]

★ ★ ★ ★ ★

To assuage her loneliness, Gladys invited Epstein to come and stay to sculpt a head of the duke. He was her main link with the art world and Gladys had been to his studio in London. Through him she became acquainted with Matthew Smith, buying his painting of red and white flowers in a vase for £50 in October 1927.

Epstein arrived at the palace on 27 July, and Gladys took him round to decide where the duke's bust should be placed. They settled on a niche in the entrance hall. At dinner there was a heated discussion as to what the duke should wear. Gladys noted: 'Epstein & I are of firm opinion it must be strictly modern – of its time. Sunny leans towards the picturesque because he hates the hard line of a collar.'[13]

Even at Blenheim, Epstein dressed in the bohemian clothes of his calling and the rumour soon spread that the duke had ordered the staff to have all of them laundered. He was apprehended several times by the gamekeepers, and enjoyed informing them that he was a guest at the palace, which, as he wrote 'always produced a comic forehead salute of flunkeys and apologies'. However, the duke made quite clear that Epstein was Gladys's guest, not his.

Differences arose at every turn. Gladys liked to have an organist come to play an hour of Bach in the morning to inspire Epstein at his work. This irritated Marlborough, who preferred jazz and announced that his idea of a great man was Luigi who ran a fashionable night-club. One day the duke showed Epstein the chapel at Blenheim where the sculptor detected no evidence of Christianity. He said as much to the duke, who retorted: 'The Marlboroughs are worshipped here.'[14]

During the next ten days he sat regularly, often for five hours a day. By the end of the month Gladys noted: 'The Bust takes on a great finesse of modelling & surface since yesterday.'[15] He was exhausted by the long sittings, which contributed to his general irritability. As the bust neared completion, Gladys had to agree that he looked a decade older than his fifty-two years.

But a row ensued about the base, Marlborough wanting to look like a Roman with bare shoulders, while Gladys and Epstein insisted on a costume. There was an acrimonious exchange, everyone got cross, and the sculpture was left as a head and neck. Epstein also attempted a second study of Gladys. This is a remarkable head, because she allowed herself to be depicted with the ravages of the paraffin wax in full evidence. It confirms her love for realism in art, with no concession to flattery. However, she never owned it.

Gladys prevailed on Epstein to finish Marlborough's bust, and work resumed in January 1926. The duke agreed to pose in Epstein's London studio, wearing his Garter robes and, at Gladys's suggestion, the hands were added. Marlborough wrote: 'He is getting on famously and he will do a fine work. The man has immense talent and is in a good temper and very pleased with the result of his efforts.'[16] As the sculptor's work approached completion, Marlborough wrote again:

We have discarded the chain [collar of the Order of the Garter] as it will be in the way – and spoil the lines of the cloak – which are good. The hands are coming out well – and are very Epsteiny – but at his best – E has taken great pains and I see a great improvement in his sense of beauty. I am tired from the ordeal and I shall be thankful when I am free. He keeps the cloak but does not work on the Garter Badge. He wanted my uniform coat – but I told him that my servant wd give notice if I did not bring it back.[17]

When completed, the bust was placed in the entrance hall at Blenheim where it has provoked contrary opinions ever since. Marlborough used to say to young Churchill cousins: 'People will think I won the Battle of Blenheim!' A society friend, who particularly disliked Gladys, said that it 'showed very much the public image'. She thought it a horrible way to be remembered. 'He was pompous, but I know masses of Dukes and unless they are particularly intelligent, they are very pompous.'[18] Sir Shane Leslie thought it brought out Marlborough's religious spirit 'as it were a Quixote designed by Greco',[19] while Maurice Ashley recalled that by the 1930s the duke 'disliked it intensely'.[20] While Blenheim profited from a bust of the duke and later of Ivor Churchill, Epstein emerged disillusioned from his efforts, 'out of spirits, and out of pocket . . .'[21]

★ ★ ★ ★ ★

On 16 October 1923 Gladys had the second of three miscarriages and retreated to the Prince's Hotel in Brighton to recuperate. She always believed this miscarriage was the result of a squabble with Marlborough in the early months of pregnancy, during which she fell against a stool. She was horrified that he allowed workmen to carry on their noisy labour when she was ill. In January 1924, after a visit to Mentmore, Gladys had an operation for appendicitis. Gradually she regained her strength, sitting up in an armchair and venturing out for ten-minute walks. In February she went to Brighton again to stay for three weeks at the Metropole Hotel, 'a very frowzly hotel famous in divorce courts as the place where defaulting husbands put up for a night with "a lady other than their wife". Certainly, one must be pushed by very interested or passionate impulses to put up with such grubby surroundings!'[22]

Gladys was alone for most of the time, though Marlborough joined her occasionally. Early in her stay she received a letter from him primarily dealing with his time of arrival, but including:

I am much disturbed by your letter. You are evidently far from well . . . Pray take care of yourself. I devoutly hope that change will do you good at Brighton. B & I are both here – both well.[23]

The letter annoyed her and she added at the foot of it: 'This is the kind of letter M. writes to help an invalid in hours of illness and loneliness.'[24]

Brighton was not empty of friends. Gladys found Lady Alexandra Curzon there, the Marquess and Marchioness of Milford Haven and Lord Alastair Innes-Ker. Lady Sackville invited her to several good lunches and she gave a lunch in return at the Metropole, after which she noted with disgust her annoyance at her fellow hotel guests: 'Great clouds of middle-class people all full of money, appetites & vulgarity.'[25] All in all she was unhappy and found even keeping her diaries disappointing: 'They do not ever tell one the weather, but there are too many things I don't want to say and the rest I forget.'[26]

★ ★ ★ ★ ★

Restored to health, Gladys returned to society, to lunch parties, to the Churchills and to Blenheim. There was some excitement in March when Winston Churchill, who had lost his seat in Parliament in the general election of October 1922, stood in a by-election for the Abbey division of Westminster. On the day, Gladys went out to see the fun 'but saw nothing but a string of cars filled with men with hooters'. Winston, standing as an Independent and anti-Socialist, was defeated by a mere forty-three votes. The duke advised him to stay detached from the Tories until he could command terms and 'get hold of the title deeds'. The following Sunday he joined the Marlboroughs for a wet day in Brighton and left by the same train as Blandford. Gladys was amused to observe as he left, 'WSC "maided" at the station by a familiar person called Locker-Lampson,* lately in the service of Ld Birkenhead',[27] as she put it.

Gladys was much occupied with this kind of gossip. She found Lord Haldane rejuvenated by ten years of being lord chancellor, Lord Buckmaster on the other hand 'very strained & ill at ease',[28] and related a tale about the Earls and Countesses of Derby and Pembroke.

---

* Commander Oliver Locker-Lampson, MP (1880–1954).

'I hear that the Derbys wdnt have Reggie Pembroke at Knowsley . . . so his wife is there & he is staying at Eaton for the Lincolnshire.'[29] In solitude in 1946, she added: '& it was said that she & Ld D . . .'[30]

In April 1924, Gladys found another solution to the boredom of Blenheim by beginning work on the rock garden. This garden had been laid down by the 5th Duke as 'a bold and rugged background' to his other horticultural plans. It was situated at the foot of the lake near Capability Brown's grand cascade, about as far away from the palace and its inhabitants as possible. Over many months, Gladys supervised the moving of rocks, the placing of steps, the clearing of undergrowth and the planting of saxifrages. At its best the rock garden was a mass of yellow flowers. Sometimes Gladys drove friends to see it in her little estate car. Not everyone enjoyed the experience as the garden was so plentifully populated with snakes that it was sometimes possible to see several slithering about at once. Her usual accomplice in the work was a local craftsman, Bert Timms, who lived at Hanborough and was later immortalised as a canephor on the West Water Terrace. They sat together at a druid's table and ate a picnic lunch. At this time, as earlier in her life, Gladys would chain-smoke, but rewarded Bert with chocolates for not following her example. Gladys enjoyed the rock garden enormously, but had to give up her work there after her third miscarriage in 1925 as she no longer had the strength. Now nature has reconverted her solitary haven to its former overgrown state.

1924 continued with uninspiring social events, though Gladys enjoyed the visit of Douglas Fairbanks and Mary Pickford on 20 April. Another visit for Paris was planned for June and she looked forward to it eagerly, as did her old 'Anaconda', Walter Berry. He had lately torn up a letter of hers, on the mournful grounds that she would never come any more. He fully understood her sense of tedium. For some time he had been trying to entice her back to Paris: 'Aren't you EVER coming back? How can you spend all your days in Hyperboria? What are you brain-cells working on?' He hoped to 'de-Blenheimise' Gladys. When plans for the visit were finalised, Berry assured her: 'Of course you'll be in at everything – and we'll gala day and night.'[31]

The Marlboroughs arrived in Paris on 12 June, as planned. Gladys was thrilled – 'in such a state of joy as never was'.[32] She promptly deserted her husband at the Gare du Nord and disappeared into the Métro 'to instantly feel & hear France, Paris itself'. For the rest of the month it was a revival: 'All my friends come beaming with joy to welcome me.'[33] There were parties for polo matches organised by the Princesse de Polignac, lunches with the Duchesse de Broglie and Thérèse Murat, dinners, dances, balls, opera, ballets and the Grand Prix. The duke returned to London on 30 June and that night Gladys dined with her 'Anaconda'. The next day she, too, left for London. 'Return to dismal England,' she wrote. 'Already at Folkestone, I am hit by the brutality and complete lack of politeness.' Depression engulfed her and during dinner it hit her that she was back in England, far from Paris, and lost anew.[34] She remained gloomy until a snatched visit to Versailles and Paris in September.

On 4 August her step-grandmother, Marraine Baldwin, died, and she received $45,716.09 of a bequest of $50,000. She commented to her uncle Charley in Colorado Springs that she believed Edith and her husband had 'really squeezed' old Mrs Baldwin dry.

On the last day of 1924, Gladys felt so ill that she did not get up. She had become pregnant for the third time but with no more success than before. A nurse was summoned to help her through several days of pain and illness. On 3 January 1925, she noted that the nurse thought 'no immediate devil expected', but the following day she became frightened and the doctor was sent for. Her final miscarriage occurred at three o'clock on the morning of 5 January, a month before her forty-fourth birthday.

Three hours later she awoke with a dreadful pain in both eyes, which had been burnt by the chloroform. The left eye was quite seriously damaged and still paining her as late as 1930. More seriously, the doctor told her that another miscarriage might cost her her life. But she wanted no children.

The early months of 1925 were given to recuperation and listless entertaining as Gladys was hostess to Lady Cunard, Lord Berners, Harold Nicolson and the Birkenheads. In March there was a lunch party for John Masefield and his wife, and Sir Frederick and Lady Keeble.

As neighbours from Boar's Hill, the Keebles were frequent visitors, usually coming to parties, but sometimes, when Blenheim was enduring an open day, they would be summoned for lunch in an underground room to which the duke and Gladys had retreated, though the tourists usually found them there. Lady Keeble was the dramatic actress Lillah McCarthy, famed for roles in Shakespeare, Galsworthy, Shaw and Masefield plays. She wrote that Gladys, 'wittiest and most brilliant of women, would make us all feel witty and brilliant'.[35] At this lunch a 'great fight' took place over Masefield's forthcoming play *The Trial of Jesus*, ending with him telling Lady Keeble: 'The Gospels cannot be translated.' On 9 May Gladys went to see the play and noted 'very adverse criticism on all sides'.

Gladys cannot be considered happy at this time. At the end of April she confided to her uncle in Colorado Springs:

No, life is not always a bed of roses & a husband impatient of anything which interferes with his arrangements makes it no easier.

Really I conclude that matrimony is a difficult & tricky business & that its success implies giving up all one's personal existence – that living in an anodyne atmosphere flat as a steppe is the best one can hope it to be . . .

This is the first time I have stayed up for dinner & I am very tired. This huge house seems to envelop me in chill spaces & like a mole I want to tunnel myself in warm darkness & fly in dreams to wild places & laughing dreams. Don't think I have melancholia because I say this. No, I have none of that only I do so wonder as most of us do what on earth life is for & what it is really meant to mean & to lead to. I fancy it is that *existence* is still that of the cave dweller's and that *life* is within us alone, a lovely glowing thing, un-interpretable, un-understandable, invisible, intangible, (un-shapeable), except to one's *self*. It is a great treasure & like treasures it must be hidden.[36]

Work began on the East Water Terraces in 1925, Marlborough keen 'to make a liaison between the façade of Vanbrugh and the water-line of the lake made by Brown'.[37] Gladys's influence was important since she had spent so much of her early life in Italy, which explains the arrival of the Bernini fountain, and the statues. She spent many hours watching progress and photographing the trees arriving in horse-drawn carts, and the Venuses being hauled down from motor-trucks and put in place. It is her unsung contribution to Blenheim's landscape – her taste, backed by Consuelo's money.

The summer passed with Gladys suffering from measles, a visit from ex-King Manoel and Queen Auguste Viktoria of Portugal and a trip to France. Once again Gladys found herself surrounded by old friends – Jacques-Émile Blanche, Albert Flament, Princess Soutzo, Elsie de Wolfe and Walter Berry. In August Lady Lee of Fareham described going to Blenheim as 'a strange and somewhat depressing experience'. Lord Lee could not decide what interested him most, Gladys or the house – while Lady Lee wrote of Gladys:

> She is very intelligent and striking in appearance, with vivid colouring and enormous blue eyes, but she is not really beautiful, as she has a heavy chin which looks like almost scarred and a coarse crooked mouth. She has also attempted to acquire a classic Grecian profile, by, it is said, having paraffin wax injected under the skin of her nose, but this appears to have got somewhat out of place.[38]

Gladys told the Lees that she was never tired, had no nerves, was not a snob and had 'no sense of possession'. They had heard a rumour that she had once declared she wanted to be a *grande cocotte*. Lady Lee concluded that Gladys was not immoral 'but merely unmoral'. She came away thinking 'she is very executive and competent and more than a match for the Duke whom A [Lord Lee] has always thought a very poor creature . . .'[39]

Interlude

McCALL'S

Gladys often hinted that she wrote articles and short stories, possibly under a pseudonym, but in old age she dismissed any such activity, including acting and playing the piano, as too much effort. However, presumably at the suggestion of Djuna Barnes, who interviewed her at Blenheim in 1922, she did write an article entitled '*The* DUCHESS LOOKS *at* LIFE – *and* LOVE'.[1] It was advertised: 'No man has ever wrecked his life on the ordinary conception of a vampire – says the beautiful American-born wife of one of England's noblest titles in this revelatory article which she has written especially for *McCall's*.'

She wrote with sardonic whimsicality about the effects of vampires on men, describing the 'typical enchantress' and sending up the kind of fatal woman that might appear in a novel by Elinor Glyn: 'the halls are mournful with the lamentations of lovers . . . she is pictured as languishing away in uncertainty and sustained only by smelling salts from Arabia'. Writing in a pre-Abdication era, Gladys was certain that no man had wrecked his life or the life of his country for love of such a conception of a vampire. 'The ship does not go ashore on the lighthouse. It goes ashore on that smiling stretch of calm, blue, gentle and caressing water just above the sand bar.' She maintained that men sought empty women to fill them with 'complete and faithful reflections' of themselves, while pointing out that the true enchantress did not wear her ambitions on her sleeve.

She then launched into an onslaught on 'the psychology of beauty and its relation to their success in life'. She maintained that women did not appreciate or use their beauty correctly, and put forward a strong case that true beauty was not an endeavour to maintain youth, 'with its bland lack of expression', but should be 'a perfect reflection' of the history of a woman's life, no matter what her calling. She liked a face to 'tell of the mind and soul behind it'. To support the argument, she wrote of the great actress, Eleanora Duse:

Such a face had Duse. What a beautiful woman she was! How ghost-ridden, how encircled, how engulfed! How she surrounded the abyss of her existence, how she championed her soul, and the tragedy that had claimed her for its own, with what pride she kept the evidence in her face, in her body, in the movement of her hands!

Gladys was all for women stressing the points that indicated their personality, even enhancing themselves with rouge and scent if it helped, but she was depressed by the almost universal fear women had of expressing individuality: 'And you cannot be beautiful and fearful, not with this kind of fear. Fear of man, perhaps, of *le monde* never, simply because it destroys every vestige of woman's individuality.' Referring obliquely to herself, she wrote that beauty of feature was of course a blessing: 'If God has been good, if He has given you a Greek nose, a perfect mouth, and wide set eyes, so much the better. But what use is it, if you do not know to what it is been [*sic*], if it does not, in its very aspect, tell the condition of the soul that is behind it.'

She was especially critical of the lack of originality in Anglo-Saxon women's way of dressing. She was aware that in Paris fashion was 'restless and unsatisfied' and forever changing, but regretted that

in Anglo-Saxon countries women make the mistake of thinking that originality in clothes is akin to freakishness, something "not quite nice." Let such women go to Paris and pass south and over the hills to Italy. When they return to their native country they may not be afraid to express their individuality in clothes, merely because the Rue de la Paix does not make that particular thing at the moment.

She concluded:

The woman who, like Duse, can lead a public life and live a private existence, this is the woman who has power and significance of character. A public life is a very difficult one, particularly in the higher circles of society. One may desire to be frank, and yet one can say so little. There is so short a time for one's meditations, there is so little privacy in which to know and to cultivate the thing that you are, that it takes a very strong nature to live in public and yet to have a private reality.

And finally she set out her philosophy, one that she would pursue to a final end in later life:

Seclusion is a blessed thing and through it one may become anything. It gave us religion, it gave us value, and it makes here and there those rare, those amazing, those ever precious women, who have come into the world, and gone out of it unafraid and glorious in their pride. They are life's successful women – the beautiful and the possessed.

21

RELIGION AND DECLINE

I have not changed my view that the human bal masqué *is* temps manqué, *I am afraid.*

Gladys to Hermann von Keyserling

Of all unlikely issues, it was religion that ultimately derailed Gladys's marriage. Sunny Marlborough had started his life as 'a total pagan', but for some time he had been anxious to become a Roman Catholic. His cousin Sir Shane Leslie thought him 'a sad and lonely man. A mystical sense had isolated him from most of his friends and family.'[1] Winston Churchill stressed his need for contact with 'the sublime and the supernatural' and how this had led him to seek sanctuary within the Church of Rome.[2]

Gladys had been furious when, in October 1922 there occurred the 'Bish row'.[3] This was one of those unnecessary issues that caused general unpleasantness. As lord lieutenant of Oxfordshire, the duke was an ex-officio member of the Oxford Diocesan Conference. The Bishop of Oxford, or the 'disgusting old Bish', as Gladys called him, publicly forbade the duke to attend any of the Diocesan Conference's meetings because he did not have 'full status as a communicant', being both divorced and remarried. The bishop stated that his marriage to Gladys was not recognised by the Church.

Gladys was incensed beyond words at the 'monstrous & uncalled for attack by the one now called here "Burgundy Burge"'. She told Lady Ottoline Morrell that the issue belonged to an era 'B.C.', and reeked of 1858, and that the attack had been inspired by Lord Saye and Sele, an Oxford county councillor, nicknamed by Gladys 'Lord Stay and Steal'.[4]

The duke had been accepted as a communicant in parishes in Oxfordshire and London and, having expressed no wish to attend the conference, the bishop's attack was in questionable taste. The press accused him of making 'a public pariah' of the duke, and his mother, an Ulster Hamilton and staunch Protestant, wrote to Gladys: 'I think the Bishop of Oxford behaved very wrongly, it was not religion, or religious what he did.'[5]

Gladys enlisted the help of her novelist friend Ethel Boileau to append her signature to a letter to the bishop. This had added weight since Mrs Boileau was the daughter and granddaughter of clergymen and had only been married once. Gladys decried the bigotry in the Church and the dissatisfaction of its members:

> I sometimes wonder & with despair if the priests of the Anglican Church know anything of the needs of the human heart – of its bitter loneliness – its painful struggle after right doing & its dumb despairs nearer to man in the tremendous mystery of the Sacrament. We ask that they sd help us to live more bravely, courageously and fully, & they hold out empty forms from which all life has long departed – a rigid ecclesiasticism which is far from the tender & merciful spirit of Christ our Master. My Lord, that Master turned once to his disciples and told them that 'The Sabbath was made for man & not man for the Sabbath.' I am impelled to ask you 'is the Church of England made for man – or is man made for the Church of England?'

She feared they were approaching 'the parting of the ways', and that unless the Church of England recognised that marriages could be annulled, a large number of its members would be driven away.[6]

The outburst soon died down, but it drove the melancholy duke to turn to Catholicism. He was instructed by Father C. C. Martindale, a Jesuit priest, later at the fashionable Catholic church at Farm Street, a balding figure with round glasses and a cleft chin, who talked with 'slow, decided and rather affected speech'.[7] Martindale was responsible for many celebrated conversions in the 1920s.

The priest was naturally cautious, but he was soon impressed by the duke's 'almost disconcertingly vivid perception of the existence and primacy of the Spiritual'.[8] However, on account of his divorce from Consuelo, he could not receive him. The duke took to attending mass as a non-communicant and became a generous supporter of Catholic causes. Normally Father Martindale saw him at Campion

Hill, but later he visited Blenheim. There was a notable dinner during the stay of King Manoel and Queen Auguste Viktoria of Portugal in May 1925. At the end of the evening, the duke showed Martindale his jewelled crucifix. Martindale judged him 'a lonely and sad man'.[9]

Martindale was never sure if Gladys was a Catholic – and neither was the duke. He knew that her upbringing in Rome and elsewhere in Europe had exposed her to Catholicism, but she eluded all his attempts to find out. When driving him from Blenheim to Heythrop, she suddenly turned and said: 'I don't believe that you are English.' He asked why not and she replied: 'Well, because you are so flexible.'[10] He felt that they had not yet confronted a principle that demanded a show of rigidity from him. He concluded that Gladys was capable of saying pretty much anything she liked.

The duke's situation changed in 1925 when Consuelo, by then Madame Balsan, applied to the Sacra Romana Rota, the Supreme Court of Justice of the Holy See in Rome, to have her first marriage annulled. This was quietly achieved on 29 July 1926. However, news slipped out, and on 11 November the story was splashed over the front page of the *New York Times*, causing an outcry that lasted for four weeks.

Bishop Manning harangued his congregation in New York, J. L. Garvin of the *Observer* argued that annulment made Blandford and Ivor illegitimate, and questions were asked as to whether a marriage that had produced two sons could be annulled on grounds of coercion. Suggestions were made that Vanderbilt money had been handed to the Rota as a bribe; the name of Winthrop Rutherfurd* was brought up as Consuelo had produced thirty-one early letters from him, and Father Martindale made clear that the duke had not asked for the annulment and all that he had paid was his train fare to London to corroborate evidence.

In the end all parties were satisfied. Consuelo's mother got as near the truth as anyone when she commented: 'This is merely one of those adjustments that come into the lives of people.'[11] Marlborough

---

* Rutherfurd was tracked down by the press and admitted: 'Yes, some 50 years ago I knew Miss Vanderbilt and I was one of her great admirers.' [*Boston Globe*, 25 November 1926]. Even so, Consuelo disguised him as 'X' in her 1953 memoirs, *The Glitter and the Gold*.

was free to be received into the Roman Catholic Church. This was done at a private ceremony in the archbishop's house at Westminster on 1 February 1927 in the presence of Gladys and others. Cardinal Bourne blessed her wedding-ring and she and the duke confirmed their consent to marriage. In gratitude, the duke gave Father Martindale the first present he agreed to accept: the Cellini crucifix he had shown him at Blenheim the night the King of Portugal dined. But Gladys remained resentful of all Catholic priests, and Niall, Duke of Argyll, an eccentric High Anglican, heard that she had screamed and left the room when Ronald Knox, a Catholic convert, and the Newman company dined at Blenheim. She told Argyll that the Roman Catholics in Britain were 'a secret political society'.[12]

Unfortunately, relations between the Marlboroughs declined after the conversion. Gladys's fears of pregnancy were aggravated by the restrictions imposed on Marlborough by his new religion, and she found that his temper, previously directed at outsiders, was increasingly directed at her.

In November 1927 she sought advice from Abbé Mugnier, who replied that the duke was just undergoing a physical crisis following his conversion and assured Gladys that he had seen many similar cases. He was sorry she was unhappy and wished she would return to Paris,[13] but even Paris was sad now, for Walter Berry had died on 21 October.

It required Gladys's uncle, Charley Baldwin, to alert Gladys to news of Walter Berry's will, details of which were published in an American newspaper. Berry loved Gladys so much that he left her $20,000, his Gauguin of Martinique, the Degas of the girl brushing her hair, a Toulouse-Lautrec of the back view of a girl seated in a chair and a leather box that had belonged to Marie-Antoinette.

★ ★ ★ ★ ★

The late years of the 1920s veered between the good and the bad. In the summer of 1926 the Marlboroughs visited Italy, explored the Villa d'Este and saw the sculptor, Canonica, in his studio. They visited the Camastras in Capri, Pompeii, and in September 1927, lunched with Mussolini at the Grand Hotel in Rome. Gladys photographed Il Duce, posing in aggressive stance, and captioned it 'Rome & its Caesar'.

On 28 February 1928, Gladys had her finest hour as Duchess of Marlborough when she gave a Leap Year Eve Ball at their new London home, 7 Carlton House Terrace. She dressed as a green pierrette with a Dresden shepherdess hat, welcomed Winston Churchill in a toga, Lord Birkenhead as a cardinal and Duff Cooper as a French Apache. Her coup was to secure the presence of the Prince of Wales, in a domino and mask.[14] The duke was delighted to entertain the heir to the throne after so many years of ostracism from the court. He 'turned into a combination of Romeo & Chevalier Bayard for quite 3 days,' wrote Gladys. 'I was allowed to express several opinions a day & no taunt abt my dislike of persons like Mr & Mrs Redmond McGrath was forthcoming.'[15]

Hermann von Keyserling materialised in the spring of 1927. He was now a world-famous philosopher and lecturer. He had hoped she would attend his lectures in London in 1926. She had explained: 'Yes my life is a very busy one, but it is probably not as full as it used to be because I have less opportunity to be alone. You see I have not changed my view that the human *bal masqué* is *temps manqué*, I am afraid.'[16]

Keyserling was now convinced that she never read any of the books he sent her, in particular not the *Veg zur Vollendong* concerning Emil Ludwig she had particularly requested. He did not realise how crushed her spirits were when, in 1929, he urged her to visit South America, 'a great continent as rich in Soul & Life as North America in material goods'.[17] That Christmas he wrote asking, as in 1908, for a photo: 'I think you know that I am the most faithful of all friends. I am practically beyond space or time. And yet I love landmarks.'[18] But Gladys sent no photos and the two fell silent for another seventeen years.

Lily de Clermont-Tonnerre could still make Blenheim look romantic. She came there in 1928:

> Silver-gilt vases modelled by Germain adorned the lunch-table one morning. The red roses, overflowing them, made a frame round the Duchess of Marlborough, so that she looked like a heroine of Shakespeare's: Rosalind in the Rose Bower. And the Duchess with her customary animation and wit entertained the Duke sitting opposite her with her paradoxes and anecdotes.[19]

Nevertheless Lily was not unaware of the conflict between Blenheim and Gladys. Sometimes the palace won, and Gladys became a solemn, dignified duchess:

At other times, light as an elf, she frisks across the flowerbeds, laughs, sheds sunlight on everything and passes with her dog through the court of honour . . . and the Palace is annihilated before so much grace and beauty.[20]

And Gladys enjoyed a last literary friendship – with the celebrated Irish novelist George Moore. Physically he was of a type well-known to her, with a high forehead, a long nose, a white walrus moustache and the dignity of an ageing sage. He loved society women. When young in the 1870s, he had tried to be an artist in Paris and had been a friend of Manet and Degas. Instead, along with Bernard Shaw, Oscar Wilde and Yeats, he had remade English literature at the end of the nineteenth century. As a young man, he had enjoyed an affair with the as yet unmarried Lady Cunard, which involved trysts in hotel bedrooms. Now in his mid-seventies, he enjoyed the attention of London society. Due to various ailments, he could be cantankerous, but one of his joys was asking young female visitors to stand naked before him.

Gladys was a kind friend to him when he was struggling to complete his last work, *Aphrodite in Aulis*. A regular flow of game arrived at Ebury Street from Blenheim to sustain him. 'Two pheasants in splendid plumage announced to me that I was not forgotten and preened my feathers for a while,'[21] he wrote. Moore had expressed a wish to see Blenheim and Gladys often invited him. She called frequently at 121 Ebury Street. Moore was always eager to see her 'and the Duke who often appears in my imagination'.[22]

In the late 1920s he fell seriously ill with prostate trouble, but pressed on with his book. In June 1929 Gladys sent him flowers. As he finished his work, he told her: 'I shall become a spectator of life, asthetising [sic] the days away in some village by the sea.'[23] His last letters showed him in a state of depression, which he hoped her 'gay voice' would dispel. In June 1930 he confessed: 'I can compose no longer. For the moment at least composition and Ebury Street terrify me like a nightmare and to escape I am going to Paris for a fortnight.'[24] After that, ill-health confined him to Ebury Street, while Gladys had her own demons. George Moore survived until 21 January 1933, a month before his eighty-first birthday.

★ ★ ★ ★ ★

In the last years of the 1920s Sunny Marlborough became increasingly bitter and disillusioned after years spent with two wives who denied him the affection he did not know how to seek. When he sold some papers to the Americans, he regretted that the injection of American ideas into Britain was a thing of the past: 'Europe, and its traditions, no longer appeals with the same force and vigour to the American feminine mind as it did in the closing years of the Victorian era.'[25]

But Gladys marked her years at Blenheim in two further ways. In August 1928 she invited the decorative and portrait painter Colin Gill* to paint her eyes on the ceiling of the portico, having first seen his work in a mural in St Stephen's Hall, Westminster. The eyes are depicted in six panels, three blue and three brown. Gladys mounted the scaffold and gave the painter a blue scarf the same colour as her eyes for him to work from. Those eyes still gaze down on whosoever enters the palace. When the Water Terraces were completed in 1930, two lead sphinxes were placed opposite each other on the first terrace. These are the work of W. Ward Willis† and bear Gladys's features.‡

In 1930 Gladys made a final effort to be sociable. She gave a dinner-party at Carlton House Terrace on 6 March to which the duke invited Arnold Bennett. Bennett and Gladys took to each other at once, and he admired her French pictures. She told him he was the first person to have done so. Later he fell to discussing one of them with her husband. The duke assured him it was a Van Gogh, Bennett was convinced it was a Cézanne, and Gladys confirmed this. Bennett concluded that he had enjoyed talking to her, 'but the bulk of the 20 guests seemed to me to have no interest whatever except sexual. I mean there were a few beautiful creatures.'[26]

Then Gladys arranged for a conversation piece, in which well-known authors would be portrayed together at tea or seated around card tables, to be photographed at Carlton House Terrace. This idea followed the success of a similar venture at Sir Philip Sassoon's house,

---

* Colin Gill (1892–1940), a cousin of Eric Gill, the first British artist to be awarded the Rome scholarship in decorative painting, served in the Royal Garrison Artillery in the First World War, and was later an official war artist. He painted Bernard Shaw in the 1920s, and Queen Elizabeth in 1938.

† (Samuel) William Ward Willis (1868–1948), artist and sculptor, known for war memorials and statuettes of racehorses and dogs.

‡ Until recently these were the only images of Gladys at Blenheim.

and her old friend Frankie Birrell assisted her in gathering a group of leading writers. Several declined but Lytton Strachey, Augustine Birrell, Harold Nicolson, David Garnett, Edward James, Edith Sitwell, Raymond Mortimer, Lord Berners and Chips Channon all appeared on the day.

The session was a fiasco from the start. The guests were assailed by Gladys's spaniels, then had to wait while the American photographer wrestled with the duke's complaints. First he forbade the use of a spiked tripod on the parquet floor. The spikes were removed, the tripod collapsed and was then fitted with India-rubber bases. Flashlight bulbs were vetoed lest the smoke would dirty the ceiling or damage the paintings. This was solved by the photographer finding transparent balloons into which the bulbs could explode.

David Garnett's eyes were caught by a 'ravishingly beautiful Chinese woman'. Lytton Strachey did not know who she was and Raymond Mortimer misinformed him that she was the actress Anna May Wong. Garnett was disappointed to learn that she was not the celebrated actress and then thought she was the daughter of the Chinese ambassador in Washington.* She was apparently the wife of the American photographer. Garnett confessed later: 'For a day or two I felt slightly sick from the violence of my attraction and the bitterness of my disappointment.'[27]

After the lengthy session, the duke served sherry downstairs and asked Garnett if he seriously thought any writer worth immortalising in this way. Garnett thanked Gladys for an afternoon 'unlike any afternoon I've spent in my life', and recommended that she invite Henry Lamb, John Banting or Vanessa Bell to paint a picture from one of the photographs. But Lytton Strachey went home, complaining: 'The exhaustion was terrific, the idiocy intense. Oh dear, Oh dear, Oh dear!'[28]

Gladys went to Eaton Hall for the Grand National and astonished the Duchess of Westminster's guests by calling for housemaid's steps and perching on them to photograph the guests at table. From there she went to Yorkshire to stay at Richmond with Lady Serena James, where she met Lady Serena's extraordinary cousin, Eve Fairfax. Ten years older than Gladys, Eve had left Yorkshire as a young girl and lived in Rodin's house in Paris. At the behest of her one-time fiancé

---

* Probably Mai Mai Sze, daughter of Dr. Alfred Sze.

Lord Grimthorpe, Rodin had sculpted a famous bust of her. Thereafter she became one of Yorkshire's most celebrated figures, travelling from country house to country house, accompanied by a 'visiting' book, given her by Lady Diana Manners in 1911. Gladys signed it twice.

The parties continued in Oxfordshire and London. Lady Keeble portrayed the Ethiopian saint, Ephigenia, in the open air at Blenheim. Rain poured down but the crowd remained motionless throughout the performance. On 30 June Gladys gave a dinner-party in London at which Edith Sitwell and Evelyn Waugh were present. Edith Sitwell sent her a book that included 'Gold Coast Customs': 'I set store by it. And you will understand it. Hardly anyone does.'[29] Evelyn Waugh noted two ambassadors at the dinner and 'about 40 hard-faced middle-aged peers and peeresses'. Gladys looked 'very battered with fine diamonds', while Marlborough wore his Garter riband and a silk turban over a bandaged eye. As Waugh left, Gladys turned to him and declared: 'Ah, you are like Marlborough. He has such a mundane mind. He will go to any party for which he is sent a printed invitation.'[30]

★ ★ ★ ★ ★

Gladys had been a dog lover since her early days, so when she found herself too weak to continue shifting rocks in the rock garden, she went to Crufts and saw how much her friends Lorna, Countess Howe, and Lady Mainwaring enjoyed showing their animals. In 1930 her uncle, Charley Baldwin, visited her and gave her some money to restart the Blenheim spaniels.

Gladys's agile mind now turned to the exciting task of breeding a champion. She entered into the business methodically and diligently, listing long, neat pedigrees, buying and selling dogs all over the country and in consequence making endless new friends, many unmet and unseen. Letters poured in from diverse places such as Exmouth, Wilmslow, Brighton and Colwyn Bay, reporting the safe arrival of a 'pup', and the happy wagging of tails in new homes. Gladys was assisted in her task by Mrs Agnes (Cherry) Grylls, who came to run the kennels at Blenheim, and in December 1932 she became patron of the King Charles Spaniel Club.

The spaniels were documented at birth: 'Babylas at 12:30' on 30 April – 'light 3 blotches'. They had romantic and imaginative names:

Benita, Ghandi, Rita, Dragée, Daffodil, Zona, Aloma, Bacchus, Bettysan, and her favourite, Snowflake.

The breeding arrangements contrasted sharply with the state of Blenheim. Lady Gwendoline Churchill's daughter, Clarissa (now the Countess of Avon), remembers a visit to the palace when she was about nine. When they arrived, she was amazed to find the Great Hall divided into dog coops and reeking most terribly. Gradually the pens spread to other rooms, partly in the same spirit of spite that caused her on another occasion to point to the duke's favourite topiary and command the gardener to 'savage it'.[31] The duke objected to the dogs on the grounds that Gladys devoted all her time to them, and allowed them to create squalor everywhere. He cursed and swore at them and searched for new stains on the carpets to show his guests.* He was disappointed if he did not find any.

Gladys was completely distanced from her earlier life. Abbé Mugnier described her as a prisoner of the grandeur of Blenheim. In 1931 Albert Flament worried that letters did not reach her: 'Your "edifice" is so vast . . . So many Duchesses of Marlborough have lived there before you!'[32] In the same year she heard that her old nurse Irma had fallen gravely ill. She immediately went to Paris, moved Irma to a nursing home and stayed with her for ten days until she died. She never went abroad again.

In the summer her favourite spaniel, Snowflake, was mated twice. At the end of July Gladys could feel the puppies and very early on 8 August they began to drop. Gladys stayed while a puppy 'of unequalled beauty' was still-born and a second born by Caesarean section the following day. But Snowflake never recovered. Her temperature rose and then she fell quiet. She did not respond to brandy on the tongue. To Gladys's everlasting sorrow Snowflake 'passed away quietly, never fully recovering consciousness since operation'.[33]

On that day Gladys wrote, 'My Snuzzles! My Danduzeau! The pain, the agony of it all!'[34] Three months later she was still writing about 'Little Danduzeau – never, never will I forget you or lose the pain of your death, my Snow, little dear Snu!'[35] In her unhappiness she feared she had caused the death by mating Snowflake too soon. Twice

---

* The myth persists that Gladys ordered doors to be cut between the state rooms to facilitate their peregrinations, but there is no contemporary or later evidence for this.

she went to London to persuade Marlborough to have the spaniel stuffed. He agreed, but the result proved nothing like the original.

★ ★ ★ ★ ★

On 13 November Gladys gave a 'coming-of-age party' to celebrate the duke's sixtieth birthday, though in fact he was only fifty-nine. The guests included old friends and neighbours, such as Lord Berners, the Earl and Countess of Carnarvon, Sir Frederick and Lady Keeble, John Masefield and his wife, Frank Pakenham (later Lord Longford) and Lord David Cecil.

One guest recalled Marlborough wearing a gold and yellow coat and the Garter and whirling round the dance floor with Constance FitzRoy, who became so giddy that she fainted. Winston Churchill and the new Lord Birkenhead (who had succeeded his father in September), surveyed the scene, smoking enormous cigars. The celebrations included a bonfire 100 feet high, which took three weeks to construct, a torchlight procession and dancing in open air. The court-yard in front of the palace was filled with glittering fairy lights, which the Marlboroughs watched from the steps. Gladys paid a local major £10.9.0d. for eggs for the party and employed Ambrose's band at a cost of £116.5.0d.

But all was not well. One night at a dinner, the duke was regaling the guests with his political views. From the other end of the table Gladys suddenly shouted at him: 'Shut up! You know nothing about politics. I've slept with every prime minister in Europe and most kings. You are not qualified to speak.' He dug nervously into his dinner. On another occasion she instigated a discussion about Communism, ingeniously involving the footmen in the conversation and creating general discom-fort. And at yet another dinner she produced a revolver and placed it beside her. A startled guest enquired: 'Duchess, what are you going to do with that?' to which she replied: 'Oh! I don't know, I might just shoot Marlborough!'[36]

22

THE UNUSUAL LIFE

The Duke of Marlborough left Gladys living alone at Blenheim in 1931. This was largely due to his general disenchantment with her, but now that the terraces were completed, he somewhat lost interest in the estate. He spent more time in London and renewed his interest in racing, explaining to his cousin, Winston: 'As you may have perceived of late, I have placed more confidence in the capacity of quadrupeds than in bipeds.'[1] He purchased the racehorse Andrea, which carried his colours in the Derby of 1932, won the St James's Palace Stakes at Ascot and, at Newbury, dead-heated in the Lingfield Park Plate, then won the Norwich Handicap.

Gladys now looked extraordinary and behaved eccentrically, but she grasped the situation that was enveloping her. When she hit back at Marlborough, she did so with venom. She accused him of unkindness, an ungovernable temper, and of being 'a very frightened rabbit where public exposure is possible'.[2] His predilection for night-clubs left him vulnerable to obvious and sordid comments. He had been in awe of, and flirting with, Mrs Redmond McGrath[*] since 1929, and Phyllis de Janzé, now aged thirty-nine, who had been his mistress, seemingly in 1919.[†]

'Gladdy' McGrath, by then fifty-two, was a woman with 'a natural vitality and zest for life that was extraordinarily infectious',[3] and had been divorced from her first husband, Andrew Kingsmill, a

---

[*] Gladys McGrath (1880–1940), daughter of Robert Johnson, married (1) 1904, Andrew Kingsmill, and (2) 1920, Commander Redmond McGrath, RN. She died tragically in hospital, having been rescued by her husband from her house, when it was bombed in the Second World War.

[†] She was with Marlborough when Lord Wimborne rented I Tatti in June 1919. They attended a concert at the Dorchester together in March 1932.

lieutenant-colonel in the Grenadier Guards, in a not unsensational case. During the Great War she had suggested that he might like to get himself killed so that she could find happiness with her then lover. As stated in court, he was unwilling to oblige. The presence of her next husband, Commander Redmond McGrath, described by Lord Birkenhead as a 'man of great height, of a leathery, weather-beaten countenance and deep, booming voice',[4] at her lunch table, in her home and in her bed, when her husband was still serving his country, prompted the judge to grant a divorce nisi. They married in 1920. She was sketched by John Singer Sargent, and her portrait painted by Ambrose McEvoy. The pair were soon established figures on the social scene.

Then there was the duke's unfulfilled romantic interest in the glamorous Canadian actress from Montréal, Frances 'Bunny' Doble, wife of Sir Anthony Lindsay-Hogg, 2nd Baronet, which was extant by 1932. Her raffish husband had turned his hand to steeple-chasing and horse-breeding, flying and fast cars, and had been obliged to resign from the Grenadier Guards for marrying an actress. They had a young son, but in the summer of 1932 she was granted a judicial separation on the grounds that her husband was cruel and had struck her six weeks after they married. When Gladys employed detectives to follow the duke, they found Bunny deep in a love affair with young Lord Birkenhead (who so admired McGrath). He was often observed leaving her house in the middle of the night.

Gladys also believed him interested in Teresa Jungman, one of the celebrated 'bright young people', as a small group of the wilder younger members of society were known. One day Gladys rushed into the room and put a ring on the girl's finger: 'The Duke's too mean to give you one, so I will!'[5]

Marlborough stayed away from Blenheim as much as possible. On rare visits, he stayed in a hotel and lunched at the Bear in Woodstock. When his mother, Albertha, Lady Blandford, died in January 1932, Gladys joined him for the funeral but that was it. Gladys was hurt when the duke yelled at her at lunch one day: 'Bah! I have no consideration for you and never have had.'[6]

Another problem was money. Gladys had enjoyed the benefit of a good income from the Deacon trust, which, at one point, had produced income of $30,000 a year for the surviving sisters. It suffered badly in the crash of 1929 and she lost her own means of support. Forced to rely on the duke for funds, which were seldom forthcoming, she took to wearing old court-dresses held up with safety-pins. She had a nineteen-year-old musquash remodelled, and also sported a patched and faded squirrel coat made for her in 1925. She complained about Marlborough's meanness, claiming to have made 150 small silk lampshades, pin-cushions for the bedrooms, and with exemplary efficiency to have mended, renovated and repaired the palace furniture, saving him, as he admitted, £600 a year.

The duke looked 'harassed and worried' at Newmarket in October 1932, according to Ivor Churchill, aware that Gladys was on the point of suing for divorce. 'That bitch Gladys was on his tracks there but we avoided an encounter,' he wrote. Evidently the duke was allowing himself to be pursued with a writ from the Treasury for non-payment of £8,000 of Super Tax, which Ivor thought was a ruse to make himself look impoverished when Gladys came after him for money.[7] Ivor was disinclined to get involved in the crisis, judging that his father and Gladys had 'lived in a world of their own creation too long to understand the customs of ordinary mortals or the rules of conduct usually considered reasonable by them'.[8]

Siegfried Sassoon offered Gladys words of encouragement: 'I am dreadfully sorry that you are unhappy, but I have an idea that you are a courageous person, so you have that to help you.'[9] In December Gladys appealed to Father Martindale, but he claimed that he hardly ever saw the duke and knew nothing of his private life. He suggested that Gladys should go away but hoped there would be no separation or divorce. The thought of further publicity made him 'seasick'.[10]

On 12 December 1932 Marlborough offered Carlton House Terrace for the reception at Diana Churchill's[*] wedding. Gladys refused to attend the service, but went to the reception, skilfully avoiding playing the charade of being seen in public as 'united husband and wife'.[11] A fortnight later, around Christmas, there were fierce rows at Blenheim, after which Marlborough forbade Gladys to come to Carlton House Terrace and declared he never wanted to see

* Diana Churchill (1904-63), daughter of Winston Churchill. Married John Milner Bailey in 1932. Divorced 1935. Later married to Duncan Sandys. She committed suicide.

her again. When he left the luncheon table on New Year's Day 1933 for London, he patted Gladys on the shoulder to look well before his guests, then walked out, taking the butler, under-butler, valet, chef and kitchen-maid with him. It was a pitiful conclusion to a relation-ship of thirty-five years.

Gladys remained alone at the palace with a handful of servants, many of whom took advantage of her plight to cause additional misery and mischief. In January 1933, angry communications between lawyers began. The duke declined to buy Gladys a new car, and refused to dismiss servants of long service, simply because they displeased Gladys. On 21 April he made a proposal via his solicitors. It began by accusing Gladys of creating difficulties, disrupting 'the tranquillity' of the duke, and failing to fortify him 'in the task of handling with circumspection the routine of household management, or indeed the responsibilities of administering the affairs of the Blenheim Estates'.[12]

The duke proposed to close Blenheim on 1 June and offered a suit-able furnished residence with kennels for the dogs, and an allowance of £2,500 per annum. Or Gladys could find her own residence, in which case he would provide £3,000 a year. Gladys was first repre-sented by Withers and from September 1933 by John T. Lewis Woods, and the duke throughout by Kenneth Brown, Baker, Baker. They made a counter-proposal and suggested that they be in touch with the duke's financial advisers.

In preparing his case, the duke levelled a general accusation of insanity against Gladys and made play of the fact that she harboured a revolver. He told neighbours that she chased him around the palace with it. Gladys once took a young friend, Sir Shane Leslie's daughter Anita,* to her bedroom and showed her the revolver, explaining that it was to shoot her husband if he ever came to her room. Interestingly, in October 1933, Gladys's lawyers confirmed receipt of 'the toy pistol, which is a flash lamp'.[13]

---

* Anita Leslie remembered Gladys looking like 'a beautiful frog' and admired her 'wicked astringent wit'. As Gladys's troubles grew worse Anita Leslie wrote to her: 'I never met anyone before who could think like you . . . I just long to be with a real person.' Clare Sheridan told her she thought Gladys had 'the brain of a man', and Anita Leslie wondered if this was a compliment.

As early as January 1933, the distinguished Oxford physician, Sir Farquhar Buzzard, wrote that Gladys's eccentric behaviour during the previous two years 'had led to great difficulties in the domestic life at Blenheim with the result that the Duke is suffering from considerable nervous strain'. He advised the duke 'to keep away from Blenheim'.[14]

In contrast, Gladys took a statement from Dr Raby, who merely alluded to the duke being concerned about 'a profound melancholy which had taken hold' of her, 'caused as he thought by a strong sceptical and pessimistic attitude of mind and which he strongly feared might lead to anything'.[15] The duke's lawyers weighed in:

> The conduct of Her Grace is – to say the least – most strange and her mode of living seems inconsistent with the position one is entitled to expect from a person in her station of life. She appears to do things which it is difficult to regard as normal and whether her actions and her strange conduct are, as some of the evidence suggests, the result of drugs is a matter for still further investigation.[16]

They declared that there were twenty dogs, five of which were kept in the living room and the bedroom of the palace, 'spoiling, by their habits, some valuable antique covers'. They concluded:

> In addition the carrying of a revolver, the walking about with it at night and other important incidents are indicative of a strange mind and gives rise and credence for persons to remark, as they do, that Her Grace is strange.[17]

And they claimed that Gladys, now aged fifty-two, was 'in her temper and fury making it as uncomfortable as is possible for the servants who remain, and some of the servants have been almost in tears in consequence of your client's effort to right dog filth in her bedroom'.[18]

Edith Hollis, caretaker for the Bothy, a house on the Blenheim estate, for the previous eight years, was prepared to testify that dogs lived in four rooms, that carpets were spoilt, settees damaged, and the legs of chairs from their 'filthy habits', that twenty or thirty maids had left, and that for four years the duchess had possessed a six-chambered six-inch revolver, which she had seen on several occasions. She would cite an incident with the revolver from July 1932. In her car Gladys had announced: 'Oh Heavens, the safety catch is not on it.' She had then pointed the revolver directly at Mrs Hollis, some fifteen inches from her face, saying: 'Would I not like to have a pop at someone? This is for road bandits.' There were further stories of Gladys 'foaming at the mouth', shouting at Mrs Hollis, and on roaming in the Long Library on night, about to give fire, convinced that she had strayed on a burglar.

The duke's chauffeur was prepared to state that Gladys could be, by turns, charming to everyone, but at other times 'she would be very dogmatic and excitable, waving her hands about, especially when expressing her disapproval.' On one occasion she produced a society magazine and pointed out: 'This is one of His Grace's last year's flames.' There were other statements about people who visited her, such as Dr Raby, who came three or four times a week in a period of three to four months.[19] His visits supported the allegation that Gladys took drugs.

In March 1933 Gladys turned to her stepson, Ivor, for help. He explained that he wanted to show friendliness 'without being actively disloyal to my father'.[20] In April Gladys made it quite clear that she 'would not under any circumstances bear to live with [the duke] again'. Her solicitors proposed that she should be granted an annuity of £10,000 and provided with a suitable residence, furnished 'in a way suitable to the needs of our client'.[21] The proposal was rejected; but Gladys waited, advised that a divorce petition might not be successful, and could be disadvantageous financially.

Gladys was still at Blenheim in May 1933, claiming to have but nine pounds in her bank account. One weekend she expected nine guests, but at the last minute she received a telegram from Marlborough forbidding her to receive them. Rather than have them turned away at the gate, she cancelled the invitations. Marlborough's solicitors then informed her that Blenheim was to be closed down at the end of the month and the cook, butler and kitchen-maid dismissed. Her solicitors protested that no suitable provision had been made for her. Neither had she anywhere to go, since the duke had made clear that if she arrived at Carlton House Terrace she would be thrown out. 'The action of the Duke in this matter is most humiliating to the Duchess, harsh and cruel,' they wrote.[22]

Gladys was in London for a while, but returned to Oxford, putting up in a hotel and going over to Blenheim each day from 26 May, eventually moving back in for two nights. Three days later she summoned a van and a motor to remove her possessions and her dogs. The agent, Mr Sacré, who had been left in charge at the palace, questioned the authority of Mrs Grylls, who was supervising the loading. Gladys was obliged to call for a young solicitor from Withers & Co. to come down to see that 'no further insolences' were done to her. After his arrival, the agent, secretary and housekeeper went to ground. The vans were loaded. Gladys, nothing if not formidable in the face of adversity, stood on the steps of the palace photographing the scene. 'Goodbye to all that!' she wrote on one of the pictures, and noted: 'It was a lovely day.'[23]

The following afternoon Princess Lida Thurn und Taxis* arrived at Blenheim and Gladys left in a car with her. She went to Seaford House, Southampton, to recover, and never again crossed the threshold of Blenheim Palace. Quiet days followed.

Throughout June and July Gladys occupied a room at the Carlton Hotel in the Haymarket. On 1 June Marlborough's solicitors informed her that the duke would no longer be responsible for her bills. 'We shall be glad to hear that your client will observe this request,' they concluded, 'as our client does not wish to take other steps to make this fact generally known.'[24] A so-called voluntary allowance of £250 a month was paid to her.

Support came to Gladys from Lily de Clermont-Tonnerre, who declared Marlborough's behaviour 'scandalous'.[25] She urged Gladys to hold firm to her rights and hoped that she would not forget Paris or Paris friends. Gladys began to move in society once more to prove she was normal. In June she found time to discuss Proust with Harold Nicolson; she attended Wimbledon, and on 14 July she went alone to the wedding of Chips Channon to Lady Honor Guinness.

The duke, meanwhile, was swift to return to Blenheim where he reclaimed the rooms so recently occupied by spaniels. In July his sister Norah came to stay with him and found him alone there, 'glad to

---

* Princess Lida von Thurn und Taxis (1875-1965), born as Eleanor Nicolls, a millionaire American, twice married, and the subject of many matrimonial and financial controversies.

have the house again to *himself*.[26] The bad state of the palace fuelled the Churchills and the establishment in circulating stories that Gladys was mad. The duke told Dorothy Hilton-Green* that Gladys was impossible, and would 'certainly be locked up within a year';[27] to which Mrs Hilton-Green laughed and replied that, on the contrary, Gladys was an extremely intelligent woman, far more so than he or any of his family had ever been. But the sad truth was that such accusations reduced Gladys from 'a woman full of life' to 'a broken woman, in health and spirits'.[28]

He was anxious to find out who Gladys had invited to Blenheim, but she had removed the visitors' book. When it came back, the duke had it engraved 'Family Heirloom' to prevent its further travels as and when future duchesses departed (and several did). Meanwhile, his eccentric way of dress caused comment. Ethel Boileau told Gladys: 'I hear Ogpu† looked too extraordinary at the Newmarket sales last week in a golfing jerkin with zip-fastening – Also he went to a public dinner the other day in slippers.'[29]

Following the duke's departure for Blenheim, Gladys was instructed by her lawyers to move into 7 Carlton House Terrace to protect her valuable possessions there. Much to the duke's annoyance, she began a vigil, which lasted nearly ten days from 27 July, during which time Diana Guinness, Patrick Balfour and the Duchess of Hamilton and Brandon came to call on her. She was visited by her doctor, and fruit, eggs and the *Daily Telegraph* were delivered regularly to the house.

Events took a sinister turn on the morning of Saturday, 5 August, in the midst of an uncomfortably hot bank-holiday weekend. The butler knocked on Gladys's door to inform her that the head housemaid, who was apparently in the habit of entertaining a lover at the house, had obeyed secret instructions from Marlborough and admitted three men. These individuals, smoking pipes and cigarettes, proceeded to lock up the linen closets, the glass and china closet, to cut off the electric light, throw the food out of the larder and lock that too.

---

* Dorothy Hilton-Green (1890–1966), daughter of Lord Henry Grosvenor.
† A joke name for the duke, adopted by Gladys, OGPU being the secret police of the Soviet Union from 1922 to 1934.

Gladys rang the police, then succeeded in contacting some friends, who promptly came to join her at the house. One of them was Herbert Pell, an American friend of her family, who used to take her and her sisters out driving in Italy in happier days. He gave up a holiday at Cowes with his family to come to her rescue. Here is Gladys's account of her altercation with the men:

> I then went downstairs & found the 3 men with their hats & caps on their heads, smoking & laughing loudly together in the inner hall. I asked them who they were and they answered 'Is Gryce the dook of Marlborough' had given the whole house into their hands. I said I did not believe them & they must leave at once. One said 'No we won't, we've a right down here & you can only have the use of the bedroom.'
>
> He had a pipe in his mouth as he spoke. I said 'Please take that pipe out of your mouth & you others put your cigarettes out.' He turned away & spoke the following words to me over his shoulder with the pipe still between his teeth, he said 'you have no right in this house. We are here with the Dook's orders.' I then reached for the pipe & knocked it out of his mouth & the others threw their cigarettes behind the stove in the lobby![30]

Gladys telephoned Blenheim and spoke to Phyllis de Janzé. She asked her to 'felicitate Marlborough on his procedure'.[31] Over the next few days the telephone, the gas and the lift ceased to operate, and the surly detectives began to wedge the basement door to prevent Gladys and her friends coming down. Meanwhile Gladys ate cold dinners by candlelight, water for baths was heated by coal, water for tea and coffee was boiled in a saucepan over a coal fire and, after the gas was cut off, all food came from cans smuggled in by a kind neighbour.

At length the situation became intolerable. Vans arrived to take away Gladys's possessions on 8 August, lawyers talked furtively outside, and a journalist from the *Daily Express* loitered for a story. At ten fifteen that night Gladys and her friends left the house, while the butler made a last-minute check to see nothing further was amiss. Gladys went back to the Carlton Hotel.

Two days later, with a flourish of the pen, Marlborough made a new will, cutting Gladys out once and for all. The solicitors resumed their flow of letters with renewed enthusiasm, each 'regretting' the action of the other's client, failing to 'understand' the accusations made, and refusing to budge on either side. Gladys was forbidden to take anything more from Blenheim without prior appointment. Methodically she listed her claims, which included the stuffed remains of poor Snowflake, still in dispute as late as May 1938.

News of Gladys's precipitous departure travelled to Florence where Berenson heard the story from her sister, Dorothy Pálffy. Nicky Mariano, Berenson's secretary, gathered that Marlborough wanted to remarry. But the hoped-for bride, 'Bunny' Doble, remained married to Sir Anthony Lindsay-Hogg until the following year. Lord Birkenhead, a more welcome suitor, whose mistress she had been for two years, then dropped her summarily and proceeded to marry Sheila Berry, daughter of Lord Camrose, in May 1935.

Support poured in for Gladys. The Duchess of Hamilton offered to have her dogs in Scotland and the Princesse de Polignac hoped that 'satisfactory arrangements may be made to ensure' her future comfort.[32] Lily de Clermont-Tonnerre was horrified to read an account of what had happened and urged Gladys to 'try and stand the nasty circumstances for a time' as she was in the right. 'I think M has lost his head and all sense of decency!' she declared.[33] 'But what an adventure, dear Gladys!!'[34] wrote Édith de Beaumont; and Ida Mathews, who ran a nursing home for cats and dogs, offered any help she could give: 'Your Grace, remember the happiest time of my life was with you. And how I have regretted ever leaving "Your Grace's" services . . .'[35]

But the best letter came from the extraordinary Viscountess Churchill in Paris. Verena Churchill was a sister of the 'Yellow' Earl of Lonsdale; she had survived a sensational marital feud with her husband, which had involved gun play, the hiring of Arabs to kidnap children, threats of disinheritance and the scattering of virtually all their material possessions, only to become a disciple of the Theosophists and a close friend of a creature called Kathleen Ellis, a woman with hypnotic grey eyes who practised automatic writing. Verena Churchill spent her last years alone and deserted.* In this crisis, Verena was Gladys's keenest ally:

---

* For an account of these dramas see *All My Sins Remembered* by Viscount Churchill.

I feel full sympathy for you . . . Both [Kathleen Ellis] and I know all
the ungentleman-like tricks that the family we both had the misfortune to marry into can do – the lies and spite – are you now called a
lunatic as I was? – such an easy thing to say & such an unchivalrous lie
to start . . . I feel so deeply for you for it is so horrible to see one's
name in all the papers & unless anyone knows the ways of the Churchill
family AS I DO how could anyone know the truth – I do not even
have to ask about it all – for I know Churchills only fight women and
children & persecute them – but never men in any position to retali-
ate . . . Why not leave it all & come to Paris later on – one gets so tired
of all their lies and malice – But in time of course lies are shown up
– It is all a question of time 'For the wheel of God grinds slowly but
it grinds exceeding small.'* . . . I wonder if your letters are opened as
mine were. If so I hope they will like this one.[36]

---

* A misquotation from Longfellow's *Retribution. From the Sinngedichte of Friedrich von
Logau*: 'Though the mills of God grind slowly, yet they grind exceeding small;
Though with patience He stands waiting, with exactness grinds He all.'

Gladys as a bride, 1921.

Blenheim Palace with the 'crooked lawn'.

A house party on 8 July 1923, photographed by Gladys. In attendance, among others, was Winston Churchill (partly hidden behind Lord Birkenhead, left), Lytton Strachey (bearded left) and on the right the Duke in a white suit.

Gladys learning to use a 'cine'.

The Duke, less than well.

A 'selfie' of Gladys with her
Russian Imperial tiara, 1927.

Gladys, a portrait.

The Duke with Monet
at Giverny, 1924.

A conversation piece at Carlton House Terrace, 1930, featuring
(left to right) Edward James, Harold Nicolson, Lord Berners, Edith Sitwell,
Chips Channon (hidden), Raymond Mortimer and Gladys.

The Duke in the rock garden at Blenheim.

A rooftop view from Blenheim, photographed by Gladys.

Colin Gill and his assistant painting Gladys's eye under the portico, 1928.

The Duke studying a statue on the new terrace.

The Duke turning away from Gladys's sphinx.

'Goodbye to all that' – Gladys's departure from Blenheim, May 1933.

'The Noble Duke of Marlborough's Ignoble Antics', during the siege of August 1933.

What Gladys called 'the unusual scenes' at Carlton House Terrace in August 1933. She was under siege. Detectives locked the basement. Finally she had to leave.

Happy Blenheim spaniels.

Mrs 'Cherry' Grylls, Gladys's companion at Mixbury and Chacombe.

Andrei Kwiatkowsky at Chacombe, photographed by the author.

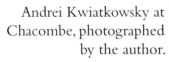

23

LITIGATION AND DEATH

Gladys mustered a strong case against the duke. Since May 1933 she had provided the famous agent Maud West* with photographs of the duke and she soon had detectives monitoring him. On at least two occasions, Gladys joined the detectives in the hunt. They 'commenced observations', noting the comings and goings of a gentleman in a grey overcoat and brown felt hat – confirmed to be the duke. On 27 May he was variously spotted at 44 Connaught Street, the home of Frances Doble; at 18 Chapel Street, the home of Phyllis de Janzé; and later at Lower Grove, Grove End Road, where Mrs Redmond McGrath lived. In June Maud West's detective agency monitored Frances Doble's house, where a young man was frequently seen – young Lord Birkenhead – not the duke.

On the night of 19 July, Gladys was called from the Carlton Hotel when the duke took a fair-haired lady back to Carlton House Terrace, and saw him escort her back to a service flat in Queen's Gate some time later.

On 1 August he was observed attempting to visit 18 Chapel Street, and later Lower Grove House in St John's Wood. He went in, as did another gentleman, and both left at 1.20 a.m. On 19 August he was seen leaving the Chatham Grill with 'Miss Doble'. More promisingly he was seen to kiss a lady in a taxi several times on 19 September.

The most damning evidence was extracted from a taxi driver. The duke had been dancing with 'a fair young girl dressed in green',[1] presently identified as a nineteen-year-old dancing teacher,[†] at the Café de Paris, after which they both entered a taxi at 1.10 a.m. on the night

---

* Her extraordinary life has been told in Susannah Stapleton's *The Adventures of Maud West, Lady Detective* (Picador, 2019).
† Freda Mavis Deeming (1913–69), twice married.

of 22/3 June. The driver was at first told to drive to Compton House in Devonshire Street, but then told to head slowly towards Kensington:

> During the journey I could see through the glass, and on occasions turned round, when I could see them kissing and cuddling; he was messing her about, and she had her clothes disarranged with her dress up to her waist . . . I heard the lady say while in the cab, 'Don't be silly, haven't you had enough?' After the lady alighted she rearranged her clothes and hair. In my opinion sexual intercourse took place in the cab because she laid right back and he on top of her . . . I often pick up couples of this description from the Café de Paris.[2]

In November the celebrated QC Sir Patrick Hastings gave his opinion that the cab driver's testimony was sound, adding that the man 'went so far as to say he could feel the motion of the springs at the back of the cab, which moved as though there was an act of adultery taking place, and moreover the position of the parties would convince him this was so'.[3]

Gladys's divorce petition, which was never served, listed many grievances – that the duke had treated her 'with great neglect, cruelty and unkindness and frequently assaulted her', that he had only visited her on rare occasions in the past three years, showing her a complete lack of consideration: 'He has treated her as a nonentity in her own house, has frequently violently abused her and his general conduct towards her has seriously affected her health.' The incident of the black eye on 6 May 1927 was cited (and a witness statement obtained from Lady Ravensdale); he was accused of 'knocking her down and kicking her in the ribs' at Carlton House Terrace in the same year, that around Christmas 1932 he 'flew into a violent rage, made grimaces [at her] and told her to run away with any man she liked', and that on 5 August 1933 he had made their London home uninhabitable, cut off the water and electric light, 'thereby terrifying [her] and causing her great alarm and distress, injuring her health'.[4]

Affidavits were obtained from a number of the staff at Blenheim, and Gladys herself prepared a statement for the court room which, if delivered, would have hit the headlines of every national newspaper. After listing many iniquities, her hardest description was to liken him to the villain in *Hatter's Castle*, the then popular novel by A. J. Cronin:

The keynote of the Duke of Marlborough's character I found in Brodie in 'Hatter's Castle' and his mood towards me is – 'I'll wipe them out as I destroy all who offend me. I'll smash everybody that interferes with me. Let them try to do it. Whatever comes I am still myself.'

A black, vicious personal pride like a disease that gets worse and worse.[5]

Solicitors' letters crossed throughout 1933 and 1934; the financial settlement was the subject of much haggling. Gladys pressed for a court case to 'let a little air into the stuffy atmosphere prevalent about my affairs & possessions'.[6] One picture in dispute was by Jozev Israëls. Gladys was furious that Marlborough would not hand it over:

I cannot imagine why you did this thing except as another general exhibition of your unwarranted ungrateful & terrifying hatred of me who have served you during my whole life with such unselfish & absolute devotion & love.[7]

Gladys stayed either at Carlton Hotel or with friends. Mrs Stobart Whetherly often invited her to Ebrington Manor, and in March 1934, she visited York, where she wrote in Eve Fairfax's book a quotation from Baudelaire: '*Conseil d'un poète – soyez toujours ivre, de vin, de vertu ou de poésie, à votre guise.*'*[8]

By and large, Gladys adopted a philosophical acceptance of her plight, writing in an album: 'After the foregoing horrors – life went on – it always does!'[9] She made an occasional foray into society. Dressed in pale pink, she attended Lady Londonderry's Eve of Session party and the next day took her place at the Opening of Parliament. She ran into Winston Churchill at a dinner in aid of the Ex-Services Welfare Society at the Mansion House, attended by the Duke of York. Churchill informed the duke that they had exchanged a quite polite: 'How d'you do'.[10]

Worries included writs from department stores, Cartier suing for non-payment of bills in March 1934, while in November 1933 a

---

* 'Advice of a poet – be drunk always, on wine, virtue or poetry, according to your taste.'

libellous cartoon appeared in a magazine called *Hooey*. This showed two rose trees intertwined and kissing. On one side a gardener was talking to a stout lady and in the background was a large house. The caption read: 'I guess we shouldn't have planted the Duchess of Marlborough and the Rev. H. Robertson Page in the same bed.' Though the choice of her name had clearly been random, and Mr Page had been president of the National Rose Society in the United States and had never met Gladys, she sued the distributors in an attempt to have her name cleared. The action was not heard until January 1935, which meant she had to endure a further fourteen months of legal correspondence.[11]

In May 1934 Gladys took a much-needed rest-cure.

★ ★ ★ ★ ★

DEATH OF THE DUKE

Just as divorce proceedings were ramping up, there came disturbing news from Blenheim. The duke's health had gone into sharp decline. On 25 May F. V. Enoch, the electrician at Blenheim, warned Gladys:

> He is in a very poor way now – looks as though he might die any day. We all think that he won't last very much longer. We understand that he is going to town for a few weeks & then going abroad, but his plans are so quickly changed.[12]

The duke went to France to see doctors, but his case was hopeless. They sent him home to die. He crossed back to England on the same boat as Ian Malcolm, who observed what he called 'the cross of Fate'[13] on his forehead. The duke was ill with inoperable cancer, which had originated near the liver. He was a difficult patient to treat and would cut his doctor short with the words: 'I know I have a filthy inside and my tongue is always dirty but that is nothing to worry about, look at me. I am a much better man than most people of my age.'[14] On a last visit to Blenheim, he called on his neighbour at Coombe, Ursula Cottrell-Dormer. He asked her: 'Tell me – do I look as ill as everyone says? Do you think I look pale or yellow?' She was horrified when he struggled to get into his car.[15]

Soon after this, he chanced to meet Lord Castlerosse in the street. 'I am feeling seedy,' he said. Castlerosse said he hoped the warm weather would do him good, but forgetting his advice to Proust, the duke merely shook his head. Castlerosse was interested in the duke's obsession with his health: he never immersed himself fully in a hot bath for fear of cardiac arrest, he danced for exercise, seldom smiled, and ate and drank in moderation. 'Valetudinarians seem to die young,' commented Castlerosse, 'and the duke was no exception.'[16]

Back in London, the duke gave a last dinner party at Carlton House Terrace. A maid at the house telegraphed Gladys regularly with news of his decline. Shortly before his death he was visited by his sister, Lady Lilian Grenfell, and told her he hoped to recover. But Ivor noted that his father spent much time lying on his sofa, 'prattling away' about the past, not strong enough to see people, but not seem-ingly in pain, which was fortunate since he believed suffering to be part of Christian life and refused morphia. Only when he was uncon-scious was it administered.

His strength ebbed away. On the last night of his life he gave a tea-party for close friends, including Winston Churchill. Father Martindale later testified that he took the sacraments seriously: '. . . after his confes-sions he would be like an old man; he would lean upon one's arm; and after his Communions he would be as it were dazed with the magni-tude of the mystery to which he had been admitted'.[17]

Marlborough died painlessly on Saturday, 30 June 1934, at the age of sixty-two. Blandford succeeded to the title as 10th Duke.

Long obituaries were published in the newspapers, listing his accom-plishments. Winston Churchill wrote some lines about his 'oldest and dearest friend'[18] for *The Times*, and Castlerosse noted perceptively:

> To me he was a pathetic figure like a lonely peacock struggling through deserted gardens . . . The Duke of Marlborough was the last duke who firmly believed that strawberry leaves could effectively cover a multi-tude of sins.
>
> I for one shall miss him, and it is a sadness for me to think that this man of brains spent his life sowing seed after seed where none can ever grow.*[19]

---

* Marlborough's brother-in-law, Sir Robert Gresley, was infuriated by Castlerosse's article and described him as a bounder.

A general theme in the letters of condolence was that the duke had been a 'disappointed' man. Lord Londonderry thought his childhood had been mismanaged, and that pessimism had set in.

Muriel Warde, the girl he should have married, wrote to Winston Churchill, making the point that, though he was 'whimsical and difficult', he had a 'charming and delightful character', which only those who really loved him appreciated. She had seen him most days, even two days before he died. She added a sinister note, which shows how extreme feelings had become, but echoed that written by the Comtesse Greffulhe in 1907:

> I think he half knew – it was the end tho' too weak to concentrate on anything except the past & thank God he never mentioned Gladys to me again, so I hope that horror had been forgotten, I mean the idea that she was working in her mind to kill him . . .[20]

Marlborough's funeral was held at Farm Street with Churchills present in force. King George V, who had long kept the duke at arm's length, was politely represented by the Marquess of Salisbury, an honour due to the duke as a lord lieutenant and Knight of the Garter. Hovering at the portal of the church, Father Martindale (who gave an address) dreaded that Gladys, or even Consuelo, might suddenly appear, draped in widow's weeds, but neither came. Inside the church, the Protestant mourners were confused by the candles they were given to hold and some burnt their fingers, not daring to extinguish the flickering symbols.

After the service the coffin was conveyed to Blenheim for burial in the chapel that had so confused Epstein when he saw it. Shane Leslie was one of those present and was much moved as he followed the hearse through the long avenues that Marlborough had planted. He walked beside Winston Churchill and they discussed the survival of the spirit. Later Churchill greeted Blandford and addressed him sonorously: '*Le Duc est mort. Vive le Duc.*' Churchill also consoled Lady Lindsay-Hogg (Frances Doble) with kind words to her on the train. Meanwhile, Enoch reported to Gladys: 'The attendance at the funeral was very small and there were only 56 wreaths altogether.'[21]

Inadvertently Gladys had now become the duke's widow. She remained in the country. Nancy Mitford and her sister Diana Guinness noticed the sadness that fell over her, despite recent bitterness. Many wrote to her, some aware of the separation, others not. Gladys acknowledged all the letters, even the remote ones, which helped her through this difficult time. Lady Edward Spencer-Churchill, Marlborough's great-aunt by marriage, wrote to her:

> I know you will feel deeply the termination of a life that for many years had been closely connected with yours. Blenheim looked very lovely yesterday in bright sunshine when it gave its last welcome to the owner who loved it so well.[22]

Lily de Clermont-Tonnerre wrote:

> Of course you must feel it and only remember the best period of your lives . . . You shall no more be upset by him, and stay for ever – the one who adorned his home for many years![23]

Ethel Boileau hoped it had not been too much of a shock: 'I hope at least he had time to be sorry – and feel some regret.'[24]

Perhaps the strangest letter of sympathy came from Nell St John Montague,* the society clairvoyant, who had predicted the blood to be shed at the wedding of King Alfonso and Queen Ena of Spain in 1906 and the sinking of *Titanic* in 1912. She wrote to Gladys: 'Yes, I remember *very* vividly telling you that I saw you would soon be freed of the Duke's death . . .'[25]

---

* Nell St John Montague (1875-1944), born Eleanor Lucie-Smith, married Henry Standish Barry. She predicted her own violent death from a bomb, and in contemporary obituaries, it was stated that Lord Louis Mountbatten was destined to die in a watery grave.

PART FOUR
Renunciation

And finally the renunciation of all that
(Renunciation, it says, is the most rewarding stage)[*]

Chacombe Grange Farm

Gladys in 1935

24

MIXBURY

The new Duke of Marlborough, the tenth to bear the title, left a house he loved in Leicestershire to move into Blenheim, the second largest house in England, but still with only one bathroom. He described the interior as having been 'neglected' and he was beset with death duties.

Writing memoirs in later life (as yet unpublished), the new duke was less than generous to Gladys. He dismissed her: 'She really became more and more impossible and my father very soon tired of her.' He cited her work in the Rock Garden as causing disruption to the outdoor staff, and the misuse of the Bow Window Room as a whelping ground for her favourite bitches. He claimed that not only were carpets and curtains ruined, but floorboards needed replacing. He accused her of removing many things from Blenheim. He wrote that his father led a 'solitary' life at Blenheim, and blamed her for 'the rapid deterioration in his health', which happened soon after the separation, and 'was to end in his death'. But he, or perhaps his collaborator, David Green,* praised the sphinxes: 'They remain to this day magnificent, perpetuating on his part an infatuation and on hers the serenity and composure of classical beauty.'†¹

On 4 August 1934 Consuelo returned to Blenheim, one of the palace's first visitors under the new regime. She saw the completion of Marlborough's constructions, made possible by Vanderbilt funds.

---

* In the autumn of 1947 David Green was about to embark on a history of Blenheim for *Country Life* and asked Mr Sacré, the land agent, what he thought about getting in touch with Gladys. Sacré advised against this, describing her as 'a dangerous woman . . . since all the trouble caused by her and her Blenheim spaniels'. [David Green unpublished diary, Bodleian Library.]

† Writing in the early 1970s, he noted dismissively: 'She is still alive but since she was only a few years younger than my mother she must now be of a great age.'

For the rest of her life, she enjoyed her role as mother of the duke, paid many happy visits there to her son and grandchildren, and helped Blenheim by paying for a complete overhaul of the palace.*

Gladys, now Dowager Duchess of Marlborough, seemed to the world to have disappeared into smoke. She adopted the name of Mrs Spencer, 'half of "Spencer-Churchill" as a joke name I took for use in the derelict hamlet of Chacombe for fun'.[2] Sometimes she signed herself 'The widow Marlborough', explaining, 'I like that way of appellation better than the meaningless & slightly absurd "Duchess".' She was anxious to sever all connections with Blenheim and was, of course, at liberty to adopt any name she liked: 'I loathe & detest that of M. & I spent enough money trying to get rid of it.'[3]

Because Gladys had remained hidden during Marlborough's obsequies, journalists began to sense a story and went in search of her. They traced her to Mixbury, a small village near Brackley in Northamptonshire. They sniffed about for a while and then investigated Town Farm, officially occupied by Mrs Grylls, who was still looking after dogs, some of which were hers and some Gladys's. The journalists discovered that Gladys did her own shopping in the village stores, wearing a smocked overall. When one of them attempted to enter Town Farm, an upper window opened and Gladys tipped a jug of water on to his head. Presently, security guards took up position around the house until the furore had died down. Reports of this incident appeared in newspapers, stories of a hermit's life and a hundred spaniels, unfortunately becoming a well-remembered and often exaggerated tale, which ended by implying that Gladys had gone crazy and greeted all visitors in this fashion. In Paris Abbé Mugnier reported to Berenson:

> Yesterday the old Princesse de Polignac informed me that the ex-Gladys Deacon and now also ex-Duchess of Marlborough has lost her head. She lives near London and when a visitor presents himself, she tips water from a window to invite him to take his leave. Poor

---

* Nevertheless, in March 1945, the duke contemplated selling the palace and discussed this with Winston Churchill, who agreed that modern life would 'make it increasingly difficult for any private person to live in so splendid a setting'. [Churchill to the 10th Duke, 1 March 1945 – quoted in *The Churchill Papers, Volume 21* (Hillsdale College Press, Michigan, USA, 2018), p. 578.]

woman! She no longer has her much vaunted beauty and now the rest is taken from her without pity. It makes one think of a famous myth by Ovid or the like.[4]

This, his own experiences and other gossip prompted Berenson to speak dismissively of Gladys in old age:

By now all people have deserted her, and nothing remains of her but a myth – she was, in former days, like Venus' cat – that cat who, made into a beautiful woman by the grace of the goddess, but could not remain in the company of women because she would suddenly spring and devour any little mouse that appeared. Gladys Deacon's mouse was the need to dominate, to crush under her heel the heads of those who were weaker than she. Thus no sooner would she see a possible victim than she forgot everything else, even her deepest interests, and would set out to pursue him until she had led him to his end. This is what ruined her.[5]

The bucket-of-water story certainly contained elements of a myth. Gladys's account presents a different picture. She explained to her lawyer:

Three creatures, a burly bully, a camera man among others formed a party who pestered Mrs Grylls all day. They put a chauffeur at the gate to warn them when Mrs Grylls was not in the house & getting over a fence, she found them *battering* (I mean literally *battering*) at the front door which was locked. She said 'What you again? Please leave my premises (she holds the lease by the bye in her name.) The bully, furious, replied shouting 'No, I refuse to go until I see who is in this house' & pounded at the door again, as one wd not a barn. She was ½ hour trying to get them out. Finally the woman said to the bully who said he wd stay there all night 'Come on Ronnie it's no use' – they had a hearty tea at the village shop talking & laughing trying to make a scandal. They went to Finmere to phone their stuff which I have not seen. They took photos from over the wall.

Some others were prowling around all day, questioning all the villagers, breaking into their premises DEMANDING as if it were by divine gift to see me.

You note the 'with a hundred dogs'. I have 3 of mine, the rest belong to Mrs Grylls. She is up in the air now abt dog licences for her 20 . . . You never saw outside of a film, the bullying, trespassing, impudence, insolence of these creatures. More will come.[6]

The Princesse de Navarro (the former actress, Mary Anderson, who lived in Broadway, Worcestershire) came to support Gladys in the siege, and Mrs Grylls proved admirable.

For some years Mrs Agnes Evelyn Innocent (Cherry) Gerveys Grylls was Gladys's staunch friend and companion. Born in 1876, she came from Launceston, the eldest daughter of Canon Edward Townend, one-time vicar of St Peter's, Fulham. In 1920 she had married Charles Reginald Gerveys Grylls, a widowed lawyer, and when she herself was widowed in 1926, she found herself short of money. Always an ardent dog breeder, she had taken it up professionally. Since 1930 Gladys had employed her to manage the kennels at Blenheim. She always called Gladys 'Your Grace', though she signed herself 'Yours affectionately' or 'Yours with love'. Besides looking after the dogs, she wrote letters to the agent on Gladys's behalf demanding the return of certain remaining possessions.

When dealing with Blenheim, they were greatly assisted by the electrician, Enoch, who went diligently about his business, saying nothing, but noting the whereabouts of Gladys's possessions, passing on lists of guests, dates of sales of the late duke's chattels, and news of modernisations at the palace. He 'cultivated the Queen',[7] which meant he kept in with the housekeeper, and he proved a splendid actor: 'The Queen informed me today you were staying at Hethe, near Bicester. Imagine my astonishment!!'[8] On another occasion he was asked if he knew where Gladys was: 'Of course I was quite ignorant,'[9] he assured her. Sometimes he slipped away to see her in person, but he had to be careful. Not long afterwards he went to work for Lord Leconfield at Petworth, where for some years Gladys rewarded his loyalty with small Christmas gifts.

More than anything Gladys wanted to be free to start a new life, quite unconnected from Blenheim and the Marlboroughs. She was disgusted by the attitude of the new duchess, who opened letters sent to her at Blenheim, then forwarded them, writing in a disguised hand 'opened in error', as though they had been redirected by a servant. Gladys regretted that she had not cultivated powerful allies:

> I quite see how I need them myself now. I know the strength of social opinion very well. I know what curs these in-laws are – what a one the late Duke was! . . . Blandford & Ivor are very rich – that will always gild with sunshine every mean thing they do for everyone.[10]

As she began to create a new life, Gladys was entertaining and philosophical about her fall from society:

> I say to myself 'Horatio, to what base uses art thou returned!'* But of course it's all my fault for being the only one who ever believed the late duke of M. was other than what the world called him all his life![11]

When Gladys went to stay with the Westminsters at Eaton Hall in March 1934, those guests who had once posed for her camera took on a distant air and in some pictures ignored the photographer altogether. Gladys realised that they were no longer interested in her now she no longer had Blenheim. But Lady Serena James remained a kind friend and invited her for Christmas in 1934.† In January 1935 she was back at Mixbury, where she and Mrs Grylls pulled a solitary cracker on Twelfth Night.

At the end of January 1935 the *Hooey* court case was heard in London. Gladys reverted to the style of Dowager Duchess of Marlborough, and a pressman snapped her in the law courts, dressed in a black coat with a fur collar and an elegant little hat. It is the last public photograph of her. Gladys stepped into the witness box in an atmosphere described as 'a mixture of distaste and embarrassment'. She told the court that the cartoon suggested her adultery with a clergyman, and she had come to clear the name of a family, which, in reality, she held in no esteem whatsoever:

---

* A mild misquotation from Hamlet in the churchyard: 'To what base uses we may return, Horatio!' (Act V, scene i).

† Another distant support disappeared when her uncle, Charles Baldwin, died after a long illness in Colorado Springs, on 29 October 1934.

I am in no way bringing this action for money not being in the least interested in whether damages are given or not but I do care for the good name of the House of Marlborough and I bring this action purely to clear the vile reflection on my character and that name.

The Lord Chief Justice, Lord Hewart, was convinced that nobody was attempting to assail Gladys's reputation and asked: 'Is this lamentable action really to go on?' She was asked if it would have made any difference had the various newsagents and distributors apologised. She stressed that circumstances necessitated full publicity to clear her name. Lord Hewart commented: 'I take a very serious view of this case – very,' and adjourned it until the following day.

The case resulted in full apologies being offered and a fixed sum handed over. The court retained 'the foul emanation from the printing press', and Lord Hewart said he hoped the publication would not discredit the profession of journalism which, he added, 'as everyone knows contains a great number of able and conscientious gentlemen'.[12] Gladys was awarded £150.

Gladys never entered the public eye again, though she was often in London, lunching at Simpson's, the Berkeley or the Ritz. In the country she attended the Bicester meet, the National Hunt Festival at Cheltenham, and the Richmond Show. In February 1935 a man stole a photograph of the bookbinder, Marius Michel, from her, which required police and legal action. He was arrested, and after telling a pack of lies in court, duly found guilty.

The Blenheim Estate Company was compulsorily wound up since Marlborough had left multiple bad and unnecessary debts, some by design to make him look poorer than he was. On 8 April Robert Bruce-Lockhart heard talk of the new duke having 'compounded with his father's creditors'.[13] As late as 1938 Gladys was advised that it would be useless to make further claims against Marlborough's estate as it was insolvent. Meanwhile items such as kennels and pictures continued to arrive from Blenheim and polite if somewhat reserved letters were exchanged between Gladys and her stepson.

1935 was the year of George V's Silver Jubilee, but Gladys ignored the festivities. She spent her time planting antirrhinums and sweet peas, burning dead grass and blackberrying, according to the season.

In September she noted that she was becoming 'quite a carpenter'.[14] Edward VIII came and went, and she remained at Mixbury.

Following the death of George V, the Coronation of Edward VIII was planned, and Gladys investigated the possibility of taking her seat in Westminster Abbey as a dowager duchess. As early as June 1936 Gladys applied to the Earl Marshal for a letter of summons to attend. The request was granted and in due course the summons, tickets and instructions arrived. Gladys began to search for a duchess's robe, 'the cape to be powdered with four Rows of Ermine, the edging five inches in breadth, the Train two yards . . .' It proved no easy matter to find one. The Army & Navy Stores reported that all known sources of supply had been explored without success. Finally, N. Clarkson of Wardour Street, who advertised 'Every requisite for stage and film,' offered the hire of a robe for thirty-five guineas.

Sadly, at the very last minute, Gladys lost her nerve and decided she could not face the ceremony. She telegraphed the Earl Marshal, pleading 'sudden indisposition', and seat number 23 in the duchesses' block was reassigned.

25

THE 'WITCH' OF CHACOMBE

*Seclusion is a blessed thing and through it one may become
anything.*

Gladys, *McCall's*, July 1927

Gladys's move to Chacombe set her on the path to becoming a total
recluse, a state with which she was quite familiar, having disappeared
into seclusion several times in her early life. But this was final.

In 1938 her lease on Town Farm, Mixbury, expired. She liked the
area and began 'an appalling hunt' for a new home. In October she
found Grange Farm, Chacombe, and bought it from Gertrude Mabel
Railton for £1,400. The house was built of Hornton stone in a small
village two and a half miles north-east of Banbury on the road to
Northampton. It occupied the entire central island of the village,
with a yard at the front, a garden beside it and a large orchard behind.
She settled in happily, as she wrote to her artist friend, Jean Marchand:

> It is charming, with a thatched roof, its stone walls covered with roses,
> an apricot tree and an old pear tree. There is a small but very pretty
> garden with three large asparagus patches and around the yard are the
> small farm buildings. Behind – an orchard which must be ravishing
> when in flower.
>
> Inside everything is small but pretty and peaceful – a very small
> library and drawing-room, a dining-room, a kitchen and dairy,
> three bedrooms full of light, electricity and a pretty, apple-green
> bathroom.
>
> In short all that we did not have in Mixbury.[1]

Gladys built an annexe to the library for her books, including the
fine collection of Marius Michels, and Rodin's *Faunesse debout* statue.

Boldini's portrait of her mother dominated the dining room. There were also works by Jean Marchand, one of them a landscape:

> You have no idea how much it has improved. The colour seems to me to have become more profound, and in its entirety it gives off a force and harmony which delights me at every hour.[2]

As she spread her collection of pictures about the little cottage, she was happy again:

> Just imagine, how I leap from one to other, admiring them, saying good morning to them – I owe money on many but too bad, one mustn't think of that.[3]

Gladys was delighted to find that Chacombe was only ten minutes from the cinema in Banbury. The disadvantages were that water was scarce in summer, the local girls worked in cloth manufacturers' – not as maids – and the house was close to the factories and would be in danger in wartime. As early as January 1939, Gladys was convinced that war would come.

Gladys and Mrs Grylls set themselves to work. They painted the house, pruned the roses and had the dairy ceiling mended. The house was re-thatched and a pergola constructed from the front door to the gate. In early days friends were invited to dinner, a Mr Draper coming over from a nearby village to act as butler.

From time to time Gladys employed some of the villagers to do odd jobs and gardening. Some found her too strict a task-master, but others were fascinated by her and she won their loyalty and affection. One man was set to work knocking together coffins for her spaniels when they died. If she trusted a servant, she gave him the freedom of the house, let him read her old diaries, and related hair-raising stories of her past life. From these stories the late duke never emerged well.

Gladys was now fifty-eight, and becoming increasingly eccentric. She dressed in old wellington boots and straw hats, which in winter she changed for a sou'wester. She adopted this look to discourage burglars, who would have been greatly surprised by the treasures concealed in Chacombe Grange Farm. One day a villager was chatting to Mrs Grylls over the gate and thought she saw a farm-hand beckoning to her across the yard. 'That's not a farm-hand,' said Mrs Grylls. 'That's the duchess.' Gladys applied paint to her legs to keep flies out of her boots when she was working outside. This caused the rumour that she was saucy, wearing garters. She ate a lot of mashed potatoes, but refused to touch cow's milk.

A flock of geese, accidentally knockèd down to Gladys at a local auction, was unpopular in the village. They attacked all comers without discrimination. Not everyone in Chacombe appreciated Gladys's nocturnal strolls around the village with her dogs. She became a poultry farmer. Some of the villagers referred to her as 'Old Dutch'. Others went further: 'The witch.'

War was declared on 3 September 1939 and Gladys remained in Chacombe for the duration. She made no contribution to the 'war effort' and was at times questioned by the local constabulary for refusing to black out her windows. These complaints she referred to Winston Churchill, whose recent rise to power left her unimpressed. 'He was the right man for the time because he was showy and that's what they wanted,'[4] she recalled. In her eyes he compared badly to Hitler, whose magnetism had stirred the whole world to arms. She expressed her sympathy with the Nazi leader by naming one of her cats 'Itler. It turned out to be well named as it stole the chickens' food.

When not working in her farmyard or looking after her dogs, Gladys read voraciously, Émile Ollivier one day, Gustave Schlumberger on Byzantium another, both of them old friends. Books arrived regularly from *The Times* Book Club, and she scoured several daily newspapers and magazines. She added to her collection of Sitwells, acquired Berenson's *Sketch for a Self Portrait* (1949) and, later on, Consuelo's memoirs, *The Glitter and the Gold* (1953).

Not long into the war, relations between Gladys and Mrs Grylls became strained. They ceased to speak, and one day Gladys told her that she hated the sight of her. In November 1941 Mrs Grylls succumbed to the strain and fled, pleading that she was ill and worn out, her nerves at breaking point, and her spirit broken. 'I simply went to pieces & couldn't get on with anything,'[5] she explained. She was convinced Gladys was glad that she had left.

Nevertheless, Mrs Grylls remained in regular contact. She urged Gladys to give up the geese, which would be stolen if food became scarce, and Gladys sold them. Gladys took on the running of the hens, the cooking, farm-work, and the care of the dogs. Mrs Grylls admired her strength of mind, and how she coped with the burden of work, survived a car accident, a sprained foot, later a scalded foot and her general condition of loneliness. In 1942 she wrote to Gladys about the fortune-teller, whom she blamed for being such a bad influence on her life:

> Last night I had a dream about you & the dogs. You were at a house – all comfortably furnished. I was with you & the dogs & you were very busy writing a book – you looked so well again and happy – I *wish* it were true.[6]

Mrs Grylls urged Gladys to give up her way of life in favour of 'a little rest & comfort'. But Gladys was determined not to give in. She became a bee-keeper in 1943 without great success, and during these years her spaniels died, one after another, from insufficient food. Mrs Grylls commiserated on their deaths.

Next Gladys was helped by May Hobbs, a good-looking evacuee from London. Though Mrs Hobbs found her exacting and mean, obliging her to pay for eggs from the farm, she was soon fascinated by her enigmatic employer. Her conclusion was that Gladys was a shrewd judge of character, and very capable, but that her talents were wasted. Gladys claimed that she was writing books under an assumed name, a ruse first tried on Berenson in 1908. She also told Mrs Hobbs that when she cut her face, she had stitched it herself in front of the mirror. Books were better cared for – they were kept warm by electric stoves, running twenty-four hours a day. Sometimes Mrs Hobbs cooked dinner for Gladys and left it in an outhouse for her to collect in the hours of darkness.

Once Mrs Hobbs was sent into the attic to work and became intrigued by Gladys's albums. She found a photograph of the duke captioned 'Himself'. She misread one caption – a photo of Jean Jardine, seated in the duke's lap, which she thought said 'tart'. She knew she was not meant to look and fortunately her instinct warned her that Gladys was about to approach. She closed the book just in time.

With ever-growing suspicion, the villagers thought Mrs Hobbs was in danger, even suggesting that she might be murdered. But Mrs Hobbs loved to listen to the stories, and after one of Gladys's late-night visits to her cottage, she noticed that her eyes still shone blue in the silvery light of the moon.

After some years Mrs Hobbs felt she should return to London for a better job. She went to see Gladys with her husband and they talked for four hours before summoning up courage to say she was leaving. Gladys told her she knew that was why they had come, and added: 'Everyone I love lets me down.'*

In April 1941 Maury Paul, the American gossip writer, asserted that the three surviving Deacon sisters were no longer in touch. Though Gladys never saw her sisters after the 1920s, they still corresponded. Maury Paul suggested that Dorothy was 'an ardent Nazi', who believed that 'Hitler and Nazism should rule the earth!' and was said to be 'high in Nazi councils'[7] in Vienna. Edith was in the United States, and occasionally sent Gladys food parcels. Dorothy was in the middle of war-torn Europe. There is a shocking story that Edith told her daughters, explaining that Aunt Dorothy loved good soap, and needed to have it. If by telling stories to Nazi officers in Vienna, she could get it, then surely this was understandable?[8] Early in the war, it was to Dorothy that Gladys revealed her early enthusiasm for Chacombe had waned:

> I am still in this hole of a house. I have broken my left arm, trying to do the work I can find no one to undertake & am fed up & will have to do housework as well . . . I went to London 10 days ago about my arm – I did nothing but sleep & eat while I was there with intervals at the dentist & having my hair 'permed' for tidiness. I hate country life. One becomes brutalized with work or for the rich with boredom & it is no wonder where live what 'brain' is abt. One wdn't know a war was on even, in the country . . .
>
> Marlborough is hanging abt nightclubs at present, too much champagne & very fat. Mary haggard & lined was a general or something†

---

* Mrs Hobbs was drawn to revisit Chacombe several times in later years to see how Gladys was. On one visit, Gladys threw her arms round her, thrilled to see her. Mrs Hobbs introduced her son, and Gladys pronounced him very bright and said he would go far. Shortly afterwards he won a scholarship to Cambridge.
† Bert, 10th Duke of Marlborough, used to say that he never knew what uniform his wife would appear in at breakfast. She was heavily involved in the Red Cross.

like that but is now expecting a miracle child in August.* At her age not only an undertaking poor thing . . .

I suppose the Americans are too busy trying on gas-masks. How utterly absurd they are with their terror of invasion. I think they think it is being fashionable to which end they'd sell their soul I always think.[9]

There were two more visits to London in August and December 1943, when Gladys stayed at the Ritz. It was on the second visit that Chips Channon had his strange encounter with her in the Bond Street jeweller's shop. Gladys often visited jewellers to buy and sell jewels to supplement her income.† Chips described Gladys as she examined a ruby clip:

I saw an extraordinary marionette of a woman – or was it a man? It wore grey flannel trousers, a wide leather belt, masculine overcoat, and a man's brown felt hat, and had a really frightening appearance, but the hair was golden dyed and long: what is wrongly known as platinum; the mouth was a scarlet scar . . .

Chips suddenly recognised Gladys and went over to greet her. She took his hand nervously and asked: '*Est-ce que je vous connais, Monsieur?*'
He replied: 'Yes, I am Chips.'
He got a strange reaction:

She looked at me, stared vacantly with those famous turquoise eyes that once drove men insane with desire and muttered '*Je n'ai jamais entendu ce nom-là.*'

In an instant she threw down the clip she was holding and bolted from the shop, leaving the social MP in a state of confusion. As it happens, she was perfectly aware of who he was. Her response was

---

* Blenheim was a school during the war, so the duke and duchess lived in but two rooms of the palace. When 'Porchy', 6th Earl of Carnarvon came to stay, they were obliged to share a room for one night. The result was Lord Charles Spencer-Churchill (1940–2016), who was born on 11 July 1940.
† After her death, Gladys's jewels were sold for over £452,000 (in 1978).

well acted. When asked in old age if she would talk to Chips should he approach her, she replied: 'Certainly not! I can be very stiff – completely oblivious if I want to be!' and then laughed.[10] No doubt Chips dined out on his encounter with a 'mad' Gladys.

The war raged on into 1944, Gladys absorbed in her daily menial tasks. Enemy aeroplanes flew overhead in February and in June a fox killed all but two of her chickens. The long-awaited Anglo-American invasion took place in Europe and hordes of Londoners arrived in the Banbury area, some of whom told Gladys they had not slept for fifteen days. At sixty-three, Gladys was finding life hard. She burnt her feet and ankles so badly that they took eleven weeks to heal. The bed sheets fell to pieces and she could not replace them. In October 1944 Mrs Grylls came to see her for a few days, again leaving all of a sudden, 'distracted with worry'[11] about her old employer and friend.

In February 1945 some German prisoners-of-war came to Chacombe, and helped Gladys prune her apple trees. She found them 'at once knowledgeable, quick and well behaved'. She wrote asking for more to come and kept in touch with them when they returned to their former lives. She was deeply shocked when friends were killed – the two sons of Lady Lansdowne, and Tom Mitford, and when Elizabeth Bibesco, Asquith's daughter, died. She followed the progress of the war with keen interest, her diaries as much concerned with her local life as the happenings in Europe. She noted raids on Berlin, cut out photos of the bombed casino at Monte Carlo and other press reports:

> What is depression? Is it only fatigue? Lovely day, frost last night. Is the war ending or not? Rumania & Bulgaria mysteries.[12]

> . . . War drones on & I feel I cannot complain abt even my hateful existence in the face of all the unhappiness. First day of Spring & a lovely one – as has been the rule for weeks past.[13]

She heard the news of Hitler's fall on the ten forty-five Foreign Service news on 1 May, and on the same day noted: 'Revolting photos in press today showing Mussolini and Clara Petacci hanging half–stripped & by the feet, then in Milan on the ground with brutes spitting on them.'[14] She followed the fates of the various enemy war leaders and the doings of Churchill:

Winston hands in resignation morning & retakes office afternoon. Labour people think it was clever trap laid for their leaders & they fell into it.*[15]

On 4 April 1946 Gladys's old suitor, Hermann von Keyserling, wrote to her from Upper Bavaria, where, following a bad time in the war, he had fallen on hard times:

Dear Gladys – In case you are alive as I hope you are (I am at Harthausen only for a cure), please answer to the adress [sic] on the other side of this letter. If not, please suggest to some heir of yours to do so. I have lost *everything*, all my books, ms, etc,† but now I am living a new life; the one I anticipated even when I knew you first, at Innsbruck, in 1908 . . .'[16]

For many years Keyserling had been active with the School of Wisdom in Darmstadt. Now he invited Gladys to come and address the school as an 'important woman'. He told her: 'Men have wrought such havoc, have concentrated entirely on the destructive side of life, so it is up to you, inspired by a few sages, to build us a better world.'[17]

Having been out of touch with Gladys since 1929, and knowing her for a bad correspondent, he ended on a note both pessimistic and optimistic: 'In case there is no answer I will consider you dead & look forward to a meeting in a better place than this world is.'[18] The letter was sent to Blenheim and forwarded to Chacombe. But the philosopher was more gravely ill than he realised, and by the time the letter arrived, he was dead. He went to that 'better place' on 26 April 1946, aged sixty-five.

Gladys stayed on at Chacombe, gradually barricading the property with elaborate fortifications, partly to deter local village boys, who

---

* The Labour Party refused to continue the wartime coalition government so on 23 May Churchill resigned, only to form an interim National Government the same day. He was defeated at the polls on 5 July 1945.

† Yet now his papers are in the library of the University of Darmstadt.

had thrown stones at the house, believing her to be a witch. Once Gladys emerged with a shot-gun, but maintained it was not loaded. Her brain remained acutely active, but she looked terrible, with no teeth, matted hair, uncut fingernails, and tramp-like clothes. This was in contrast to her neat handwriting, the meticulously kept diaries with press-cuttings neatly glued in, and to her thoughtful, articulate letters. There can seldom have been a more extreme contrast between physical appearance and mental capacity.

In extreme old age Gladys said: 'There are some things that happen to you, and it cuts you off. After that you don't care any more.'[19] This did not refer to her ruined face but to her failed marriage, with its accompanying horrors and insults and its harrowing aftermath.

In 1942 Gladys was saddened to hear that her friend Ethel Boileau had died. Ethel combined life at Ketteringham Park, in Norfolk, with being 'probably the best-selling woman novelist of the day',[20] as her publishers declared – though now she is forgotten.* Gladys first met her in 1917, four years before she married Marlborough. At that time Ethel, though married, had been desperately in love with a man called Reggie† who was 'playing her up'. This had made her so unhappy that she had contemplated suicide. Gladys had exhorted her with the words: 'Take your courage in both hands and hold your heart high.' Many years later, Ethel had reminded Gladys of her help:

> The mental and spiritual stiffening you gave me then I cannot explain to you, because it was not done deliberately by you but was the result of your own nature – so radiant and detached and serene which threw a mysterious charm over everything you touched, and reconciled one to life in a queer way . . .[21]

Ethel Boileau was convinced that Gladys had taught her 'the greatest of all values in life – that of detachment, that sure and certain core

---

* Ethel made an oblique reference to Gladys in her novel *Turnip Tops* (Hutchinson, 1932), p. 29 – 'And the M————s to; it took me a long time to forget her face; she was a brave woman if ever there was one.'
† This could be the Hon. Reginald Fellowes, coincidentally the one-time lover of Consuelo.

in oneself which lifts one above the chances and bitterness of life'.[22]
She prayed that the cruelty Gladys had suffered at Marlborough's
hands would never result in her losing that detachment.

On 19 May 1947, Gladys glanced at her diary for 1924:

Look it's today – 23 years later 1947 – again Monday the 19th! Well the
existence of 1924 passed away 9 years later like a black heavy cloud
leaving such a disgusted pain that for years & even now I cannot bear
to brush by it in thought. I had then no idea of how 'dirty' are so many
people. Marlborough stealing the one nice thing I had the Corot* - In
another place his son's doings – Ivor unwilling to make a statement the
picture was mine, that his father had said so to & before him over &
over again & before Blandford too. Well I feel cleaner not being in
such contact & certainly happier.[23]

Gladys now preferred the occasional company of village folk and
was grateful for any kindness shown her. Mrs Speed, who lived at
Chacombe and had worked in the house, cooked her a hearty meal
for Christmas in 1946. Gladys wrote in her diary:

England's presents continue innumerous in 1946 but given by needy
people are most gratifying. A pair of bedsocks, a bottle of bathsalts, a
good dinner, a basket of fruit.
   The rich guests of yesteryear – nothing.[24]

Most of all she loved animals. Two years after her little dog Coronie
died, she wrote:

It is so hard to love cruel, calculating, selfish human beings who bring
only pain to one – & it is so easy to love the defenceless & devoted like
you.[25]

Gladys fed the animals on healthy meat from the butcher, while
she lived on boiled cabbage, drawing on an iron determination to
survive.

---

* The Corot, which Gladys had owned even when she lived in Nice, was never
returned to her.

Visitors to Grange Farm were not usually made welcome. Mrs Grylls, who found that life after her time with Gladys had proved no more than a series of dull episodes, visited her several times, especially when she moved to look after her old friend, Mrs Bull, at Castle House, Buckingham. She stayed with Gladys for two months at the end of 1947. But when she came to collect some of her things in 1948, she was put through the process of waiting for three-quarters of an hour before she was admitted inside. Mrs Grylls remained in touch with Gladys until May 1951. The following year, on 28 September 1952, her body was found in the Thames off County Hall. The inquest produced insufficient evidence to explain why she had come to be in the water. She was seventy-five.

Lady Sophia Schilizzi, daughter of the 11th Earl Waldegrave, moved to Chacombe House in 1947. One night she met Gladys on one of her nocturnal peregrinations, dressed in dirty wellington boots, a black Molyneux gown and what resembled a witch's pointed hat. Gladys immediately said: 'You look like something out of a book!' but Lady Sophia was too nonplussed to ask which one. Gladys called on her one evening when she saw the light on and related strange tales. Subsequently she telephoned Lady Sophia several times between midnight and 3 a.m. to ask if she knew how to make strawberry jam. Lady Sophia had to say she preferred to make it by daylight.[26]

Gladys occasionally wrote to her sisters, but they were largely unaware of her condition. In 1938 Dorothy wrote of the 'strange life she leads, full of remote sadness.'[27] In 1943, Edith's husband, Harry Gray, wrote from New York that they had had no news since 1940, but presumed Gladys was still at Chacombe. Dorothy worried that her aunt Virginia kept press cuttings out in Colorado about her and Gladys's life, aware that they had both interested the public for some reason, though they now lived quiet lives. In 1947 Dorothy was surprised to find Gladys still fighting her step-son, the Duke of Marlborough, about a red lacquer table.

Gladys's niece 'Betka', Dorothy's daughter, came to see her in November 1946 and knocked several times at the door. Nothing happened so she went away and made enquiries at the local pub. During a final attempt to stir Gladys, the front door suddenly opened ajar. Betka pushed it and, to her considerable astonishment, came face to face with her aunt. Simultaneously a dozen cats flew out and scuttled from the darkness through her legs into the daylight. Gladys yelled at her: 'Get out! Leave me alone!' Then, just as suddenly, she made a complete volte-face and spoke in a well-modulated voice: 'If you would be so kind as to wait outside, I will join you.' True to her word, she emerged a few minutes later, wrapped in a shawl and chatted for twenty minutes or so in a mixture of English and German.

She knew who her visitor was, but little of the minutiae of her life, which had been difficult – Betka had spent two months in a prisoner-of-war camp with her husband, who had died tragically in Switzerland in July 1945, just after the war had ended. Gladys asked no questions. For all she cared, her niece could have dropped from the sky. But she must have liked her since spontaneously she gave her a cheque for £25.* Then, just as suddenly as before, she darted back into the house, slammed the door and was gone.[28]

---

* This astonished Dorothy: 'She sent Betka a $100 cheque which I find amazing as she has never been known to give anyone anything in her life.' [Dorothy to Virginia Baldwin, 3 January 1947.]

26

THE POLE

A recluse needs at least one ally. One day in 1951 a young man was bicycling through Chacombe on his way from work. Gladys was trying to mend the front gate. She spotted him and cried out, commanding him to help her. He promptly dismounted and came over. The two fell into conversation and she discovered that he was Polish – a DP (displaced person), who had settled in the area. Because Gladys was an exacting task-master she had never retained an English servant for long; neither had she taken the English to her heart. But here was a man who knew how to obey. Moments later she was ordering him to come and work for her. He protested that he had a job, to which Gladys replied: 'Very well, you will come at weekends.' She would pay him a pound for half a day's work.

The young man was Andrei Kwiatkowsky, then in his twenties, whose father had, by coincidence, worked on the Mankiewicze estate of Prince Karol Radziwill, brother of Dorothy's erstwhile husband, Aba Radziwill. During the war, Andrei had been the victim of Russian press-gangs, forced to assist in building their army's route through the Finnish marshes at Mannerheim. He escaped and made his way to England. On his arrival he secured a job in a factory and married a girl from Liverpool. She produced two sons, who later made their father proud by securing good jobs.

Gladys inspired Andrei's total loyalty, which continued until the day she died. He spoke five languages, so they often conversed in German and were thus not understood by the villagers. He tended the garden and undertook a number of odd jobs around the farm buildings. For the first two years Gladys did not allow him into her house, and there were days when she would open an upper-storey window and lower garden implements on a rope. At the end of the day the process was reversed. She had adopted Proustian hours, sleeping during the day and rising at about five in the afternoon. Andrei started work at midday, pottering around the garden on his own.

Gladys liked to steal up on him to see if she could catch him idling, but Andrei always knew when she was about to appear. She would unbolt the kitchen door, a lengthy process, due to the profusion of locks and chains. A host of cats would scamper out and perch on the walls. The sight of a cat heralded Gladys's arrival as clearly as white smoke from the Vatican announces the election of a new pope. Thereafter Gladys would accompany Andrei around the garden, giving him specific instructions as to what was to be done. At other times she might summon him from the upper window, her cry ringing out over the neighbourhood: 'Andrei! Come here!'

One of his duties was to turn the wheels of two Austin Sevens that stood on blocks in one of the barns. They were never driven, and chickens roosted in them. One day she asked him if he had performed this task. He replied that he had. 'No, you haven't,' she snapped. 'I marked them with a crayon!' She would get him to inject thistles with wax, he knew not why, without telling him the effect this had had on her own face, passing that off as a car accident.

Once, she wanted to go for a walk around the village. She tied a sack around her middle, over her boiler suit, put a fisherman's hat on her head and, being somewhat lame, took his arm and they set off. The extraordinary pair were in the middle of their excursion when a red Midland bus passed by. The driver was so astonished that he nearly drove his passengers into a ditch.

The fortuitous arrival of Andrei meant that Gladys could retire indoors and never come out again. Meat, milk, newspapers and other essentials were delivered to the house. Instructions to tradesmen were written on a blackboard, which was placed outside the house in the small hours of the night. Business affairs were dealt with by Gladys's bank manager, Mr S. B. Cooper, of Lloyds Bank, St James's. Though she was often out of contact for months and refused to sign forms or pay her taxes, he remained a patient and loyal ally. Unquestionably, he had a soft spot for his strange and difficult client. To a letter from Gladys in 1953, in which she expressed mistrust of the tax authorities and others in classical terms, he replied:

We can understand your feelings of mistrust but are hopeful that you could perhaps, to continue the excursion into Greek mythology, look upon us as a modern Olympus, offering you all possible protection from Scylla and Charybdis.[1]

In time Andrei was admitted into Gladys's strange domain. He found the drawing room in good condition. Here were her pictures and her books, with the stove alight twenty-four hours a day. Sometimes Gladys sat in a chair in this room, with her feet up, smoking a pipe, the cats clambering over her. She had had all her teeth taken out in 1948, and Andrei was astonished when she dropped her false ones on the floor, then simply picked them up and replaced them in her mouth without washing them. Near her chair stood a refrigerator, delivered in good condition but never connected. Any cat that died was put inside it to await solemn burial in a corner of the garden.

The dining room was piled high with newspapers and periodicals. Upstairs, her bed had collapsed and the broken mattress she lay on was filled with old books. Her famous revolver lay nearby and it was not unknown for Gladys to take pot-shots from the upper windows with a shot-gun. The plumbing in the house had been a thing of the past for many years. The main area of occupation was the kitchen where Gladys would stand over a huge cauldron providing food for her cats and eating from it herself. Joints of meat from the butcher were stored in one corner and invariably went off before they were touched, or Gladys would attempt to cook a herring, forget about it, and let it burn to a frazzle. Medicine of one kind or another lived in a cupboard outside her bedroom, everything meticulously marked.

The house was fortified. Heavy black curtains now covered all the windows and once a year Andrei was ordered to drench them in oil to prevent the moths from eating them. All the doors were bolted and a small chopper stood by the main door lest some too persistent visitor should present himself. Outside, the house was surrounded by yards of chicken- and pig-wire.

Villagers had mixed reactions to Gladys. Sue Woodford lived with her parents in a thatched cottage opposite Gladys's garden. She wrote that there was little sign of Gladys by daylight, but at night as she lay in bed, sometimes a torch-light would play on the ceiling of her room as Gladys wandered by. Sue described her clothes: 'Combinations, not unlike those worn by the cowboys in old Western films, were her "undies" and a cotton wraparound overall on top with a sleeveless leather jerkin (like those coalmen wear) completed her outfit. Her feet were encased in down-at-heel wellingtons which were liberally studded with red bicycle puncture-repair patches, and the whole ensemble was topped by a black sou'wester hat.'[2] Believing her to be a witch, some of the villagers ordered their children not to accept apples from her, lest they were poisoned. Such was her reputation that children were scared to pass her gates and ran by at speed, as if passing the 'Boo' Radley house in *To Kill a Mockingbird*.

Friends attempted to visit from time to time. Most of them were avoided. If they left visiting cards, Gladys threw them into the fire. If they happened to catch a glimpse of her, they invariably scurried off of their own accord. No doubt most of these visitors came out of curiosity. Others had more complicated missions. Her sister Dorothy never came to see her, but kept abreast of Gladys's antics and relayed news of her to Berenson and others. Following her 1946 visit, her niece Betka appears to have taken no further interest in her until many years later. Dorothy alerted her son, Count John Pálffy, to Gladys's existence. He was interested in her intellectual past and concerned as to the whereabouts, safety and ultimate destination of her valuable collection of art. Sue Woodford remembered his second visit in 1955 'smartly dressed in a suit, collar and tie and he smelt of a very pleasant after-shave not usually worn by men forty-odd years ago'.[3] At first Gladys shouted from her bedroom window that he was no nephew of hers and he should leave an old woman in peace. Thanks to Sue Woodford's mother, he was eventually allowed in, and they chatted for some time. His cousin, Milo Gray, reported to her aunt Virginia Baldwin (by then Princess Tchkotoua):

> She made him seem a little more welcome. They chatted together all afternoon and she told John she was quite happy leading the strange life she does of a recluse and wanted very little else.
>
> She is still very bitter about the Marlboroughs and refuses to discuss any part of her past life. Her house is small and littered every-where with newspapers which she reads avidly, not only English

papers, but French, Spanish and German newspapers as well and John said there was nothing in her house that could possibly remind one of her life with Marlborough. She kept nothing and wants nothing of that side of her life and becomes angry at the slightest suggestion of it.

She sounds strange in one sense and yet quite happy and peaceful in another and John said he almost envied her. As far as her health goes, she is not too well as she has broken her back about a year ago and for many months had to wear a 'corset' but told him she found this uncomfortable and so has refused to wear it in spite of the doctor's orders.[4]

Pálffy urged Gladys to see a specialist in Oxford about a nasty sore on her face.

He came again in 1958, was admitted into the house, and stayed talking to her for several hours, finding her wise and detached, if a little cynical. He was amazed at her strength. On one occasion she was about to pick up some poultry boxes and he offered to help. They were too heavy for him. He felt her piercing blue eyes on him as he struggled. She then picked both up casually and carried them across the room. As they talked, so night began to fall. Gladys turned on no lights but watched him become increasingly uncomfortable and nervous. He could tell that she was enjoying his discomfort.[5]

Though forgotten by the world, there were occasional intrusions. In 1948, as Dowager Duchess of Marlborough, she had been invited to the King's garden party at Buckingham Palace. She did not go. Nor was she forgotten by Consuelo, now Madame Balsan, living with her balloonist husband Jacques Balsan, who was so successfully sustained by monkey-gland injections that he propelled himself onto numerous young ladies.* When Consuelo came to publish the English edition of The Glitter and the Gold, she excised Gladys's name from the story about the Crown Prince of Prussia, disguising her as 'a young American girl'. Consuelo had been warned that Gladys had sued over

---

* He pinned (Laura) Countess of Dudley to the floor, when she was in hospital, recovering from an operation. One of Consuelo's granddaughters was told to lock her bedroom door. She saw the handle turning in the night.

the *Hooey* libel, and told her editor: 'As she is now rather mad one must be careful.'[6]

In 1959 Sir Shane Leslie, nephew of Lady Randolph Churchill, began to wonder what had happened to Gladys. He obtained news of her from the local Catholic priest, Father John Maunsell, in whose parish Chacombe lay. He urged him to visit her, and armed him with a letter of introduction, which recalled staying at Blenheim years before: 'Time passes but the memory of your beauty descends the ages. I am sure you will find Father Maunsell a sympathetic friend.'[7]

Father Maunsell called on Gladys about once every two months for about six years. He experienced some difficulty in getting her to admit she was a Catholic, telling him she had been baptised Protestant and Catholic the same day, the second baptism unknown to her father. Finally, she admitted: 'Yes, I am a Catholic, but a bad one.' Father Maunsell then contacted Father Martindale, in retirement in Petworth, hoping he might visit her. But Martindale regretted that he was too ill; neither did he think it would do much good. He urged Father Maunsell to keep in touch with Gladys and, when the time came, to give her the sacraments and a Catholic burial.

In 1960 Sir Shane himself materialised, staying with Edward Courage and his wife at Edgcote House. Mr Courage drove Sir Shane and Father Maunsell the short distance to Chacombe and Sir Shane was allowed in. He came out after half an hour, upset by her state. His verdict was that she was very poor, full of grievances, but certainly not insane. He approached the Apostolic Delegate in Great Britain, hoping he might persuade Gladys to accept the sacraments, which would bring her 'consolation that at the present time she knows nothing about',[8] but the Most Reverend Gerald O'Hara was too busy for that expedition.

In August 1961, Edith's daughter, Milo Gray, came to England for the first time and telephoned her aunt to make a date with her. She came to Chacombe and waited in the farmyard for Gladys to let her in. The house remained silent but Milo had the uncanny feeling that Gladys was watching her. Finally she gave up, and wrote an aggrieved letter particularly since she had come such a long way to see her. Gladys sent Andrei to the post office with a telegram, which read: 'Dear Heart, Don't be a silly-bill. Of course I wanted to see you but

I was ill.'⁹ When Count Pálffy brought his young bride, she was left sitting on the wall, the door closed against them.

Gladys did not celebrate Christmas, but excused Andrei his duties during the holiday. She marked the season by offering him some fine white Burgundy. To his horror, she poured the wine into two plastic tumblers, which did little to enhance its taste. He did not mind when she declared: 'You were born a peasant and you'll die a peasant, but me, I'm a duchess!' She warned him to trust nobody. 'Friendship doesn't last,' she said. On a good day she would regale him with stories about Russian grand dukes kissing first the tips of her fingers, then her hand, and then all up her arm. When they reached her shoulder, they were firmly halted.

The rate of domestic accidents increased as Gladys approached her eightieth year. She broke her shoulder in a fall, did nothing about it, and presently it set itself. On a few occasions she hurt herself so badly that the doctor had to drive her to hospital, but she always refused to stay in overnight. When movement became more of a problem, Andrei dressed her wounds.

Every morning he came to the house, carried Gladys upstairs and put her to bed. When she was safely installed there, he underwent the daily ritual of locking the house, keys like the garden implements lowered down and pulled back from an upper window. Although he did not have an easy time, Andrei loved working for Gladys, and when later he visited her in hospital, he used to recall with nostalgia 'the good old days at Chacombe'.

Gladys never lost her sense of time or her ability to digest news from the outside world. If an item interested her, she cut it from the newspaper and found a home for it. A cock robin was killed when he flew into a store window in Wisconsin. Beside his dead body stood his mate on solitary guard until the evening traffic frightened her away. Gladys folded the photograph into a book by Berenson, correctly dating it: '17 April 1961 (Budget Day)'. Almost the only entry in her diary that year was to be found in October: 'Day the great bomb was sailed into space.'*¹⁰

The winter of 1961 proved especially bad. Gladys's fear of

---

* The Russians launched Tsar Bomba in the Arctic Ocean on 30 October 1961, then the world's most powerful bomb.

intruders increased, and the sight of a village boy stealing an apple from her orchard was invested with sinister significance. She would call the police in the middle of the night complaining of strange happenings. Concern for her condition grew apace. Andrei's care remained constant throughout, and undoubtedly he saved her life that winter. One night, sitting in the darkness, she wrote in an old diary:

I am left alone in this house!!!! Unable to move!!

None of such a monstrous abandoning of a completely helpless, wounded woman unable to move cd happen except in England.[11]

Yet there remained one thing that meant more to her than anything else — something she had valued all her life: her freedom. For this reason she refused to have anyone living with her or to move from her house. For Gladys there was no compromise, despite the entreaties of Andrei and others.

Unbeknown to her, however, plans were being made on her behalf. Her nephew came again in 1962 (his third visit). He maintained that the local police and health authorities would not permit Gladys to live alone, unaided and unprotected 'in practically inhuman circumstances in her house'. He described her as something of a 'public nuisance', this time citing police, fire brigade and health authorities. Since she refused to change her *modus vivendi*, he decided that she should be taken into St Andrew's Hospital, Northampton.[12] He might also have been worried how the world would perceive family neglect of her if she came to a tragic end.

A further worry was that Gladys might set fire to her house and that her pictures, sculptures, jewellery, furniture and books would be lost – an Aladdin's cave of treasures and a valuable inheritance. He had been helping her with her finances since about 1955. This included persuading her to pass over the $5,000 inheritance from her cousin, Eugene Higgins, and various other funds, totalling over $22,000. These he was managing on her behalf.[13]

Gladys was taken away on the night of 15 March 1962. The irony of the date did not escape her: the Ides of March (about which the soothsayer warned Caesar in vain). Cars drew up outside the house. People moved about in the yard. Pressure was put on Andrei to unlock the door. Four men in white coats took hold of Gladys, who fought like a wild animal cornered in its lair, and dragged her from the house. She cried out to Andrei, who stood petrified and helpless in a corner of the yard.

Gladys was driven away.

27

'A VAST LUNATIC ASYLUM'

I have long been ill since I was dragged out of my room by force, only partly dressed in not even a dressing-gown & stockings or slippers – the kidnappers refused to give any information or even speak & dragged me after a gallant fight by me down the stairs by 3 men grabbing my feet & making me lose my balance into their hands [by] which I was lugged out to a waiting [car] pushed into it & quickly taken away, frozen to the bone (15th of March) & brought here – No doctors, 2 women tore my clothes off, put me to bed.[1]

Thus begins Gladys's account of her transfer to St Andrew's Hospital, Northampton, which, did she but know it, was to be her home for the next fifteen and a half years. She arrived in the Rolls-Royce invariably sent to collect new patients.

In the confusing world in which she found herself, Gladys reverted from being Mrs Spencer to her ducal status. Since the 10th Duke's wife, Mary, had died in May 1961, she was within her rights to call herself 'Duchess of Marlborough', rather than Dowager.

St Andrew's was an imposing Georgian mansion, set in 100 acres of the Nene Valley. It described itself as 'a private psychiatric hospital independent of the National Health Service'. Gladys called it 'a vast lunatic asylum'.[2] It had been opened by the 3rd Earl Spencer in 1838 as Northampton General Lunatic Asylum, accommodating fifty-two paupers and thirty private patients. In 1863 a chapel was built in Northamptonshire stone to the design of Sir George Gilbert Scott. Extensions had been added over the years – a golf course and tennis courts, a gymnasium, a swimming pool, occupational-therapy units, dental clinics, a physiotherapy department and even a beauty salon. Colefax & Fowler had decorated the front hall.

Patients came to St Andrew's from all over the world. It still retains a reputation as the repository for members of the British aristocracy unable to cope with everyday life. Walking along its extensive corridors is to observe on doors the names of unknown members of well-known families, patients from the peerage, from distant branches of royal families, and from the professional classes.

Its most famous inmate was the poet, John Clare, admitted in 1837, who died there in 1864. Another poet, J. K. Stephen (cousin of Virginia Woolf), was committed in November 1891. When he heard of the death of his former pupil, HRH the Duke of Clarence, the following February, he became manic, refused to eat and soon died.

More recently, the hospital had housed the Hon. Violet Gibson, the woman who shot Mussolini in 1926, winging him in the nose but failing to kill him. She was detained there from 1927 until she died in 1956. Then there was Lucia Joyce, daughter of James Joyce, and said to be his muse for *Finnegans Wake*. She arrived in 1951 and was visited at least once by her younger lover, Samuel Beckett. She died there in 1982.*

Gladys began her new life in a south-facing room on the second floor of the Cedars, a villa in the grounds, built in the early 1900s. Her physical condition horrified the matron, who declared that she could not remember a patient ever admitted in such a dirty state, but she was soon enjoying a regular bath, even demanding one. For five months she suffered from a respiratory tract infection, which nearly cost her her life.

Gladys was eighty-one years old. She hated her new life. She continually demanded to be allowed to return to Chacombe. Unfortunately her persistent demands earned her a reputation as a difficult and aggressive patient. It was felt that to discharge her was

---

* Other patients included Lady Tatiana Mountbatten (1917–88), a first cousin of the Duke of Edinburgh; the beautiful Diana (Drummond) Astor (1926–82), wife of the Hon. John Astor, suffering from premature senility; Foreign Office wife Diana Bromley (1918–72), who poisoned her two young sons in a fit of melancholia; the Earl of Leicester (1908–76), later contained at Holkham; Lady Griselda Balfour (1924–77), daughter of the 12th Earl of Airlie; the Hon Mavis Portal (1926–85), daughter of Marshal of the RAF Viscount Portal of Hungerford; and, briefly, John Buckmaster (1915–83), the erratic son of Dame Gladys Cooper, who later killed himself in America.

not in her best interests as her life at Chacombe had been so eccentric. She was suspicious by nature and refused to sign any documents, and she was without friends to advise her or present alternatives. She made attempts to escape and had to be restrained, none of which helped her cause. Her sole ally was Andrei, and she even blamed him for letting her be taken from her home. She said to him: 'I forgive, but I don't forget.'[3]

By the time she entered St Andrew's, her youngest sister, Dorothy Pálffy, had died (in August 1960), which left the other sister, Edith Gray, still alive until 1965, as her next of kin by law. However, there was no love lost between Edith and Gladys, due to Gladys's disdainful behaviour in the early 1900s, and Edith had not seen her since the 1920s. Edith did nothing to help her sister in her hour of need.

It appears that Gladys had not left a will. This left six beneficiaries in the next generation. They were Edith's three daughters, of whom Audrey and Alison had had nothing to do with her, while the other sister, Milo, had attempted to visit at Chacombe in 1961. There was Dorothy's daughter, Betka (Tomaszewska), who considered herself, with some justification, to be the favourite niece. But on Edith's instructions she was not informed about Gladys's fate. Then there were Dorothy's Pálffy son and daughter, John and Caja. Count Pálffy had involved himself in Gladys's affairs, while Caja played no part. None of these relations lived in the United Kingdom.

It was on the instructions of John Pálffy that Gladys was put into St Andrew's Hospital, and for this she never forgave him. Because he lived abroad, he had been assisted in negotiations with Gladys by his business partner, Dick Joscelyne,* who had first met Gladys some eight years before. He had acted as intermediary.

Gladys had two personal links to the outside world: her bank manager at Lloyds Bank, St James's, Terence Woodford-Smith, with whom she corresponded regularly, he reassuring her that she had not been abandoned, and her ever-loyal ally, Andrei. Over the years various lawyers were involved, representing different members of the family. The key figure at St Andrew's Hospital was Dr Daniel

---

* Richard Andrew Joscelyne (1909–92), m. 1940 Jean Symons (1916–2011), a businessman with Gray Dawes & Co.

O'Connell, the medical superintendent.* He soon decided that Gladys was suffering from persecution mania and delusions. Having read Gladys's diaries of the time and some of the correspondence, I am not convinced that he was right.

Hardly had Gladys gone to St Andrew's than her family put their heads together. There exist dozens of letters written between them from that day until the day she died – and beyond – primarily concerned with the fate of her valuable art collection and other possessions, and outlining strategies to be employed when she died.

The family's first mission was to get Gladys to sign a Power of Attorney in favour of Dick Joscelyne so that he could manage her affairs. They were paying her hospital bills and were naturally anxious that she should pay these herself. Not surprisingly, Gladys had no intention of signing such a document. This was deemed to indicate persecution mania at work.

In an attempt to persuade Gladys, Joscelyne arrived at the hospital on 14 April 1962, four weeks after her incarceration. He had a meeting with Dr O'Connell, who showed him a note that she had written, demanding to know who had committed her. The doctor then went into her room at the Cedars, but she shouted that Joscelyne was 'a liar and a thief'.[4] The doctor advised him not to go in, so he confined himself to sneaking a glimpse of her sitting in bed, her face turned away from him. The doctor told him that Gladys was 'a very difficult, aggressive patient'. He said they would be happy to keep her for the rest of her life, and that she needed day and night nursing 'or she may walk out and fall down'.[5] It was thought her stay in the hospital would cost £2,000 to £2,500 a year.

Dick Joscelyne had sympathy for Gladys in her plight and took it upon himself to sort out her house, get it repainted and pulled into order, and he took steps to safeguard her possessions. He spent some days at Chacombe and the extent of its squalor was determined. He removed the chicken- and pig-wire with which Gladys had barricaded the house. A massive cleaning operation was undertaken, disposing of enough rubbish to fill two five-ton trucks, including loads of newspapers, poultry-feed bags, tins full and empty, and between 300 and 400 pots of jam, some of which were nearly ten years old. The house was

* Daniel J. O'Connell (1903–68). He retired in 1966.

redecorated, which enraged Gladys when she heard about it in November. The geese were given away. A plan was conceived to have Gladys's cats 'put out of the way', since they were ailing.[6]

A tomato-sauce carton, discovered in a long-deserted cat's bed, revealed an exquisite silver snuff box. A sapphire pin and a necklace of pinkish pearls were found in a pigskin case in the attic. A Kelmscott Chaucer, cited as 'one of the great books of the world',[7] and destined to sell at Christie's for £32,000, came to light, as did a book of sexually explicit drawings by D. H. Lawrence and a 1526 Erasmus. The ground floor alone produced thousands of pounds of valuables lurking in the muck. Joscelyne found some diaries, which her nephew wanted destroyed unread, but fortunately they were preserved.

Joscelyne reported that he was taking steps to have the pictures inspected for insurance purposes, considering that to be the next most important issue now that Gladys was safe in St Andrew's.[8] Presently, Leggatt Brothers recommended that they be brought to London for storage and possible restoration.

Joscelyne's letters reveal that he was worried that he should have done more to help Gladys while she was at Chacombe, but then, as he said, no one had done anything, neither the villagers nor the neighbours in big houses – only Andrei, who had cared for her for eight years despite frequent accusations and abuse.

The money issue became more concerning to the family as the hospital bills and other expenses mounted, and they instructed that Gladys's well-being should be managed 'in the most economical and expeditious manner'.[9] Gladys was by no means bankrupt. Besides her house and possessions, she still received a third of the income from the Edward Parker Deacon Trust in Boston, with assets of about $360,000 at the time of her death; also a reluctant £2,000 a year from the Marlboroughs; and some income from British securities held in London.

It was clear that Gladys was not going to sign any legal documents, the only alternative being that her affairs should be taken into receivership. On 1 May 1962 Dr O'Connell reported that Gladys was about to apply to the Mental Health Review Tribunal 'to investigate the legality of her detention'. He was not concerned, believing her detention to be valid. When pressed to sign a Power of Attorney, she informed the doctor of her nephew's 'many iniquities' and his 'total unsuitability for such a trust'.[10] But Gladys did not submit her application at that time, Dr O'Connell presuming that she mistrusted the process.[11]

Gladys then appealed to her niece, Milo Gray, in America, in the letter quoted at the opening of this chapter. She asked for the address of her sister Edith as her next of kin, and warned Milo not to trust her '1/2 relative, Palfi'.* Since her arrival, she told her, she had been suffering from broncho-pneumonia and a priest had been summoned to see her. She declared that she was fed up, 'in utter weariness of all this comic opera of the unadult Palfi & his myrmidons'.[12]

Milo informed Gladys that her mother was travelling all summer and would be hard to contact. Gladys replied: 'I am glad but rather shocked at your mother off to so many places with which she has neither friends nor interests. It is of course pleasant to get away from the general "buzz" I suppose.'[13]

Next Gladys told Dr O'Connell that Pálffy and Joscelyne 'were members of a plot which led to her admission' to St Andrew's, and would not admit she was 'in any way mentally disturbed'.[14] The family's line was that the local police, fire brigade and health authorities did not permit Gladys to continue living in practically inhuman conditions and that she was a public nuisance. So she had been transferred to St Andrew's, where the staff could cope with her particular state of mind.[15] On 8 June Gladys's sister Edith, far away in the United States, signed a document authorising Gladys to be taken into receivership.

Since Gladys refused to place herself voluntarily into the hands of Dick Joscelyne, an application was made to the Court of Protection† to have this done on their instructions. Even then, Joscelyne asked whether a final effort could not be made to get her back to Chacombe, now tidied and repainted: 'It just seems to me a terrible waste and altogether a very sad situation that this old lady should

---

* This was a reference to Dorothy's parentage. Gladys made several mentions of her as her 'half-sister' over the years, believing her to be the daughter of Émile Abeille, the Frenchman her father had disposed of with three pistol shots in February 1892.
† The Court of Protection has extensive powers and looks after patients who cannot manage their own affairs. One of its roles is to oversee the assets of mental patients that need to be protected.

spend the last years of her life in a Lunatic Asylum.'[16] But the idea was not explored.

While it was hoped that a notice of receivership need not be served on Gladys, Dr O'Connell pointed out that nobody could claim she was incapable of understanding such a notice. Finally he wondered whether her objection to Joscelyne could be ascribed to 'delusional intensity' but was not sure that this plan would work.[17]

Gladys's niece, Milo Gray came to London in November and visited her aunt. This visit was not a success. She brought Gladys some scent. 'Don't you realise you only give scent to whores?' said Gladys, rejecting it.[18]

Plans were well set for the final takeover of Gladys, her affairs and her possessions. But then the family got a shock. On 12 December 1962 Dick Joscelyne had an interview with Raymond Jennings, master of the Court of Protection. He told Joscelyne that Gladys had written to the court making the following points:

1) I am fully in possession of my mental faculties.
2) I wish to see my solicitor.
3) I do not wish Mr Richard Joscelyne to have anything to do with my affairs.[19]

The master told Joscelyne that if he appointed him as receiver, then Gladys could appeal and an appeal judge might question his handling of the issue. He explained that the government tried to take account of the patient's wishes. Instead, the master appointed the Official Solicitor as receiver. Gladys was informed about this, but found Dr O'Connell evasive. When she asked him direct questions, he parried them, 'parroting his everlasting "I have no power or authority" . . .'[20]

The order was delayed until 21 January 1963, leaving Joscelyne with two alternatives: to influence Gladys's solicitor to persuade her to withdraw her demands, or to try to persuade the master of the court to disregard her request and appoint him instead.[21]

The family approached the master through solicitors and set out their mission to have Joscelyne appointed:

A. Having by now quite a detailed knowledge of Gladys's affairs and having already been of substantial help in arranging same, and

   B. In order to reassure the immediate family that Gladys's affairs in
      receivership be properly, intelligently and economically maintained
      in the interest of Gladys and her eventual estate.[22]

On 16 February Mr Phillips, of Stockton, Sons & Fortescue, visited
Gladys at St Andrew's. He was from a firm of solicitors Gladys had
used in the past. He was introduced to her as 'someone who had been
sent to explain the intentions of the Court of Protection and to ascertain the Patient's wishes'. Gladys was at first annoyed that Mr Fortescue
himself had not come, but it was explained that he had retired. This
she accepted.

In a meeting of an hour and ten minutes, Phillips explained that
the Court of Protection was 'a sort of branch of the High Court',
prompting Gladys to ask: 'Judge – do you mean a Master in Lunacy?'
She told him she disliked all her relatives, both in America and
England, distrusted American citizens, and believed that American
businessmen were trying to get a foothold in Britain by buying
English properties. She described her nephew as 'a softener' and
Joscelyne as 'a tool' of the Americans. At the end of the meeting she
conceded that Joscelyne was a 'poor fellow' and that all she had against
him was that he was under her nephew's influence. Her parting thrust
was: 'I am English by marriage and I am proud of it. I want American
influence wiped out of my affairs.'[23]

Gladys was later angered to find that Phillips was working for both
sides. He did not report her annoyance that some of her money had
been transferred to the USA via Hong Kong.[24] She therefore wrote
to the Court of Protection, refusing to have anything to do with her
nephew or Joscelyne, forbidding them and any Grays 'to come in past
the gates', and asking for details of all her financial transactions since
March 1962.[25]

The family were not pleased by this news. They sent a message to
the Court of Protection, signed by five of her relatives with the same
message about her personal welfare and business affairs being over-
seen by Joscelyne.[26] But the master concluded that he had to have
regard for the duchess's 'expressed objections' to Joscelyne, even if
these were 'entirely unreasonable'.[27] Therefore he placed Gladys's
affairs in the hands of the Official Solicitor, operative from three
weeks. The family had the right to appeal.

As it happens, Gladys's objections were very far from unreasonable. She might have been paranoid, but she was quite right to suggest that the family had plans which involved her personal possessions.

The family appealed in vain, at which point, on the advice of the Court of Protection, Gladys submitted her application to the Mental Health Review Tribunal seeking her discharge from St Andrew's. For some weeks between 26 March and 29 July her diary expressed the genuine hope that she would be allowed to go home, though there were numerous delays and from Andrei she heard disturbing accounts of her family rifling through her house.

Dr O'Connell was determined to squash Gladys's appeal for release. He wrote to her nephew to garner support, asking him to outline the conditions under which she lived at Chacombe, her state of cleanliness and capability of looking after herself.[28] Count Pálffy's reply outlined her way of life at Chacombe and suggested that if she were released she might well die in a tragic way. He stated that the family were unanimous in their view that it would be undesirable for his aunt to be discharged from St Andrew's Hospital where she was well cared for.

On 7 June 1963 the Mental Health Review Tribunal met and decided that Gladys was 'properly detained' in the hospital.[29] A month later, Gladys heard about this. She wrote in her diary:

> Food continues awful but it seems these 10 old people gobble any & everything. Am getting more depressed especially as Home News are that my side has been *roulé en grand* [thoroughly routed] so I will be imprisoned here all my life . . . Tribunal end was kept *secret from me* – WHY?[30]

★ ★ ★ ★ ★

Although Gladys was not permitted to leave the hospital, she did succeed in frustrating her family's plans concerning her possessions. While still at Chacombe, her nephew had tried to persuade her to allow him to take her pictures to Switzerland to avoid death duties. With her apparent agreement, a letter was concocted about taking the 'cats' to 'the vet'. The cats were the pictures, while the vet was Mr Joscelyne. Gladys knew this letter was somewhere in the house and told Andrei to find it. Eventually he did.

She then wrote to the Lord Chancellor and he sent the Official Solicitor to see her. She produced the letter from her nightgown and explained its significance. As a result the Official Solicitor oversaw all Gladys's affairs for the rest of her life and the family could touch nothing.

Gladys was never told that in March 1965 her house was sold to pay for her livelihood, and to insure her possessions. Her pictures were at first stored with T. R. Rogers in London, but later in an underground vault at Battersea under the aegis of the Royal Bank of Scotland.

Her cats were destroyed and a vast quantity of furniture and other items were stored in Banbury. The inventory stretches to more than 500 pieces. She, who had assets of considerable value and no dependants, spent her last years in a small hospital room with an iron bed.

28

LAST ENCOUNTER

Gladys kept a diary at the hospital, a small pink plastic book. It gives a devastating account of life in a psychiatric hospital, at times made alarming by the behaviour of the more seriously disturbed patients. In it she recorded her interest in world affairs, gleaned from newspapers, and occasionally revealed the particular sense of humour and observation that had made her so alluring in earlier life. A graphologist, shown her handwriting, gave his opinion that she had mental initiative, alertness, confidence, leadership, though a confused thought pattern. She was spontaneous but irrational, her moods changed quickly; she was energetic.*

The nurses aggravated her and, in turn, she made their lives difficult. One nurse had such scant knowledge of history that she thought Gladys had spent her early life in the French Revolution. Another was accused of removing private papers from a drawer. In the midst of this, Matron arrived:

> At that moment the *Arch Yapper* walked in, evidently been listening outside the door secretly & starts a loud & constant flow of un-understandable yapp. Finally my heart thumping my ribs, I yelled to her 'The Dess. of Marlborough to Miss Anderson - get out of the room *at once*' & out she went still yapping.[1]

Hair washing and inspections were treated as an assault on the rights of the individual. Matron brought health visitors one day. They marched in 'to see beef on a Duchess'.[2]

---

* He also looked at her handwriting when she was forty, when it showed confidence, leadership and drive. She was self-sufficient and a logical thinker, with an ability to administrate and with common sense. There was a certain controlled sensitivity.

Gladys largely ignored her fellow inmates or 'the mads': 'Oh dear what a dead set of people,'[3] she wrote. From time to time she was pleased to note 'quiet of all lunatics, not a sound'. When Princess Alexandra was married in April 1963, she who had attended the Duke of York's wedding in 1923, observed: 'All these women in the English state of excitement over "Royal Marriages". In the sun 82. Poor wedding guests – no wonder they looked furious.'[4]

Gladys followed the Argyll divorce case, the Profumo affair, the H-bomb, the actions of President Kennedy and even the fluctuations of the New York Stock Exchange. On the Cuban Missile crisis she wrote: 'I think Cuba may be a teeth showing by Kennedy',[5] and later: 'Cuba still looks like electioneering.'[6] She was pleased to find her political judgement still sound: 'As I surmised last Tuesday, Cuba was nothing but cold war & so it is continuing.'[7] She was excited by the election of Pope Paul VI, sent him 'a telegram of real joy'[8] and was thrilled when he flew to meet the head of the Orthodox Church, the first ever aeroplane flight by a reigning pope:*

> The Pope's journey – its terrific fatigue, his cheerful endurance of it, that part of his journey finished today – King Hussein has been splen- did through it . . . I feel my heart uplifted & yet like a gaffed fish.[9]

Andrei remained a faithful visitor throughout these years. He went on to work for the new owners of her house at Chacombe, and brought flowers from her garden and gifts of food. He always put on his Sunday best for his visits. Though offered compensation for his travel, he stated proudly: 'I go there on *my* wheels.'[10]

Besides reading, Gladys loved the birds. She encouraged the pigeons to fly to the windowsill, where she fed them. Sometimes they flew into her room and the nurses got used to seeing Gladys sitting in bed, surrounded by them. She was upset when accidents occurred. One day a bird flew from a plinth and killed itself hitting a table – 'a half-grown starling so pretty and so hurt'.[11]

She watched racing. 'Gold Cup day for the free,'[12] she wrote, and

---

* Pope Paul visited the white-bearded Ecumenical Patriarch Athenagoras between 5 and 6 January 1964, in the first such meeting for 500 years.

proudly recorded several winners. The deaths of old friends upset her: 'depressed to read Vita Sackville died over the weekend'.[13] Occasionally she noted happenings at Blenheim and the travels of 'Blandford', while even 'poor' Consuelo was now viewed more favourably.

Christmas remained a sad time, but Gladys was entertained by the picture of the superintendent and the matron making a 'whistle stop with good wishes' and then 'speeding away in a large grey car'.[14] Sometimes depression overcame her: 'Feel so unhappy here, wish me dead.'[15]

The Official Solicitor sent occasional visitors, but they never got past her initial onslaughts. In 1964 one such found her 'in great form', recounting her triumphs against 'the enemy' – he presumed the staff at the hospital. A year before, her conversation had centred on 'getting out of this hell' but now he believed she was reconciled to staying.[16] A report from St Andrew's in 1968 indicated that Gladys was in good health, could still converse 'brilliantly' on current events, was reading several daily newspapers from cover to cover and was considered likely to live for a number of years.

As old age advanced, she was moved from the Cedars to a psycho-geriatric ward in the main block, where she had her own room, often remaining there all day. She broke her hip in January 1971 and spent her ninetieth birthday in Northampton General Hospital. She made a remarkable recovery and was soon walking the corridors of St Andrew's again with the use of a zimmer frame. She remained demanding but the nurses found her 'a very likeable character'.

And so, in O'Connell Ward at St Andrew's Hospital, Gladys lived on into her nineties. She took to a wheelchair as her mode of transport, although she could walk if she wanted to. She stayed alive due to a phenomenal appetite, an extraordinary will to live, yet nothing to live for. She had a super-human resistance to illness and accidents, rising like a phoenix from breakages, influenza and comas, to the astonishment of all. Many times the doctors brought out the death-certificate book, many times the last rites were said, but she survived them. She lived on and on, seemingly indestructible.

★ ★ ★ ★ ★

O'Connell Ward marked the end of Gladys's long journey through life, a voyage that began in Paris, raised her to the heights of fame as a radiant beauty, took her to Blenheim, then allowed her to drop into the black squalor of an Augean stable at Chacombe. Throughout her life she was content to be alone, and in old age her spirit was unbroken. Looking at illustrations of works of art, she would say: 'Look at that! Despair! Artists always despair because they never attain. But I'm not like that.'

Often she shone brightly, but then she fizzled out. And yet she would rise to shine again. She even shone for me in those last years in the hospital.

Gladys was ninety-four when I met her. I believe she allowed me to become a friend because I was too young to have had any connection with that past life. She said once: 'I seem to have had two lives, the past and the present.' She did her best to put the former out of mind. But I wonder if she did not have extraordinary visions and memories floating about in that beautifully shaped head to sustain her. It is easy to paint a grim picture, but she had lived a fuller and more varied life than most.

For years, Andrei had been her only regular visitor and friend. Sometimes she pretended to be asleep but he could spot Gladys secretly observing him. When it suited her she would suddenly 'wake up', exclaiming, 'How long have you been there?' I once sat beside her for so long that I fell asleep myself.

Some of the nurses were special favourites. She nicknamed Sister Dillon 'Mrs England' or 'The English Nurse', and Staff Nurse Battle was called 'Franka'. Less politely, one of the male staff was dubbed 'Fat Doctor' or '*Le Gros*'.

Visiting her had some alarming elements. I only communicated with a few of the patients, while Gladys ignored the lot. With one lady, Joy, I learnt that when she approached, with a tortured expression and hand outstretched, you had to say, 'Lovely - Lily of the Valley,' and then she would be happy. Otherwise she menaced you and became agitated. One memorable day, one of the ladies 'streaked' along the corridor – 'naked as a jaybird', as the Ray Stevens hit song put it. I never turned my back on any of them. Once I came in to see Gladys and she asked me where I had come from. I pointed to the door, but she thought I meant the room where the mad women sat. She said: 'No, you're not like that. They have thoughts but they can't direct them. Their thoughts come out, wee & wee . . .' She gestured as thoughts spun off left and right into the ether. 'There is a chasm between sanity and madness,' she said. 'Madness is an inability to balance or impress.'

Normally, I found Gladys in the Green Room. When she recognised me, she would take my hand and, without seeming to exert pressure, hold it in a vice-like grip. This continued until she was confident that I had settled down and was not about to disappear. We often talked alone in the doctor's office, and after she was seated comfortably, I would hand over the *nonnettes* (two packets of currant buns) and a box of After Eight, which were then concealed in her basket for late-night consumption. Conversation often began with strange tales about the iniquities of the hospital or the fate of the old ladies in the ward. Once she told me: 'They're all in the kissing halls, you know.'

I said: 'You mean like the women of the Pigalle?'

'Heavens, no!' she replied. 'Not even as good as that!'

This was my cue to produce a book. She loved looking through books, especially on art or artists, and on good days would concentrate closely on the pictures. She enjoyed a good conversation and stipulated: 'Don't mix with fools. Fools rub off on you like bad dye.' She told me she dreamt a lot, sometimes good dreams, sometimes bad. 'I wake up panting,' she said, 'and find myself *here* – in this hospital.'

During the years I was there, from 1975 to 1977, Gladys took in the arrival of Concorde, the 1976 earthquake in Italy, the separation of Princess Margaret and Lord Snowdon, and the demise of Mao in China. If she had missed something, she was never short of an answer. In May 1976, my father asked her who she thought would be the next President of the United States. She answered: 'To be honest I haven't been following the campaign, but you can be sure it will be the worst possible man!' Some weeks later I told her that Harold Wilson, the retiring Labour prime minister, was to be installed as a Knight of the Garter at Windsor. She commented: 'Well, he had been prime minister for ten years. Of course he is of very common birth, but I like him. He does his best, which is more than can be said for the rest of them. He's a good Liberal.'

I asked: 'You mean Labour by name, Liberal by politics?'

'Well, of course. He had to get the votes, didn't he?'

Gladys hated going into the garden, but one hot Sunday afternoon she was wheeled there with the other inmates and we sat in the sun, eating chocolate ice-cream. There were often curious happenings as a backdrop to our conversations such as when a jet of 'water' shot out from under one lady patient sitting in a nearby canvas chair. I asked Gladys: 'What is the highest form of knowledge?'

She thought for a moment and then said: 'Knowledge of science is the most important thing. But don't be a scientist. It's all new discoveries. The newest thing is held. You be a banker. Bankers have a finger in every pie. They can do anything.'

I protested that I did not have a good head for figures. 'That's perhaps because you don't like them much,' she said. 'It is a passion that can be very profitable, I'm told.'

'Well, what would a banker say to Epstein?' I pressed on. 'They would have nothing in common.'

'Epstein!' she cried. 'Honestly! Epstein was pained and unhappy. He used to cry over me. He was never happy doing what he did. He always wanted to do something else. You know, I think that's why he veered so much towards ugliness in his work . . . No, you be a banker. That way you'll always have a good dinner every night. I worry about that sometimes. Otherwise you'll end up in a place like this!'

I quote these vignettes to show the quality of her mind, when she was calm, relaxed and interested. Of course there were bad days too, when she was tired or distressed. Once I was only with her for ten minutes before she said: '*Kommen Sie ein andere Tag.*' ('Come another day.') I learnt never to take anything for granted. After a stroll in the garden, I drove the hour and a half back to London.

Gladys was forever keen to escape from the hospital and frequently asked me to help her. Fortunately, I had been schooled that trust is built by telling the truth, so I always said I couldn't, but told her when I was next coming and kept to that. One day she said: 'You take me downstairs and put me in your car.' I asked where we would go. 'Out into the world,' she answered.

In September 1976 Gladys suffered a bad fall and was transferred to Northampton General Hospital for an operation. She was ninety-five and survived it. Finding herself in different surroundings, she thought I had pulled off a miraculous coup. She was somewhat more than angry to find herself back at St Andrew's.

There were times when I brought visitors, my parents and my sister, and once Miron Grindea, editor of *ADAM*. Dorothy's grandson, Georges-Charles Tomaszewski, came as a forerunner, and later his mother, Betka, materialised after many years. She had tried to visit Gladys in the late 1960s but Gladys had declared: 'That woman is not my niece. My niece is a little girl.' Betka asked me to bring her and her husband, and she then made at least one more visit. I was not surprised when the ever-patient Sister Dillon said she preferred dealing with the patients.

I was always anxious in case Gladys broke off friendship with me, aware that she had done this so often in her life, with people like the Duke of Connaught, Montesquiou and Berenson. I survived one incident when, claiming not to have recognised me, she tipped a glass of water over me. There was another unpleasant incident after her return to St Andrew's, when she spat at me, something I succeeded in blanking from my memory until I found the account in my diary.

Then on the Sunday morning of 1 May 1977, I thought it was all over. A terrible scene occurred when I showed her an Helleu drawing of Helena Rubinstein. She threw it across the room, then engaged me in a charade similar to that inflicted on the Duke of Norfolk in 1903. She was to be Napoleon and I was to be a peasant. My imitation was hopelessly bad, not least because it had to be done in French. She watched me become increasingly self-conscious, and exhorted me: 'Do you need wine? Do you need gin? Do you need hashish?' Then she launched into one of the most fluent onslaughts on my character that I have ever had the misfortune to endure. She folded her arms and 'went to sleep'.

I had no alternative so went out into the garden where I sat forlornly on a seat by myself. My diary records:

I felt so miserable, rejected etc, and then one of those strange, wonderful things happened. An old, old man came up to me. He spoke briefly about the weather and the peacefulness and the beauty of the garden. Then he asked how old I was. '25,' I replied.

'How old do you think I am?' he asked.

I said: 'A little older than me. Sixty?'

'I was born on 21 May 1890,' he replied. 'That means I am about to be 87.'

I said: 'And you must remember the Diamond Jubilee of Queen Victoria?'

He sat down and told me that he had lived at Chewton Mendip. At the Jubilee there had been terrific parties and certain persons had got somewhat drunk at the end of the day. It transpired that he'd been at Westminster and then worked for Winston Churchill at the Board of Trade. His name was Richard Allenby [Arabin] Shore.*

He asked why I was there, and upon my explaining that I was visiting the Duchess of Marlborough 'who lives here', he asked: 'As a patient?' laying euphemisms aside.

I explained what had happened. He was marvellous. He said: 'Oh! Don't break it off, don't give up. Women are all the same. They're very difficult. You arrive next week with a box of chocolates and you'll be all right.' He said this with clearly inestimable wisdom. Then he was gone.[17]

Mr Shore's advice proved sound, though it was five weeks later that I returned somewhat nervously. Gladys simply said: 'I am glad to see you. I thought you'd given me up.'

I replied, 'No,' and we resumed our friendship, though I was careful not to provoke such a reaction again.

Sister Dillon was robustly unsympathetic. 'You ought to know the duchess's ways by now,' she said.

Late that summer Gladys suffered a bad fever and the last rites were read. Again she survived them, but time was running out.

The ninth of October 1977 was a Sunday and Gladys was in the same chair in which I had first met her two and a half years before. Her head was down and her feet were up on another chair. She was drowsy, but perked up briefly when I gave her the box of After Eights. She was hard to hear, but said, 'I don't want to die.' When I asked her how she was, she replied: 'I'm very far from well.'

We tried to look at books, but she was too tired. Then she asked me for my hands and clutched them tightly for about two minutes. I

---

* Richard Arabin Shore (1890–1985), born in Weymouth, served in the First World War as a gunner, Royal Canadian Horse Artillery Brigade, later a civil servant. He did a curious thing in marrying a widow twenty-five years his senior, in 1935, Sidonie Brodie (1865–1945), daughter of HE Field Marshal von Neuber, Austrian Army, and widow of Wilfred Brodie.

kissed her on the left forehead and her eyes widened – not really permitted that! Then I kissed her hand, and this was deemed more correct. The ominous feeling came over me that we would not meet again.

I stood back and looked at her. She smiled at me, nodding slightly as I waved goodbye. I stole another glance at her as I left the Green Room, and closed the door. She looked extraordinarily like an Epstein – a sculpture with pink skin, blue eyes and white hair. The other ladies were at lunch, and so Gladys was all alone.

On my way out, by chance I met my old friend, Mr Shore. We had a short chat and he said he had often wondered how I was getting along. Presently he wandered away, and I drove to London.* At home I wrote to Gladys's niece, Milo, to say: 'Gladys sat mellow in the chair . . . and I had the distinct feeling that it was our last meeting. If this is the beginning of the end, then Gladys is peaceful and untroubled. She is, as it were, just slowly going to sleep as at the end of a very long day.'

Four days later, on Thursday, 13 October, at eleven o'clock at night, Gladys died peacefully in her sleep. A requiem mass was said at St Gregory's Church, Northampton, in the presence of a tiny group of mourners. Then they took her to Chacombe churchyard where Father Maunsell officiated at the interment. Only six wreaths lay on the coffin, one from Blenheim: 'With deepest sympathy from the Marlborough family', one from me.

Her niece Betka and her husband were at the funeral, and Andrei stood sadly by the grave. Also present were Mr John Schilizzi, as church warden, his wife Lady Sophia, and Joan Rees, the London solicitor administering the estate. A small crowd of villagers gathered outside the church to witness the return of the lady of the Grange.

★ ★ ★ ★ ★

Hardly had Gladys died than the long-made plans to dispose of her estate ground into action. Her family converged on Christie's for a meeting, later described as one of the most unpleasant gatherings ever

---

* After Gladys's death, he sent me a message of sympathy. I wrote to him and received in return a long, rambling letter. I remember my encounter with him with considerable gratitude. What a kind man!

conducted at King Street, on account of the hostility between certain members. It was agreed that all her possessions, now released by the Court of Protection, would fall to the auctioneer's hammer. There was a series of sales in the course of 1978. Her jewellery raised £452,755 in one hour, a sapphire single-stone ring of 12.86 carats fetching £105,000 (about £8,165 per carat). The so-called 'Marlborough Diamond', originally 48.01 carats, was sold for £60,000 (and stolen from Graff's in Brompton Road in 1980). A tiara, not identified as having been bought as part of the Russian Imperial jewels in 1928, was instantly authenticated and sold to Madame Marcos of the Philippines. In another sale, Rodin's *Faunesse Debout* fetched £17,000, and a previously unrecorded Toulouse-Lautrec (the one left to her by Walter Berry) £58,000. By the end of the season the total stood at £784,000.

A stone was placed in Chacombe churchyard to mark the grave. The inscription read: GLADYS MARIE DEACON, DOWAGER DUCHESS OF MARLBOROUGH 1881-1977. Above the name, to the slight concern of the local vicar but at my suggestion, the stone-mason carved a representation of Gladys's eye, a copy of that painted by Colin Gill in the portico at Blenheim fifty years before.

★ ★ ★ ★ ★

The name of Gladys Deacon evokes the image of a beautiful girl with a devastating sense of humour, abundant charm and the quick conversation that enabled her to monopolise great men at the dinner-table. Eventually most of those whom Gladys charmed became suspicious and searched for what lay behind the façade, and they turned away from her. Or did she turn them away? She survived the ghastly drama of her face, but she did not weather her Pyrrhic victory in winning Marlborough. How sad that she did not wed someone who might have fulfilled the demands for which Marlborough was so inadequate. She paid a high price for her coronet.

Her marriage failed as many of those Anglo-American matches failed. The British Establishment can be witheringly unkind to those they do not understand and they were remorselessly unforgiving of her. She ended her days disillusioned, but not despairing.

From one of the suitcases in which Gladys kept her letters emerged a poem written in 1901. It is impossible to know who wrote it, but

the author knew well the young girl to whom he gave it and understood her. The poem is no masterpiece, but it was written with love
and inspired by a unique personality that influenced the lives and
works of so many great and gifted men.

Sweet and Twenty

Bright, sweet and fair, with a head that's sometimes level
A wit most rare, with more than a spice of devil.
And large round eyes that appear so intent and true,
She looks so wise while she inwardly laughs at you.
Sometimes she affects a look like a Madonna;
Then one quite expects a halo to grow on her:
Inconsequent – in every succeeding minute
Her mind is bent on something and how to win it;
Withal, such charm, you'll forget she's sometimes selfish,
Your rage she'll calm with a sweetness almost elfish;
Young men and old men lie down and bow before her;
Young girls and old dames all equally adore her;
All things that bore her are wished by her in Hades,
You won't want more now to guess her name is Gladys.

Appendix

GLADYS'S ANCESTORS

THE DEACONS

The Deacons were Gladys's paternal family. They originated in Burlington, New Jersey, with her great-grandfather, David Deacon, who became a captain in the United States Navy and served with distinction under Commodore Edward Preble, one of the most romantic and legendary figures from the early history of that navy. David Deacon was one of 'Preble's boys' and took part in the Tripoli campaign against Barbary pirates in the summer of 1804. He was later imprisoned by the British in the war of 1812 and interned at Little York.

In August 1824, Margaret, Countess of Blessington,* Lord Byron's friend, came to Naples. David Deacon was serving under Commodore Crichton in his ship. The countess was impressed by how 'exceedingly gentlemanly, well informed and intelligent'[1] the officers were. A few days later the captain was one of the officers who went to dine with the countess: 'They are sensible and agreeable men: one, a Captain Deacon, has his son on board, a very fine and interesting child, eight or ten years of age. It was pleasant to see the kindness and gentleness displayed towards this boy, by the messmates of his father.'[2] David had named his second son Edward Preble after the commodore. Gladys's father owned the countess's letters to E. P. Deacon and used to bother William James on the matter.[3]

David Deacon bequeathed 'the farm near Erie commonly called Kent Farm on Walnut Creek by purchase from the estate at a fair valuation'. He showed sound judgement in the distribution of his

---

* Marguerite Power Farmer Gardiner, Countess of Blessington (1789–1849), author, born in Ireland.

323

assets, insisting that 'my sons receive as good an education as the property I leave them will afford – being more desirous that they should be well educated than that the money should be reserved to spend after they are of age'.[4] He died on 22 February 1840.

Edward Preble Deacon, Gladys's grandfather, had a varied career, climbing several rungs of the social ladder in his short life of thirty-eight years. In the late 1830s he had a whaleboat business with his brother Adolphe. But on an excursion at Port Sheldon, Adolphe was the victim of over-exposure, 'uttered a groan, fell violently on the deck in convulsions' and presently expired.[5] Edward Preble Deacon was then engaged in lumbering in Michigan, and later took up the post of attaché to the United States Legation in Boston under General Lewis Cass.

Arriving in Boston he exuded an aura of mystery. One rumour had it that he was a Frenchman because he had travelled abroad, but Mrs Charles Pelham Curtis,[*] a rich socialite, described him as 'a handsome, attractive man, but without visible property . . . coming from one of the Middle States'.[6] On 20 November 1841, at Hudson, New York, he made a most advantageous marriage with Sarah Annabella Parker, daughter of Peter Parker, a rich merchant living at 46 Beacon Street, and a member of the well-known family of Boston Parkers. Hence their son, who was Gladys's father, liked to call himself Edward Parker Deacon, because it sounded grander, and his youngest daughter, Dorothy, went a step further and hyphenated the names.

Edward Parker Deacon had a brother, Harleston (1848-1926), and a sister, Ida (1847-83), whose grave is in the same Newport cemetery as Mr Deacon's (and his daughter, Edith Gray's). 'Harl', as his brother called him, stepped forward to help the family at various times of trouble.

THE PARKERS

The Parkers descended from Nathaniel Parker, born in Dedham, Massachusetts, in 1670, the son of Samuel Parker, of English birth. Peter Parker decided that his daughter and son-in-law should live in

---

[*] Caroline Gardiner Curtis (1827-1917), daughter of Thomas Graves Cary and Mary Ann Cushing Perkins.

a magnificent dwelling and was prepared to finance this. Thus Deacon House was built between 1846 and 1848, occupying an entire block on the corner of Washington Street, between Worcester and East Concord Streets in Boston's South End. The house was designed by Jean Lemoulnier, adorned with a mansard roof, and was an early example of French architecture in Boston, which, until then, had looked to England for inspiration. It was surrounded by a high brick wall with a porter's lodge on one side of the double gates on Concord Street.

Edward Preble Deacon had acquired avant-garde tastes and he undertook two extended shopping trips to France, taking advantage of the sales of royal estates following the 1848 Revolution. The result was that whole rooms and fabulous furnishings were shipped over by the boatload and earned the house the reputation as 'a wonder of the mid-century'. Among the more spectacular embellishments were a large square piece of Gobelin tapestry representing 'Victory', which hung by the oak staircase in the hall, and four large oil-paintings by Fragonard on the 'History of Love'. From the salon with its mirrors, gilded panels and candelabra, great parlours extended one beyond another in a glorious vista. The Marie Antoinette Boudoir, an oval room, was covered with thirteen panels in pale silk damask, its ceiling bearing a painting by Fragonard. The dining room had a cabinet containing a Sèvres china tea service presented by the City of Paris to Marie Antoinette. The house was lit by 400 candles.

Yet the treasures were amply contrasted with dismal curiosities, for the house had more than its share of dingy green velvet draperies and ancient breastplates and shields surrounded by divers diabolical weapons.

The poet Henry Longfellow visited the house in 1848 and described it as 'the most beautiful private house I ever beheld. It haunts me like a vision.'[7] Caroline Curtis recalled a fine ball at the house and 'some charming small dances, ending in a supper, announced to us by tall French footmen in livery'.[8]

Sarahann Parker brought social status and wealth to the Deacons. She and her husband would have been splendid characters in an early Henry James novel – Sarahann, a dull, rich, unattractive bride, the victim of Edward Preble Deacon, a dashing profiteer. They produced two sons and a daughter: one of the sons was Gladys's father, born on

2 October 1844. Their marriage lasted a mere ten years, for Edward Preble Deacon, remembered as 'the chief attraction'[9] of Deacon House, died of consumption in Savannah, Georgia, on 1 March 1851. At his death, he was worth $90,000. Gladys's father was left in the care of his mother and his rich Parker grandparents, and lived on in Deacon House until 1861. The house was briefly reopened for one last party, given to celebrate his return from the Civil War in 1865.[10]

As recorded, Sarahann was an epileptic who ended her days in a lunatic asylum in Isleworth, Middlesex, in 1900. Her simple grey marble stone in the now derelict Isleworth Cemetery spells her Christian names wrongly, and bears the significant message: 'In Peace'.

Deacon House itself fared little better. It sank into a state of decrepitude and ghostly stories grew up about it. One nocturnal visitor told a mysterious tale of a tall lady, dressed in rich, flowered brocade, who swept through the empty rooms at dead of night, holding high a tiny lamp, which glimmered above her head. The willowy shade did not appreciate being disturbed. Turning her eyes full on the intruder, she raised her hand with a commanding gesture towards the door.[11]

Peter Parker died in 1870. The contents of Deacon House were put up for sale in February 1871, and thirteen thousand people bought tickets to view its much discussed but rarely seen interiors.[12] Thus the contents of Deacon House fell to an auctioneer's hammer over three days and raised $22,250. Today only the rear façade survives, while a later structure looms behind garish shop-fronts and shields an empty house, as deserted and forgotten as the family who once lived there.

THE BALDWINS

In contrast to the adventurous Deacons and the fashionable Parkers, the Baldwins were a grand New England family with a considerable fortune, her share of which Florence, Gladys's mother, contrived to squander by 1918. Originally from Aston Clinton in Buckinghamshire, they had been in America since 1638. Florence's father was Rear-Admiral Charles H. Baldwin (1822–88), said to be the richest man in the US Navy. His grandfather, Captain Daniel Baldwin, had been a Captain of the Revolution, a close ally of George Washington and a founder member of the Society of the Cincinnati. The admiral's naval career was determined when, as a lad building toy castles at home in New York, he chanced on the novels of Captain Frederick Marryat. The books kindled in him the ambition to be a sailor and led to a successful career in the American Navy. Thus Gladys had naval ancestors on both sides.

The admiral was by no means a modest man. In his later years at Snug Harbor on Bellevue Avenue, Newport, Rhode Island, he enjoyed telling tales of his naval career and in particular the taking over of California in 1846:

> After six weeks of beating against the trade-wind, which is constant all summer, we reached Monterey, capital of California, several hours ahead of the English. I was ordered ashore with a boat's crew, and raised the American flag over the Cuartel. Next day the squadron sailed for Yerba Buena [now San Francisco] and I was left behind in command of a hundred sailors. That act of raising the American flag brought into the Union the territory between British Columbia, the Rocky Mountains, and what is now Mexico – about the size of the whole of Europe, if you leave Russia out![13]

In 1854 Baldwin resigned from the navy and was given command of the Vanderbilt Nicaraguan steamers, which plied between New York and the Pacific Ocean. A warm friendship developed between Baldwin and 'Commodore' Vanderbilt, a friendship that was to be echoed in the mutual fondness of their respective progeny, Gladys and Consuelo, who both married the same duke. While Admiral Baldwin was deeply grateful to the commodore and warmly disposed towards him, he could not help looking down on the Vanderbilts as a clan. It is reported that he once chopped off his daughter Florence's hair for the crime of having danced with a Vanderbilt at a party. The admiral later commanded the largest ship in the US Navy, SS *Vanderbilt*, in the Civil War at the express wish of the commodore.

Admiral Baldwin passed some years in California as Fleet Captain of the Northern Pacific Squadron and was a special partner in the commission firm of Edward L. G. Steele & Co. He became a rear-admiral in 1879 and, due to his considerable fortune, earned the reputation of a generous host. Alas, his genial disposition deserted him when he took to sea. He became a stern disciplinarian and it was unwise to transgress aboard one of his ships. No man sent for court martial was ever reprieved and the sentences meted out were an ugly deterrent to future offenders. For assaulting an officer of police, a wretched first-class fireman was sentenced 'to be confined for thirty days in double irons on bread and water with full rations every fifth day; to lose one month's pay, amounting to thirty-five dollars: and to perform extra duty and be deprived of liberty for three months'. Approving the sentence, the admiral felt compelled to add: 'I consider the punishment awarded as exceedingly light for the offence which the accused has committed.'[14] He preferred to order sixty lashes.

The climax of the admiral's career inspired from him behaviour less than worthy of his rank. Because he was the most distinguished American in the vicinity he was appointed to attend the Coronation of Tsar Alexander III of Russia in 1883 and to 'indicate the friendship of the United States for the Czar and the Russian people'. The admiral sailed to Kronstadt and progressed to Moscow. The night before the ceremony he began to get anxious as his invitation had not arrived. In a report to the secretary of the navy he gave his version of what occurred:

> No invitations having come at midnight, I notified the minister; and at seven o'clock the next morning I received from him cards of admission to the Tribune which was said to be opposite to the Church in which the Emperor was to be crowned, and which was occupied by Attachés of Legations, Russian officers, etc., etc. (I may here state that the ceremony was to begin at 8 o'clock, and we were required to be in full dress and were two miles from the Kremlin.) Of course I could not attend in such an inferior position. Although the Church in which the Coronation took place was small, accommodating about three hundred people, still, all the Ambassadors, Foreign Ministers, their wives, daughters, Secretaries of Legations, and all Military Attachés were invited; – consequently I have the mortification to report that I was not able to be present at this great and important ceremony.[15]

Later the representative of the United States Legation at St Petersburg gave his account, describing the admiral's conduct as having been in most questionable taste:

From this office I drove to the Admiral's house, though it was then 2
a.m. when he had doubtless retired, and arousing him, gave him my
message with the assurance in the name of the Chamberlain that he
would be taken to his place at the ceremony. The Admiral replied that
'he would accept no invitation given at the 11th hour; that he preferred
taking his coffee comfortably at home', and nothing I could say had
any influence on his decision.[16]

The boycotting of the ceremony did not prevent the admiral from
expressing his opinions about it. A few weeks afterwards, he told Mrs
Mary King Waddington, the American wife of a French diplomat,
that it was 'all show (not much of it) and hollow'. They entered into
heated discussion and Mrs Waddington concluded: 'I fancy he always
takes the opposite side on principle.'[17]

When the admiral died in November 1888, five hundred marines
escorted his coffin to the funeral at St Thomas's Church, Fifth Avenue.
He was laid to rest in the family vault at St Mark's-in-the-Bowery in
downtown New York.

Personal Postscript

Gladys had a considerable impact on my life. I was lucky to find her and I venture to suggest that it was not bad for her when I appeared. She was ninety-four and I was twenty-three. I am confident that I cheered up the last two years of her life. Had I not become involved, she would have remained in the obscurity in which she had chosen to live for the last forty years of her life.

I was in Florence in October 1977, on my way to research at I Tatti, when I heard that she had died. I was unable to return to England for the funeral, and when I attempted to go into an empty church for some quiet time while the service was going on, the door was locked. Instead I sat in my car.

My aunt Margaret wrote to me: 'I am sorry for you, because you have lost a friend but of course you will be able to give her a lasting gift if you can tell of her life and the influences she had on so many talented people, even geniuses . . . As a last tribute to Gladys, you proved to her that she could still attract & hold people even in extreme old age.'[1] Sister Dillon, my great ally at St Andrew's Hospital, replied to a letter I wrote her: 'Take comfort in knowing that you brought some happiness back into her life. Your visits meant so much to her, and were always eagerly awaited.'[2]

The first edition of *Gladys* received largely favourable reviews and reached the right homes. One of its readers was Sir Cecil Beaton, then living at Broadchalke. He had the book read to him between September and November 1979. He was seeking a biographer and I was sent down to visit him in December. He chose me, which I often thought was Gladys's posthumous gift to me. I went to see him again on 15 January 1980. He died three days later. As I set off on another adventure, I thought for the first time that perhaps I was not going to be a failure in life.

I remained interested in Gladys over the years that followed. When I went to Rome in 1988, I explored her part of the city, the Palazzo Farnese, and visited the graveyard where her mother is buried. The family and the team at Blenheim became gradually more accepting of her, and I became accepted as a curious living link to a lost era in its history. The eyes in the portico were restored in 2008, a first step in the reintegration of Gladys into the palace's history.

In 2011 an exhibition was staged in the Long Library, so I played a part in bringing her back to the palace from which she had been evicted in 1933. I was allowed to make a speech and could not resist saying that, if Gladys could be brought back to Blenheim, the duke and I should stage exhibitions in trouble spots in the world such as Iraq and Afghanistan, since, after this act of reconciliation, anything was surely possible.

The exhibition also inspired a touching reunion with Sister Dillon. Blenheim wrote to St Andrew's Hospital for comments. Three came, all anonymous. One said:

> Hugo Vickers, who was writing her biography, used to come and see her and she was always in a good mood after he left her, recalling her earlier years.[3]

Another stated: 'I remember Hugo Vickers, the author, visited her regularly as he was writing a book about her and built up a lovely relationship with her.'[4] That had to have been from Sister Dillon. She was alive. I wrote to her and she brought eighteen of her family to see the exhibition at Blenheim. We had not met since 1977 and, I confess, it was an emotional reunion. Sister Dillon died in 2018. I know I could never have got through to Gladys without her support over those two years between 1975 and 1977, and I dedicate this edition to her memory.

At difficult times in my life, I have escaped back into Gladys's world. I owned most of her private papers, and would occasionally type out letters and documents. I went to Florence in 2014, tried to find Audrey's grave, visited the Villa d'Este at Tivoli, which I had seen in Gladys's photographs, and, wishing to visit Caprarola, found myself giving a lecture in the palace about the time her mother lived there. In 2018 I returned to research at Villa I Tatti, and, with the help of my daughter Alice, then aged seventeen, we finally found Audrey's grave. I was also glad to be asked to write about Gladys for the *Dictionary of National Biography*. At the eleventh hour, I found the fascinating cache of letters in the Comtesse Greffulhe papers in Paris. Even after that I flew off to explore the Charles and Virginia Baldwin papers in the Penrose Library in Colorado Springs, and was not disappointed.

Now that this book is finished, Gladys's papers, of which I have been the custodian for forty years, find a permanent home in the Blenheim Palace Archives.

And all this came from the stray reading of a page in Chips Channon's diary, way back in 1968, when I was sixteen years old.

Acknowledgements

I have been working on this book for a long time (arguably forty years) and I risk forgetting those who have helped me along the way. There are many that I want to thank:

Tom Perrin for commissioning it. He felt that the time had come to bring Gladys to a new readership in a new generation, and thus guided the shape of this version from the start. Tom created Zuleika in 2017 and as I write, has had many successes, most notably with Anne Glenconner's *Lady in Waiting* in 2019 – which reached number 1 on Amazon, and he also brought *The Quest for Queen Mary* to life in 2018 (it had languished in a drawer for ten years). I consider that his list should be examined very closely as he has backed a number of other books of which more mainstream publishers and agents have not always seen the potential. Indeed, I was told that a new edition of Gladys would be 'a labour of love'. It certainly has been that, but it has also received lots of encouragement.

Rowena Webb at Hodder took Queen Mary on and also took on Gladys. It has been a joy to work with Rowena and her team – in particular Ian Wong, who has masterminded the editing, Hazel Orme, doyenne of copy-editors, Juliet Brightmore, Caitriona Horne, Eleni Lawrence and Karen Geary.

Blenheim Palace were not keen on Gladys back in the 1970s, though when the first edition came out, the 11th Duke and his then wife, Rosita, began to take an interest in her story. In 2008 the late Duke agreed to the suggestion of Alexander Muir (grandson of the 10th Duke and a trustee) that her eyes should be restored in the portico, and also to Alexander's suggestion of a major exhibition based around Gladys's life at the palace in 2011. Alexander Muir has played a vital role in the reintegration of Gladys.

I would also like to thank the present Duke and Duchess, and Lady

Henrietta Spencer-Churchill for their support with subsequent projects since then. It has been one of the most rewarding experiences of my life to see Gladys 'restored' to Blenheim, a process that still has more potential adventures.

At Blenheim I would like to thank Dominic Hare, Heather Carter, John Hoy, Dr Alexa Frost, Boun Norton and Richard Cragg for their help. Karen Wiseman was immensely supportive before she left in 2018, and throughout this time, Antonia Keaney has been a joy to work with – and again we have many future plans cooking. While working on my book, Michael Waterhouse and Karen Wiseman produced a biography of the 9th Duke, greatly to be welcomed. Mike was another grandson of the 10th Duke who helped reverse the traditional view of Gladys at Blenheim.

I have received copious help from others – Nicolas Cavaillès, for help over Audrey Deacon and Catherine Pozzi; Mary Jane Cryan, who arranged a visit and lecture at Caprarola, & Luciano Passini at Caprarola; Celia Lee for help over Jean Hamilton; Claudia Rosencrantz & the Degas drawing (now at Pallandt House); Caroline Weber, for help over the Comtesse Greffulhe; Ilaria Della Monica for help with the Berensons, and for an enjoyable few days researching once more at Villa I Tatti; Barbara Guidi, for help with Boldini (& the wonderful Boldini exhibition in Ferrara in 2019); Tim Morris and his team at the Peaks Pike District Library, Colorado Springs, for help with Charles & Virginia Baldwin; Jessica James for showing me round Colorado Springs School (the Baldwin home in Colorado Springs); Rainer von Hessen, for help, advice and translations with Keyserling and Hofmannsthal; Dr Francis de Marneffe, who showed me round the McLean Hospital, Boston; Rick Hutto for identifying elusive characters in the book; Robert Nedelkoff, a walking encyclopaedia, specifically for help with Djuna Barnes; Caterina Fiorani at the Archivio Fondazione Camillo Caetani for help with Roffredo Caetani; Olivia Varig over Hofmannsthal; Julia Bolton Holloway in Florence; Patricia Hageman over F. Marion Crawford; Carol DeBoer-Langworthy over Neith Boyce; Jennifer Petro over Abeille; Michael Frease (Claremont); Allen Packwood (Churchill Archives); Mrs Christine Sturgess, for kindly showing me round Chacombe Grange in its present incarnation; Nicola Vivian (another Zuleika author) for her advice and moral support; Susannah Stapleton with Maud West; Sara Hiorns, Adam Zamosyki, Antony Green, Sue Woodford and many more besides.

It has been nice being in touch with members of Gladys's family. Milo Gray remained a close friend until her death in 2015; also Countess Lila Pálffy, Gina Pálffy-Szokoloczy & Philippe Szokoloczy, Domino Szokoloczy (who helped scan photos); Alexander Valtorta-Méndez (grandson of Caja Pálffy); Towny Gray and his sister, Pam Reese; and unmet but in touch – Melinda Murray & Wendy Chapin.

Many people helped me with the first edition of Gladys, including in particular her nephew and nieces (above all, Milo Gray, who was a constant help throughout my research), the staff of St Andrew's Hospital, Northampton (and in particular, Sister June Dillon), Andrei Kwiatkowsky (her Polish helper), David Green at Blenheim Palace, and many literary figures of the day, whom I consulted, including Paul Morand, David Garnett, Comte Louis Gautier-Vignal, Professor Philip Kolb, Philippe Jullian and Stuart Preston. I was also helped by other biographers, in England, France and the United States, including Professors Leon Edel, Ernest Samuels and Sir Harold Acton. I worked in a number of libraries. All are listed in *Gladys, Duchess of Marlborough*, and specific quotes are cited in this volume.

In producing this book, it has been a great joy to have the help of my children, in particular Alice, who came on the trip to Fiesole, and helped me research at Villa I Tatti. Arthur typed several draft chapters and scanned images, and George also scanned, but more importantly saved the day with numerous computer crises and saved the day when my computer crashed – with impeccable timing – just as I was in the last week of tying everything together. Without him, I would have been heading to Northampton . . .

Copyrights

For copyrights, permission was given for the last edition from the heirs of HRH The Duke of Connaught, the 9th Duke of Marlborough and Consuelo Vanderbilt, and Mary Berenson.

For this edition, I would like to thank the following for access to and use of material in their archives –

Blenheim Palace Heritage Foundation –
The papers of the 9th Duke of Marlborough.

Churchill Archives Centre –
Letters to Sir Winston Churchill.

Biblioteca Berenson, Villa I Tatti, &
The Harvard University Center for Italian Renaissance Studies –
The papers of Bernard Berenson.

Lilly Library, Indiana University –
Letters from Mary Berenson to her mother, Hannah Whitall Smith.

Archives Nationales of Paris –
The papers of the Comtesse Greffulhe (quoted by kind permission of Laure de Gramont).

Also to Austen Gray – Towny and his sister, Pamela – for permission to quote from letters written by Milo Gray, and their grandmother Edith.

Manuscript Sources

UK

Author's papers –
The Gladys Deacon papers – letters, diaries, albums, press cuttings, financial and legal papers, currently in the possession of the author, but soon to go to Blenheim Palace Archives.
The papers of Charles & Virginia Baldwin (relating to Gladys, her mother, step-grandmother & sisters).
Hugo Vickers private papers, diaries and notes.
The letters of Niall, 10th Duke of Argyll.

Blenheim Palace Archives –
  The papers of the 9th Duke of Marlborough (letters from Gladys, & papers relating to Consuelo Vanderbilt).

Bodleian Library –
  The papers of David Green (quoted with permission of his family).

British Library –
  The papers of Lady Ottoline Morrell.

Churchill College, Cambridge –
  The papers of Sir Winston Churchill.

France

Bibliothèque Nationale –
  The papers of Comte Robert de Montesquiou.
  The papers of Anatole France.

Archives Nationales –
  The papers of the Comtesse Greffulhe.

Germany

Technische Universität Darmstadt –
  The papers of Count Hermann Keyserling (Das Hermann-Keyserling-Archiv der ULB).

Italy

Villa I Tatti, Settignano –
  The papers of Bernard Berenson.
  Copies of the letters from Mary Berenson to Hannah Whitall Smith (the originals being in the Lilly Library, Indiana University).

The USA

The papers of the late Mrs Austen T. Gray (now held by her family).

Humanities Research Center, The University of Texas at Austin –
    The papers of Lady Ottoline Morrell.

Boston Athenaeum –
    Papers and books relating to the Deacons in Boston.

Library of Congress, Washington –
    Papers relating to the 9th Duke of Marlborough and Winston
    Churchill.

Peaks Pike District Library, Colorado Springs –
    The papers of Charles & Virginia Baldwin.

Since 2019 I have been running an Instagram page for Gladys, posting
a daily image from her collection, which can be followed at
@gladysdeacon or found online at www.instagram.com/gladysdeacon/.

Sources

Archive Sources

ANP – Archives Nationales, Paris.

ATG – Papers in possession of the late Mrs Austen T. Gray, still in the possession of her family, USA.

BNP – Bibliothèque Nationale, Paris.

BPA – Blenheim Palace Archives.

CAB – Baldwin Family Papers, 1853-1955 [1911-1926] MSS 0263, Pikes Peak Library Special Collections, Colorado Springs, USA.

CCC – Churchill College, Cambridge.

GDP – Gladys Deacon Papers (currently in the possession of the author, but presently to go to the Blenheim Palace Archives.

HRC – Humanities Research Center, Texas, USA.

HVP – Hugo Vickers's personally owned papers.

LL – Lilly Library, Indiana University, USA.

VIT – Bernard Berenson Archives, Villa I Tatti, Settignano.

Papers marked 'formerly in GDP' mean either those which were regrettably sold at auction, or 'borrowed' by a member of Gladys's family and never returned. In certain cases there are copies in HVP.

Names

BB – Bernard Berenson
C – Consuelo Vanderbilt Balsan
EPD – Edward Parker Deacon
FB – Florence Baldwin
G – Gladys Deacon
HV – Hugo Vickers

SOURCES

HWS – Hannah Whitall Smith
M – 9th Duke of Marlborough
MB – Mary Berenson
WSC – Winston Churchill

Photographs are from the author's collection, additional source Alamy, inset p. 5 above.

Every reasonable effort has been made to trace copyright holders, but if there are any errors or omissions, Hodder & Stoughton will be pleased to insert the appropriate acknowledgement in any subsequent printings or editions.

Notes

Introduction

1 Robert Rhodes James (ed.), *Chips*, p. 382.
2 Ibid.
3 HV, diary, 22 March 1968.
4 Ibid., 9 June 1975.
5 Ibid., 6 July 1975.
6 Ibid., 20 February 1976.
7 Ibid., 20 February 1976.
8 Ibid., 7 March 1976.

1. A Remarkable Young Person

Based on newspaper accounts for 1892, notably the *New York Times*, 18 November 1892; *L'Affaire Deacon* in A. Bataille, *Causes Criminelles et Mondaines 1892* (Paris, 1893), pp. 161–86; and letters from Bernard Berenson to Mary Berenson, 9 July 1904, 14 August 1908, and 19 November 1916 (VIT); *Drame de Cannes* (246) *Note concernant Madame Deacon* – Fonds Montesquiou (BNP); and newspaper accounts in 1892, including *The News* (Newport), 19 February and 21 May; *The Times*, 19, 20, 23 and 29 February; 11 March and 21 May; *Daily Telegraph*, 20, 23 and 29 February; 28 May; and *New York Times*, 20, 25, 29 February, and 22 May.

1 'Heartbreaks of Society', *American Weekly*, 21 August 1949.
2 FB to G, 6 February 1914 [formerly in GDP].
3 G, conversation with the author, 7 February 1976.
4 G to M, 3 October 1918 [BPA].
5 Ibid., Tuesday night, undated but 18 June 1918 [BPA].
6 EPD to George B. Peck Jr, Boston, 17 March 1867.
7 Unidentified press cutting sent by Rick Hutto.
8 Virginia Baldwin to G, New York, 19 February 1935 [GDP].
9 Henry James to Thomas Sergeant Perry, 2 November 1879, in Walker and Zacharias, p. 35.
10 Admiral C.H. Baldwin to Charles A. Baldwin, Paris, 11 May 1885 [CAB].

11 G to M, 4 October 1918. [BPA].

12 Sue Woodford, 'My Memories of the "Old Dutch"' (*Chacombe Chimes*, September 1997), p. 10.

13 Admiral C.H. Baldwin's Will, dated 13 January 1888 [CAB].

14 *New York Tribune*, 30 November 1919.

15 *Daily News*, 2 September 1934.

16 *Daily Telegraph*, 23 February 1892.

17 *International Herald Tribune* (Paris edition), 21 May 1892.

2. Murder in the South of France

1 Gramont, *Au Temps des Équipages,* p. 96.

2 Castellane, p. 104.

3 *Daily Telegraph*, 23 February 1892.

4 MB to HWS, I Tatti, 2 March 1901 [LL].

5 *New York Times*, 21 February 1892.

6 Matthieson and Murdock, p. 116.

7 Ibid., p. 308.

8 Dumas statement, 19 May 1892, quoted in *Daily Telegraph*, 20 May 1892.

9 *The Guardian*, 21 May 1892.

10 *International Herald Tribune* (Paris edition), 21 May 1892.

11 Ibid.

12 *New York Times*, 21 May 1892.

3. America

1 EPD to G, 30 March 1892 [GDP].

2 Gladys to FB, 2 April 1892 [formerly in GDP].

3 Sister to FB, 2 April 1892 [GDP].

4 Coolidge, 17 June 1892.

5 EPD to G, 24 September 1892 [GDP].

6 *San Francisco Chronicle*, 29 December 1892.

7 G to FB, 14 March 1893 [formerly in GDP].

8 *New York Times*, 24 March 1893.

9 G to FB, 19 November 1893 [formerly in GDP].

10 The late David McKibbin (1906-78), conversation with the author, Boston, 25 March 1976.

11 William James to Henry James, Chocorua, 5 July 1897, in Skrupskelis and Berkeley, p. 10.

12 G to FB, *circa* 1895 [formerly in GDP].

13 *New York Times*, 4 January 1894.

14 Reported by G to FB, 19 May 1893 [formerly in GDP].

15 G to FB, 22 October 1893 [formerly in GDP].

16 G, diary, 8 February 1894 [formerly in GDP].

17 G to FB, 23 April 1895 [formerly in GDP].

18 *Boston Globe*, 25 August 1895.

19 Ibid., 22 September 1895.

20 G to FB, 16 October 1895 [formerly in GDP].

21 Mrs Agnes Grylls to G, 25 October 1942 [GDP].

22 G to FB, undated but 1896 [formerly in GDP].

23 Quoted in the *San Francisco Chronicle*, 13 December 1897.

24 Henry James to EPD, 6 June 1897 [copy in GDP]; also in Edel, pp. 44-5.

25 William James to Henry James, Chocorua, 5 July 1897, in Skrupskelis and Berkeley, Vol 3, p. 10.

26 Henry James to William James, Dunwich, Saxmundham, Suffolk, 7 August 1897, related in Edel, (ed.), Vol IV, pp. 54-5, & Skrupskelis and Berkeley,*Correspondence of William & Henry James, Volume 3*, p. 15.

27 G, conversation with the author, 26 March 1977.

28 *San Francisco Chronicle*, 25 February 1900.

29 *New York Times*, August 1897.

30 EPD, copy of medical opinion by Charles L. Dana, MD (1897) [ATG].

31 *The News*, 24 August 1897.

32 Edward Cowles to W. P. Blake, 9 September 1897 [ATG].

33 Ibid.

34 *San Francisco Chronicle*, 15 April 1898.

35 MB to HWS, I Tatti, 2 March 1901 [LL].

36 *Boston Globe*, 30 July 1901.

37 *New York Tribune*, 9 July 1901.

4. Paris in the Belle Epoque

1 G, conversation with the author, 11 March 1977.

2 G to FB, 17 October 1897 [formerly in GDP].

3 G to Audrey, undated but 1898 [formerly in GDP].

4 G to FB, 8 December 1898 [formerly in GDP].

5 G, conversation with the author, 11 March 1977.

6 Unidentified press cutting, 11 February 1902 [ATG].

7 G, conversation with the author, 19 January 1977.

8 Ibid., 19 March 1977.

9 Unidentified press cutting, 11 February 1902

10 Gladys, Duchess of Marlborough, article, *McCall's,* July 1927.

11 Berenson, *The Passionate Sightseer*, p. 167.

12 Paul Helleu to Gabriel Yturri, undated but October 1901 [Fonds Montesquiou, BNP].

13 G to Montesquiou, undated but December 1901 [Fonds Montesquiou, BNP].

14 G to BB, undated but 1899 [VIT].
15 *San Francisco Chronicle*, 25 February 1900.
16 Jullian, *Robert de Montesquiou*, p. 203.
17 G, conversation with the author, 26 February 1977.
18 Schlumberger, p. 172.
19 Clermont-Tonnerre, *Robert de Montesquiou et Marcel Proust*, p. 61.
20 G to BB, undated but 1900 [VIT].
21 Secrest, p. 217.
22 G to BB, undated but spring 1900 [VIT].
23 MB to HWS, 14 November 1901 [LL].
24 G to BB (undated but December 1901) [VIT].
25 Gramont, *Years of Plenty*, p. 64.

5. The Berensons

 1 MB to BB, 31 December 1901 [VIT].
 2 Ibid., 1 January 1902 [VIT].
 3 G, conversation with the author, 1976.
 4 G to BB, undated but 1900 [VIT].
 5 Ibid., undated but a Saturday late in 1900 [VIT].
 6 MB to HWS, 28 February 1901 [LL].
 7 The late Stephen Tennant to author, 17 September 1980.
 8 MB to HWS, 2 March 1901 [LL].
 9 Ibid., 4 March 1901 [LL].
10 Ibid., 10 March 1901 [LL].
11 Mariano, pp. 91-2.
12 BB to MB, 21 April 1901 [VIT].
13 MB, diary, 13 March 1902 [VIT].
14 MB to HWS, I Tatti, 11 March 1902 [LL].
15 Ibid. [LL].
16 Ibid., March 1902 [LL].
17 Ibid., 14 March 1902 [LL].
18 Ibid., 22 March 1902 [LL].
19 Ibid., 25 March 1902 [LL].
20 MB, diary, 26 March 1902 [VIT].
21 MB to HWS, I Tatti,, 2 April 1902 [LL].
22 Ibid., 21 April 1902 [LL].
23 MB to Alys Russell, I Tatti, 2 April 1902 [LL].

Interlude: *Cecilia*

 1 Sermoneta, p. 103.
 2 Crawford, p. 27.

3 Ibid., p. 46.
4 Sermoneta, p. 103.
5 F. Marion Crawford, quoted in Sermoneta, p. 104.

6. The Marlboroughs

1 Balsan, p. 98.
2 G, conversation with the author, 1976.
3 Marchioness of Lansdowne to G, Bowood, undated but 31 January 1922 [GDP].
4 Lady Boileau to G, Ketteringham Park, Wymondham, 18 July 1933 [GDP].
5 7th Marquess of Londonderry to WSC, 2 July 1934 [CHAR 1/255, CCC].
6 Quoted in full in Waterhouse and Wiseman, pp. 8-12.
7 M to WSC, undated but 1906 [CHAR 1/57/22-23, CCC].
8 M to G, Majestic Hotel, Harrogate, undated but August 1901 [GDP].
9 Balsan, p. 102.
10 M to G, Majestic Hotel, Harrogate, undated but August 1901 [GDP].
11 Balsan, p. 116.
12 Inscription in the book, the Long Library, Blenheim.
13 Blenheim Palace Visitors' Book.
14 Balsan, p. 117.
15 Consuelo (Duchess of Marlborough) to G, Blenheim Palace, 25 October 1901 [GDP].
16 MB to HWS, 8 March 1902 [LL].
17 Trevelyan, p. 325.
18 Chapman-Huston, *The Private Diaries of Daisy, Princess of Pless,* p. 89
19 MB to BB, 1 September 1901 [VIT].
20 Consuelo to G, undated [GDP].
21 G to BB, undated but October 1901 [VIT].
22 Ibid.
23 Consuelo to G, Blenheim Palace, 6 January 1902 [GDP].

7. The London Season – 1902

1 MB diary, 8 May 1902, quoted in Samuels, p. 333.
2 *Buffalo Courier,* New York, 25 June 1911.
3 Aimée Lowther (1869-1935) to G, 10 Montpelier Crescent, Brighton, 2 July 1934 [GDP].
4 MB to HWS, I Tatti, April 11 1902 [LL].
5 G to BB, undated but December 1902/January 1903 [VIT].
6 MB to HWS, I Tatti, 19 April 1902 [LL].
7 *The Lady,* 24 May 1902.
8 MB, diary, 19 June 1902 [VIT].

9 Derived from MB to HWS, 16 May 1904 [LL].

10 G to FB, summer 1902 [formerly in GDP].

11 *Le Matin*, 11–13 August 1902.

12 Ibid., 14 August 1902.

13 Ibid.

14 Albert Flament, *La Revue de Paris – Tableaux de Paris* – Article on La Comtesse Potocka, 1931, p. 697.

8. 'Death or Permanent Disfigurement'

1 *Boston Globe*, 13 February 1903.

2 FB to BB, undated but 1900 [VIT].

3 G to BB, Ugbrooke Park, November 1902 [VIT].

4 Bibesco, *La Vie d'une Amitié, Volume 1*, pp. 8–16.

5 Dodge Luhan, pp. 241-2.

6 Notes et Réflexions Inédités de Robert de Montesquiou, 4e accueil, Ombres Portées – 229 note concernant Miss Gladys Deacon, *Américanisme* [Fonds Montesquiou, BNP].

7 Goldberg (ed.), Volume 4, pp. 1-9.

8 MB to HWS, Gazzada Prov. di Como, 23 October 1902 [LL].

9 *Boston Globe*, 13 February 1903.

10 G to BB, undated but early 1903 [VIT].

11 Ibid.

12 Ibid., 11 February 1903 [VIT].

13 MB to HWS, I Tatti, 29 April 1903 [LL].

14 MB to BB, 4 April 1903 [VIT].

15 Ibid., 5 April 1903 [VIT].

16 FB to MB, 8 April 1903 [VIT].

17 MB to BB, 8 April 1903 [VIT].

18 BB to MB, 7 April 1903 [VIT].

19 *San Francisco Examiner*, 16 August 1903.

20 Copy of letter, Logan Pearsall Smith to MB, MB's diary, 27 May 1903 [VIT].

21 MB to HWS, I Tatti, 27 May 1903 [LL].

22 G to BB, undated but summer 1903 [VIT].

23 G to Robert de Montesquiou, undated but 14 June 1903 [Fonds Montesquiou, BNP].

24 Celia Lee, Jean, *Lady Hamilton, A Biography from her Diaries*, privately published, 2001, p. 252.

25 Chapman-Huston (ed.), *The Private Diaries of Daisy, Princess of Pless 1873-1914*, p. 115.

26 Recorded in MB to BB, 27 July 1903 [VIT].

27 MB to HWS, New York, 17 December 1903 [LL].

28 G to BB, undated but September 1903 [VIT].

29 MB to HWS, New York, 17 December 1903 [LL].
30 *The Lady*, 19 November 1903.
31 Ettie Desborough to A. J. Balfour, 25 February 1904, DE/rv/C1085/10 [Hertfordshire Archives] – quoted in Davenport-Hines, pp. 153-4.
32 Joseph, p. 107.
33 Cavaillès, p. 230.
34 Paulhan (ed.), p. 241.

9. The Death of Audrey

1 G, diary, 22 May 1945, in 1923 diary [GDP].
2 Note by the Comtesse Greffulhe, 5 June 1907, Gladys Deacon file [Fonds Greffulhe, ANP].
3 Audrey Deacon to Catherine Pozzi, 21 January 1904, in Cavaillès, p. 237.
4 Amy Turton, diary of Audrey's illness, 9 April 1904 [GDP].
5 Ibid.
6 MB to HWS, I Tatti, 10 May 1904 [LL].
7 MB to Isabella Stewart Gardner, 27 May 1904; quoted in Hadley, p. 337.
8 BB to Isabella Stewart Gardner, 23 May 1904; ibid., p. 336.
9 MB to HWS, I Tatti, 13 May 1904 [LL].
10 Ibid., 16 May 1904 [LL].
11 Ibid.
12 Ibid.
13 Ibid., 17 May 1904 [LL].
14 Ibid., 19 May 1904 [LL].
15 Ibid., 21 May 1904 [LL].
16 Ibid.
17 Amy Turton, diary of Audrey's illness, 20 May 1904 [GDP].
18 Ibid., 21 May 1904 [GDP].
19 MB to HWS, I Tatti, 21 May 1904 [LL].
20 Amy Turton. diary of Audrey's illness, 22 May 1904 [GDP].
21 Ibid.
22 MB to HWS, I Tatti, 24 May 1904 [LL].
23 Ibid., 25 May 1904 [LL].
24 BB to Isabella Stewart Gardner, 23 May 1904, quoted in Hadley, p. 336.
25 Amy Turton to G, undated but summer 1904 [GDP].
26 Joseph (ed.), p. 107.
27 Copy of G to C, undated but 1904 [GDP].
28 G to Robert de Montesquiou, 1905, quoted in Robert de Montesquiou, *Le Chancelier des Fleurs* (privately printed, 1908), [Fonds Montesquiou, BNP].

Interlude: *The Eternal Spring*

1 Boyce, p. 189.
2 Ibid, p. 147.
3 Ibid., p. 24.
4 Ibid., pp. 24-5.
5 Ibid., p. 153.
6 Ibid., p. 79.
7 MB to HWS, November 1907 [LL].
8 Neith Boyce, diary, 29 June 1903, quoted in DeBoer-Langworthy, p. 240.
9 Ibid., 5 August 1903, p. 256.
10 Ibid., 6 August 1903, p. 256.

10. Roman Days

1 Rhodes James, p. 382.
2 G, conversation with the author, 20 February 1976.
3 Carlo Placci to MB, 10 January 1904 [VIT].
4 Dodge Luhan, pp. 241-2.
5 Edith Deacon to G, Palazzo Borghese, Rome, undated but 1904-8 [GDP].
6 Dom Pedro de Carvalho to the Comtesse Greffulhe, Rome, 20 February 1905 [Fonds Greffulhe, ANP].
7 *San Francisco Examiner*, 5 February 1928.
8 MB to HWS, Palazzo Borghese, Rome, 27 March 1905 [LL].
9 Varé, p. 100.
10 Hadley, p. 471.
11 MB to HWS, I Tatti, 7 June 1904 [LL].
12 Gramont, *Years of Plenty*, p. 21.
13 Dom Pedro de Carvalho to the Comtesse Greffulhe, Davos, 8 February 1904 [Fonds Greffulhe, ANP].
14 Ibid., Rome, 21 December 1904 [Fonds Greffulhe, ANP].
15 The late Donna Julia Brambilla, conversation with the author, Washington, 29 March 1976.
16 Trevelyan, pp. 355-6.
17 The Comtesse Greffulhe to Roffredo Caetani, quoted in Hillerin, p. 335.
18 The Comtesse Greffulhe to the Duke of Sermoneta (1904), quoted in ibid., p. 335.
19 BB to MB, August 1904 [VIT].
20 G to BB, 24 June 1906 [VIT].
21 *Washington Post,* 3 April 1910.
22 MB to HWS, I Tatti, 17 January and 14 March 1905 [LL].
23 G to Robert de Montesquiou, undated [Fonds Montesquiou, BNP].
24 Ibid., July 1905 [Fonds Montesquiou, BNP].
25 FB to Robert de Montesquiou, 18 July 1905 [Fonds Montesquiou, BNP].

26 BB to MB, 20 June 1904 [VIT].

27 G to BB, letter folded inside BB to MB, 20 June 1904 [VIT].

28 G to BB, undated but *circa* 3 July 1904 [VIT].

29 BB to G, 7 July 1904 [formerly in GDP].

30 G to BB, undated but *circa* 3 July 1904) [VIT].

31 G, draft letter (possibly to the Duke of Marlborough), undated but summer 1904 [GDP].

32 The Duke of Camastra to G, 7 September 1933 [GDP].

33 Ibid., Vallombrosa, undated but 1904 [GDP].

34 Ibid.

35 BB to MB, 19 August 1904 [VIT].

36 G to BB, undated but August 1904 [VIT].

37 MB to BB, 30 August 1904 [VIT].

38 G to BB, undated but 22 August 1904 [VIT].

39 BB to MB, 10 January 1905 [VIT].

40 MB to HWS, I Tatti, 16 January 1905 [LL].

41 Ibid., Palazzo Borghese, Rome, 23 March 1905 [LL].

42 Ibid., 27 March 1905 [LL].

43 Ibid., 25 March 1905 [LL].

44 MB, diary, 28 March 1905 [VIT].

45 BB to MB, 15 August 1905 [VIT].

46 G to BB, 18 December 1905 [VIT].

47 Trevelyan, p. 324.

Interlude: Marcel Proust

1 Marcel Proust to Madame Gaston de Caillavet, Versailles, 8 December 1906, quoted in Kolb,, *Tome VI*, p. 311; and in Painter, p. 63.

2 Proust to Madame Emile Straus, Versailles, soon after 26 October 1906, quoted in Kolb, *Tome VI* , p. 257.

3 Proust to Reynaldo Hahn, 7 January 1907, quoted in Kolb, *Tome VII*, p. 23.

4 Proust to G, undated but 24 July 1918 [formerly in GDP], quoted in Kolb, *Tome XVII*, p. 318.

5 G to the Comtesse Greffulhe, Hôtel La Pérouse, Paris, 2 July 1907 [Fonds Greffulhe, ANP].

6 The Duchesse de Clermont-Tonnerre, *Marcel Proust*, pp. 38-42.

7 Proust to the Duchesse de Clermont-Tonnerre, after 20 June 1907, quoted in Kolb, *Tome VII*, pp. 190-4.

8 Duchesse de Clermont-Tonnerre, *R. de Montesquiou & M. Proust*, p. 137. Also Proust to the Duchesse de Clermont-Tonnerre, just before 7 July 1907, quoted in the appendix to Kolb, *Tome XIX*, pp. 708-9.

9 G, conversation with the author, 1976.

11. Separation

1 W. T. Stead to G, *The Review of Reviews,* 15 December 1910.
2 C to G, Sunderland House, London, 13 July 1904 [GDP].
3 Ibid.
4 M to C, October 1906 [BPA].
5 William Kissam Vanderbilt to M, 10 rue Leroux, Paris XVI, 11 October 1906 [BPA].
6 William Fletcher, statement [BPA].
7 G, conversation with the author, 1976.
8 G to M, Paris, 27 May 1918 [BPA].
9 Trevelyan, p. 332.
10 Balsan, p. 136.
11 M to WSC, Monday, undated but 1907 [CHAR 1 /57 / 22-23 – Churchill Papers, CCC].
12 Magnus, pp. 405-6.
13 Pringle, p. 117.
14 MB to BB, 18 August 1905 [VIT].
15 MB to HWS, I Tatti, 27 May 1906 [LL].
16 Ibid., 10 June 1906 [LL].
17 MB to BB, 22 October 1906 [VIT].
18 Dom Pedro de Carvalho to the Comtesse Greffulhe, Davos, May 1907 [Fonds Greffulhe, ANP].
19 G to the Comtesse Greffulhe, Palazzo Borghese, Rome, undated [Fonds Greffulhe, ANP].
20 Notes by Dr Henri Favre, Gladys Deacon file [Fonds Greffulhe, ANP].
21 Observation Graphologique, Gladys Deacon file [Fonds Greffulhe, ANP].
22 G to the Comtesse Greffulhe, Palazzo Borghese, Rome, July 1907 [Fonds Greffulhe, ANP].
23 Ibid., 14 October 1907 [Fonds Greffulhe, ANP].
24 Note by the Comtesse Greffulhe, 8 June 1907, Gladys Deacon file [Fonds Greffulhe, ANP].
25 Gramont, *Mémoires II,* p. 54.
26 Gramont, *Pomp and Circumstance,* p. 22.
27 G, conversation with the author, 1976.
28 Ibid.
29 Jullian, *Oscar Wilde,* p. 236.
30 The Baronne (Madeleine) Deslandes to G, 7 rue Christophe Colombe, Paris, 14 December, undated [GDP].
31 Stein, p. 60.
32 Burns, pp. 281-4.
33 G, conversation with the author, 1976.
34 MB to BB, 18 June 1909 [VIT].
35 Reported in BB to MB, 31 August 1907 [VIT].

36 G, conversation with the author, 14 July 1976.
37 BB to MB, 7 August 1907 [VIT].
38 Ibid., 9 August 1907 [VIT].
39 Ibid., 20 August 1907 [VIT].
40 WSC to the Countess of Lytton, 19 September 1907, quoted in Randolph S. Churchill, pp. 679–80.
41 G to author, 10 February and 10 September 1976.

Interlude: Caprarola

1 FB to Rodin, 1911 [Rodin Museum, Hôtel Biron, Paris].
2 FB to G, undated [formerly in GDP].
3 Ibid., Caprarola, 23 April 1914 [formerly in GDP].
4 Edith Wharton to BB, undated [VIT].
5 MB to BB, undated [VIT].
6 MB to HWS, Grand Hotel, Rome, 26 April 1910 [LL].
7 Ibid., Palazzo Farnese, Caprarola, 9 June 1911 [LL].
8 BB to Isabella Stewart Gardner, Rome, 11 May 1910, quoted in Hadley, p. 471.

12. The Chinaman

1 Hermann von Keyserling to G, various letters, spring 1908 [GDP].
2 Keyserling, drafts for letters to G, 1908 [Keyserling Archives, University of Darmstadt].
3 G to Keyserling, April 1908 (Keyserling Archives, University of Darmstadt).
4 Keyserling to G, undated, 1908 [GDP].
5 Keyserling to G, Thursday evening, undated, 1908 [GDP].
6 Hermann von Keyserling, *The World in the Making*, p. 20.
7 Schlumberger, p. 178.
8 Gramont, *Years of Plenty*, p. 57.
9 Keyserling to G, undated, 1908 [GDP].
10 Ibid.
11 Keyserling to G, Saturday evening, undated, 1908 [GDP].
12 Ibid., 12 May 1908 [GDP].
13 Ibid., undated, 1908 [GDP].
14 Ibid., 24 May 1908 [GDP].
15 Rosa de Fitz-James to Keyserling, 8 August 1908 [Keyserling Archives, University of Darmstadt].
16 Ibid., 30 May 1908 [Keyserling Archives, University of Darmstadt].
17 Keyserling to G, Bad Kissingen, 3 June 1908 [GDP].
18 Ibid.
19 G to Keyserling, Palazzo Borghese, Rome, Saturday afternoon, undated but 6 June 1908 [Keyserling Archives, University of Darmstadt].

20 Keyserling to G, Bad Kissingen, 12 June 1908 [GDP].

21 MB to HWS, Hotel St James and d'Albany, Paris, 26 June 1908 [LL].

22 MB to BB, 20 July 1908 [VIT].

23 Rosa de Fitz-James to Keyserling, 18 July [1908], [Keyserling Archives, University of Darmstadt].

24 Ibid., Kallwang, Steichmark, summer 1908 [Keyserling Archives, University of Darmstadt].

25 G to WSC, Hôtel Barblan, Sils [16 August] 1908 [CHAR 1/76, CCC].

26 BB to MB, August 1908 [VIT].

27 G, draft letter to Keyserling, undated but September 1908 [copy in GDP].

28 Keyserling to G, undated, 1908 [GDP].

29 G to Keyserling, Hôtel de l'Europe, Venice, Wednesday evening, undated [Keyserling Archives, University of Darmstadt].

30 Keyserling to G, 20 September 1908 [GDP].

31 Keyserling to Countess Marguerite Bismarck, Rayküll (Estonia), 31 December 1908 [Keyserling Archive, University of Darmstadt].

32 G to Rosa de Fitz-James, Hôtel de la Pérouse, Paris, and Rosa to Keyserling, January, undated but 1909 [Keyserling Archives, University of Darmstadt].

Interlude: *The Marriage of Zobeïde*

Material in this interlude is derived from the three Hofmannsthal volumes, Hofmannsthal & Nostitz, *Briefwechsel* (S. Fischer, Verlag, Vienna, 1965), & Hoppe (works cited), & also Michael Hamburger, *Hofmannsthal – Three Essays* (Princeton University Press, USA), 1972.

1 Hoppe, p. 407.

2 Hofmannsthal and Hélène von Nostitz, *Briefwechse,* pp. 70-71.

3 Hofmannsthal, *Aufzeichnungen* (1959), pp. 160–1.

4 Ibid., p. 161.

5 Hofmannsthal to Gertrude, 30 March 1906, quoted in Hofmannsthal, *Aufzeichnungen. Hrsg. von Rudolf Hirsch und Ellen Ritte* (Frankfurt am Main, 2013)

6 Ibid.

7 Ibid.

8 Hofmannsthal to G, undated [formerly in GDP].

9 Hoppe, p. 90.

13. The Comtesse Greffulhe and the Sisters

1 G to M, Rome, dated '13th I think', but 13 November 1908 [copy of draft in GDP].

2 Dom Pedro de Carvalho to the Comtesse Greffulhe, Rome, 26 May 1909 [Fonds Greffulhe, ANP].

3 MB to Senda Berenson, I Tatti, 25 May 1909 [LL].

4 MB to HWS, I Tatti, 25 May 1909 [LL].

5 Ibid., 30 May 1909 [LL].

6 Ibid., 5 June 1909 [LL].

7 Ibid., 7 June 1909 [LL].

8 BB to MB, Hôtel St James, Paris, 21 June 1909 [VIT].

9 Ibid., Hôtel Ritz, Paris, 26 October 1910 [VIT].

10 *Washington Post*, 24 July 1910.

11 G to the Comtesse Greffulhe, Paris, undated but 1910 [Fonds Greffulhe, ANP].

12 Ibid., Caprarola, 29 October 1909 [Fonds Greffulhe, ANP].

13 Ibid., 31 May 1910 [Fonds Greffulhe, ANP].

14 Ibid., Paris, undated but 19 May 1910 [Fonds Greffulhe, ANP].

15 Ibid., undated, but 1910 [Fonds Greffulhe, ANP].

16 Ibid., Caprarola, August 1910 [Fonds Greffulhe, ANP].

17 MB to HWS, Grand Hotel, Rome, 26 April 1910 [LL].

18 MB to Isabella Stewart Gardner, 5 June 1910, quoted Hadley, pp. 471-2.

19 MB to HWS, Grand Hotel, Rome, 26 April 1910 [LL].

20 Ibid., I Tatti, 18 April 1910 [LL].

21 Ibid., Grand Hotel, Rome, 26 April 1910 [LL].

22 Ibid., I Tatti, 5 June 1910 [LL].

23 Gabriac to Robert de Montesquiou, 1910, [Fonds Montesquiou, BNP].

24 G to the Comtesse Greffulhe, Paris, 28 May 1910 [Fonds Greffulhe, ANP].

25 Ibid. Thursday, undated but July 1910 [Fonds Greffulhe, ANP].

26 MB to HWS, Palazzo Farnese, Caprarola, 9 June 1911 [LL].

27 MB to Isabella Stewart Gardner, 28 October 1911, quoted in Hadley, p. 493.

28 FB to Charles A. Baldwin, Palazzo Borghese, 4 January 1911 [CAB].

29 Ibid., 5 June 1910, p. 473.

30 William P. Blake to Charles A. Baldwin, Boston, 6 January 1911 [HVP].

31 FB to G 22 February 1911 [formerly in GDP].

32 FB to Charles A. Baldwin, Palazzo Borghese, Rome, 4 January 1911 [CAB].

33 FB to Charles A. Baldwin, Hôtel Célerina & Cresta Palace, Célerina, 15 August 1911. [CAB]

34 *Washington Post*, 5 February 1911.

35 *San Francisco Examiner*, 25 June 1911.

36 FB to G, 1 January 1911 [formerly in GDP].

37 MB to HWS, Grand Hotel, Rome, 23 April 1911 [LL].

14. Enter the Duke

1 *San Francisco Examiner*, 25 June 1911.

2 Ibid.

3 G to M, undated but August 1911 [copy in GDP].

4 BB to Hermann von Keyserling, Hotel Cavour Milan, 19 June 1911 [Keyserling Archives, University of Darmstadt].

5 BB to Keyserling, Copesham, Esher, 9 July 1911 [Keyserling Archives, University of Darmstadt].

6 MB to Isabella Stewart Gardner, 28 October 1911, quoted in Hadley, p. 493.

7 Ibid.

8 Ibid., 10 April 1912, quoted in ibid., p. 493.

9 G to FB, Hôtel de la Pérouse, Paris, 11 November 1911 [copy in GDP].

10 Prince Roffredo Caetani to G, 28 October 1913 [GDP].

11 G to FB, Hôtel de la Pérouse, Paris, 11 November 1911 [copy in GDP].

12 FB to G, Caprarola, 12 October 1912 [formerly in GDP].

13 Ibid., 25 December 1912 [formerly in GDP].

14 Marraine Baldwin to Charley Baldwin, 14 May 1912 [CAB].

15 G to FB, 1912 [formerly in GDP].

16 These and subsequent quotes relating to Marthe Bibesco from Marthe Bibesco, *La Vie d'une Amitié* (Plon, 1957), pp. 8-16.

17 Ibid., p. 9.

18 M to G, Blenheim, 1 September 1912 [GDP].

19 The late Stephen Tennant, conversation with the author, 18 September 1980.

20 M to G, Blenheim, 14 September 1912 [GDP].

21 Ibid.

22 Ibid., 27 July 1912 [GDP].

23 Ibid., undated but August 1912 [GDP].

24 Ibid., Marlborough Club, London, 25 August 1912 [GDP].

25 G to M, 16 April 1914 [BPA].

26 M to G, Beaulieu-sur-Mer, April 1913 [GDP].

27 Ibid.

28 BB to MB, July 1913 [VIT].

29 MB to BB, undated [VIT].

Interlude: Rodin and Monet

1 G to Auguste Rodin, 11 Savile Row, London [Musée Rodin, Paris].

2 G, conversation with the author, 20 June 1976.

3 Ibid.

4 G to Rodin [Musée Rodin, Paris].

5 Rodin to G, 77 rue de Varenne, undated but 1912 [formerly in GDP].

6 Ibid., 182 rue de l'Université, Paris, 20 July 1912 [formerly in GDP].

7 G to Rodin, 1914 [Musée Rodin, Paris].

8 Rodin to G, Hill Hall, Theydon Mount, Epping, undated but October 1914 [formerly in GDP].

9 G to Rodin, 1916 [Musée Rodin, Paris].

10 FB to G, January 1917 [formerly in GDP].

11 G to Rodin, 11 Savile Row, London, 17 February 1917 [Musée Rodin, Paris].

12 G to M, Sunday evening, undated but July 1916 [BPA].

13 Gladys photograph album, number IV [GDP].

15. The Great War, 1914-1916

This includes material from the Duke of Marlborough to Gladys, 1914-15; Florence Baldwin to Gladys, and letters between Mary and Bernard Berenson, June, August, September and December 1915; also *New York Times*, 19 April and 26 July 1915.

1 Ralph Curtis to Isabella Stewart Gardner, undated, but 1914 [Gardner Museum, Boston].

2 G to the Crown Prince of Prussia, 23 Quai Voltaire, 1914 [found in GDP].

3 G to FB, dated Tuesday 24th November, [GDP].

4 Ibid., 30 November 1914 [formerly in GDP].

5 Ibid.

6 Trevelyan, p.367.

7 FB to G, December 1914 [formerly in GDP].

8 Ibid., Thursday, December 1914 [formerly in GDP].

9 Ibid., 27 January 1915 [formerly in GDP].

10 'Mother of Deacon Beauties Makes Castle a Workshop', American press cutting in Charles Baldwin collection, September 1918 [HVP].

11 MB to BB, 25 September 1915 [VIT].

12 Ibid., 28 September 1915 [VIT].

13 M to G, Blenheim Palace, Wednesday, undated but 1915 [GDP].

14 Ibid., Tuesday, undated but 1915 [GDP].

15 Ibid., July 1915 [GDP].

16 WSC to the Marquess of Lansdowne, 6 July 1915, quoted in Martin S. Gilbert (ed.), *Volume III, Companion Part 2 Documents*, pp. 1078-9.

17 The Marquess of Lansdowne to WSC, Lansdowne House, 7 July 1915, quoted in ibid., p. 1079.

18 M to G, Blenheim, 16 July 1915 [GDP].

19 M to WSC, undated but after 16 July 1915, quoted in Gilbert (ed.), *Volume III, Companion Part 2*, p. 1080.

20 G to M, Lausanne, 20 October 1915 [BPA].

21 MB to BB, 22 February 1916 [GDP].

22 Lord Bertie of Thame, p. 289.

23 M to G, early 1916 [GDP].

24 Ibid., Blenheim Palace, 6 February 1916 [GDP].

25 FB to G, undated but 1916 [GDP].

26 M to G, 5 May 1916 [GDP].

27 G to M, 31 May 1916 [BPA].

28 M to G, 29 May 1916 [GDP].

29 G to M, 5 June 1916 [BPA].

30 FB to G, July 1916 [GDP].

31 G to M, Paris, 29 July 1916 [BPA].

32 Ibid., Sunday evening, undated but July 1916 [BPA].

33 M to G, 9 August 1916 [GDP].

34 G to M, Paris, 17 July 1916 [BPA].

35 Ibid., Sunday evening, undated but July 1916 [BPA].

36 FB to Charles Baldwin, Caprarola, 7 July 1916 [CAB].

37 Marraine Baldwin to Virginia Baldwin, NY, 8 November 1916 [CAB].

38 Edith to Charles Baldwin, Newport, [undated but November] 1916 [CAB].

39 G to M, 18 September 1916 [BPA].

40 Ibid., 19 September 1916 [BPA].

41 Abbé Mugnier to BB, undated, 1916 [VIT].

42 Giraudoux, p. 108.

43 M to G, 15 Great College Street, Saturday, undated, but December 1916 [GDP].

Interlude: Epstein

1 Buckle, p. 88; and Lady Epstein to author, 7 January 1976.

2 Ibid.

3 Epstein, p. 96.

4 Ibid., pp. 95–6.

5 M to G, 4 March 1918 [GDP].

16. Armistice, 1917–1918

Based on letters from the Duke of Marlborough to Gladys, Florence Baldwin to Gladys, Walter Berry to Gladys, material in R.W. B. Lewis, *Edith Wharton* (Constable, 1975) and the *New York Times*, 18 July 1918; and *Collection Edgar Degas* (Galerie Georges Petit, Paris, 1918).

1 G to M, March 1917 [BPA].

2 M to G, 16 June 1917 [GDP].

3 G to M, 11 March 1918 [BPA].

4 G to FB, March 1918 [formerly in GDP].

5 Ibid., 15 May 1918 [formerly in GDP].

6 G to M, Paris, 21 March 1918 [BPA].

7 G to FB, 15 May 1918 [formerly in GDP].

8 G to M, undated but May 1918 [BPA].

9 Ibid., 27 May 1918 [BPA].

10 G, conversation with the author, 1976.

11 BB to MB, Paris, 12 or 13 October 1918 [VIT].

12 Lewis, p. 329.

13 Walter Berry to Gladys, undated 1918 [formerly in GDP].

14 Elsie de Wolfe to BB, May 1918 [VIT].

15 FB to MB, 29 June 1918 [VIT].

16 Ibid., undated 1918 [VIT].

17 The late Lady Gladwyn (Cynthia Noble) to author, 1978.

18 Marcel Proust to G, undated but 24 July 1918, original letter sold, but published in Philip Kolb (ed.), *Tome XVII*, pp. 318-19.

19 G to WSC, Hôtel Sarciron, Le Mont-Dore, 3 July 1921 [CHAR1/143, CCC].

17. The Irish Duke

1 G to M, Nice, 8 February 1919 [BPA].

2 Boldini to G, 41 rue Berthier, Paris, 3 August 1919 [formerly in GDP].

3 G to M, 'Rathole', 23 quai Voltaire, Paris, 4 July 1918 [GDP].

4 Anita Leslie, p. 216.

5 HRH The Duke of Connaught to G, Hôtel des Réserves, Beaulieu, 20 March 1919 [GDP].

6 Ibid., 2 April 1919 [GDP].

7 Ibid., 9 April 1919 [GDP].

8 Ibid., 11 April 1919 [GDP].

9 Frankland, p. 365.

10 HRH The Duke of Connaught to G, Bagshot Park, Easter Day, 20 April 1919 [GDP].

11 Ibid., 24 April 1919 [GDP].

12 Morra, pp. 58-9.

13 Ibid.

14 Harold Nicolson, diary, quoted in Harold Nicolson, *The Peacemaking*, pp. 318-9.

15 HRH The Duke of Connaught to G, Clarence House, 14 May 1919 [GDP].

16 Ibid., 14 July 1919 [GDP].

17 Ibid., 22 July 1919 [GDP].

18 *Buffalo Times*, 4 January 1920.

19 HRH The Duke of Connaught to G, Clarence House, 18 December 1919 [GDP].

20 Ibid., Hôtel California, Cannes, 29 December 1919 [GDP].

21 Ibid., 30 December 1919 – first letter [GDP].

22 Ibid., second letter [GDP].

23 *Daily Graphic*, 1 January 1920.

24 Central News statement, 19 March 1920.

25 HRH The Duke of Connaught to G, Hôtel Ritz, Paris, 17 April 1920 [GDP].

26 G to HRH The Duke of Connaught, 4 May 1920 [copy in her hand in GDP].

27 HRH The Duke of Connaught to G, Hôtel Ritz, Paris, 17 April 1920 [GDP].

Interlude: Robert Trevelyan

1 The late David Garnett, letter to author, 24 November 1975.
2 Mariano, p. 24.
3 The late Julian Trevelyan, letter to author, Durham Wharf, Hammersmith Terrace, London W6, 13 December 1975 [HRV].
4 G, conversation with the author, 1976.
5 The late David Garnett, letter to author, 24 November 1975 [HRV].
6 Francis Birrell to G, Mission Anglo-Américaine de la Société des Amis, Paris, 22 September 1919 [formerly in GDP].
7 Francis Birrell to G, 1 October 1919 [formerly in GDP].
8 Roger Fry to G, 17 Dalmeny Avenue, London N2, 25 January 1920 [formerly in GDP].
9 Edmond Jaloux to G, Villa Saint-Jacques, 20 June 1920 [formerly in GDP].
10 Nigel Nicolson (ed,), *The Question of Things Happening – The Letters of Virginia Woolf, Vol. II 1919–1922*, p. 494.
11 Ibid., p. 499.
12 Mariano, pp. 25-6.

18. Paris Wedding

1 M to Jennie Cornwallis-West, 27 June 1921 [CHAR 28/134/86, CCC].
2 M to G, 10 November 1920 [GDP].
3 Edmond Jaloux to G, undated but 1920 [GDP].
4 G, conversation with the author, 1976.
5 M to G, 2 June 1921 [GDP].
6 M to WSC, 15 Great College Street, 7 June 1921 [CHAR1/138/41, CCC].
7 M to G, 2 June 1921 [GDP].
8 Bibesco, *La Vie d'une Amitié, Vol. 1*, p. 8.
9 Schlumberger, p. 183.
10 Marcel Proust, letter to M. and Mme Sydney Schiff, 17 October 1921, quoted in Kolb, *Tome XX*, p. 485.
11 Proust, undated letter, quoted in André Maurois, *Le Visiteur du Soir* (Palatine, 1947), p. XX.
12 Proust, letter to La Princesse Soutzo, 16 June 1921, Kolb (ed.), *Tome XX*, pp. 343-4.
13 Edmond Jaloux to Proust, 3 June 1922, quoted in Philip Kolb (ed.), *Correspondance de Marcel Proust 1922, Tome XXI* (Plon, 1993), p. 246.

14 *New York Times*, 25 June 1921.

15 *Daily Express*, 25 June 1921.

16 *The Times*, 27 June 1921.

17 *New York Times*, 26 June 1921.

18 Ibid.

19 Marthe Bibesco to Abbé Mugnier, 5 July 1921, quoted in Bibesco, *La Vie d'une Amitié, Vol. 1*, p. 449.

20 Linda Lee Porter to BB, quoted in MB, letter to Isabella Stewart Gardner, Vallombrosa, 21 August 1921, quoted in Hadley, p. 634.

21 G, diary, 2 June 1922 [GDP].

19. Blenheim

1 The late Lady Epstein, conversation with the author, 7 January 1976.

2 Green, *Blenheim Palace Guide Book*, p. 37.

3 *McCall's* magazine, quoted in Herring, p. 98.

4 Carnarvon, p. 140.

5 The late Countess of Longford, conversation with the author, Windsor, 13 June 1977.

6 Clermont-Tonnerre, *Pomp and Circumstance*, p. 283.

7 Unpublished memoirs of 10th Duke of Marlborough, David Green manuscript [BPA].

8 G, diary, 9 October 1922 [GDP].

9 Marchioness Curzon of Kedleston, 1 Carlton House Terrace, SW1, 27 June 1921 [CHAR 28/134/85 (850), CCC].

10 G, conversation with the author, 1976.

11 Ibid.

12 G, diary, 21 July 1921 [GDP].

13 Lady Ottoline Morrell, diary, 26 September 1921 [British Museum].

14 The late Julian Vinogradoff to the author, 25 January 1978.

15 G, conversation with the author, 19 March 1977.

16 G to Lady Ottoline Morrell, 13 June 1922 [HRC].

17 G, diary, 6 January 1921 [GDP].

18 Ibid., 10 January 1922 [GDP].

19 Ibid., 14 January 1922 [GDP].

20 Ibid., 16 January 1922 [GDP}.

21 M to G, 15 Great College Street, London, 12 January 1922 [GDP].

22 Ibid., 6 February 1922 [GDP].

23 G to Lady Ottoline Morrell, 13 June 1922 [HRC].

24 The late Paul Maze, conversation with the author, 16 January 1976.

25 G to Lady Ottoline Morrell, 13 June 1922 [HRC].

26 G, diary, 12 June 1922 [GDP].

27 Birkenhead, p. 128.

28 G, diary, 25 June 1922 [GDP].

29 Ibid., 18 July 1922 [GDP].

30 G to Lady Ottoline Morrell, 2 August 1922 [HRC].

31 G, diary, 8 August 1922 [GDP].

32 Ibid., 21 August 1922 [GDP].

33 Ibid., 2 September 1922 [GDP].

34 Ibid., 3 September 1922 [GDP].

35 Ibid., Interlaken, 5 September 1922 [GDP].

36 Ibid., Jungfrau, 6 September 1922 [GDP].

37 Ibid., Interlaken, 9 September 1922 [GDP].

38 Ibid., 11 September 1922 [GDP].

39 G to Lady Ottoline Morrell, 27 September 1922 [HRC].

40 G, diary, 27 September 1922 [GDP].

20. The Usual Life

1 G to Lady Ottoline Morrell, 27 September 1922 [HRC].

2 G, diary, 5 October 1922 [GDP].

3 Ibid., 9 October 1922 [GDP].

4 Ibid., 6 October 1922 [GDP].

5 Lady Ottoline Morrell, diary, 13 November 1922 [British Library].

6 G, diary, 18 November 1922 [GDP].

7 Ibid., 27 December 1922 [GDP].

8 Ibid., 13 February 1923 [GDP].

9 Ibid., 25 June 1923 [GDP].

10 G, conversation with the author, 1976.

11 Holroyd, *Lytton Strachey, Volume II*, p. 469.

12 Lytton Strachey to G, 5 November 1929 [formerly in GDP].

13 G, diary, 27 July 1923 [GDP].

14 Epstein, p. 95.

15 G, diary, 31 July 1923 [GDP].

16 M to G, White's, 18 January 1926 [GDP].

17 Ibid., 15 Great College Street, 22 or 29 January 1926 [GDP].

18 The late Helen, Lady Dashwood, conversation with the author, 1975.

19 Shane Leslie, pp. 237-8.

20 Ashley, p. 4.

21 Epstein, p. 96.

22 G, diary, 8 February 1924 [GDP].

23 M to G, Blenheim, Sunday, February 1924 [GDP].

24 Note on M's letter of Sunday, February 1924 [GDP].

25 G, diary, 23 February 1924 [GDP].

26 Ibid., 25 February 1924 [GDP].

27 Ibid., 23 March 1924 [GDP].

28 Ibid., 26 March 1924 [GDP].
29 Ibid., 29 March 1924 [GDP].
30 Ibid., 29 March 1946, in 1924 diary [GDP].
31 Walter Berry to G, undated [formerly in GDP].
32 G, diary, 12 June 1924 [GDP].
33 Ibid., 14 June 1924 [GDP].
34 Ibid., 1 July 1924 [GDP].
35 McCarthy, pp. 254-5.
36 G to Charles Baldwin, Blenheim Palace, 30 April 1925 [CAB].
37 Green, *Blenheim Palace* (Country Life, 1951), pp. 205-6.
38 Clark, pp. 261-2.
39 Ibid., p. 262.

Interlude: *McCall's*

1 *McCall's*, July 1927, p. 30.

21. Religion and Decline

1 Shane Leslie, pp. 236-7.
2 WSC and C.C. Martindale, S. J., *Charles, IXth Duke of Marlborough, K.G.*, p. 9.
3 G, diary, 21 October 1922 [GDP].
4 G to Lady Ottoline Morrell, 25 October 1925 [HRC].
5 Albertha, Lady Blandford to G, 108 Park Street, London, 14 April 1925 [GDP].
6 Copy of letter dated 29 October 1922 [GDP].
7 *The Times*, 19 March 1963.
8 *Charles, IXth Duke of Marlborough, K.G.*, p. 15.
9 Caraman, p. 158.
10 Father C. C. Martindale to Father John V. F. Maunsell, 11 May 1959 [courtesy of the late Father Maunsell].
11 *New York Times*, 17 November 1926.
12 10th Duke of Argyll to the Rev Bartholomew Hack, 2 Observatory Gardens, London, W8, 26 November 1927 [HVP].
13 Abbé Mugnier to G, 8 November 1927 [formerly in GDP].
14 *The Lady*, 8 March 1928.
15 G to Maurice Alexander, 1 October 1934 (copy of letter) [GDP].
16 G to Hermann von Keyserling, Blenheim Palace, 6 February 1926 [Keyserling Papers, University of Darmstadt].
17 Hermann von Keyserling to G, Darmstadt, 21 December 1929 [GDP].
18 Ibid.
19 Clermont-Tonnerre, *Pomp and Circumstance*, pp. 280-5.

20 Ibid.

21 George Moore to G, 15 December 1927 [formerly in GDP].

22 Ibid.

23 Ibid., 10 December 1929 [formerly in GDP].

24 Ibid., 28 June 1930 [formerly in GDP].

25 M to Hon. Hubert Putnam, 4 January 1929 [Library of Congress, Washington].

26 Bennett, pp. 292–3.

27 Garnett, pp. 24–6.

28 Holroyd, p. 650.

29 Edith Sitwell to G,, undated but 1930 [formerly in GDP].

30 Davie (ed.), p. 318.

31 The late David Green to author, 5 May 1976.

32 Albert Flament, Paris, to G, 12 March 1931 [copy in GDP].

33 G, diary, 10 August 1931 [GDP].

34 Ibid.

35 Ibid., 8 November 1931 [GDP].

36 The late Anita Leslie to author, 1976.

22. The Unusual Life

1 M to WSC, 7 Carlton House Terrace, SW1, 28 May 1932 [CHAR 2/573 A–B (39), CCC].

2 G, divorce statement to Withers & Co., May 1933 [GDP].

3 Appreciation by Peter Stewart, *The Times*, 23 October 1940.

4 Tribute by the Earl of Birkenhead, *The Times*, 1 April 1960.

5 The late Loelia, Duchess of Westminster to author, 30 March 1981.

6 G, divorce statement [GDP].

7 Lord Ivor Spencer-Churchill to WSC, 4 John Street, Mayfair, W1, Thursday, October 1932 [CHAR 2/573 A–B (34), CCC].

8 Ibid., 23 February, undated but 1933 [CHAR 2/573 A–B (20) CCC].

9 Siegfried Sassoon to G, Ossemsley Manor, Christchurch, Hants, 16 November 1932 [formerly in GDP].

10 Father C. C. Martindale to G, 114 Mount Street, London, 28 December 1932 [GDP].

11 G, divorce statement [GDP].

12 Kenneth Brown, Baker, Baker, to G, Essex House, London WC2, 21 April 1933 [GDP].

13 John T. Lewis & Woods, 54 Chancery Lane, WC2, to G, 5 October 1933 [GDP].

14 Sir E. Farquhar Buzzard to Sir Reginald Poole, Lewis & Lewis, 5 January 1933 [BPA].

15 Dr John P. Raby, 117 Woodstock Road, Oxford, to G, 2 May 1933 [GDP].

16 Kenneth Brown, Baker, Baker, statement, 24 March 1933 [GDP].
17 Ibid.
18 Kenneth Brown, Baker, Baker to Withers, Essex House, 10 May 1933 [GDP].
19 Various statements prepared for the duke's divorce [BPA].
20 Lord Ivor Spencer-Churchill to Gladys, 23 March 1933 [GDP].
21 Kenneth Brown, Baker, Baker to Withers, 1933 [GDP].
22 Kenneth Brown, Baker, Baker to Withers, 1933 [GDP].
23 Gladys, photograph album, IV [GDP].
24 Kenneth Brown, Baker Baker to Withers, 1 June 1933 [GDP].
25 The Duchesse de Clermont-Tonnerre to G, 67 rue Raynouard, Paris, 19 June 1933 [GDP].
26 Whish, pp. 168-9.
27 Dorothy Hilton-Green, divorce statement to Withers & Co., 1933 [GDP].
28 Agnes Grylls, divorce statement to Withers & Co., 8 May 1933 [GDP].
29 Lady Boileau to G, Ketteringham Park, Wymondham, 18 July 1933 [GDP].
30 G, photograph album, IV [GDP].
31 G, letter to lawyer [GDP].
32 Winaretta, Princesse de Polignac to G, La Vigne Mohimont, Ardennes, August 1933 [GDP].
33 The Duchesse de Clermont-Tonnerre to G, Grand Hôtel, Beau-Rivage, Annecy, 11 August 1933 [GDP].
34 The Comtesse (Étienne) de Beaumont to Gladys, 2 rue Duroc, Paris, 26 August 1933 [GDP].
35 Ida Matthews to G, 1933 [GDP].
36 Viscountess Churchill to G, 10 August 1933 [GDP].

23. Litigation and Death

1 Report re Carlton House Terrace, 22 June 1933 [GDP].
2 Sworn statement from Emanuel Ricardo, taxi driver relating to the evening of 22/3 June 1933, given 10 August 1933 [GDP].
3 Note by John T. Lewis & Woods, to the clerk to Sir Patrick Hastings KC, 8 November 1933 [GDP].
4 Petition for Judicial Separation, by Her Grace the Duchess of Marlborough to the Rt Hon. the President, in the High Court of Justice, Probate Divorce and Admiralty Division (Divorce), August 1933 [GDP].
5 G, divorce statement to Withers & Co., 1933 [GDP].
6 G to her lawyer [GDP].
7 G to M, 1933 [copy in GDP].
8 Eve Fairfax's visiting book, seen by the author in the Retreat, York, 12 March 1977.
9 G, photograph album, IV [GDP].

10 Derived from WSC to M, 20 March 1934 (Churchill papers 8/484 – CCC), Gilbert (ed.), *The Churchill Documents, Volume,* p. 736.

11 Several *Hooey* files [GDP].

12 F. V. Enoch to G, 1934 [GDP].

13 Sir Ian Malcolm to WSC, The Travellers [Club], Paris, July 1934 [CHAR 1/255/63, CCC].

14 F. V. Enoch to G, 1934 [GDP].

15 Ursula Cottrell-Dormer to G, Coombe, Oxfordshire, 12 July 1934 [GDP].

16 *Sunday Express,* 1 July 1934.

17 *Charles, IXth Duke of Marlborough,* p. 16.

18 Ibid., p. 5.

19 *Sunday Express,* 1 July 1934.

20 Muriel Warde (formerly Wilson) to WSC, Tranby Croft, Hull, Monday night, undated, but 2 July 1934 [CHAR 1/255, CCC].

21 F. V. Enoch to G, July 1934 [GDP].

22 Lady Edward Spencer-Churchill to G, 4 July 1934 [GDP].

23 The Duchesse de Clermont-Tonnerre to G, 69 rue Raynouard, Paris, 1 July 1934 [GDP].

24 Lady Boileau to G, Ketteringham Park, Wymondham, 1 July 1934 [GDP].

25 Nell St John Montague to G, 24A Harrington Road, SW7, 18 July 1934 [GDP].

24. Mixbury

1 Unpublished memoirs of 10th Duke of Marlborough, David Green manuscript [BPA].

2 Gladys to Milo Gray, 12 May 1962 [HVP].

3 Gladys, to her lawyer [GDP].

4 Abbé Mugnier to BB, 31 December 1934 [VIT].

5 Morra, pp. 88–9.

6 G to Lieutenant-Colonel Maurice Alexander, 27 August 1934 [copy in GDP].

7 F. V. Enoch to G, 1934 [GDP].

8 Ibid.

9 Ibid.

10 G to Lieutenant-Colonel Maurice Alexander, 27 August 1934 [copy in GDP].

11 Ibid.

12 *The Times,* 1 February 1933.

13 Young (ed.), p. 318.

14 G, diary, 27 September 1935 [GDP].

25. The 'Witch' of Chacombe

Based on conversations with the late Andrei Kwiatkowsky, 1975-7, with members of Gladys's family, certain villagers at Chacombe, and letters in the collection of the late Reverend Father John V. F. Maunsell (1914-99).

1 G to Jean Marchand, Chacombe, 19 January 1939 [copy in GDP].
2 Ibid.
3 Ibid.
4 G, conversation with the author, 20 February 1976.
5 Mrs Agnes 'Cherry' Grylls to G, Longwood, Sunninghill, Ascot, 13 November 1941 [GDP].
6 Ibid., 25 October 1942 [GDP].
7 *San Francisco Examiner*, 23 April 1941.
8 The late Milo Gray to author, March 1976.
9 G to Countess (Dorothy) Pálffy, 4 June 1940 [copy in GDP].
10 G, conversation with the author, 21 May 1976.
11 Mrs Agnes 'Cherry' Grylls to Gladys, Longwood, Sunninghill, Ascot, 17 November 1944 [GDP].
12 G, diary, 13 March 1945, in 1923 diary, [GDP].
13 Ibid., 21 March 1945, in 1923 diary [GDP].
14 Ibid., 1 May 1945, in 1923 diary [GDP].
15 Ibid., 24 May 1945, in 1923 diary [GDP].
16 Hermann von Keyserling to G, Harthausen, bei 13 Badaibling, Upper Bavaria, 4 April 1946 [GDP].
17 Ibid.
18 Ibid.
19 G, conversation with the author, 10 April 1977.
20 Hutchinson advertisement, *Observer*, 25 February 1934.
21 Lady Boileau to G, Ketteringham Park, Wymondham, 7 July 1933 [GDP].
22 Ibid., 9 May 1933 [GDP].
23 G, diary, 19 May 1947, in 1924 diary [GDP].
24 Ibid., 25 December 1946, in 1924 diary [GDP].
25 Ibid., 15 February 1946, in 1924 diary [GDP].
26 The late Lady Sophia Schilizzi, conversation with the author, London, 27 February 1979.
27 Dorothy to Virginia Baldwin, 1 December 1938 [CAB].
28 Mrs Elisabeth Tomaszewska, conversation with the author, London, November 1976.

26. The Pole

1 S. B. Cooper, Lloyds Bank, St James's Street, London, to G, 21 January 1953 [GDP].

2 Sue Woodford, 'My Memories of the "Old Dutch"', (*Chacombe Chimes*, September 1997), p. 10.

3 Ibid., p. 11.

4 Milo Gray to Virginia Tchkotoua, August 1955 [CAB].

5 The late Count John Pálffy, conversation with the author, Lausanne, 9 June 1975.

6 C to Marguerite Hoyle, 5 August 1952, quoted in Mackenzie Stuart, pp. 489-90.

7 Sir Shane Leslie to Father John V. F. Maunsell, 15 May 1959 [GDP].

8 Most Reverend Gerald O'Hara to Father Maunsell, 22 September 1960 [courtesy of Father Maunsell].

9 G to Milo Gray, telegram, August 1961 [HVP].

10 G, diary, 31 October 1961, written under 24 October 1951 [GDP].

11 G, diary, entry written for 7 November 1944 – but later [GDP].

12 Derived from Count John Pálffy letter to R. A. Joscelyne, 18 May 1962 [HVP].

13 Derived from Count John Pálffy letter to G, 9 April 1957 [copy in HVP].

27. 'A Vast Lunatic Asylum'

This chapter is based on family correspondence now in the possession of the author.

1 G to Milo Gray, 6 May 1962 [HVP].

2 G to Milo Gray, 6 May 1962 [HVP].

3 The late Andrei Kwiatkowsky to the author, 1975. [HVP]

4 R. A. Joscelyne to Milo Gray, 17 April 1962 [HVP].

5 Ibid.

6 R. A. Joscelyne to Count John Pálffy, 21 June 1962; and John Pálffy to R. A. Joscelyne, 27 June 1962 [HVP].

7 Christie's catalogue, July 1978.

8 R. A. Joscelyne to Count John Pálffy, 30 April 1962. [HVP].

9 Count John Pálffy to the Official Solicitor, 14 January 1963 [copy in HVP].

10 Dr D. J. O'Connell, medical superintendent, St Andrew's Hospital, to R. A. Joscelyne, 1 May 1962 [HVP].

11 Ibid., 31 May 1962 [HVP].

12 G to Milo Gray, St Andrew's Hospital, Northampton, dated 12 May, but 12 June 1962 [HVP].

13 Ibid.

14 Dr D. J. O'Connell, medical superintendent, St Andrew's Hospital, to Messrs Elvy Robb & Co., 16a St James's Street, SW1, 21 May 1962 [HVP].

15 Count John Pálffy to R. A. Joscelyne, 18 May 1962 [HVP].

16 R. A. Joscelyne to Count John Pálffy, 11 July 1962 [HVP].

17 Dr D. J. O'Connell, medical superintendent, St Andrew's Hospital, to Waltons & Morse, Count John Pálffy's solicitors, 20 August 1962 [HVP].

18 The late Milo Gray, conversation with the author, 30 August 1975.

19 Contained in a letter, R. A. Joscelyne to Mr and Mrs Austen T. Gray, 40 St Mary Axe, London EC3, 13 December 1962 [HVP].

20 G, diary, 29 January 1963 [copy in GDP].

21 R. A. Joscelyne to Mr and Mrs Austen T. Gray, 40 St Mary Axe, London EC3, 13 December 1962 [HVP].

22 Count John Pálffy to R. A. Joscelyne, 14 January 1963 [HVP].

23 Stockton, Sons & Fortescue, Doddington, Oxford, to Waltons & Morse, 18 February 1963 [HVP].

24 G, diary, 16 February 1963 [copy in GDP].

25 Ibid., 18 February 1963 [copy in GDP].

26 Count John Pálffy to R. A. Joscelyne, 1 March 1963 [HVP].

27 R. B. Sharp to Count John Pálffy, 12 March 1963 [HVP].

28 Dr D. J. O'Connell, medical superintendent, St Andrew's Hospital, to Count John Pálffy, 18 April 1963 [HVP].

29 Ibid., 24 June 1963 [HVP].

30 G, diary, 29 July 1963 [copy in GDP].

28. Last Encounter

1 G, diary, 28 January 1963 [copy in GDP].

2 Ibid., 28 February 1963 [copy in GDP].

3 Ibid., 15 March 1963 [copy in GDP].

4 Ibid., 23 April 1963 [copy in GDP].

5 Ibid., 24 October 1963 [copy in GDP].

6 Ibid., 27 October 1963 [copy in GDP].

7 Ibid., 29 October 1963 [copy in GDP].

8 Ibid., 22 June 1963 [copy in GDP].

9 Ibid., 7 and 8 January 1964 [copy in GDP].

10 The late Andrei Kwiatkowsky, conversation with the author, 1975.

11 G, diary, 31 December 1963 [copy in GDP].

12 Ibid., 21 June 1963 [copy in GDP].

13 Ibid., 4 June 1962 [copy in GDP].

14 Ibid., 25 December 1963 [copy in GDP].

15 Ibid., 10 June 1963 [copy in GDP].

16 Dr A. Tandy Cannon to N. H. Turner, Official Solicitor, 25 September 1964 [ATG].

17 HV diary, 1 May 1977 [HVP].

Appendix: Gladys's Ancestors

1 Edith Clay, p. 110.
2 Ibid., pp. 115–16.
3 William James, letter to Henry James, Chocorna, 5 July 1897, quoted in Skrupskelis and Berkeley, *Volume 3*, p 10.
4 Will of David Deacon, September 1823 [ATG].
5 Edward Preble Deacon to David Deacon, 27 July 1839 [ATG]
6 Curtis, p. 22.
7 Henry Wadsworth Longfellow, 1848, quoted in Shannon, p. 120.
8 Curtis, p. 23.
9 Ibid., p. 24.
10 Anon [J. O. Field], *Uncensored Recollections*, p. 322.
11 *Boston Morning Journal*, 2 and 3 February 1871.
12 *Governor Henry Lippitt House Museum Newsletter*, spring 1992, Vol. 2, article by John A. Neale.
13 Elliott, p. 244.
14 European Station Order no 7, USS *Lancaster*, Smyrna, Turkey, 30 April 1884 [ATG].
15 Report by Admiral Charles Baldwin to the Hon. W. E. Chandler, secretary of the Navy, Washington, DC, 22 June 1883 [ATG].
16 Mr Wurtz, Legation Department of US, St Petersburg, to Navy Department, 9 October 1883 [ATG].
17 Waddington, pp. 137–8.

Personal Postscript

1 The late Margaret Vickers, Hampshire to author, 17 October 1977 [HVP].
2 The late Sister June Dillon, Northampton, to author, 31 October 1977 [HVP].
3 Note by 'J', student nurse, St Andrew's Hospital, Northampton, 2011 [HVP].
4 Note by 'J', ward sister, St Andrew's Hospital, Northampton, 2011 [HVP].

Bibliography

Books

Albaret, Céleste, *Monsieur Proust*, Collins & Harvill Press, 1976.

Ashley, Maurice, *Churchill as Historian,* Secker & Warburg, 1968.

Asquith, Lady Cynthia, *Diaries 1915-18*, Hutchinson, 1968.

Baldwin, C. C., *Baldwin Genealogy Supplement*, Cleveland, USA, 1881 & 1889.

Balsan, Consuelo Vanderbilt, *The Glitter and the Gold*, Heinemann, 1953.

Baring-Gould, S., *A Book of the Riviera,* Methuen, 1905.

Barker, Richard H., *Marcel Proust – A Biography*, Faber & Faber, 1959.

Bataille, A., *Causes Criminelles et Mondaines 1892*, Paris, 1893.

Batchellor, T. B., *Glimpses of Italian Court Life*, Doubleday, NY, 1905.

Beam, Alex, *Gracefully Insane*, Public Affairs, NY, 2001.

Beebe, Lucius, *The Big Spenders*, Doubleday, NY, 1966.

Bennett, Arnold, *Letters to His Nephew*, Heinemann, 1936.

Berenson, Bernard, *Sketch for a Self Portrait*, Constable, 1949.

—, *The Passionate Sightseer*, Thames & Hudson, 1960.

Bertie of Thame, Lord, *The Diary of Lord Bertie of Thame, 1914-18,* Hodder & Stoughton, 1924.

Bibesco, Marthe, *La Vie d'Une Amitié (Vol I),* Plon, Paris, 1951–57.

Birkenhead, The Earl of, *F. E., The Life of F. E. Smith*, Eyre & Spottiswoode, 1959.

—, *The Prof in Two Worlds*, Collins, 1961.

Bithell, Jethro, *Modern German Literature 1880-1950*, Methuen, 1959.

Blanche, Jacques-Émile, *Portraits of A Lifetime*, Dent, 1937.

Boileau, Ethel, *Turnip Tops*, Hutchinson, 1933.

Bonnet, Henri, *Marcel Proust 1907 à 1914*, A. G. Nizet, Paris, 1971.

Bonvicini, O.F., *Caprarola, Il Palazzo e La Villa Farnese*, Rome, 1973.

Boyce, Neith, *The Eternal Spring*, Fox, Duffield & Co, NY, 1906.

Buckle, Richard, *Jacob Epstein Sculptor*, Faber & Faber, 1963.

Bunting, Bainbridge, *Houses of Boston's Back Bay*, Harvard Paperbacks, 1967.

Burns, Edward, *Staying on Alone – The Letters of Alice B. Toklas*, Angus & Robertson, 1974.

Butler, Ruth, *Hidden in the Shadow of the Master*, Yale University Press, 2010.

—, *Rodin – The Shape of Genius*, Yale University Press, 1993.

Buzzoni, Andrea, *Museo Giovanni Boldini*, Fondazione Ferrara Arte, 1997.

Cameron, Roderick, *The Golden Riviera*, Weidenfeld & Nicolson, 1975.

Caraman, Philip, *C. C. Martindale*, Longmans, 1967.

Cardona, Emilia, *Vie de Jean Boldini*, Eugéne Figuière, Paris, 1931.

Carnarvon, Earl of, *No Regrets*, Weidenfeld & Nicolson, 1976.

Castellane, Boni de, *Comment J'ai découvert l'Amérique*, Crés, Paris, 1925.

Cavaillès, Nicolas, *L'Élégance et le Chaos*, Non Lieu, Paris, 2011, p. 230.

Chapman-Huston, D. (ed), *Daisy, Princess of Pless by Herself*, John Murray, 1928.

—, *The Private Diaries of Daisy, Princess of Pless 1873-1914*, John Murray, Albemarle Library, 1950.

Churchill, Randolph S., *Winston S. Churchill, Companion Volume II*, Houghton Mifflin, Boston, 1969.

Churchill, Viscount, *All My Sins Remembered*, Heinemann, 1964.

Churchilll, W. S., & Martindale, C. C., *Charles IX Duke of Marlborough Tributes*, Burns & Oats, 1934.

Clark, Alan (ed), *A Good Innings – The Private Papers of Viscount Lee of Fareham*, John Murray, 1974.

Clay, Edith (ed), *Lady Blessington at Naples*, Hamish Hamilton, 1979.

Clermont-Tonnerre, E de, (Gramont, E de), *Au Temps des Équipages*, Les Cahiers Rouges, Grasset, Paris, 2017.

—, *Marcel Proust*, Flammarion, Paris, 1925.

—, *Memoires, Vol. II*, Bernard Grasset, Paris, 1929.

—, *Pomp & Circumstance*, Jonathan Cape, 1929.

—, *Robert de Montesquiou et Marcel Proust*, Flammarion, Paris, 1925.

—, *Years of Plenty*, Jonathan Cape, 1931.

Coolidge, T. Jefferson, *Autobiography 1857-1900*, privately printed, Boston, 1902.

Crawford, Francis Marion, *Cecilia*, Macmillan, 1902.

Cronin, A. J., *Hatter's Castle*, Victor Gollancz, 1931.

Curtis, Caroline Gardiner, *Memories of Fifty Years in the Last Century*, Boston, 1947.

Curzon of Kedleston, Marchioness, *Reminiscences*, Hutchinson, 1955.

Darroch, Sandra Jobson, *Ottoline*, Chatto & Windus, 1976.

Davenport-Hines, Richard, *Ettie*, Weidenfeld & Nicolson, 2008.

Davie, Michael (ed), *The Diaries of Evelyn Waugh*, Weidenfeld & Nicolson, 1976.

DeBoer-Langworthy, Carol (ed), *The Modern World of Neith Boyce*, University of New Mexico, Albuquerque, USA, 2003.

de Cossé-Brissac, Anne, *La Comtesse Greffulhe*, Perrin, Paris, 1991.

de Diesbach, Ghislain, *La Princesse Bibesco*, Perrin, Paris, 1986.

—, *Proust*, Perrin, Paris, 1991.

de la Gándara Serristori, *Memorie di Hortense*, Baldini Castoldi Dalai, Italy, 2007.

de Stoekl, Agnes, *My Dear Marquis*, John Murray, 1952.

Dodge Luhan, Mabel, *European Experiences*, Harcourt, NY, 1935.

Downing, Ben, *Queen Bee of Tuscany*, Farrar, Straus & Giroux, NY, 2013.

Dunn, Richard M., *Geoffrey Scott and the Berenson Circle*, The Edwin Mellen Press, NY, 1998.

Edel, Leon (ed), *Henry James Letters, Volume IV, 1895-1916*, The Belknap Press, USA, 1984.

Elliott, Maud Howe, *This was my Newport*, The Mythology Co, A. Marshall Jones, USA, 1944.

Epstein, Jacob, *An Autobiography*, Vista Books, 1963.

Field, J. O. [Anon], *Uncensored Recollections*, Lippincott, Phidelphia, 1924.

Fourquières, André de, *Fantômes du Faubourg St Honoré*, Oeuvres Libres, Paris, no 353, December 1956.

—, *Mon Paris et Ses Parisiens Vol. I*, Horay, Paris, 1953.

Frankland, Noble, *Witness of a Century*, Shepheard-Walwyn Ltd, 1993.

Frazier, Adrian, *George Moore*, Yale University Press, 2000.

Frease, J. Michael, *The Colorado Springs School's Historic Trianon*, privately printed, Colorado Springs, USA, 2007.

Gardiner, Stephen, *Epstein – Artist Against the Establishment*, Michael Joseph, 1992.

Garnett, David, *The Familiar Faces*, Chatto & Windus, 1962.

Garten, H. F., *Modern German Drama*, Methuen, 1959.

Gautier-Vignal, *Proust Connu et Inconnu*, Robert Laffont, Paris, 1976.

Gilbert, Martin S. (ed.), *Winston S. Churchill, Volume III, Companion Part 2 Documents May 1915-December 1916*, Heinemann, 1972.

—, *The Churchill Documents – Volume 12: The Wilderness Years 1929-1935*, Hillsdale College Press, Michigan, USA, 1981.

—, *The Churchill Documents – Volume 21: The Shadows of Victory*, Hillsdale College Press, Michigan, USA, 2018.

Giraudoux, Jean, *Souvenir de Deux Existences*, Bernard Grasset, Paris, 1975.

Glendinning, Victoria, *Edith Sitwell*, Weidenfeld & Nicolson, 1981.

—, *Vita*, Weidenfeld & Nicolson, 1983.

Gramont – *see* Clermont-Tonnerre.

Graves, Charles, *Royal Riviera*, Heinemann, 1957.

Green, David, *Blenheim Palace*, Country Life, 1951.

—, *Blenheim Palace*, Blenheim Estate Office, 1973.

—, *Blenheim Park & Gardens*, Blenheim Estate Office, 1972.

Guidi, Barbara, *Boldini a Parigi*, Fondazione Ferrara Arte, 2019.

—, *Boldini e la Moda*, Fondazione Ferrara Arte, 2019.

Hadley, Rollin Van H. (ed), *The Letters of Bernard Berenson and Isabella Stewart Gardner 1887-1924*, Northeastern University Press, Boston, 1987.

Hageman, Patricia S., *F. Marion Crawford*, Word Association Publishers, USA, 2016.

Hamilton, Edith, *Mythology*, Mentor (New American Library), 1969.

Harrison, Michael, *Lord of London*, W. H. Allen, 1966.

Hayman, Ronald, *Proust*, Heinemann, 1990.

Herring, Philip, *Djuna*, Viking, 1995.

Hillerin, Laure, *La Comtesse Greffulhe, L'Ombre des Guermantes*, Flammarion, Paris, 2014.

Hofmannsthal, Hugo von, *Aufzeichnungen*, S. Fischer Verlag, 1959.

—, *Aufzeichnungen. Hrsg. von Rudolf Hirsch und Ellen Ritter in Zusammenarbeit mit Konrad Heumann und Peter Michael Braunwarth*, Frankfurt am Main, 2013.

—, *Briefe 1900-09*, Bermann-Fischer Verlag, Vienna, 1937.

Hofmannsthal, Hugo von & von Nostitz, Hélène, *Briefwechsel*, S. Fischer Verlag, Vienna, 1965.

Holroyd, Michael, *Lytton Strachey, Vol. II*, Heinemann, 1969.

Hone, Joseph, *The Life of George Moore*, Victor Gollancz, 1936.

Hoppe, Manfred (ed), Hugo von Hofmannsthal, *Sämtliche Werke V – Dramen 3*, S. Fischer Verlag, Frankfurt, 1992.

Hoyt, Edwin P., *The Vanderbilts and their Fortunes*, Frederick Muller, 1963.

Hughes-Hallett, Lucy, *Gabriele d'Annunzio*, Knopf, NY, 2013.

Ives, Colta et al, *The Private Collection of Edgar Degas*, The Metropolitan Museum of Art, NY, 1997.

Jonas, Klaus W., *The Life of Crown Prince William*, Routledge & Kegan Paul, 1961.

Joseph, Lawrence, *La Flamme et la Cendre*, Gallimard, Paris, 2006.

Jullian, Philippe, *D'Annunzio*, Pall Mall, 1972.

—, *Oscar Wilde*, Constable, 1969.

—, *Robert de Montesquiou*, Secker & Warburg, 1967.

Keyserling, Hermann von, *The World in the Making*, Jonathan Cape, 1927.

Kiel, Hanna, *Looking at Pictures with Bernard Berenson*, Harry N. Abrams, NY, 1974.

Kilham, Walter H., *Boston After Bullfinch*, Cambridge, Mass, 1946.

Kolb, Philip (ed), *Corréspondance de Marcel Proust, 1906 Tome VI*, Plon, Paris, 1980.

—, *Corréspondance de Marcel Proust, 1907 Tome VII*, Plon, Paris, 1981.

—, *Corréspondance de Marcel Proust, 1918 Tome XVII*, Plon, Paris, 1989.

—, *Corréspondance de Marcel Proust 1920 Tome XIX*, Plon, Paris, 1991.

—, *Corréspondance de Marcel Proust 1921, Tome XX*, Plon, 1992.

—, *Corréspondance de Marcel Proust 1922, Tome XX1*, Plon, Paris, 1993.

—, *Lettres à Reynaldo Hahn*, Gallimard, Paris, 1956.

Lees-Milne, James, *Ancestral Voices*, Chatto & Windus, 1975.

Leslie, Anita, *Edwardians in Love*, Hutchinson, 1972.

Leslie, Sir Shane, *Long Shadows*, John Murray, 1966.

Lewis, R.W. B., *Edith Wharton*, Constable, 1975.

Linzee, John William, *History of Peter Parker and Sarah Ruggles of Roxbury, Mass*, privately printed, Boston, 1913.

McCarthy, Lillah, *Myself & My Friends*, Thornton Butterworth, 1933.

Mackenzie Stuart, Amanda, *Consuelo & Alva*, Harper Collins, 2005.

Maclay, E. S., *A History of the United States Navy 1775-1893 (3 vols)*, Bliss, Sands & Foster, London, 1894.

Magnus, Philip, *King Edward VII*, E. P. Dutton, NY, 1964.

Mariano, Nicky, *Forty Years with Berenson*, Hamish Hamilton, 1966.

Masson, Georgiana, *Italian Gardens*, Thames & Hudson, 1961.

—, *Italian Villas and Palaces*, Thames & Hudson, 1959.

Matthiessen, F. O., & Murdock, Kenneth B., *The Notebooks of Henry James*, Oxford University Press, 1947.

Maurois, André, *The Chelsea Way*, Weidenfeld & Nicolson, 1966.

Montesquiou, Robert de, *Le Chancelier des Fleurs*, privately printed, 1908.

—, *Les Paons*, Édition Définitive, Paris, 1908.

—, *Paul Helleu – Peintre et Graveur*, H. Floury, Paris, 1913.

Morand, Paul, *Le Visiteur du Soir*, Palatine, Geneva, 1947.

Morra, Umberto, *Colloqui con Berenson*, Garzanti, Milan, 1963.

Mosley, Sir Oswald, *My Life*, Nelson, 1968.

Nicolson, Harold, *Diaries and Letters 1930-39*, Collins, 1966.

—, *The Peace-Making*, Constable, 1933.

Nicolson, Nigel, *The Question of Things Happening – The Letters of Virginia Woolf Vol. II 1919-22*, Hogarth Press, 1976.

Otis-Skinner, Cornelia, *Elegant Wits and Grand Horizontals*, Michael Joseph, 1962.

Painter, George D., *Marcel Proust – A Biography, Vol. II*, Chatto & Windus, 1973.

Papi, Stefano, & Rhodes, Alexandra, *Famous Jewelry Collectors*, Thames & Hudson, 1999.

Parks, Mercedes Gallagher, *Introduction to Keyserling*, Jonathan Cape, 1934.

Paulhan, Claire (ed), *Catherine Pozzi – Journal de Jeunesse 1893-1906*, Éditions Claire Paulhan, 1997.

Pickvance, Ronald, *Gauguin*, Fondation Pierre Gionadda, Martigny, Switzerland, 1998.

Plesch, Etti, *Horses & Husbands*, The Dovecote Press, 2007.

Poniatowski, Prince, *D'un Siècle à l'Autre*, Presses de la Cité, Paris, 1948.

Pringle, Henry F., *Theodore Roosevelt*, Jonathan Cape, 1932.

Proust, Marcel, *The Guermantes Way, Part II*, Chatto & Windus, 1925.

Rappazzini, Francesco, *Élisabeth de Gramont*, Fayard, Paris, 2004.

Recupero, Jacob, *Il Palazzo Farnese di Caprarola*, Bonecchi Edizione, 'Il Turismo', Florence, 1977.

Rhodes James, Robert (ed), *Chips – The Diaries of Sir Henry Channon*, Weidenfeld & Nicolson, 1967.

Risset, Jacqueline, *La Rivista Botteghe Oscure e Marguerite Chapin*, Fondazione Camillo Caetani, Rome, 2007.

Roumania, Queen Marie of, *The Story of My Life (Vols I & II)*, Cassell, 1934.

Rowse, A. L., *The Later Churchills*, Macmillan, 1958.

Sams, William, *Court Anecdotes*, London, 1825.

Samuels, Ernest, *Bernard Berenson – The Making of a Connoisseur*, The Belknap Press, USA, 1979.

Schnadelbach, R. Terry, *Hidden Lives, Secret Gardens,* Laud Press, USA, 2009.

Schlumberger, Gustave, *Mes Souvenirs, Vol II,* Plon, Paris, 1934.

Secrest, Meryle, *Between Me and Life*, Macdonald & Jane's, 1976.

Sermoneta, Duchess of, *Things Past*, Hutchinson, 1929.

Shannon, Hope J., *Legendary Locals of Boston's South End*, Arcadia, 2014.

Skrupskelis, Ignas K. & Berkeley, Elizabeth M. (eds), *The Correspondence of William & Henry James, Volume 3*, University of Virginia Press, USA, 1994.

Sparks, Edward I., *The Riviera*, J. & A. Churchill, 1879.

Sprague, Marshall, *Newport in the Rockies*, Swallow Press, Ohio University Press, USA, 1997.

Stapleton, Susannah, *The Adventures of Maud West – Lady Detective*, Picador, 2019.

Stein, Gertrude, *The Autobiography of Alice B. Toklas*, The Bodley Head, 1933.

Strachey, Barbara, *Remarkable Relations*, Victor Gollancz, 1980.

Strachey, Barbara, & Samuels Ernest (eds), *Mary Berenson – A Self Portrait from her Letters & Diaries*, Victor Gollancz, 1993.

Trevelyan, Raleigh, *Princes Under the Volcano*, William Morrow & Co, NY, 1973.

Varé, Daniele, *Ghosts of the Spanish Steps*, John Murray, 1955.

Vickers, Hugo, *Gladys, Duchess of Marlborough*, Weidenfeld & Nicolson, 1979 & Hamish Hamilton, 1987.

Waddington, Mary King, *Letters of a Diplomat's Wife 1883-1900*, Smith, Elder & Co, 1904.

Walker, Jonathan, *The Blue Beast*, The History Press, 2012.

Walker, Peter A. & Zacharias, Greg W. (eds), *The Complete Letters of Henry James*, University of Nebraska, USA, 2015.

Waterhouse, Michael, & Wiseman, Karen, *The Churchill Who Saved Blenheim*, Unicorn, 2019.

Weber, Caroline, *Proust's Duchess*, Alfred A. Knopf, NY, 2018.

Wecter, Dixon, *The Saga of American Society*, Charles Scribner, NY, 1970.

Westminster, Loelia Duchess of, *Grace and Favour*, Weidenfeld & Nicolson, 1961.

Wharton, Edith, *Italian Villas and their Gardens*, John Lane: The Bodley Head, 1904.

Whish, Violet, *Partners in Friendship*, Wyman & Sons, 1949.

Whistler, James McNeil, *The Baronet and the Butterfly*, Valentine, Paris, 1899.

Whitehill, Walter Muir, *Boston – A Topographical History*, Harvard, Mass, 1968.

Young, Kenneth B. (ed), *The Diaries of Robert Bruce Lockhart 1915-38, Vol I*, Macmillan, 1973.

Catalogues & Periodicals

American Weekly, 21 August 1949.

Catalogue Collection Edgar Degas 26-27 mars 1918, Galerie Georges Petit, Paris, 1918.

Chacombe Chimes, September 1997.

BIBLIOGRAPHY

Christie's, *A Casket of Highly Important Jewels*, 5 July 1978.

—, *Impressionist and Modern Drawings*, 27 June 1978.

—, *Impressionist and Modern Paintings*, 27 June 1978.

—, *Nineteenth and Twentieth Century Printed Books*, 26 July 1978.

Dermal Fillers, Volume 4, Karger, 2018.

Governor Henry Lippitt House Museum Newsletter, Spring 1992, Vol. 2.

Grindea, Myron, *Adam International Review, no 260*, 1957.

La Revue de Paris – Tableaux de Paris, 1931.

The Month, April 1953 (New Series, Vol. IX, no 4).

The Review of Reviews, 15 December 1910.

Index